KIERKEGAARD AND HIS GERMAN CONTEMPORARIES

TOME II: THEOLOGY

Kierkegaard Research: Sources, Reception and Resources
Volume 6, Tome II

Kierkegaard Research: Sources, Reception and Resources
is a publication of the Søren Kierkegaard Research Centre

This volume was published with the generous financial support
of the Danish Agency for Science, Technology and Innovation

Kierkegaard and His German Contemporaries

Tome II: Theology

Edited by
JON STEWART

ASHGATE

Published by
Ashgate Publishing Limited
Gower House
Croft Road
Aldershot
Hampshire GU11 3HR
England

Ashgate Publishing Company
Suite 420
101 Cherry Street
Burlington, VT 05401-4405
USA

Ashgate website: http://www.ashgate.com

British Library Cataloguing in Publication Data
Kierkegaard and his German contemporaries
Tome 2: Theology. - (Kierkegaard research : sources, reception and resources ; v. 6)
1. Kierkegaard, Søren, 1813-1855 2. Kierkegaard, Søren, 1813-1855 - Friends and associates 3. Philosophy, German - 19th century
I. Stewart, Jon (Jon Bartley)
198.9

Library of Congress Cataloging-in-Publication Data
Kierkegaard and his German contemporaries / edited by Jon Stewart.
p. cm. -- (Kierkegaard research ; v. 6)
Includes bibliographical references and index.
ISBN 978-0-7546-6132-0 (hardcover) 1. Kierkegaard, Søren, 1813-1855. 2. Philosophy, German--19th century. I. Stewart, Jon (Jon Bartley)

B4377.K4552 2007
198'.9--dc22

2006034593

ISBN-13: 978-0-7546-6132-0

Cover design by Katalin Nun.

Printed and bound in Great Britain by TJ International Ltd, Padstow, Cornwall.

Contents

List of Contributors

Christine Axt-Piscalar, Theologische Fakultät, Georg-August-Universität, Platz der Göttinger Sieben 2, 37073 Göttingen, Germany.

Lee C. Barrett, Lancaster Theological Seminary, 555 West James Street, 17603 Lancaster, PA, USA.

Stephan Bitter, Falkenweg 10, 45478 Mülheim an der Ruhr, Germany.

Richard E. Crouter, Department of Religion, Carleton College, One North College Street, Northfield, MN 55057, USA.

David James, School of Politics, Howard College Campus, University of KwaZulu-Natal, Durban 4041, South Africa.

Christoph Kronabel, Heidelberg Innovation, Im Neuenheimer Feld 581, 69120 Heidelberg, Germany.

Douglas Moggach, School of Political Studies and Department of Philosophy, University of Ottawa, Ottawa, Canada, K1N 6N5.

George Pattison, Christ Church, Oxford OX1 1DP, England.

David D. Possen, Committee on Social Thought, University of Chicago, 1130 East 59th Street, Chicago, IL 60637, USA.

Heiko Schulz, Theologische Fakultät, Duisburg-Essen Universität, Universitätsstr. 12, 45117 Essen, Germany.

Jon Stewart, Søren Kierkegaard Research Centre, Farvergade 27D, 1463 Copenhagen K, Denmark.

List of Abbreviations

Danish Abbreviations

B&A *Breve og Aktstykker vedrørende Søren Kierkegaard*, ed. by Niels Thulstrup, vols. 1–2, Copenhagen: Munksgaard 1953–54.

Bl.art. *S. Kierkegaard's Bladartikler, med Bilag samlede efter Forfatterens Død, udgivne som Supplement til hans øvrige Skrifter*, ed. by Rasmus Nielsen, Copenhagen 1857.

EP *Af Søren Kierkegaards Efterladte Papirer*, vols. 1–9, ed. by H.P. Barfod and Hermann Gottsched, Copenhagen 1869–81.

Pap. *Søren Kierkegaards Papirer*, vols. I to XI–3, ed. by Peter Andreas Heiberg, Victor Kuhr and Einer Torsting, Copenhagen: Gyldendalske Boghandel, Nordisk Forlag 1909–48; second, expanded ed., vols. I to XI–3, by Niels Thulstrup, vols. XII to XIII supplementary volumes, ed. by Niels Thulstrup, vols. XIV to XVI index by Niels Jørgen Cappelørn, Copenhagen: Gyldendal 1968–78.

SKS *Søren Kierkegaards Skrifter*, ed. by Niels Jørgen Cappelørn, Joakim Garff, Jette Knudsen, Johnny Kondrup, Alastair McKinnon and Finn Hauberg Mortensen, Copenhagen: Gads Forlag 1997ff.

SV1 *Samlede Værker*, ed. by A.B. Drachmann, Johan Ludvig Heiberg and H.O. Lange, vols. I–XIV, Copenhagen: Gyldendalske Boghandels Forlag 1901–06.

English Abbreviations

AN *Armed Neutrality*, trans. by Howard V. Hong and Edna H. Hong, Princeton: Princeton University Press 1998.

AR *On Authority and Revelation, The Book on Adler*, trans. by Walter Lowrie, Princeton: Princeton University Press 1955.

ASKB *The Auctioneer's Sales Record of the Library of Søren Kierkegaard*, ed. by H.P. Rohde, Copenhagen: The Royal Library 1967.

BA	*The Book on Adler*, trans. by Howard V. Hong and Edna H. Hong, Princeton: Princeton University Press 1998.
C	*The Crisis and a Crisis in the Life of an Actress*, trans. by Howard V. Hong and Edna H. Hong, Princeton: Princeton University Press 1997.
CA	*The Concept of Anxiety*, trans. by Reidar Thomte in collaboration with Albert B. Anderson, Princeton: Princeton University Press 1980.
CD	*Christian Discourses*, trans. by Howard V. Hong and Edna H. Hong, Princeton: Princeton University Press 1997.
CI	*The Concept of Irony*, trans. by Howard V. Hong and Edna H. Hong, Princeton: Princeton University Press 1989.
CIC	*The Concept of Irony*, trans. with an Introduction and Notes by Lee M. Capel, London: Collins 1966.
COR	*The Corsair Affair; Articles Related to the Writings*, trans. by Howard V. Hong and Edna H. Hong, Princeton: Princeton University Press 1982.
CUP1	*Concluding Unscientific Postscript*, vol. 1, trans. by Howard V. Hong and Edna H. Hong, Princeton: Princeton University Press 1982.
CUP2	*Concluding Unscientific Postscript*, vol. 2, trans. by Howard V. Hong and Edna H. Hong, Princeton: Princeton University Press 1982.
EO1	*Either/Or*, Part I, trans. by Howard V. Hong and Edna H. Hong, Princeton: Princeton University Press 1987.
EO2	*Either/Or*, Part II, trans. by Howard V. Hong and Edna H. Hong, Princeton: Princeton University Press 1987.
EOP	*Either/Or*, trans. by Alastair Hannay, Harmondsworth: Penguin Books 1992.
EPW	*Early Polemical Writings*, includes: *From the Papers of One Still Living*; *Articles from Student Days*; *The Battle Between the Old and the New Soap-Cellars*, trans. by Julia Watkin, Princeton: Princeton University Press 1990.
EUD	*Eighteen Upbuilding Discourses*, trans. by Howard V. Hong and Edna H. Hong, Princeton: Princeton University Press 1990.
FSE	*For Self-Examination*, trans. by Howard V. Hong and Edna H. Hong, Princeton: Princeton University Press 1990.

FT *Fear and Trembling*, trans. by Howard V. Hong and Edna H. Hong, Princeton: Princeton University Press 1983.

FTP *Fear and Trembling*, trans. by Alastair Hannay, London and New York: Penguin Books 1985.

JC *Johannes Climacus, or De Omnibus dubitandum est*, trans. by Howard V. Hong and Edna H. Hong, Princeton: Princeton University Press 1985.

JFY *Judge for Yourself!*, trans. by Howard V. Hong and Edna H. Hong, Princeton: Princeton University Press 1990.

JP *Søren Kierkegaard's Journals and Papers*, ed. and trans. by Howard V. Hong and Edna H. Hong, assisted by Gregor Malantschuk, vols. 1–6, vol. 7 Index and Composite Collation, Bloomington and London: Indiana University Press 1967–78.

KAC *Kierkegaard's Attack upon "Christendom," 1854–1855*, trans. by Walter Lowrie, Princeton: Princeton University Press 1944.

LD *Letters and Documents*, trans. by Henrik Rosenmeier, Princeton: Princeton University Press 1978.

M *The Moment and Late Writings*, trans. by Howard V. Hong and Edna H. Hong, Princeton: Princeton University Press 1998.

P *Prefaces/Writing Sampler*, trans. by Todd W. Nichol, Princeton: Princeton University Press 1997.

PC *Practice in Christianity*, trans. by Howard V. Hong and Edna H. Hong, Princeton: Princeton University Press 1991.

PF *Philosophical Fragments*, trans. by Howard V. Hong and Edna H. Hong, Princeton: Princeton University Press 1985.

PJ *Papers and Journals: A Selection*, trans. with introductions and notes by Alastair Hannay, London and New York: Penguin Books 1996.

PLR *Prefaces: Light Reading for Certain Classes as the Occasion May Require*, trans. by William McDonald, Tallahassee: Florida State University Press 1989.

PLS *Concluding Unscientific Postscript*, trans. by David F. Swenson and Walter Lowrie, Princeton: Princeton University Press 1941.

PV *The Point of View* including *On My Work as an Author*, *The Point of View for My Work as an Author*, and *Armed Neutrality*, trans. by Howard V. Hong and Edna H. Hong, Princeton: Princeton University Press 1998.

PVL *The Point of View for My Work as an Author* including *On My Work as an Author*, trans. by Walter Lowrie. New York and London: Oxford University Press 1939.

R *Repetition*, trans. by Howard V. Hong and Edna H. Hong, Princeton: Princeton University Press 1983.

SBL *Notes of Schelling's Berlin Lectures*, trans. by Howard V. Hong and Edna H. Hong, Princeton: Princeton University Press 1989.

SLW *Stages on Life's Way*, trans. by Howard V. Hong and Edna H. Hong, Princeton: Princeton University Press 1988.

SUD *The Sickness unto Death*, trans. by Howard V. Hong and Edna H. Hong, Princeton: Princeton University Press 1980.

SUDP *The Sickness unto Death*, trans. by Alastair Hannay, London and New York: Penguin Books 1989.

TA *Two Ages: The Age of Revolution and the Present Age. A Literary Review*, trans. by Howard V. Hong and Edna H. Hong, Princeton: Princeton University Press 1978.

TD *Three Discourses on Imagined Occasions*, trans. by Howard V. Hong and Edna H. Hong, Princeton: Princeton University Press 1993.

UD *Upbuilding Discourses in Various Spirits*, trans. by Howard V. Hong and Edna H. Hong, Princeton: Princeton University Press 1993.

WA *Without Authority* including *The Lily in the Field and the Bird of the Air*, *Two Ethical-Religious Essays*, *Three Discourses at the Communion on Fridays*, *An Upbuilding Discourse*, *Two Discourses at the Communion on Fridays*, trans. by Howard V. Hong and Edna H. Hong, Princeton: Princeton University Press 1997.

WL *Works of Love*, trans. by Howard V. Hong and Edna H. Hong, Princeton: Princeton University Press 1995.

Bruno Bauer:

Biblical Narrative, Freedom and Anxiety

David James and Douglas Moggach

I. Bruno Bauer

Bruno Bauer (1809–82), theologian, philosopher, and historian, was a leader of the left-Hegelian or republican school in the 1840s. The left Hegelians, such as Feuerbach (1804–72), Arnold Ruge (1802–80), and the early Marx, went beyond Hegel in their demand for popular sovereignty and in their explicit criticisms of irrational religious beliefs and practices.[1] Bauer developed an idea of republican freedom based on what he called universal self-consciousness, the capacity of thought to be self-determining not only in the maxims it adopted (as in Kantian morality), but in its ability to shape the external world, struggling against all obstacles to freedom posed by outmoded political, social, and religious institutions and relations. Genuine freedom depended on the capacity of subjects to rise above their particular desires and to subject these to rational control, thus promoting a universal interest in their own lives and actions. Bauer wrote extensively on the origins of Christianity and its relation to the culture of classical antiquity. In *Herr Dr. Hengstenberg*[2] and *Religion des Alten Testaments*,[3] Bauer attacked conventional depictions of the continuity between Christianity and Judaism. Viewing religion as the unfolding of human self-consciousness, he distinguished the irrational prescriptions of the Mosaic law, and its particularistic appeal to a chosen people, from the new, inclusive, universalistic spirit of the gospels. By 1840, and notably in his three-volume *Kritik der evangelischen Geschichte der Synoptiker* (1841–42),[4] Bauer's attitude toward Christianity became increasingly

---

The authors express their thanks to the Social Science and Humanities Research Council of Canada for its generous support for this article.

1 See Douglas Moggach (ed.), *The New Hegelians: Politics and Philosophy in the Hegelian School*, Cambridge: Cambridge University Press 2005.

2 Bruno Bauer, *Herr Dr. Hengstenberg. Ein Beitrag zur Kritik des religiösen Bewußtseins. Kritische Briefe über den Gegensatz des Gesetzes und des Evangeliums*, Berlin: Ferdinand Dümmler 1839.

3 Bauer, *Kritik der Geschichte der Offenbarung. Die Religion des Alten Testaments in der geschichtlichen Entwicklung ihrer Prinzipien dargestellt*, vols. 1–2, Berlin: Ferdinand Dümmler 1838.

4 Bauer, *Kritik der evangelischen Geschichte der Synoptiker*, vols. 1–3, Leipzig: Otto Wigand 1841–42 (vol. 3 was published with the title *Kritik der evangelischen Geschichte der Synoptiker und des Johannes*, Braunschweig: Friedrich Otto 1842).

negative, as he identified it practically as a bulwark of the oppressive Restoration political order and theoretically as a self-denial of freedom. In further studies, Bauer traced the evolution of Christian doctrine from Stoic and late Hellenistic sources, dating the earliest gospel to the reign of the emperor Hadrian (117–38).[5]

II. *Bauer's* Zeitschrift für spekulative Theologie

Bauer's views in the 1830s were not so explicitly republican, and his attitude toward religion was far more conciliatory. Even so, he was probing in his criticisms of the defective logic of orthodox religious positions. In Kierkegaard's works Bauer's name is mentioned several times in connection with a journal which he edited and to which Kierkegaard subscribed. The journal in question is the *Zeitschrift für spekulative Theologie*, of which three volumes appeared between 1836 and 1838.[6] Kierkegaard's references to this journal for the most part concern the writings of various right and center Hegelians, such as Daub,[7] Erdmann,[8] and Rosenkranz,[9] rather than Bauer's own writings. The journal did, however, contain some articles that Bauer himself wrote, along with some reviews and other texts by him.[10] Moreover, Kierkegaard refers directly to one of these articles, "Die Urgeschichte der Menschheit nach dem biblischen Berichte der Genesis, kritisch untersucht."[11] This article must therefore form the starting-point for any attempt to determine the nature of Kierkegaard's relation to Bauer.

Kierkegaard mentions the article in question in an undated journal entry from 1838–39.[12] Although Kierkegaard refers to an excerpt from "Die Urgeschichte der Menschheit," the journal entry reads more like a summary of some problems that Bauer raises in connection with the Genesis account of the prehistory of man than an excerpt from the article itself. One of these problems concerns what Bauer calls the double account [*Doppelbericht*] of the Creation which is given in Genesis.[13] He argues that the Genesis account of the Creation is a double one because, when

---

5 Bauer, *Kritik der paulinischen Briefe*, Berlin: Gustav Hempel 1850–51; *Kritik der Evangelien und Geschichte ihres Ursprungs*, Parts 1–4 in vols. 1–2, Berlin: Gustav Hempel 1850–51 (4th part under the title *Die theologische Erklärung der Evangelien*, Berlin: Gustav Hempel 1852).

6 *Zeitschrift für spekulative Theologie*, vols. 1–3, ed. by Bruno Bauer, Berlin: Ferdinand Dümmler 1836–37 (*ASKB* 354–357).

7 *SKS* 4, 279 / *PF*, 80. *SKS* 17, 223, DD:13 / *JP* 1, 279. *SKS* 17, 213, DD:2 / *JP* 2, 1233. *SKS* 17, 222, DD:12 / *JP* 3, 3605.

8 *SKS* 1, 154n / *CI*, 102n. *Pap.* IV B 1, 146 / *JC*, 167n. *Pap.* IV B 12, p. 174 / *PF*, Supplement, 251. *SKS* 17, 219, DD:8 / *JP* 4, 3998.

9 *SKS* 17, 213, DD:1 / *JP* 2, 2211. *SKS* 17, 219f., DD:10 / *JP* 5, 5222.

10 Bauer's contributions to this journal are listed in a comprehensive bibliography compiled by Aldo Zanardo, "Bruno Bauer hegeliano e giovane hegeliano," in *Rivista Critica di Storia della Filosofia*, 1965, pp. 1–57.

11 "Die Urgeschichte der Menschheit nach dem biblischen Berichte der Genesis, kritisch untersucht," *Zeitschrift für spekulative Theologie*, op. cit., vol. 3, no. 1, 1837, pp. 125–210.

12 *SKS* 18, 372, KK:8 / *JP* 5, 5355. The excerpt itself is not given in *JP*.

13 *Zeitschrift für spekulative Theologie*, op. cit., vol. 3, no. 1, 1837, p. 131.

understood in literal terms, it must be thought to contain two conflicting accounts of the appearance of man and the relation of his appearance to the rest of creation.

These conflicting accounts of the Creation are as follows: the first chapter of Genesis, which for Bauer consists of a determinate sequence of events (that is, a series of discrete acts through which God created heaven and earth, then light, and so forth), contains an account of the Creation in which the creation of man forms the final crowning moment of the whole sequence of events; so that all the lower stages of finite being, which precede the creation of man in this biblical narrative, are seen as presuppositions of the appearance of man.[14] Yet, in the second chapter of Genesis, man is described as already formed before the creation of both the vegetable kingdom and the rest of the animal kingdom; and Bauer here cites the fact that the appearance of the Garden of Eden is described as taking place after the creation of man, as well as the fact that man is said to be in the Garden of Eden before the beasts of the field and the birds of the air have been formed.[15]

When Bauer speaks of the Genesis account of the Creation as a double one, he must therefore be understood as identifying an incompatibility between biblical narrative and the human understanding, which cannot simultaneously assert two conflicting accounts of the same set of events: for us, the creation of the plants and animals must either precede or follow the creation of man. One may, perhaps, dispute Bauer's characterization of the creation of the plants and animals as presuppositions of the appearance of man on the grounds that he neither sufficiently explains nor justifies this claim. Nevertheless, the fact remains that the Genesis account of the Creation, which claims that the creation of the plants and animals both precedes and follows the appearance of man, appears to violate one of the main logical principles governing the human understanding: the law of the excluded middle.

Kierkegaard seems to have been struck by the way in which Bauer shows that the double nature of the Genesis account of the Creation involves a contradiction, for in the journal entry mentioned above he offers a summary of Bauer's argument. He also refers to an attempt to remove the contradiction which Bauer expressly rejects: the argument that the narrative involves a step back, with the creation of the animals being mentioned only later as an afterthought; in other words, in the second chapter of Genesis, the creation of the plants and animals is still thought to precede the appearance of man, even though it is only mentioned after the appearance of man in the narrative itself. Bauer rejects this explanation in the case of the creation of the animals on the grounds that the narrative itself describes their creation as motivated by Adam's loneliness.[16]

The contradiction outlined above is one between two differing accounts of the same set of events. Yet Bauer also argues that the individual accounts of the Creation can be seen as self-contradictory, so that a literal understanding of biblical narrative again becomes impossible.[17] To support this claim, Bauer gives the example of the difference between the individual days, which, in the biblical narrative of the

14 Ibid.

15 Ibid., pp. 131f.

16 Ibid., p. 132.

17 Ibid., p. 133.

Creation, is made to contradict the absolute mechanism of the universe, since in the first chapter of Genesis the difference between the days is assumed to exist before that which makes the difference between them possible, that is, the solar system and its movements. Bauer is here referring to the fact that it is only on the fourth day that God is said to have created the solar system (Genesis 1:14). According to Bauer, the way in which the real possibility of the days is posited only on the fourth day of the Creation contradicts the difference between the preceding days and the whole order of creation as presented in the seven days' work. The problem here is that what is conditioned is taken to exist prior to the condition of its possibility, thus violating our understanding of the relation between a condition and that of which it is the condition. Kierkegaard also mentions in his journal Bauer's account of this example of an incompatibility between biblical narrative and the logical principles governing human thought, thus suggesting once more that he was struck by Bauer's presentation of this problem.

The idea that biblical narrative is incompatible with some of the main logical principles governing the human understanding suggests a link with Kierkegaard's own thought because he accepts that some of the main teachings of Christianity do indeed represent an offense to the human understanding. One of the most important examples that he gives of such offense is the paradox of the Incarnation, which he describes as the absolute paradox as expressed in the thesis that "God has existed in human form, was born, grew up etc."[18] According to Kierkegaard, the Incarnation is a paradox because the eternal is by its very nature unhistorical, and yet the eternal must be thought to become historical once the god comes into existence as an individual human being at a specific moment in time. In this particular case the historical is therefore not something historical in the ordinary sense of the term, but is instead the historical that has become historical only against its nature.[19] In other words, the eternal is essentially unhistorical in the sense that it is not subject to the conditions which temporality imposes on finite things; yet, in the Incarnation, the eternal itself becomes subject to these same conditions in complete opposition to our understanding of the essential nature of the eternal. Once again the law of the excluded middle comes into play, since the god is thought to be either unhistorical or historical, eternal or temporal. Consequently, Kierkegaard describes the juxtaposition of the eternal and the temporal that is found in the Incarnation as "a break with all thinking."[20] He does not think, however, that there is any way of resolving the paradox, unlike Bauer's teacher, Hegel, who accepts that the idea of Christ as the God-man presents a contradiction to the understanding,[21] but also thinks that this contradiction can be overcome at the level of speculative philosophy, with its purely conceptual grasp of reality.

While Bauer may not have been the first person to alert Kierkegaard to the way in which the teachings of Christianity represent an offense to the human understanding,

---

18 *SKS* 7, 198 / *CUP1*, 217.

19 *SKS* 7, 526 / *CUP1*, 578.

20 *SKS* 7, 526 / *CUP1*, 579.

21 Cf. G.W.F. Hegel, *Vorlesungen über die Philosophie der Religion*, vols. 1–3, ed. by Walter Jaeschke, Hamburg: Meiner Verlag 1993–95, vol. 1: *Die Vollendete Religion*, p. 239.

we have seen that there is good reason for thinking that Kierkegaard found Bauer's presentation of this problem in the "Die Urgeschichte der Menschheit" especially provocative. Yet the extent to which Bauer's article influenced Kierkegaard's own thought may have been even greater, and we now intend to suggest that Kierkegaard's reading of Bauer's article may also have provoked him into developing a response to the idea that the teachings of Christianity must be viewed as myths because they represent an offense to the human understanding.

The fact that Kierkegaard thought of Bauer as someone who reduces biblical narrative to the status of myth is suggested by some remarks that he makes in connection with a review of his dissertation on irony in the journal *Fædrelandet* written by Andreas Frederik Beck (1816–61), an assistant professor of philosophy at the University of Copenhagen. Kierkegaard expresses his great surprise at finding himself included among the followers of D.F. Strauss in Beck's book *The Concept of Myth or the Form of the Religious Spirit*,[22] and he then mentions Bauer together with Strauss and Feuerbach.[23] While Kierkegaard's main aim in mentioning Beck's inclusion of him among the followers of Strauss may have been to demonstrate Beck's failure to understand his dissertation on irony, he thus also shows that he views Bauer as a follower of Strauss, whereas in some of his early theological writings Bauer was, in fact, highly critical of certain aspects of Strauss' thought.[24] One might consider this to be evidence of a lack of familiarity on Kierkegaard's part with Bauer's own writings. However, Kierkegaard's understanding of Bauer on this point is not without some justification in the case of "Die Urgeschichte der Menschheit," since in this article Bauer does indeed treat the Genesis account of the prehistory of man as belonging to the realm of myth. For he argues that while the orthodox view is that the biblical account of the Creation rests on immediate divine revelation, it really belongs, as myth, to a pagan view of the genesis of the universe and is thus historically conditioned by such a viewpoint, even though it has subjected this presupposition (that is, the pagan view of the genesis of the universe) to a higher principle.[25] The principle in question is the power of free subjectivity, which Bauer claims was first revealed to Abraham, so that this principle cannot be seen as fully realized in the biblical account of the Creation.[26]

Thus far, we can claim with some justification that Kierkegaard views Bauer's thought as representative of at least two ideas: the idea that biblical narrative contains elements which are contrary to the logical principles governing the human understanding, and the idea that biblical narrative has the status of myth. We shall see, in fact, that Kierkegaard appears to understand the second idea as being a corollary of the first idea in the case of a thinker such as Bauer. In order to show what grounds Kierkegaard provides for making a direct link between these two ideas, we shall

---

22 Andreas Frederik Beck, *Begrebet Mythus eller den religiøse Aands Form*, Copenhagen: P.G. Philipsens Forlag 1842 (*ASKB* 424).

23 *SV1* XIII, 405 / *COR*, 10.

24 Cf. Moggach, *The Philosophy and Politics of Bruno Bauer*, Cambridge and New York: Cambridge University Press 2003, Chapter 3, especially pp. 44f. and pp. 73f.

25 *Zeitschrift für spekulative Theologie*, op. cit., vol. 3, no. 1, 1837, pp. 141–2.

26 Ibid., p. 144.

now turn to a work in which he himself looks at part of the Genesis account of the prehistory of man, namely the fall of man. The work in question is *The Concept of Anxiety*, in which, moreover, Kierkegaard provides us with yet another example of how biblical narrative represents an offense to the human understanding.

While he acknowledges that the Genesis account of sin represents an offense to the human understanding, Kierkegaard, unlike Bauer in "Die Urgeschichte der Menschheit," does not reduce the story of the Fall to the status of a myth. He instead seeks to demonstrate that the Genesis account of sin is essentially true and is therefore more than a myth. If we now turn to *The Concept of Anxiety*, we can thus discover a concrete example of the way in which Kierkegaard's reading of Bauer's article may have influenced his own thought. Moreover, in relation to the issue as to how one is to discover the truth underlying a biblical narrative such as that of the Genesis account of the Fall, we shall see that for Kierkegaard Bauer provides an example of the type of person who is not in the position to discover religious truth because he lacks inwardness.

III. Bauer's Article and The Concept of Anxiety

In *The Concept of Anxiety* Kierkegaard asks whether the concept of hereditary sin is identical with the first sin, that is, Adam's sin; and he claims that if this is the case, the task of explaining hereditary sin becomes identical with explaining Adam's sin.[27] Kierkegaard argues, however, that such an approach fantastically places Adam outside the history of the human race.[28] The main idea behind this claim appears to be that when the existence of sinfulness in the world is taken to have come about through Adam's sin, a state of affairs (that is, a state of innocence) must be presupposed in which such sinfulness was absent; the fall of man is thereby understood as a consequence of the loss of innocence, while the state of innocence must be presupposed in order to explain the possibility of its loss.[29] This in turn means that before he sinned, Adam must have been in a condition of innocence from which every subsequent individual is excluded due to the presence of sinfulness in the world, which came about through the first sin (that is, Adam's sin).

Although the connection between Kierkegaard's thoughts on sin and Bauer's treatment of the Genesis account of the Creation might seem far from obvious, there is one nevertheless, since in both cases the law of the excluded middle comes into play. In the case of Kierkegaard's argument against explaining hereditary sin in terms of Adam's sin, the point is that such an explanation would make Adam both part of the human race and not part of it, and it would thus appear to violate the law of the excluded middle. Kierkegaard points out that the individual is both himself and the race, that is to say, he is both a particular individual and an example of the general type human being, so that, in so far as the individual is part of the human race, what is true of every other individual human being must also be true of Adam, the first man; and, since in this respect what is true of Adam is therefore true of all individuals, that

27 *SKS* 4, 332 / *CA*, 25.

28 Ibid.

29 Ibid.

which explains Adam also explains the race.[30] If, however, Adam is understood to have been in a state of innocence from which the rest of the human race is excluded, this would no longer be the case. Consequently, Kierkegaard rejects the idea of a state of innocence which was enjoyed only by Adam and not the rest of the human race on the grounds that it would make Adam into both part of the human race and not part of it, thereby violating the law of the excluded middle. However, while Kierkegaard here avoids a contradiction by rejecting one of two mutually exclusive propositions, we shall see that he grants that the Genesis account of sin represents an offense to the human understanding.

With respect to the concept of sin, the fact that what explains Adam also explains the race implies that the essential nature of sin, or its quality, will be the same in the case of Adam as in the case of every subsequent individual who sins. Kierkegaard therefore claims that while sinfulness came into the world through the first sin (that is, Adam's sin), it is equally true of every subsequent man's first sin that through it sin comes into the world; while in relation to sin itself (that is, the quality of sin) the fact that sin was not in the world before Adam's first sin is accidental and irrelevant.[31] In other words, the quality of sin explains each individual case of sin because it is that which makes something into a sin in the first place, whereas any quantitative determination, such as whether a sin was the first one in relation to a second, third or fourth sin, is irrelevant because it does not explain the essential nature of sin.

There is, however, an important sense in which Kierkegaard thinks that sin cannot be explained. He claims, moreover, that the Genesis story of the first sin presents the only "dialectically consistent" view of the matter and that its content is concentrated in one statement: sin came into the world by a sin.[32] If this statement expresses the quality of sin, so that it is as true of every subsequent individual who sins as it is of Adam that sin comes into the world by a sin, it does so at the expense of offering a circular explanation of sin, since the explanation employs the concept of sin to explain the quality of sin, and therefore presupposes what it seeks to explain. Kierkegaard recognizes this and acknowledges that for the understanding such an explanation is an offense. He also claims, possibly with Bauer in mind, that it is therefore a myth.[33] Kierkegaard thus implies that the reduction of biblical narrative to the status of myth is motivated by an awareness of its incompatibility with the logical principles governing human thought.

The problem of circularity is, of course, different from the problems with biblical narrative which Bauer identifies in his article, "Die Urgeschichte der Menschheit," since these concern the violation of the law of the excluded middle and the relation between a condition and that of which it is the condition. Nevertheless, it still serves as an example as to how Kierkegaard accepts the view that biblical narrative appears to be irreconcilable with certain principles of human thought. Yet for Kierkegaard the offense to the human understanding that is caused by the Genesis story of the first sin does not serve to undermine this account of sin, which accords perfectly

30 *SKS* 4, 335f. / *CA*, 29.
31 *SKS* 4, 337 / *CA*, 31.
32 *SKS* 4, 338 / *CA*, 32.
33 Ibid.

with Christian dogmatics, since the latter explains the presence of sin in the world by means of the presupposition of hereditary sin.[34] However, this only partly shows why Kierkegaard thinks that biblical narrative has an underlying truth which makes it into something more than myth. He also thinks that in order to recognize the truth contained in Christian dogmatics, an individual must first be in the position to appropriate such teachings in the right way. Indeed, according to Kierkegaard, there are individuals who are not in the position to appropriate the content of Christian dogmatics because they approach biblical narrative, such as the Genesis account of the Fall, in the wrong way. By looking more closely at this issue, we shall discover another possible link between Kierkegaard's and Bauer's thought.

In *The Concept of Anxiety* Kierkegaard claims not only that the statement "sin came into the world through a sin" is as true of every subsequent individual as it is of Adam, but also that this statement implies that sin is a concrete category which is posited by the single individual as the single individual.[35] In other words, it is only through the single individual's first sin that sin comes into the world for the individual in question. Kierkegaard therefore claims that when it comes to the issue as to how sin came into the world, each man understands it solely by himself, and if he would learn it from another person, he would *eo ipso* misunderstand it.[36] This primitive relation to sin can be further illustrated with reference to Kierkegaard's introduction of the concept of anxiety into his account of sin.

Kierkegaard relates the psychological concept of anxiety, which he thinks can be both prior to sin and a consequence of the latter, to the Genesis story of the Fall of man when he turns to God's prohibition not to eat from the tree of the knowledge of good and evil. Kierkegaard points out that Adam could not have understood this prohibition because the knowledge of the distinction between good and evil could only follow as a consequence of his eating from the tree of the knowledge of good and evil.[37] Bauer makes the same point in "Die Urgeschichte der Menschheit," and, as with his account of the difference between the days in the Genesis account of the Creation, he characterizes the problem as one in which what is conditioned is understood as being prior to the condition of its possibility, which violates the relation between a condition and that of which it is the condition. Bauer also argues that an understanding of the real import of the words "good" and "evil" could only be gained through a degree of experience of life which man could not have possessed in the first moments of his existence.[38]

The offense to the human understanding is in this case, unlike the paradox of the Incarnation, one that Kierkegaard attempts to remove; for he claims that the prohibition induces anxiety because it awakens in man the possibility of freedom, or the possibility of being able.[39] Freedom's possibility is not, however, to be understood

---

34 *SKS* 4, 326f. / *CA*, 19.

35 *SKS* 4, 362 / *CA*, 57.

36 *SKS* 4, 356 / *CA*, 51.

37 *SKS* 4, 350 / *CA*, 44.

38 *Zeitschrift für spekulative Theologie*, op. cit., vol. 3, no. 1, 1837, p. 147.

39 *SKS* 4, 350 / *CA*, 44.

as the ability to choose between good and evil.[40] The possibility of "being able" should be understood instead as an awareness of the ability to choose which does not as yet involve a consciousness of the different choices that one can make; and this is why Kierkegaard calls it a higher form of ignorance.[41] This is again reminiscent of Bauer's treatment of the literal conception of the Genesis account of the Fall, for he allows that while we cannot attribute to man an insight into the distinction between good and evil in the first moments of his existence, the possibility of such an insight can be thought to lie within him.[42]

For Kierkegaard the distinction between freedom as possibility and the consciousness of being able to choose between good and evil serves as another link with the Genesis story of the Fall of man because it means that the narrative in Genesis gives the correct explanation of innocence, which is that innocence is ignorance.[43] Moreover, just as for every other individual as well as for Adam sin comes into the world through a sin, every man loses innocence in essentially the same way as Adam.[44] According to Kierkegaard, anxiety is what precedes this loss because the awakening of freedom's possibility disturbs the individual's immediate unity with his natural condition. Yet the concept of anxiety can only take us so far because freedom's possibility does not yet involve the knowledge of good and evil, and it cannot therefore explain the possibility of sin. Kierkegaard describes anxiety as the "dizziness of freedom," and he claims that freedom somehow succumbs in this dizziness only to find at the next moment that it is guilty, so that a qualitative leap must be thought to lie between the moment of anxiety and the moment of guilt.[45] The transition from anxiety to guilt is, in short, inexplicable, just as sin is a presupposition which cannot be explained.

While the presupposition of sin cannot be explained, its truth can be directly experienced, however, in the sense that the individual who makes the transition from anxiety to guilt is made to confront this presupposition as the only possible explanation of his guilt. Consequently, the truth of this presupposition can only be understood by an individual who becomes guilty and conscious of his sinfulness. In other words, an individual's understanding of sin depends on his primitive relation to sin. Since Kierkegaard thinks that the Genesis story of the first sin presents the only dialectically consistent view of the matter, he must also hold the view that such a primitive relation to sin is a precondition for a correct understanding of this story. This suggests that Kierkegaard would regard Bauer as someone who is unaware of, or unconcerned about, this primitive relation to sin, and is thus led to treat the Genesis account of the Fall as a myth. This in turn points to another important aspect of Kierkegaard's thought in which his understanding of Bauer's writings might have had a role to play: his account of the objective attitude towards the teachings of Christianity.

---

40 *SKS* 4, 354 / *CA*, 49.

41 *SKS* 4, 350 / *CA*, 45.

42 *Zeitschrift für spekulative Theologie*, op. cit., vol. 3, no. 1, 1837, p. 148.

43 *SKS* 4, 343 / *CA*, 37.

44 *SKS* 4, 342 / *CA*, 35.

45 *SKS* 4, 365 / *CA*, 61.

IV. Bauer and the Objective Attitude

In *The Concept of Anxiety* Kierkegaard refers to a free-thinker who "applies all his acumen to prove that the New Testament was not written until the second century."[46] The editors of the English translation suggest that Kierkegaard might here have had in mind Bauer's *Kritik der evangelischen Geschichte der Synoptiker*,[47] a three-volume work from 1841–42, in which Bauer challenges the historical existence of Christ, and depicts the gospels as literary creations. Bauer most explicitly advances his claim for the second-century origins of Christianity in his writings of the 1850s,[48] subsequent to Kierkegaard's *The Concept of Anxiety*, but his earlier gospel investigations already warrant the implicit conclusion that Christianity arose belatedly, so that the identification of Bauer as the object of Kierkegaard's critique is at least plausible. Such a reading provoked Kierkegaard to attack what he calls the historical-critical tendency, and perhaps to see Bauer as a spokesman for this approach. However, we have no firm evidence that Kierkegaard had at some point read Bauer's critique of the synoptics; for, unlike the various editions of the *Zeitschrift für spekulative Theologie*, there is no mention of the *Kritik der evangelischen Geschichte der Synoptiker* in the *Auction Catalogue* of Kierkegaard's library. Nevertheless, even if Kierkegaard may have had at best only a second-hand knowledge of this work, it may have helped to shape his understanding of Bauer's thought, and perhaps to channel his own thinking.

In the Preface to his extensive work on the synoptics, Bauer makes certain claims which could have reinforced Kierkegaard's view of him as someone who wishes to show that the teachings of Christianity are myths, although Bauer is careful to distance himself from this reading. For instance, Bauer argues that the task of criticism is to investigate whether the content of the synoptic gospels, and not only their form, is of a literary origin, and thus the free creation of self-consciousness.[49] Moreover, Bauer signals that he intends to give an affirmative answer to this question when he states that he looks forward to a time when what is written in the Bible [*das Bibelwort*] is recognized as the work and revelation of self-consciousness.[50] These claims suggest that the synoptic gospels do not contain any historical truths but are instead products of the human imagination. Bauer himself does not take this conclusion to imply that they are therefore to be understood as myths, however, and his critique of D.F. Strauss' work makes this distinction plain. We will explore this point subsequently. Kierkegaard, however, may have interpreted Bauer's position as equivalent to that of Strauss; and he may thereby have attributed to him the intention of seeking to reduce the content of Christianity to the status of myth, not in the sense that Bauer distinguishes the mythical from the literary, but in the sense that he treats the historical foundations, or their absence, as the essential factor in determining the truth of Christianity. This in turn suggests a link with one form of the objective

46 *SKS* 4, 442f. / *CA*, 142.

47 Cf. *CA*, 251, note 44.

48 Moggach, *The Philosophy and Politics of Bruno Bauer*, op. cit., p. 184.

49 *Kritik der evangelischen Geschichte der Synoptiker*, op. cit., vol. 1, p. xv.

50 Ibid., p. xx.

attitude which Kierkegaard criticizes in the *Concluding Unscientific Postscript*, namely the historical-critical approach to the Bible.

When Kierkegaard mentions the free-thinker who applies all his acumen to prove that the New Testament was not written until the second century, he places this figure in the same category as the man of rigid orthodoxy who applies all his diligence and learning to prove that every word in the New Testament derives from the respective apostle, since in both cases inwardness disappears. Kierkegaard refers to these two figures as analogous forms of the demonic.[51] Moreover, he remarks elsewhere that there is something demonic in wanting to attack the historical in the New Testament as if it were the main thing;[52] and, as we have suggested above, Kierkegaard may have had some grounds for thinking that this was what Bauer was doing in such works as the *Kritik der evangelischen Geschichte der Synoptiker.*

The man of rigid orthodoxy whom Kierkegaard mentions is representative of the type of attitude which busies itself with the question as to which books of the Bible are to be regarded as authoritative, thus raising concerns about the canonicity, authenticity, and integrity of the particular books of the Bible.[53] Kierkegaard argues, however, that the historical-critical enterprise which concerns itself with such matters cannot lead to an absolutely certain account of what Christian doctrine really is, since the authenticity of particular books of the Bible can be thrown into doubt by the discovery of new facts. To illustrate this problem, he describes a situation in which the authenticity of certain books of the Bible is demonstrated only for doubts to arise concerning books whose authenticity has never before been doubted.[54]

The free-thinker obviously differs from the man of rigid orthodoxy in the sense that he is not seeking to establish the truth of the historical facts on which Christianity is thought to rest, but is instead questioning the authenticity of these foundations. Moreover, if the free-thinker's historical-critical mode of enquiry leads him to cast doubt on the truth of Christianity, Kierkegaard would regard this outcome as a natural consequence of this mode of enquiry. The free-thinker is in this respect more consistent and insightful than the man of rigid orthodoxy, who persists in the futile attempt to provide a historical basis for his faith; indeed, what Kierkegaard says about the "modern mythical allegorising trend," which "summarily declares Christianity to be a myth," may equally be applied to the claims of the free-thinker, namely, that this is at least forthright behavior.[55] Since Kierkegaard appears to regard Bauer as a representative of the mythical allegorizing trend, we may suppose that he had some respect for his honest attitude towards Christianity.

Nevertheless, for Kierkegaard the free-thinker and the man of rigid orthodoxy both lack the right disposition towards the teachings of Christianity because they lack passion. Kierkegaard argues that faith requires such passion precisely because Christianity contains teachings which represent an offense to the human understanding. The teachings of Christianity therefore require a different basis than

---

51 *SKS* 4, 442 / *CA*, 142.
52 *Pap.* V B 64 / *JP* 2, 1643.
53 *SKS* 7, 32 / *CUP1*, 24.
54 *SKS* 7, 38f. / *CUP1*, 32.
55 *SKS* 7, 199 / *CUP1*, 218.

that of the type of absolute certainty which objective reasoning seeks to attain. Against the aspirations of objective knowledge, Kierkegaard claims that without risk there is no faith, and that the more objective reliability, the less inwardness, and conversely, the less objective reliability, the more inwardness.[56] The idea seems to be that the less probable or possible a belief is from the objective standpoint, the more passionately must individuals believe in it if they are not going to renounce such a belief; and by committing themselves to a belief of this kind, individuals run an increasing risk of being wrong. Consequently, Kierkegaard thinks that the historical-critical form of enquiry is irrelevant to faith, whether its intention is to demonstrate the truth of Christianity or to undermine it.[57]

We therefore need to determine to what extent Bauer can be seen as an example of the objective reasoning which Kierkegaard thinks is incompatible with genuine religious faith and a proper understanding of the true import of the teachings of Christianity. We have already seen an objective type of reasoning at work in Bauer's "Die Urgeschichte der Menschheit," since in this article Bauer seeks to demonstrate that the Genesis account of the prehistory of man is incompatible with some of the logical principles governing human thought. We now need to examine Bauer's attitude towards Christianity in so far as it can be classed as an objective one that involves a historical-critical mode of enquiry, and to determine the specificity of Bauer's position in relation to other available forms of religious criticism. Even if it cannot be proven that he is the "demonic" free-thinker whom Kierkegaard mentions in *The Concept of Anxiety*, the likelihood persists, given the historically motivated attack on Christianity in the *Kritik der evangelischen Geschichte der Synoptiker*. Bauer's treatment of certain key themes in his religious critique will provide an illuminating comparison with Kierkegaard.

V. Bauer as "Free-thinker"

We may distill from the foregoing discussion a number of issues on which Bauer and Kierkegaard offered conflicting perspectives: the Incarnation, the nature of inwardness, the mythical status of religious beliefs, and the substance of historical critique. To illustrate these differences, we must now range widely across Bauer's literary output in the 1830s and 1840s. It is here not a matter of seeking specific points of contact or reference, but of determining a fundamentally different understanding of selfhood.

Bauer himself had placed the question of the Incarnation first among the twelve theological theses which he defended in order to obtain his licentiate in Berlin on 15 March 1834.[58] Here Bauer asserted, "The concept of the person solves all controversies about the dual nature of Christ."[59] Though the arguments whereby Bauer propounded this thesis have not been preserved, it is tempting to speculate that

---

56 *SKS* 7, 192 / *CUP1*, 209.

57 *SKS* 7, 36f. / *CUP1*, 29f.

58 Ernst Barnikol, *Bruno Bauer. Darstellung und Quellen*, unpublished manuscript, Amsterdam: International Institute for Social History (ca. 1965).

59 Douglas Moggach's translation from Latin.

there is an anticipation here of the duality of particular and universal moments within human self-consciousness, which is fundamental to his later thought. Hegel himself had defined personality as the ability to give oneself one's own attributes as a matter of conscious choice, to shape contingent and particular drives into the expression of freedom, by processes of critical selection. The person is thus always dual, particular in view of the accidents and circumstances of one's life, but also universal, as the agent of practical will, able to sift and fashion this material into an integrated whole. While it is clear that in 1834 Bauer had not worked out the implications of this view for the republican project of political and social emancipation, the central importance of the moment of form, of moulding the given into a conscious product, is a constant feature of his thought. The Incarnation, as the willing descent of the universal into the particular, becomes the paradigm of the freedom of self-consciousness, and is repeated in each human subject who acts ethically and with critical awareness. The universal thus takes on a concrete and determinate shape: not only once, at a single historical moment, as Christianity imagines it, but in innumerable instances. And the universal is ours, as a property of self-consciousness, and not as the character of a separate, supramundane realm. Its appearance in the world is not a derogation from its divine status, but the fulfilment of an imperative of rational freedom.

This idea has important consequences for Bauer's thought. Already in 1829, in his prize essay on Kant's aesthetics, he attributes a relative priority to art over religion. Religion, he affirms, excludes doubt and critical consciousness, and its dogmatism is inimical to the free movement and probing of thought. Art, by contrast, depicts the activity of thought in a material element, transforming matter in light of the idea. Art is thus, too, emblematic of freedom, and of the central Hegelian idea of the effectiveness or causal power of reason in objectivity. Later, by 1840, Bauer will stress the constriction and alienation of the religious consciousness, against the emancipatory force of art. Religion portrays spirit mired in inwardness, while art displays it in triumphant conquest of the world.

And yet inwardness, for Bauer, is not thereby extinguished but enhanced. He distinguishes kinds of inwardness or subjectivity. The beautiful soul described by Schleiermacher and the pietists[60] suffers from a twofold limitation: a sense of dependence on a transcendent absolute, thus a denial of the capacity for autonomous self-direction; and, correspondingly, a view of inwardness as an obstacle to action, an impotence or refusal to sully the purity of one's intentions by transforming them into tangible deeds. This reluctance manifests the egoistic orientation that Bauer attributes to religion generally. Kierkegaard's dialectic of sin, anxiety, and guilt can be understood as a modification of this view, tracing out what the religious consciousness experiences as it acts in the world, but it shares with the inert beautiful soul the dependency on a transcendent source of value.

The kind of inwardness Bauer favors expresses his understanding of the Hegelian idea of the unity of thought and being. This idea appears now as thinking

---

60 Friedrich Schleiermacher's *Soliloquy* of 1810, cited in David Simpson, *German Aesthetic and Literary Criticism*, Cambridge: Cambridge University Press 1984, p. 12. Schleiermacher's position cannot be assimilated to that of the pietists, though Bauer tends to do so.

that transforms objectivity into a vehicle of itself and of its freedom. The creative subjectivity that initiates and sustains processes of objective transformation is what Bauer calls universal self-consciousness, a universal that is immanent in history itself as its motive force. Against the impotence of the beautiful soul, this consciousness is activist, passing into objectivity to negate the obstacles that it finds to freedom, but returning to its ideal element in self-knowledge, enriched by its struggles. If it loses itself in its products, or does not find itself confirmed and realized in its deeds, this discovery only presses it on to greater exertions, and not to lamentation, sorrow, and defeat. The inward and outward are two indissociable moments, and the inward has a highly complex structure of universal form and particular matter. This is not the empty or abstract universal, the ability to dissociate the will from all content, with which Hegel begins his account in the *Philosophy of Right*.[61] It is a concrete universal, whose positive content, the substance of what is to be willed, derives from reflection on the historical process as an ongoing struggle for emancipation from all irrational relations and institutions.[62] Each moment prescribes a series of tasks to be completed so that the knowledge and experience of freedom may advance, but the manner of their completion is open and undetermined, is itself a work of freedom.

The foregoing reflections open to two further, related questions: namely whether Bauer can be held to attribute a mythical status to the biblical accounts, and in what sense for him the historical critique of Christianity is the principal issue in assessing its role and meaning. Among the Hegelian left, it is D.F. Strauss who had depicted the gospels as the mythical manifestation of the collective experiences and struggles of the early Christian community.[63] Bauer takes issue with this approach, however, because it does not adequately demonstrate the mediation of an apparently given content into form through the labor of individual thinkers, nor does it explain the emergence of the content itself. Strauss describes not the real genetic process of the gospel narratives, but the illusory appearance of a process, reproducing the hypothesis of divine inspiration in the idea of communal production.[64] Bauer stresses instead the literary origins of the Biblical texts, not as collective myths, but as individualized aesthetic works.[65] As such, they are not falsifications or conscious deceptions, but a record of the development of self-consciousness, responding to historical problems with the resources of subjectivity then available. The creativity underlying these works does fulfill a need experienced by those who cannot themselves formulate a solution; it is not independent of the conditions of its genesis, or it would never find an audience. Even when they act within the confines of the dependent religious relation, the gospel authors manifest a formative creativity which can now be seen as a pale reflection of autonomous self-consciousness. They respond to a deeply felt problem or urging by endowing it with an aesthetic shape, giving voice to an

---

61 G.W.F. Hegel, *Grundlinien der Philosophie des Rechts*, ed. by Helmut Reichelt, Frankfurt am Main: Ullstein 1972, § 5.

62 Moggach, "'Free Means Ethical': Bruno Bauer's Critical Idealism," *The Owl of Minerva*, vol. 33, no. 1, Fall/Winter 2001–02, pp. 1–24.

63 D.F. Strauss, *Das Leben Jesu, kritisch bearbeitet*, vols. 1–2, Tübingen: Osiander 1835.

64 *Kritik der evangelischen Geschichte der Synoptiker*, op. cit., vol. 1, p. vi.

65 Ibid., p. vi and p. 69.

inarticulate need experienced by the early Christian community for a comprehension of its own origins and value. This need sets the preconditions and limits within which alienated creativity can work, and poses a range of issues which must be addressed, without stipulating the form that this solution might take. Strauss' mythical approach sees content as directly determining form, but this is to misconstrue the necessity for thought, even religious thinking, to give itself its own form. Thus, Bauer explains, the early stirrings of the Christian consciousness are satisfied by Mark's account of Christ's adult life,[66] but subsequently the community craves a more detailed story, and this need is gratified by the history of Christ's ancestry, conception, birth, and childhood. Luke and Matthew then frame a suitable narrative, while retaining as much as possible of Mark's original literary creation.[67] If Bauer and Strauss both strive to humanize the absolute, and to deny its transcendent status, they do so in two distinct ways.[68]

Bauer's way is distinct too from that of his eighteenth-century precursors. It is in the Enlightenment criticisms of religion, with Holbach, for example, that the historical and contingent presents itself as the main issue. For Bauer, it is rather a question of the comprehensive history of self-consciousness and the overcoming of alienation, with religion as a necessary if negative moment in the process: negative because it denies human creativity in favor of an alien, transcendent source; necessary because the abasement of reason before its own products is a stage in its coming to awareness of its own powers and freedom. There is, thus, a striking contrast between Holbach's 1756 *Le christianisme dévoilé*[69] and Bauer's equivalently titled *Das entdeckte Christenthum* of 1843.[70] In Holbach's Enlightenment rationalism, deceit, manipulation, and the power-seeking of the clergy are the bases of religion, but from Bauer's perspective, this superficial approach fails to engage with the profound issues of alienated self-consciousness which religion expresses. For Bauer, the ground of religion is not duplicity or gullibility, but reason's truncation and devaluation of its own activity, or the distorted projection of human attributes into a transcendent, otherworldly domain. In religion, self-consciousness appears passive, receiving dogmas and commands from another, but it is never truly so. Rather, thought deceives itself about its own activities, attributing them to an alien source.

---

66 On the temporal priority of the Pauline epistles to the gospel narratives, see *Kritik der evangelischen Geschichte der Synoptiker*, op. cit., vol. 2, p. 45.

67 *Kritik der evangelischen Geschichte der Synoptiker*, op. cit., vol. 1, p. 127. Compare *Kritik der evangelischen Geschichte der Synoptiker*, op. cit., vol. 2, pp. 45–6. On the aesthetic limitations of this literary creation, see also *Kritik der evangelischen Geschichte der Synoptiker*, op. cit., vol. 3, p. 36.

68 The foregoing contrast is drawn from the fuller exposition in D. Moggach, *The Philosophy and Politics of Bruno Bauer*, op. cit., Chapter 3.

69 Paul-Henry Thiry d'Holbach, *Le christianisme dévoilé, ou Examen des principes et des effets de la religion chrétienne* (London 1756), Reprinted in *Oeuvres philosophiques*, vols. 1– 3, Préface de Jean Claude Bourdin, Paris: Editions Alive 1998, vol. 1, pp. 1–120.

70 Bauer, *Das entdeckte Christenthum. Eine Erinnerung an das 18. Jahrhundert und ein Beitrag zur Krisis des 19ten*, Zürich and Winterthur: Verlag des literarischen Comptoirs 1843.

> Thus, the religious spirit is that splitting of self-consciousness in which its essential determinateness appears over and against it as a separate power. Before this power, self-consciousness must necessarily lose itself, for it has ejected into it its own content, and as far as it can still maintain itself for itself as ego, it feels itself as nothing before that power, just as it must consider it in turn the negation of itself.[71]

This fundamental alienation is the condition of possibility for any empirical manipulation or power relations that might define particular religious sects as they emerge historically. For Bauer, the abasement of consciousness culminates in Christianity, which he defines as the purely abstract religion, divorcing the believer from all ties of belonging to concrete communities.[72] Placing the individual in abject dependence on an absolute power (a figure Hegel had analyzed as the unhappy consciousness), Christianity drives the opposition between universal and particular to an extreme pitch, where it must be resolved, and the universal reclaimed for its rightful place as an aspect of our own thought and deeds. At the same time, through the doctrine of the Incarnation, Christianity also intimates how that resolution might be achieved. This unbearable darkness and foreshadowing is not simply a logical contradiction, like the creation stories, but defines the moving dialectic of the Christian religion, and marks its place in the historical record of emancipation, as Bauer reads it. In the 1840s, when the polemics between Restoration orthodoxy and critical progress intensify, it is the negative side that Bauer stresses more, since the positive moment of Christianity has been completely assimilated into his idea of republican freedom.

The paradox of the Incarnation graphically illustrates the key differences among the left Hegelians, on the one hand, and between them collectively and Kierkegaard, on the other. Like Ludwig Feuerbach, for whom the attributes of the deity are the projected properties and aspirations of the human genus as a whole,[73] Strauss thinks that what orthodoxy describes as the Incarnation occurs through the species collectively: over the vast expanse of historical time, the powers of the species are manifest and perfected. The universal is realized distributively over the entire species, but not in any finite individual. In contrast, Bauer thinks that the Incarnation, as the synthesis of universality and particularity, can occur in each human individual singly, to the extent that the person is capable of self-transformation in light of a universal ideal. The absolute *is*, in infinite self-consciousness, when we act with ethical awareness, and free ourselves from the grip of irrational powers and interests. This synthesis of universal and particular is not to be understood as a hubristic or impossibly rigorist objective, but as a regulative ideal, enjoining subjects to scrutinize their maxims and actions, to attain a high degree of self-awareness, and

---

71 *Kritik der evangelischen Geschichte der Synoptiker*, op. cit., vol. 1, p. 25 (Douglas Moggach's translation). Cf. ibid., pp. 240–1 and p. 307n.

72 The characterization of Christianity as the abstract religion is elaborated in Bruno Bauer (anonymous), *Die Posaune des jüngsten Gerichts über Hegel den Atheisten und Antichristen. Ein Ultimatum*, Leipzig: Otto Wigand 1841, as well as in *Das entdeckte Christentum*, op. cit. See also *Kritik der evangelischen Geschichte der Synoptiker*, op. cit., vol. 3, p. 310.

73 Ludwig Feuerbach, *Das Wesen des Christentums* (1841), ed. by Werner Schuffenhauer and Wolfgang Harich, Berlin: Akademie Verlag 1973.

to be alert to the effects of heteronomous impulses. To the extent that they do this, subjects realize the infinite in their own lives, and re-enact the rational and liberating content of the process which orthodoxy depicts as the Incarnation. In this sense, stressing the personal and inward engagement of each subject with the universal,[74] Bauer is perhaps closer to the intimate concerns of Kierkegaard, and yet they remain diametrically opposed. Against the left Hegelians, Kierkegaard denies that the divine can be made fully immanent. "God and man are two qualities separated by an infinite qualitative difference. Humanly speaking, any teaching that disregards this difference is demented—divinely understood, it is blasphemy."[75] In Kierkegaard's view, Feuerbach, Strauss and Bauer indulge in hubris when they fail to maintain the distinction between the human and divine, by reducing the latter to the former; and thus they eliminate the paradox of the Incarnation by suppressing one of its terms. For Bauer, however, the religious doctrine is a confused anticipation of a freedom newly available after millennial struggles. The task now is to secure that freedom in "the republic of self-consciousness."[76]

While "Die Urgeschichte der Menschheit" is the only text by Bauer which we know Kierkegaard read, this article features two issues which clearly preoccupied him and came to influence his own thought: the fact that Christianity can be shown to contain teachings which appear contrary to the human understanding, and the view that these teachings must therefore be viewed as myths. With respect to the former issue, there are a number of places in Kierkegaard's writings in which he himself acknowledges that the teachings of Christianity appear to violate the principles governing human thought: the violation of the law of the excluded middle, the inversion of the logical order in which a condition and that of which it is the condition stand to each other, and the problem of circularity. He even views such offense to the human understanding as being an inescapable feature of Christianity. This does not lead Kierkegaard to argue that the teachings of Christianity are myths, however; and his theory of subjective truth can be seen as a response to such a tendency, which he appears to associate with Bauer. While Bauer may not have been the first or only person to force Kierkegaard into considering the idea that the teachings of Christianity violate the logical principles governing human thought, we have seen that he was especially struck by Bauer's presentation of this problem in "Die Urgeschichte der Menschheit." This in turn means that there are good grounds for thinking that in this respect Bauer exercised an important influence on Kierkegaard.

There is no firm evidence that Kierkegaard read any of Bauer's other texts, although the fact that he owned copies of all three editions of Bauer's *Zeitschrift für spekulative Theologie* leads one to suspect that he may have read some of the other articles which Bauer wrote for this journal. As regards the suggested link between

---

74 John E. Toews, *Hegelianism. The Path Toward Dialectical Humanism, 1805–1841*, Cambridge: Cambridge University Press 1980, also stresses the importance for Bauer of personal formative activity on the self and the world.

75 *SKS* 11, 237 / *SUD*, 126.

76 Bruno Bauer, "Leiden und Freuden des theologischen Bewußtseins," in *Anekdota zur neuesten deutschen Philosophie und Publizcistik*, vols. 1–2, ed. by Arnold Ruge, Zürich and Winterthur: Verlag des literarischen Comptoirs 1843, vol. 2, p. 111 (*ASKB* 753).

the "demonic" free-thinker whom Kierkegaard mentions in *The Concept of Anxiety*, and Bauer's *Kritik der evangelischen Geschichte der Synoptiker*, we have seen that Bauer's free-thinking is *sui generis*, differing from the mythical approach of D.F. Strauss and from Enlightenment critiques by virtue of its fidelity to the central Hegelian insight of the unity of thought and being. Bauer's historical idealism defends a principle of universality against particular interests and identities, but sees this universal as fully immanent in the historical process. According to Bauer, the religious consciousness anticipates freedom, but again denies it, and reveals itself now as the adversary of emancipation. Yet, holding that autonomy can be won only by personal exertion, Bauer shares with Kierkegaard the profound concern for the inner life. The fulfillment of that inner life, however, lies not in the relation of the self to God but to historical processes of liberation, securing the accord of the outer order with the ethical will.

Bibliography

I. Bauer's Works in The Auction Catalogue *of Kierkegaard's Library*

"Der mosaische Ursprung der Gesetzgebung des Pentateuch," *Zeitschrift für spekulative Theologie*, vols. 1–3, ed. by Bruno Bauer, Berlin: Dümmler 1836–38, vol. 1, no. 1, 1836, pp. 140–81 (*ASKB* 354–357).

"Der Pantheismus innerhalb des Rationalismus und Supranaturalismus," *Zeitschrift für spekulative Theologie*, op. cit., vol. 1, no. 1, 1836, pp. 267–76.

"Der Alt-Testamentliche Hintergrund im Evangelium des Johannes," *Zeitschrift für spekulative Theologie*, op. cit., vol. 1, no. 2, 1836, pp. 158–204.

"Das 'Antitheologische' am Hegel'schen Begriff der hebräischen Religion," *Zeitschrift für spekulative Theologie*, op. cit., vol. 1, no. 2, 1836, pp. 247–56.

"Das Geständnis der Philosophie," *Zeitschrift für spekulative Theologie*, op. cit., vol. 1, no. 2, 1836, pp. 257–9.

"Die neueren Commentare zu den Psalmen," *Zeitschrift für spekulative Theologie*, op. cit., vol. 2, no. 1, 1837, pp. 217–52.

"Die Prinzipien der mosaischen Rechts- und Religions-Verfassung nach ihrem inneren Zusammenhange entwickelt," *Zeitschrift für spekulative Theologie*, op. cit., vol. 2, no. 2, 1837, pp. 297–353.

[Review of] "*Die Glaubwürdigkeit der evangelischen Geschichte zugleich eine Kritik des Lebens Jesu von Strauß*. Dargestellt von Dr. A. Tholuck. Hamburg, bei F. Perthes 1837. XVI, 463. S.," *Zeitschrift für spekulative Theologie*, op. cit., vol. 2, no. 2, 1837, pp. 405–25.

[Review of] "*Propädeutik der Neutestamentlichen Theologie* von C. Steph. Matthies. Greifswald, bei E. Mauritius 1836. S. XII, 386," *Zeitschrift für spekulative Theologie*, op. cit., vol. 2, no. 2, 1837, pp. 425–38.

[Review of] "*Die Authentie des Pentateuches*, erwiesen von Dr. E.W. Hengstenberg. Erster Band. Berlin, bei Ludwig Oehmigte 1836. S. LXXXIV. 502," *Zeitschrift für spekulative Theologie*, op. cit., vol. 2, no. 2, 1837, pp. 439–66.

"Der Begriff der göttlichen Gerechtigkeit im zweiten Theil des Jesaias," *Zeitschrift für spekulative Theologie*, op. cit., vol. 2, no. 2, 1837, pp. 78–487.

"Die Urgeschichte der Menschheit nach dem biblischen Berichte der Genesis, kritisch untersucht," *Zeitschrift für spekulative Theologie*, op. cit., vol. 3, no. 1, 1837, pp. 125–210.

[Review of] "*Vorlesungen über Glauben und Wissen als Einleitung in die Dogmatik und Religionsphilosophie*, von Dr. Joh. Ed. Erdmann, außerord. Prof. der Phil. an der Univers. zu Halle. Berlin, Duncker und Humblot. 1837. X. 276," *Zeitschrift für spekulative Theologie*, op. cit., vol. 3, no. 1, 1837, pp. 253–61.

"Apologetisches und Kritisches zum biblischen Bericht von der Urgeschichte der Menschheit," *Zeitschrift für spekulative Theologie*, op. cit., vol. 3, no. 2, 1838, pp. 435–54.

[Review of] "*Symbolik des Mosaischen Cultus* von R.Ch.W.F. Bähr. Erster Band. XII. 498. Heidelberg bei Mohr. 1837," *Zeitschrift für spekulative Theologie*, op. cit., vol. 3, no. 2, 1838, pp. 485–511.

"Leiden und Freuden des theologischen Bewußtseins," in *Anekdota zur neuesten deutschen Philosophie und Publicistik*, vols. 1–2, ed. by Arnold Ruge, Zürich and Winterthur: Verlag des Literarischen Comptoirs 1843, vol. 2, pp. 89–112 (*ASKB* 753).

[Review of] "*Bremisches Magazin für evangelische Wahrheit gegenüber dem modernen Pietismus*. Erstes Heft. Auch unter dem Titel: die verschiedenen theologischen Richtungen in der protestantischen Kirche unserer Zeit von Paniel. Bremen, bei Schünemann 1841. P. XVI. 288," in *Anekdota zur neuesten deutschen Philosophie und Publicistik*, op. cit., vol. 2, pp. 113–34.

[Review of] "*Einleitung in die Dogmengeschichte von Theodor Kliefoth*. X. 387. Parchim und Ludwigsluft, Hinstorff'sche Hofbuchhandlung," in *Anekdota zur neuesten deutschen Philosophie und Publicistik*, op. cit., vol. 2, pp. 135–59.

[Review of] "*Die Geschichte des Leben Jesu mit steter Rücksicht auf die vorhandenen Quellen* dargestellt von Dr. von Amman. Erster Band. Leipzig 1842. Vogel," in *Anekdota zur neuesten deutschen Philosophie und Publicistik*, op. cit., vol. 2, pp. 160–85.

"Das alte neue Testament," in *Anekdota zur neuesten deutschen Philosophie und Publicistik*, op. cit., vol. 2, pp. 186–93.

[ed.] *Zeitschrift für spekulative Theologie*, vols. 1–3, Berlin: Dümmler 1836–38 (*ASKB* 354–357).

II. Works in The Auction Catalogue *of Kierkegaard's Library that Discuss Bauer*

Beck, Andreas Frederik, *Begrebet Mythus eller den religiøse Aands Form*, Copenhagen: P.G. Philipsens Forlag 1842 (*ASKB* 424).

Biedermann, A. Emanuel, *Die freie Theologie oder Philosophie und Christenthum in Streit und Frieden*, Tübingen: Ludwig Friedrich Fues. 1844, p. 82; p. 183n (*ASKB* U 20).

Brøchner, Hans, *Nogle Bemærkninger om Daaben, foranledigede ved Professor Martensens Skrift: Den christelige Daab*, Copenhagen: P.G. Philipsens Forlag 1843, pp. 31–3; p. 39; p. 60 (*ASKB* U 27).

Fichte, Immanuel Hermann, "Die philosophische Litteratur der Gegenwart. Neunter Artikel. Die Radikalen in der Spekulation, mit Rücksicht auf...Bruno Bauer, *Geschichte der Politik, Cultur und Aufklärung*...," *Zeitschrift für Philosophie und spekulative Theologie*, vols. 1–16, ed. by Immanuel Hermann Fichte and Christian Hermann Weiße, Bonn et al.: Eduard Weber et al. 1837–46, vol. 13, 1844, pp. 298–304 (*ASKB* 877–911).

Helfferich, Adolph, *Die christliche Mystik in ihrer Entwickelung und in ihren Denkmalen*, vols. 1–2, Gotha: Friedrich Parthes 1842, vol. 1, p. 115 (*ASKB* 571–572).

Ruge, Arnold, "Bruno Bauer und die Lehrfreiheit," in his *Anekdota zur neuesten deutschen Philosophie und Publicistik*, op. cit., vol. 1, pp. 119–42.

Schmidt, Karl, *Das Verstandesthum und das Individuum*, Leipzig: Otto Wigand 1846 (*ASKB* 868).

Weiße, Christian Hermann, "Strauß und Bruno Bauer. Eine kritische Parallele," *Zeitschrift für Philosophie und spekulative Theologie*, op. cit., vol. 10, 1843, pp. 40–82.

III. Secondary Literature on Kierkegaard's Relation to Bauer

None.

F.C. Baur:
On the Similarity and Dissimilarity between Jesus and Socrates

David D. Possen

Ferdinand Christian Baur (1792–1860), founder and center of the group of historical-critical theologians known as the "Tübingen School," had a pivotal early influence on the development of Søren Kierkegaard's thought. Most prominently, Baur's 1837 monograph on Socrates and Jesus, *Das Christliche des Platonismus*,[1] is both cited and parodied repeatedly in Kierkegaard's 1841 dissertation, *The Concept of Irony*. Nevertheless, Kierkegaard's relation to Baur has been almost entirely ignored in the secondary literature, perhaps for one or more of the following reasons: (1) Kierkegaard does not refer to Baur in his works or journals from before 1837 or after 1841; (2) Kierkegaard appears to have owned only three of Baur's early works, together with a few associated articles, all published between 1834 and 1839; (3) Kierkegaard exhibited little interest, during the main period of his authorship (the 1840s and early 1850s), in Baur or in his school; finally, (4) Baur and the Tübingen School have attracted comparatively little scholarly attention over the last century and are now fairly obscure even to scholars of the history of Protestant theology.[2]

This article has benefited greatly from the editorial advice of Jon Stewart, the bibliographical suggestions of Richard Purkarthofer, and discussions of related material with Jonathan Lear and James Conant. I thank them all.

1 Ferdinand Christian Baur, *Das Christliche des Platonismus, oder Sokrates und Christus*, Tübingen: Ludwig Friedrich Fues 1837 (*ASKB* 422).

2 Fewer than a dozen significant studies of Baur or the Tübingen School have appeared since 1900. See Ernst Barnikol, *Ferdinand Christian Baur als rationalistisch-kirchlicher Theologe*, Berlin: Evangelische Verlagsanstalt 1970; Karl Barth, *Die protestantische Theologie im 19. Jahrhundert. Ihre Vorgeschichte und ihre Geschichte*, Zurich: Evangelischer Verlag 1946, pp. 450–8; Franz Courth, *Das Wesen des Christentums in der liberalen Theologie. Dargestellt am Werk Friedrich Schleiermachers, Ferdinand Christian Baurs und Albrecht Ritschls*, Frankfurt: Peter Lang 1977; Gustav Fraedrich, *Ferdinand Christian Baur der Begründer der Tübinger Schule, als Theologe, Schriftsteller und Charakter*, Gotha: F.A. Perthes 1909; Wolfgang Geiger, *Spekulation und Kritik. Die Geschichtstheologie Ferdinand Christian Baurs*, Munich: Christian Kaiser Verlag 1964; Horton Harris, *The Tübingen School. A Historical and Theological Investigation of the School of F.C. Baur*, 2nd ed., Grand Rapids: Baker Book House 1990 [1975]; Peter Crafts Hodgson, *The Formation of Historical Theology. A Study of Ferdinand Christian Baur*, New York: Harper & Row 1966; Frank

These facts are undeniable. Yet they are also beside the point. To Kierkegaard, Baur's book on Socrates and Jesus typified a mode of intellectual hubris—the conceit that speculative philosophy can *explain* Christian faith as a superior form of human reason—common also among the Danish Hegelians whom Kierkegaard would attack throughout his authorship. Kierkegaard's intellectual encounter with Baur deserves attention, therefore, as an early variation on his broader, lifelong polemic against such figures as Hans Lassen Martensen (1808–84), Johan Ludvig Heiberg (1791–1860), and Adolph Peter Adler (1812–69). To this end, the present essay offers a brief introduction to Baur and the Tübingen School, an overview of Kierkegaard's known references to Baur, and a detailed interpretation of the most polemical of these references, aided by a short summary of the argument of Baur's *Das Christliche des Platonismus*.

I. Baur and the Tübingen School

F.C. Baur was born in the village of Schmiden, now a Stuttgart suburb, on 21 June 1792. Thanks in part to the influence of his father, a Protestant minister of Swabian heritage, Baur gained a thorough education in Latin, Greek, and Hebrew at the evangelical seminaries of Blaubeuren (from 1805 to 1809) and Maulbronn (from 1809 to 1811), before proceeding to study philosophy and theology at the University of Tübingen (from 1811 to 1814). In 1817, after three years as a country vicar near Ulm, Baur was hired as professor at Blaubeuren. In 1826, Baur received an appointment at the Faculty of Evangelical Theology at Tübingen, where he remained until his death on 2 December 1860.

During his years as professor at Tübingen, Baur produced a continuous torrent of scholarly articles, essays, and tomes. These include monographs on Christianity's relation to ancient schools of philosophy (Pythagoreanism, Platonism, and Stoicism);[3] a theological manifesto, *Die christliche Gnosis*, which diagnoses Protestant speculative philosophy as a modern return to Gnosticism;[4] three major multi-volume histories of Christian dogma;[5] and a number of critical studies of the

Kaufmann, *Foundations of Modern Church History*, New York: Peter Lang 1992, pp. 74–148; E.P. Meijering, *F.C. Baur als Patristiker. Die Bedeutung seiner Geschichtsphilosophie und Quellenforschung*, Amsterdam: J.C. Gieben 1986; and Ernst Schneider, *Ferdinand Christian Baur in seiner Bedeutung für die Theologie*, Munich: J.F. Lehmanns Verlag 1909.

3 These texts are collected in Baur, *Drei Abhandlungen zur Geschichte der alten Philosophie und ihres Verhältnisses zum Christentum*, ed. by Eduard Zeller, Aalen: Scientia-Verlag 1978 [1876].

4 Baur, *Die christliche Gnosis oder die christliche Religionsphilosophie in ihrer geschichtlichen Entwiklung*, Tübingen: C.F. Osiander 1835 (*ASKB* 421).

5 Baur, *Die christliche Lehre von der Versöhnung, in ihrer geschichtlichen Entwicklung von der ältesten Zeit bis auf die neueste*, Tübingen: C.F. Osiander 1838 (*ASKB* 423); Baur, *Die christliche Lehre von der Dreieinigkeit und Menschwerdung Gottes in ihrer geschichtlichen Entwicklung*, vols. 1–3, Tübingen: C.F. Osiander 1841; and Baur, *Vorlesungen über die christliche Dogmengeschichte*, vols. 1–3, Leipzig: Fues's Verlag 1865–67.

books of the New Testament, with special emphasis on the letters of Paul.[6] Though Baur's posthumous fame has largely been linked to the latter texts—above all, to his role as a Church historian and New Testament critic—it is three of the former books, we shall see in Section II below, that appear to have exclusively engaged Kierkegaard's interest.

Baur is best known as the founder and nexus of the "Tübingen School," a group of Protestant scholars in and around Tübingen dedicated to promoting a historical-critical approach to scriptural interpretation, theology, and Church history.[7] It should be noted that Baur emphatically denied that his "School" was anything like a club with a rigid list of members; he insisted, instead, that "its true essence consists only in the principles...from which it first proceeded."[8] In general, what brought the Tübingen School's theologians together was their shared methodology, inspired by the speculative efforts of Schleiermacher, Schelling, and Hegel: a common commitment "to investigate critically and interpret imaginatively the historical origins, development, and 'forms' of the Christian church" while avoiding, wherever possible, resort to supernatural or miraculous explanations of events.[9] In Baur's case, this procedure led him to reject the authenticity of all but three of the Epistles of Paul and to date most of the remaining books of the New Testament to the early or middle decades of the second century A.D.[10] Meanwhile, though Baur did not court the label "Hegelian," he was at certain points in the habit—particularly during the late 1830s, his period of greatest influence on Kierkegaard—of advertising his own work as a continuation and fulfillment of Hegel's efforts to conjoin and systematize the history and philosophy of religion.[11]

---

6 Baur, *Die sogenannten Pastoralbriefe des Apostels Paulus aufs neue kritisch untersucht*, Stuttgart: J.G. Cotta'sche Verlagshandlung 1835; Baur, *Paulus, der Apostel Jesu Christi*, Stuttgart: Becher und Müller 1845; and Baur, *Kritische Untersuchungen über die kanonischen Evangelien, ihr Verhältniss zu einander, ihren Charakter und Ursprung*, Tübingen: Ludwig Friedrich Fues 1847.

7 To be clear: by this term I am not referring to the *Catholic* "Tübingen School," a later, parallel movement at Tübingen's Faculty of Catholic Theology, oriented around the figures of Johann Sebastian Drey (1777–1853) and Johann Adam Möhler (1796–1838).

8 Baur, *Die Tübinger Schule und ihre Stellung zur Gegenwart*, Tübingen: Ludwig Friedrich Fues 1859, p. 55.

9 Peter C. Hodgson, *The Formation of Historical Theology: A Study of Ferdinand Christian Baur*, op. cit., p. 88.

10 See Horton Harris, *The Tübingen School: A Historical and Theological Investigation of the School of F.C. Baur*, op. cit., p. 237.

11 For example, in an 1837 article owned by Kierkegaard, Baur describes his work in *Die christliche Gnosis* as filling in a gap comparable to "the truly monstrous leap…in the Hegelian philosophy of religion, which is also, simultaneously, a history of religion—just as I conjoin the philosophy of religion and the history of religion—from the religion of utility or of the understanding, i.e., the Roman religion, to the absolute religion, i.e., Christianity in the form it takes in the standpoint of the most recent speculative theology." Baur, "Ueber den Begriff der christlichen Religions-Philosophie, ihren Ursprung und ihre ersten Formen," *Zeitschrift für spekulative Theologie*, ed. by Bruno Bauer, vols. 1–3, Berlin: Ferdinand Dümmler 1836–38; vol. 2, no. 2, pp. 354–402, p. 392 (*ASKB* 354–357).

The principal members of the Tübingen School were recruited, almost to a man, from among Baur's students and young admirers. The best known of these are Adolf Hilgenfeld (1823–1907), Karl Reinhold Köstlin (1819–94), Karl Christian Planck (1819–80), Albert Schwegler (1819–57), Gustav Volkmar (1809–93), and Eduard Zeller (1814–1908).[12] Some sense of the religious politics of the Tübingen School can be gleaned from a brief look at two figures on the School's margins: Albrecht Ritschl (1822–89) and David Friedrich Strauss (1808–74). Ritschl broke with Baur by defending the authenticity of several Pauline epistles and other New Testament texts; he thus proved himself too conservative for the School. By contrast, Strauss openly dismissed the foundational narratives of Christianity as mere mythology; he thus proved himself too radical for the school. Strauss, as it happens, had begun his career as a star pupil of Baur's at Blaubeuren, and later became Baur's devoted friend at Tübingen. When Strauss' provocative 1835 biography of Jesus, *Das Leben Jesu*, earned notoriety both for himself and for his former professor, Baur was forced to distance himself openly from him.[13] Among modern scholars of Baur, these events have spurred a lively debate over whether or not it is appropriate to attribute to Baur, at the end of the day, an atheism or near-atheism similar to that of Strauss.[14]

The Tübingen School did not long outlast Baur's death in 1860. In biblical criticism, new methods and their champions—Wellhausen on the Old Testament, Holtzmann on the New—quickly rose to dominance. Among Protestant theologians, meanwhile, interest steadily waned in the Tübingen School's characteristic attempts to provide speculative or historical *explanations* for the origins and distinctiveness of Christian faith. As it happens, Kierkegaard himself may have been partly responsible for the latter change; or so Peter C. Hodgson has implied in his 1966 attempt to rehabilitate Baur as the pioneer of "a whole alternative approach to the problem of faith and historical knowledge typified by Protestant theology since Kierkegaard."[15] The sections that follow will work to make clearer the depth and importance of the contrast between Kierkegaard's and Baur's approaches to the problem of faith and reason.

II. Kierkegaard's Relation to Baur: Sources

At the time of his death, Kierkegaard appears to have owned only three of Baur's earlier books: *Die christliche Gnosis*, an 1835 contribution to speculative theology; *Das Christliche des Platonismus*, a brief 1837 study of the similarities and radical dissimilarity between Christianity and Platonism, between Jesus and Socrates; and *Die christliche Lehre von der Versöhnung*, an 1838 volume on the history of dogma.

---

12 For brief biographies of these figures, see Horton Harris, *The Tübingen School*, op. cit., pp. 55–100; pp. 113–33.

13 See Horton Harris, *The Tübingen School*, op. cit., pp. 27–9.

14 Of Baur's two twentieth-century American biographers, one (Hodgson) seeks to rescue him from the charge of atheism, while the other (Harris) insists on the plausibility of that charge. See Peter Hodgson, *The Formation of Historical Theology*, op. cit., pp. 2–6; Horton Harris, *The Tübingen School*, op. cit., pp. 159–63.

15 Peter Hodgson, *The Formation of Historical Theology*, op. cit., p. 279.

Of these three works, only the second is referred to substantially in Kierkegaard's writings. The first is nowhere mentioned in the journals, notebooks, or published works; and for the last, we find only rough Danish translations of two brief passages, both thematically linked to Baur's comparison of Platonism and Christianity, in a single 1838 journal entry. The remainder of this essay, accordingly, will take as its focus Kierkegaard's evolving response, between 1837 and 1841, to Baur's understanding of Christianity's relation to Platonism, and of Jesus' relation to Socrates.

Kierkegaard's earliest reference to Baur occurs in a complex journal entry (DD:75), dated 1 November 1837, where Kierkegaard records his first encounter with a translated excerpt from Baur's *Das Christliche des Platonismus*.

> In Clausen and Hohlenberg's *Tidsskrift for udenlandsk theologisk Litteratur*, 1837, no. 3., pp. 485–534, there is a fragment of an article by Baur on the Christian elements in Platonism which drives right into my own study of irony and humor; this must be the case particularly with the portion omitted from the journal, since one of its particular tasks is to develop the concept "irony." (To what extent Baur has become conscious of the Christian contrast in humor I still do not know, of course, as I have not read the article.) In his parallel between Christ and Socrates on page 529 [p. 528] there are some very good things. "Just as in paganism the divine belongs on the whole only to the subjective representation, and thus always has the human [p. 529] as its presupposition and foundation, so that precisely this, the human subjectivity of the divine, is paganism's greatest characteristic, just so even such a remarkable personality as Socrates is regarded only from the standpoint of the human."[16]

This entry was written, it should be noted, at a time when Kierkegaard was intently engaged in an effort to define irony and humor as the pagan and Christian varieties, respectively, of the comic.[17] In the words of this entry, Kierkegaard's goal was to specify "the Christian contrast in humor," over and above irony. Here Kierkegaard notes, with evident excitement, that Baur's book might fit well into his own project, inasmuch as Baur *also* aims to provide an account of how Christianity differs from the pagan thought of Socrates, irony's consummate exemplar. To this end, Kierkegaard jots down in Danish a sentence found in the concluding section of Baur's book, a section devoted to explaining the nature of the difference—in Baur's words, "the permanently unbridgeable gap"—between Christian and pagan categories.[18] In the sentence Kierkegaard cites, Baur argues that the very fact that Plato never asserts that Socrates is an incarnate god points to the essence of the contrast between paganism and Christianity: paganism moves only within the sphere of the human, whereas

16 *SKS* 17, 245–6, DD:75 / *CI*, 435.

17 For two thorough discussions of Kierkegaard's enterprise in its local context, see K. Brian Söderquist, "Kierkegaard's Contribution to the Danish Discussion of 'Irony,'" in *Kierkegaard and His Contemporaries: The Culture of Golden Age Denmark*, ed. by Jon Stewart, Berlin: Walter de Gruyter 2003 (*Kierkegaard Studies. Monograph Series*, vol. 10), pp. 78–105; K. Brian Söderquist, "Irony and Humor in Kierkegaard's Early Journals," *Kierkegaard Studies. Yearbook*, 2003, pp. 143–67.

18 Ferdinand Christian Baur, *Das Christliche des Platonismus*, op. cit., p. 147; p. 152.

Christianity countenances an irruption of the divine *into* the human sphere, namely, in the person of the God-man.

Putting all of the above together: on 1 November 1837, Kierkegaard recorded his *qualified* admiration for Baur's way of specifying the dissimilarity between Christianity and pagan thought. Kierkegaard qualified his admiration, it seems, only because he had not yet read Baur's treatment of Socratic irony, found in the first half of Baur's book.[19] Instead, Kierkegaard had read a "fragment" of the book—a Danish translation published by Henrik Nikolai Clausen (1813–94) and Matthias Hagen Hohlenberg (1797–1845)—which covered only the book's second half.[20] This fact will prove of enormous help to us, we shall see, in interpreting Kierkegaard's enigmatic passages on Baur in *The Concept of Irony*.

Before turning to those passages, however, we will briefly consider Kierkegaard's second and last journal entry on Baur (KK:6), which dates to 1838. This entry consists simply of near-verbatim translations of two passages from Baur's *Die christliche Lehre von der Versöhnung*, both on the ninth-century Irish theologian John Scotus Erigena.[21] Kierkegaard's interest in these passages can best be explained, I believe, by their relevance to Baur's understanding of the relation between Christianity and Platonism. In the first passage, Baur identifies Erigena's standpoint as one in which the dissimilarity between the divine and the human is apprehended only "as a vanishing moment"; Erigena's standpoint thus "quite strongly suggests the standpoint in which Christianity and Platonism touch one another."[22] In the second passage, Baur advises scholars not to take Erigena as the first in a new line of Christian speculation, but rather to see him as bringing to fruition "the entire older speculative development," namely, pagan philosophy.[23] Together, these passages present Erigena as a figure who is not yet fully Christian, yet stands in some sense *between* Platonism and Christianity—and thus offers a potentially useful case study for any attempt to provide a scholarly account of the "Christian contrast" to Socratic irony.

We do not know what Kierkegaard himself thought of these passages in 1838, since he merely translates them here without comment. By 1841, however, it is clear that Kierkegaard had had second thoughts about the very enterprise of attempting

---

19 This discussion can be found at Baur, *Das Christliche des Platonismus*, op. cit., pp. 27–8.

20 To be specific: the Danish translation furnished by Clausen and Hohlenberg corresponds to Ferdinand Christian Baur, *Das Christliche des Platonismus*, op. cit., pp. 83–154. See Baur, "Det Christelige i Platonismen, eller Sokrates og Christus. En religionsphilosophisk Undersøgelse," *Tidsskrift for udenlandsk theologisk Litteratur*, vols. 1–20, ed. by Henrik Nikolai Clausen and Matthias Hagen Hohlenberg Copenhagen: C.A. Reitzel 1833–52, vol. 5, 1837, pp. 485–534. I am grateful to Cynthia W. Lund of the Hong Kierkegaard Library for her assistance in clarifying this matter.

21 *SKS* 18, 360, KK:6. For the original texts, see Ferdinand Christian Baur, *Die christliche Lehre von der Versöhnung, in ihrer geschichtlichen Entwicklung von der ältesten Zeit bis auf die neueste*, Tübingen: C.F. Osiander 1838, pp. 118–20; pp. 136–8.

22 *SKS* 18, 360, KK:6; see Baur, *Die christliche Lehre von der Versöhnung*, op. cit., pp. 118–20.

23 *SKS* 18, 360, KK:6; see Baur, *Die christliche Lehre von der Versöhnung*, op. cit., pp. 116–38.

to specify this "Christian contrast" in an academic study. In Section III below, I will argue that several of Kierkegaard's remaining comments on Baur—all in the text and footnotes of *The Concept of Irony*—serve to *parody* Baur's way of attempting to do justice, in *Das Christliche des Platonismus*, to *both* the similarity and the dissimilarity between Jesus and Socrates. To appreciate Kierkegaard's parody, however, we will first need a detailed acquaintance with these enigmatic, occasionally hilarious passages.

In *The Concept of Irony*, Kierkegaard repeatedly cites Baur's *Das Christliche des Platonismus* as a perceptive work on Socrates. Thus Kierkegaard praises Baur's sensitivity to the benefits of Plato's perspective on Socrates, compared to Xenophon's;[24] Baur's way of attending to the outer form of Platonic dialogues;[25] Baur's "beautiful observation" that Socrates, in the *Symposium*, represents the unity of the comic and the tragic;[26] and, finally, Baur's way of attending to the importance of the person of Socrates in the passages on immortality in the *Phaedo*.[27] At the same time, Kierkegaard criticizes Baur for conflating Platonic myth with Athenian tradition,[28] and for overstraining several attempts to draw parallels between Socrates and Jesus.[29] Meanwhile, a third set of passages critiques Baur's general approach—namely, Baur's way of broaching the sensitive topic of the relation between Jesus and Socrates in the first place.

It is this third set of passages that will occupy our attention in the remainder of this essay, for it is here that Kierkegaard's polemic against Baur most clearly emerges. We will begin with an opening footnote, where, after praising Baur's "noteworthy" contributions on the subject of "the relation between Socrates and Christ," Kierkegaard nonetheless complains of "a modest little asthmatic doubt… that the similarity consists in dissimilarity and that there is analogy only because there is contrast."[30] Later in the text, after calling Baur's analysis of Socrates and Jesus as personalities "very productive," Kierkegaard maintains that "the main point is to insist on the infinite dissimilarity that still remains within this similarity."[31] Together, these lines indicate that the dissertation's first and perhaps most striking Latin thesis, known as "Thesis I," unmistakably refers to Baur's project. Thesis I runs as follows: "The similarity between Christ and Socrates consists essentially in their dissimilarity."[32] Though on its face this line is simply nonsensical—a similarity that is nothing other than a dissimilarity is no similarity at all—it can also be understood as a challenge to those who, like Baur, would dare to compare Jesus to Socrates, that

24 *SKS* 1, 75–7 / *CI*, 13–5.

25 *SKS* 1, 93 / *CI*, 31–2.

26 *SKS* 1, 113 / *CI*, 52.

27 *SKS* 1, 122, 128–9 / *CI*, 62, 69–70.

28 *SKS* 1, 153–4 / *CI*, 99–100.

29 *SKS* 1, 75, 113 / *CI*, 13–4, 52.

30 *SKS* 1, 76n / *CI*, 15n.

31 *SKS* 1, 265n / *CI*, 220n.

32 *SKS* 1, 65 / *CI*, 6–7. This statement is the first of 15 Latin theses attached to Kierkegaard's dissertation. In the original, it reads: *Similitudo Christum inter et Socratem in dissimilitudine praecipue est posita.*

is: "If you wish to describe the essence of the similarity between Jesus and Socrates, you do best to insist upon their *difference* from one another."

These passages are obviously polemical; but what, exactly, is the point of the polemic? Read in isolation, these passages appear simply to *rebuke* Baur for failing to pay proper regard to the infinite dissimilitude between Socrates and Christ. As it happens, Kierkegaard's commentators have almost uniformly interpreted these passages in just such a light. The classic formulation of this reading is due to Jens Himmelstrup, whose 1925 monograph on *Kierkegaards Opfattelse af Sokrates* remains the most comprehensive examination to date of Kierkegaard's relation to Baur.[33] As Himmelstrup tells it, Kierkegaard's resistance, in *The Concept of Irony*, to Baur's way of conflating Socrates and Christ foreshadows his later insistence, in such works as *Philosophical Fragments* and *The Sickness unto Death*, on defending sharper and sharper distinctions between Socratic and Christian categories.[34]

The next section offers an alternative reading, grounded in the above passages' historical and textual contexts. As I argue, Kierkegaard's true polemical purpose is to *parody* Baur, not to scold him. For Baur's book, I show below, in fact does *exactly* what Kierkegaard, in *The Concept of Irony*, seems to be accusing it of failing to do: it dampens its own emphasis on the similarity between Jesus and Socrates by means of an abrupt appeal to the *dissimilarity* between Jesus and fallen humanity.[35] The 1837 journal entry cited above (DD:75) confirms, moreover, that Kierkegaard was long aware of this apologetic turn in Baur's argument. Kierkegaard's true quarrel with Baur, I conclude, is provoked not by the latter's somehow failing to "insist on" the dissimilarity between Jesus and Socrates, but rather by the very idea that an academic study can give that dissimilarity its proper due.[36]

---

33 According to Himmelstrup, Kierkegaard's portrait of Socrates' ironic activity permits "the infinite dissimilarity to come to the fore"; Baur's portrait does not allow this. Jens Himmelstrup, *Søren Kierkegaards Opfattelse af Sokrates. En Studie i dansk Filosofis Historie*, Copenhagen: Arnold Busck 1924, pp. 219–33; p. 233. The core of Himmelstrup's reading—the idea that Kierkegaard breaks with Baur by emphasizing the dissimilarity between Socrates and Christ, which Baur elides—remains standard in the secondary literature. See Eric Ziolkowski, "From *Clouds* to *Corsair*. Kierkegaard, Aristophanes, and the Problem of Socrates," in *The Concept of Irony*, ed. by Robert L. Perkins, Macon, Georgia: Mercer University Press 2001 (*International Kierkegaard Commentary*, vol. 2), pp. 193–233; p. 210; Tonny Aagaard Olesen, "Kierkegaard's Socratic Hermeneutic in *The Concept of Irony*," in *The Concept of Irony*, ed. by Robert L. Perkins, op. cit., pp. 101–22; p. 110; David Kangas, "Conception and Concept. The Two Logics of *The Concept of Irony* and the Place of Socrates," in *Søren Kierkegaard and the Word(s): Essays on Hermeneutics and Communication*, ed. by Poul Houe and Gordon D. Marino, Copenhagen: C. A. Reitzel 2003, pp. 180–91; p. 188; Verena Peters, "Sokrates, 'Ritter der Unendlichkeit.' Sören Kierkegaards sokratisches Christentum," in *Das Lächeln des Sokrates*, ed. by Herbert Kessler, Kusterdingen: Die Graue Edition 1999 (*Sokrates-Studien*, vol. 4), pp. 271–300; pp. 275f; and Sophia Scopetea, *Kierkegaard og græciteten: En kamp med ironi*, Copenhagen: C. A. Reitzel 1995, p. 107; p. 129.

34 Jens Himmelstrup, *Søren Kierkegaards Opfattelse af Sokrates*, op. cit., pp. 233f.

35 Baur, *Das Christliche des Platonismus*, op. cit., pp. 152–4.

36 *SKS* 1, 265n / *CI*, 220n.

III. Kierkegaard's Relation to Baur Reconsidered

To see how Kierkegaard's comments on Baur in *The Concept of Irony* amount to an extended *parody* of Baur's book on Socrates and Jesus, we will need first to review, in some detail, the argument of the book in question. For as it happens, Baur's *Das Christliche des Platonismus* is a strangely bifurcated work. The book begins by amassing an impressive list of parallels between Jesus and Socrates, between Christianity and Platonism; yet it then turns aside, at the last moment, to insist on the *dissimilarity* between these persons and movements.

In the first 30 pages of *Das Christliche des Platonismus*, Baur argues that Christianity is far more closely related to Platonism than his fellow scholars have cared to admit. In particular, Baur accuses Constantin Ackermann (1799–1877), author of an 1835 book on *Das Christliche in Plato und in der platonischen Philosophie*,[37] of relying upon unverifiable assumptions about Christianity's superiority. Baur then devotes the middle sections of his book (totaling 115 pages) to an ambitious compendium of parallels between Christianity and Platonism. Yet at the book's end, just where we might expect him to conclude by reprising his thesis in triumph, Baur abruptly presents his *own* ten-page account of Christianity's radical superiority over Platonism. Oddly enough, we shall see, this apologetic turn exposes Baur to the very charge he himself has leveled against Ackermann: that of assuming Christianity's superiority without proof.

To appreciate the suddenness of Baur's switch to apologetics, it will help to take a brief tour of his opening pronouncements. Baur begins his book by championing the philosophy of religion's right to investigate the similarity between Socrates and Christ:

> Scholarship cannot relinquish the right to treat Christianity in regard to its historical point of origin, rather than simply as an isolated phenomenon, walled off on its own, called into being only by a miracle, and relating negatively toward its entire historical context. *Even the absolute must always also stand in a relative relation to that from which it differs absolutely.*[38]

The last line can be thought of as the mirror-image of Kierkegaard's Thesis I, cited above: "The similarity between Christ and Socrates consists essentially in their dissimilarity." As we have seen, Kierkegaard's Thesis I issues a challenge to any scholar who dares to compare Jesus to Socrates, for it seems to insist that the only way to describe the essence of the similarity between Jesus and Socrates is to insist upon their difference from one another. Baur, by contrast, urges scholars to *set aside* Christian doctrine's insistence upon the "absolute" dissimilarity between Christ and Socrates and to *reveal* their underlying, "relative" similarity.

Baur's target here is Ackermann, who describes the difference between Platonism and Christianity as that between possible and actual salvation. As Ackermann would have it, Socrates teaches philosophy, which "aims at salvation," while Christ provides

---

37 Constantin Ackermann, *Das Christliche in Plato und in der platonischen Philosophie*, Hamburg: F. Perthes 1835.

38 Baur, *Das Christliche des Platonismus*, op. cit., p. 1.

grace, which "effects salvation"; Socrates offers us the *idea* of escape from the cave of sin, while Christ actually sets us free.[39] Baur assails Ackermann's account as both unscholarly and wrong-headed. It is unscholarly because, as Baur sees it, Ackermann cannot possibly *prove* that Christianity and Platonism differ in salvific efficacy. "Christianity, too, can only aim at salvation, not effect it, insofar as the actual receipt of the salvation it offers remains a matter of free will...and who is to say that the Ideas of Platonism have never acquired actuality," that is, "an effective and decisive influence on human life?"[40] Ackermann's account is wrong-headed, meanwhile, inasmuch as it hastily equates the Platonists' cave and the Christians' fallenness, conflating the Platonists' understanding of evil as *error*, arising in ignorance, with the Christians' understanding of evil as *sin* arising in willful defiance.[41]

The last argument cited might remind us of Kierkegaard's later pseudonym Anti-Climacus, who draws a sharp contrast between Christianity's understanding of sin as "a position" and Socrates' understanding of sin as "ignorance."[42] However, whereas Anti-Climacus will identify this difference as Christianity's decisive break with Socratic thought, Baur sees it as merely a matter of degree. Citing *Phaedrus* 229e, Baur depicts Socrates' knowledge of his own ignorance—an awareness that drives him to ask whether he is a simple being possessed of something divine, or a beast "more monstrous than Typhon"—as compatible, even continuous, with the knowledge of sin Christianity inspires in its followers.[43] Baur explains: "Socratic philosophy and Christianity are related as self-knowledge to knowledge of sin. Neither can exist without the other. Knowledge of sin has self-knowledge as its necessary precondition[;] meanwhile, the more deeply consciousness burrows into itself, the more surely self-knowledge encounters the sin that inheres in a human being's deepest essence."[44] For Baur, in short, there is nothing radically new about Christianity's doctrine of fallenness; when Socrates asks whether he might not be more monstrous than Typhon, he is already in the act of discovering his own entanglement in sin.

Baur does not even see a decisive break between Christianity and Platonism in their differing accounts of human reconciliation to truth—for Platonists, the recollection of ideas known before birth; for Christians, the radically new provision of truth in grace. As is well known, Kierkegaard's pseudonym Johannes Climacus cites precisely this difference in sketching Christianity's departure from Socratic thought.[45] Baur, instead, admits only a "seeming contradiction" between the Platonist

---

39 Baur, *Das Christliche des Platonismus*, op. cit., p. 10. For the original source, see Constantin Ackermann, *Das Christliche in Plato*, op. cit., p. 332; *The Christian Element in Plato and in the Platonic Philosophy*, trans. by Samuel Ralph Asbury, Edinburgh: T. & T. Clark 1861, p. 259: "The essence of Christianity consists...in *saving power*, that of Platonism in *saving purpose*. In Christianity, therefore, salvation is present in deed and reality; in Platonism only in thought, as the end of striving."

40 Baur, *Das Christliche des Platonismus*, op. cit., p. 11.

41 Ibid., p. 8.

42 *SKS* 11, 201–212 / *SUD*, 87–100.

43 Baur, *Das Christliche des Platonismus*, op. cit., p. 23n.

44 Ibid., pp. 24–5.

45 *SKS* 4, 218–28 / *PF*, 9–20.

and Christian accounts of reconciliation to truth; he argues that Platonism in fact teaches, no less than does Christianity, that human beings must be reconciled to truth by means of an *external* revelation.[46] On Baur's understanding of Platonism, the truth attained by Socratic recollection is simply "the universal as the objectively given…[which] reveals and pronounces itself [to] subjective consciousness and in this way determines the human being in his willing and acting."[47]

By now it is clear that, at the start of his book, Baur assumes a series of positions sharply opposed to those that will later prove central to Kierkegaard's pseudonymous authorship. Baur rejects the notion that Christianity differs radically from paganism in its doctrines of sin and grace. Baur proceeds by offering a long list of parallels, not only between Christian and Platonist doctrine, but also between the personalities of Jesus and Socrates. Had Baur ended his book here, it would be easy to envision him standing accused by Kierkegaard, in Thesis I and elsewhere, of conflating Socrates and Christ.

Instead, Baur abruptly turns the tables. Just after allowing his comparison of Socrates and Christ to swell to fever pitch,[48] Baur suddenly undertakes to explain how Christ and Christianity differ decisively from Socrates and Platonism after all:

> All of paganism moves entirely within the sphere of the human. Hence paganism can never admit an individual who stands before the others with a decisively determining authority. Wherever the difference between the human and the divine has not been revealed, the union of this difference cannot be revealed either....[Conversely,] the human cannot raise itself to the divine unless the divine lowers itself to the human. The human is thus only at one [*Eins*, literally "one"] with the divine insofar as the divine is itself revealed in the human. This always remains the great and essential difference between the standpoints of Christianity and paganism. This is precisely what leaves open a permanently unbridgeable gap between Platonism and Christianity.[49]

On this account, the essential distinction between Christianity and paganism lies in Christians' and pagans' differing religious *capabilities*. I cannot, on my own devices, conceive of the divine in any way robust enough to reach beyond the "sphere of the human"; I can do so only insofar as the divine has penetrated the sphere of the human for me. Baur concludes that Christians can, while pre-Christian pagans such as Socrates or Plato cannot, develop a conception of the divine that succeeds in transcending the "sphere of the human."

This argument is certainly convenient for Baur. It allows him to assert a decisive difference between Platonism and Christianity, *without* having to retract any of the parallels that he has already drawn. In particular, this argument enables Baur to dismiss Plato's thought as inferior without diagnosing any particular shortcomings in it: he needs only claim that Plato did the best *anyone* could do in the absence of an incarnate God. In his book's last paragraph, in fact, Baur ascribes to Plato "a mind

46 Baur, *Das Christliche des Platonismus*, op. cit., p. 25.

47 Ibid.

48 "How near they stand to one another!" Baur cries. Baur, *Das Christliche des Platonismus*, ibid., p. 140.

49 Ibid., pp. 151–2.

open to the revelation of Christianity," foiled only because "the living combination of the divine and the human was missing."[50] What really held Plato back, it seems, was his own cosmic misfortune: God became man in Jesus, not in Socrates.

This argument's advantages to Baur are clear. It is nonetheless puzzling that he uses it, since he thereby invites the same charge of unscholarly reasoning that he himself had leveled against Ackermann. After all, how can we prove that those who call themselves Christians have in fact undergone a transformative encounter with the incarnated God? And who is to say that pre-Christian pagans such as Plato had no access to the divine's descent into the human? Baur provides no answer to the first question, and offers at best a partial answer to the second. The fact that Plato never asserted that Socrates was divine, the fact that "even as remarkable a personality as Socrates is regarded only from the standpoint of the human"—this fact, Baur claims, manifests "paganism's greatest characteristic," namely, its way of relegating the divine to "subjective representation, [which] always has the human as its presupposition and foundation."[51]

We have met the last sentence before: it is the line translated by Kierkegaard in his 1 November 1837 journal entry (DD:75). As I see it, the very fact that Kierkegaard copied this sentence verbatim into his journal—indeed after musing, in the same entry, about the extent of Baur's awareness of "the Christian contrast in humor"—indicates that he was then interested in Baur as a theorist of "the Christian contrast," as a writer who may certainly present parallels between Socrates and Christ, but who is ultimately concerned with their underlying *dissimilarity*. Such an interest would make sense historically, after all, given that by this point Kierkegaard had read only the *second* half of Baur's book, as we saw in Section II above.

It is certainly possible that Kierkegaard changed his mind about Baur at one or more points between 1837 and 1841, particularly after purchasing the book and reading its defiant opening pages. Yet I find it difficult to believe that Kierkegaard simply forgot about the book's apologetic ending. It seems much more likely that Kierkegaard wrote what he wrote, in *The Concept of Irony*, in full awareness that Baur *does* attempt to "insist upon the infinite dissimilarity that still remains within this similarity."[52] For these reasons, I propose that we approach Kierkegaard's apparent rebuke of Baur in *The Concept of Irony* with a healthy dose of skepticism.

Consider, for example, the details of Kierkegaard's *own* specification of "the infinite dissimilarity" between Jesus and Socrates in *The Concept of Irony*. Kierkegaard explains that Socrates' "relation to the world is a continuous non-relation," since his "ironic personality is actually only the outline of a personality"; by contrast, "the immediate fullness of deity resided in Christ," whose "relation to the world is so absolutely real a relation that the Church is conscious of itself as members of his body."[53] On this account, the divine Creator establishes a real, full, and immediate relation to His human creatures in and through Jesus Christ, in whose

50 Ibid., p. 153.

51 Ibid., p. 147.

52 *SKS* 1, 265n / *CI*, 220n.

53 *SKS* 1, 265n / *CI*, 220–1n.

body Christians take part. The ironist Socrates, by infinite contrast, has *no* relation to his fellow human beings.

Here it is clear that Kierkegaard, by emphasizing Socrates' "ironic personality," has more to say than does Baur about Socrates' *specific* shortcomings, *qua* ironist, relative to Jesus. However, it is still the case for Kierkegaard, as for Baur, that what makes the dissimilarity between Socrates and Jesus *infinite* is the fact that the divine penetrates the sphere of the human *only* in the case of Jesus. After all, a Socrates who abandoned irony—who acquired *some* relation to his fellow human beings, rather than none—would still differ "infinitely" from Jesus, inasmuch as the latter's relation to humanity remains the uniquely "absolutely real" relation of creator to creation. My point is that the crucial step in Kierkegaard's explanation of "the infinite dissimilarity" between Jesus and Socrates—the step that explains why their dissimilarity is *infinite*—suspiciously resembles the closing argument of Baur's book.

To recapitulate: the preponderance of the evidence suggests that Kierkegaard wrote *The Concept of Irony* in full awareness of Baur's apologetic insistence upon the infinite dissimilarity between Jesus and Socrates. If this is true, then we should not take Kierkegaard at his word in those passages where he appears to criticize Baur for failing to insist upon this dissimilarity. Instead, I propose that we read these passages as *parodying* both Baur's apologetic turn and its underlying conceit, namely, the very idea that *any* scholarly inquiry could complete itself by "factoring in" the radical newness of Christianity and its Teacher.

Suppose, for example, that Kierkegaard's Thesis I—"The similarity...consists essentially in...dissimilarity"—*mocks* how Baur's search for the essence of the similarity between Jesus and Socrates culminates and expires in his closing assertions about their dissimilarity. On this reading, Thesis I ironically champions an apologetic turn like Baur's as a hopeless prescription for scholarship: "The *correct* way to describe the essence of the similarity between Jesus and Socrates is to describe their dissimilarity." I call this prescription "hopeless" because it does not in fact depict any "way" available to scholarship. After all, the dissimilarity between Jesus and Socrates rests in the infinite difference between Christ and fallen humanity; that difference, in turn, can be explicated only in terms of *sin*; and as several of Kierkegaard's pseudonyms will later agree in insisting, sin cannot possibly be explained in a scholarly setting.[54]

Let me be clear: I am not suggesting that Kierkegaard has *nothing* to say in *The Concept of Irony* about the dissimilarity between Jesus and Socrates. Indeed, we have met, above, Kierkegaard's vivid gloss upon their infinite difference. Rather, I am claiming that, for Kierkegaard, such comments cannot be generated by scholarship alone. Kierkegaard hints at the view just stated, I believe, when he remarks that such comments have no real place in his dissertation: "I could wish (if this wish

---

54 According to Vigilius Haufniensis in *The Concept of Anxiety*, scholarship's trouble with sin is that it belongs to dogmatics: *SKS* 4, 323, 326–9 / *CA*, 16, 19–23. According to Johannes Climacus in *Philosophical Fragments*, only the god can teach the consciousness of sin: *SKS* 4, 252 / *PF*, 47. Finally, according to Anti-Climacus in *The Sickness unto Death*, we can learn of sin only by a revelation from God: *SKS* 11, 208 / *SUD*, 96.

were not already outside the scope of this study) that I would be permitted within the sphere of this inquiry to explore the relation between Socrates and Christ."[55] Here Kierkegaard impudently flouts a scholarly standard—perhaps that of his examiners—that is intolerant even of the *wish* to comment upon the dissimilarity between Jesus and Socrates. We are left to ask: what, exactly, is Kierkegaard wishing for? Is he calling for, even inaugurating, a *new* model of scholarship, one capable of exploring the dissimilarity between Socrates and Christ? Or is he directing us away from scholarship entirely?

I am skeptical of the former reading, since it makes Kierkegaard into a partisan or practitioner of just the sort of blend of conventional scholarship and apologetics that we have seen at work in Baur's closing pages. Instead, I advocate the latter reading: in *wishing* to take up Baur's theme, Kierkegaard means to point us toward a wholly *un*-scholarly concern with Socrates and Christ. As he remarks elsewhere in *The Concept of Irony*, in a discussion of the difficulty of discussing Socrates' significance as a *person*, "Grant that science and scholarship are right in ignoring such things; nevertheless, one who wants to understand the individual life cannot do so."[56] By 1841, I believe, Kierkegaard had grown disillusioned with the underlying conceit of Baur's book, namely, the very idea that scholarship can provide an account of "the Christian contrast." Kierkegaard's attack on Baur in *The Concept of Irony* amounts, in my view, to a public break with this conceit, and signals the onset of Kierkegaard's broad-based, lifelong polemic against those in Denmark who, like Baur, hoped to account for "the Christian contrast" in the terms and paragraphs of a work of speculative philosophy.

55 *SKS* 1, 76n / *CI*, 15n.

56 *SKS* 1, 215 / *CI*, 166.

Bibliography

I. F.C. Baur's Works in The Auction Catalogue *of Kierkegaard's Library*

"Ueber den Begriff der christlichen Religions-Philosophie, ihren Ursprung und ihre ersten Formen," *Zeitschrift für spekulative Theologie*, vols. 1–3, ed. by Bruno Bauer, Berlin: Dümmler 1836–38, vol. 2, no. 2, 1837, pp. 354–402 (*ASKB* 354–357).

Die christliche Gnosis oder die christliche Religionsphilosophie in ihrer geschichtlichen Entwiklung, Tübingen: C.F. Osiander 1835 (*ASKB* 421).

Das Christliche des Platonismus, oder Sokrates und Christus, Tübingen: Ludwig Friedrich Fues 1837 (*ASKB* 422).

Die christliche Lehre von der Versöhnung, in ihrer geschichtlichen Entwicklung von der ältesten Zeit bis auf die neueste, Tübingen: C.F. Osiander 1838 (*ASKB* 423).

"Katolicismens og Protestantismens Modsætning efter Principierne og Hoveddogmerne i begge Lærebegreber" [1833], *Tidsskrift for udenlandsk theologisk Litteratur*, vols. 1–20, ed. by Henrik Nikolai Clausen and Matthias Hagen Hohlenberg, Copenhagen: C.A. Reitzel 1833–52, vol. 2, 1834, pp. 227–321 (*ASKB* U 29).

"Besvarelse af Hr. Dr. Möhlers nyeste Polemik imod den protestantiske Lære og Kirke," *Tidsskrift for udenlandsk theologisk Litteratur*, op. cit., vol. 2, 1834, pp. 587–625.

"Det Christelige i Platonismen, eller Sokrates og Christus: En religionsphilosophisk Undersøgelse," *Tidsskrift for udenlandsk theologisk Litteratur*, op. cit., vol. 5, 1837, pp. 485–534.

"Menneskehedens ældste Historie efter den bibelske Beretning i Genesis," *Tidsskrift for udenlandsk theologisk Litteratur*, op. cit., vol. 6, 1838, pp. 516–62.

"Den christelige Lære om Forsoningen i dens historiske Udvikling fra den ældste Tid indtil den nyeste," *Tidsskrift for udenlandsk theologisk Litteratur*, op. cit., vol. 7, 1839, pp. 247–329.

"Paulus, Jesu Christi Apostel," *Tidsskrift for udenlandsk theologisk Litteratur*, op. cit., vol. 14, 1846, pp. 317–434.

II. Works in The Auction Catalogue *of Kierkegaard's Library that Discuss F.C. Baur*

Beck, Andreas Frederik, *Begrebet Mythus eller den religiøse Aands Form*, Copenhagen: P.G. Philipsens Forlag 1842 (*ASKB* 424).

Fischer, Carl Philipp, *Die Idee der Gottheit. Ein Versuch, den Theismus speculativ zu begründen und zu entwickeln*, Stuttgart: S.G. Liesching 1839, p. 92n (*ASKB* 512).

Günther, Anton, *Der letzte Symboliker. Eine durch die symbolischen Werke Doctor J. A. Möhler's und Doctor F.C. Baur's veranlaßte Schrift, in Briefen*, Vienna: Wallishausser 1834 (*ASKB* 521).

—— *Die Juste-Milieus in der deutschen Philosophie gegenwärtiger Zeit*, Vienna: Beck 1838, pp. 389–409 (*ASKB* 522).

Hagen, Johan Frederik, *Ægteskabet. Betragtet fra et ethisk-historiskt Standpunct*, Copenhagen: Wahlske Boghandels Forlag 1845, p. 110n (*ASKB* 534).

Hasse, F.R., "*Die christliche Gnosis oder die christliche Religionsphilosophie in ihrer geschichtlichen Entwicklung*. Von Dr. Ferdinand Christian Baur," *Zeitschrift für spekulative Theologie*, op. cit., vol. 1, no. 2, 1836, pp. 209–44.

Helfferich, Adolph, *Die christliche Mystik in ihrer Entwickelung und in ihren Denkmalen*, vols. 1–2, Gotha: Friedrich Parthes 1842, vol. 1, p. 115; p. 261 (*ASKB* 571–572).

Hundeshagen, C.V., "Den tydske Protestantisme, dens Fortid og dens nuværende Livsspørgsmaal," *Tidsskrift for udenlandsk theologisk Litteratur*, op. cit., vol. 16, 1848, pp. 125–240.

Müller, Julius, *Die christliche Lehre von der Sünde*, vols. 1–2, 3rd revised and enlarged ed., Breslau: Josef Max und Komp. 1849, vol. 1, pp. 391ff. (*ASKB* 689–690).

Rosenkranz, Karl (ed.), *Schelling. Vorlesungen, gehalten im Sommer 1842 an der Universität zu Königsberg*, Danzig: Fr. Sam. Gerhard 1843, p. 381 (*ASKB* 766).

III. Secondary Literature on Kierkegaard's Relation to F.C. Baur

Himmelstrup, Jens, *Søren Kierkegaards Opfattelse af Sokrates: En Studie i dansk Filosofis Historie*, Copenhagen: Arnold Busck 1924, pp. 219–33.

Hodgson, Peter Crafts, *The Formation of Historical Theology: A Study of Ferdinand Christian Baur*, New York: Harper & Row 1966, pp. 271–84.

Kangas, David, "Conception and Concept: The Two Logics of *The Concept of Irony* and the Place of Socrates," in *Søren Kierkegaard and the Word(s): Essays on Hermeneutics and Communication*, ed. by Poul Houe and Gordon D. Marino, Copenhagen: C.A. Reitzel 2003, pp. 180–91; p. 188.

Leemans, Victor, *Sören Kierkegaard*, Antwerp and Amsterdam: Uitgeversmij. N.V. Standaard-Boekhandel 1956, see pp. 38–41.

Olesen, Tonny Aagaard, "Kierkegaard's Socratic Hermeneutic in *The Concept of Irony*," in *The Concept of Irony*, ed. by Robert L. Perkins, Macon, Georgia: Mercer University Press 2001 (*International Kierkegaard Commentary*, vol. 2), pp. 101–22; p. 110.

Peters, Verena, "Sokrates, 'Ritter der Unendlichkeit.' Sören Kierkegaards sokratisches Christentum," in *Das Lächeln des Sokrates*, ed. by Herbert Kessler, Kusterdingen: Die Graue Edition 1999 (*Sokrates-Studien*, vol. 4), pp. 271–300; pp. 275f.

Scopetea, Sophia, *Kierkegaard og græciteten: En kamp med ironi*, Copenhagen: C.A. Reitzel 1995, p. 107; p. 129.

Ziolkowski, Eric, "From *Clouds* to *Corsair*: Kierkegaard, Aristophanes, and the Problem of Socrates," in *The Concept of Irony*, ed. by Robert L. Perkins, Macon, Georgia: Mercer University Press 2001 (*International Kierkegaard Commentary*, vol. 2), pp. 193–233; p. 210.

Bretschneider:

The Tangled Legacy of Rational Supernaturalism

Lee C. Barrett

Søren Kierkegaard's dialectical/poetic experiments did not by any means parallel the theological project of Karl Gottlieb Bretschneider, a project that by the 1830s had been eclipsed by the more influential work of Georg Wilhelm Friedrich Hegel, Friedrich Schelling, and Friedrich Schleiermacher. Nor did Kierkegaard ever deem Bretschneider significant enough to subject his theology to an extended polemical critique. Nevertheless, Bretschneider was important for Kierkegaard's intellectual development in that he helped familiarize Kierkegaard with two extremely important academic fields: the history of Christian confessional theology and the theological appropriation of a rationalism influenced by Immanuel Kant.

I. A Brief Survey of Bretschneider's Life and Works

Karl Gottlieb Bretschneider (1776–1848) was best known for promoting a distinctive type of theology often labeled "rational supernaturalism," an attempted synthesis of philosophy and historic Christian doctrines. Born in 1776 in Saxony, Bretschneider studied at the Lyceum at Chemnitz and later at the University of Leipzig, and in 1812 took a doctor of theology degree at Wittenberg. Although he was clearly academically inclined, anxiety concerning the precariousness of German universities during the Napoleonic wars motivated Bretschneider to seek a career first in parish ministry and later in ecclesiastical administration. In 1807 he served as a pastor in Schneeberg, in 1808 was promoted to ecclesial superintendent in Annaberg, and from 1816 until his death in 1848 functioned as general superintendent of Gotha. Because the territorial churches of the various German states usually operated as departments of their civil governments, Bretschneider spent a great deal of time mediating marriage disputes, attending to church school problems, adjudicating canon law, and settling controversies concerning the church tax.[1] Remarkably, during this hectic administrative career Bretschneider wrote voluminously on a wide variety of subjects including New Testament exegesis, Greek lexicography, the works of Josephus,

1 Karl Gottlieb Bretschneider, *Aus meinem Leben: Selbstbiographie*, ed. by Horst Bretschneider, Gotha: Müller 1851. English translation: "Autobiography of Dr. Karl Gottlieb Bretschneider," in *The Bibliotheca Sacra and American Biblical Repository*, Andover, Massachusetts: W.F. Draper 1852, vol. 9, pp. 657–86; vol. 10, pp. 229–63.

the history of doctrine, and the essential concepts of dogmatics. His notoriety was assured by the publication of a monograph in which he raised questions concerning the Johannine authorship of the gospel of John, although he later protested that he drew attention to critical historical issues only to stimulate research.[2] Perhaps his most ambitious project was his edition of the writings of Melanchthon which he contributed to the *Corpus Reformatorum*, a collection of the essential writings of the German reformers. Throughout his polyglot scholarly career his main purpose was to articulate and defend an irenic, latitudinarian form of Christianity that both maintained continuity with the theological traditions of the Church and also accommodated the main themes of a somewhat Kantian philosophy. His *Handbuch der Dogmatik der evangelisch-lutherischen Kirche* served as a standard textbook on Lutheran doctrine for students of theology, and was published in many editions. His popular *Manual of Religion and the History of the Christian Church* was written for a more general audience and made his rationalistic version of Lutheranism more widely available. Bretschneider's later life was vexed by disputes with conservative Lutheran confessionalists and with the new breed of Romantic pietists. He died in 1848, leaving his unfinished autobiography to be completed by his son.

II. Bretschneider's Thought

The basic dynamics of Bretschneider's theology were determined by a syncretistic blend of Wolff's rationalism, Kant's ethics and philosophy of religion, and an historicist interpretation of the Lutheran confessions. Although the Saxon church of his youth was very theologically conservative, the University of Leipzig that he attended was sympathetic to the milder forms of rationalist theology. Bretschneider's patron, the court preacher of Saxony Franz Volkmar Reinhard (1753–1812), promoted a tolerant and broad version of Christianity with the doctrinal essentials reduced to a minimum. Bretschneider's close friend at Leipzig, Heinrich Gottlieb Tzschirner (1778–1828), launched his academic career with the claim that the purpose of Christianity is not only to proclaim the gospel but also to promote natural knowledge. Such theologians as these all shared the convinction that the Church should encourage moral edification, instructing humanity in its proper civic duties so that society would gradually evolve into the kingdom of God.

Inspired by these thinkers, Bretschneider began to contend that religious propositions must be philosophically grounded. Like the earlier neologians, he maintained that the credentials of any alleged divine revelation must be evaluated by pure reason before that revelation could be legitimately believed. Philosophical principles, being more certain than revelation, must be logically prior to the propositions of any historical positive religion whose claims to truth are based on authority. Most importantly, no valid revelation could contain anything contrary to reason. Bretschneider was convinced that Christian revelation is rendered probable by the fact that its essential theological claims are suggested by both practical and

---

[2] Bretschneider, *Probabilia de evangelii et epistolarum Ioannis Apostoli*, Lipsiae: Sumtibus Jo. Ambros. Barthii 1820.

theoretic reason.[3] Acceptance of the truth-claims of Christianity is justified by the twin testimony of its moral fruits and its fulfillment of reason's quest for the unconditioned. For Bretschneider the concept of God as the sum of all perfections is naturally inherent in human reason, being presupposed by the perception of imperfection.[4] God is the unifying Idea of ideas that satisfies reason's quest for a synthesis of all forms of knowledge. God is the true, the good, and the beautiful, the object posited by the conjunction of theoretic, practical, and aesthetic reason.[5] In all his works Bretschneider subscribed to a somewhat Kantian epistemology, but he remained more optimistic than Kant that the categories of substance and causality could be intelligibly applied to the noumenal realm, generating an idea of God as the absolute cause and the fundamental substance. To this understanding of God's metaphysical perfections, practical reason adds the insight that God is also the source of our categorical duties and is the quintessence of ethical goodness. As in Kantian moral philosophy, practical reason also generates our consciousness of unconditional moral freedom, our awareness of our absolute worth as moral agents, our postulate of immortality as the condition for the possibility of endless moral progress, and our hope for a future conjunction of virtue and happiness. Belief in God's providential control of history is necessary to guarantee this eventual synthesis of moral worth and happiness.[6] Without this postulate, our lack of power over nature would cause us to despair over the prospect that the moral life and the life of the senses could never be integrated.[7]

By the first decade of the nineteenth century the Kantian theological tradition that influenced Bretschneider had divided into several factions. In a manner reminiscent of such earlier neologians as Johann Salomo Semler (1725–91), the most radical Kantians who contributed to the *Magazin für Prediger*[8] maintained that reason is entirely sufficient to establish a natural religion that need not and should not be supplemented by revelation.[9] In principle, the postulates of practical reason, the Kantian triad of God, human freedom, and immortality, are sufficient for human religious flourishing. These more rationalistic Kantians based their suspicion of revelation on Kant's claim that the virtuous will must pursue the moral good for its own sake and not for the sake of obedience to external authority. Slightly more

3 Bretschneider, *Lehrbuch der Religion und der Geschichte der christlichen Kirche für die oberen Klassen der Gymnasien*, Gotha: Justus Perthes 1824. English translation: *A Manual of Religion and of the History of the Christian Church*, London: Trübner and Co. 1857, pp. 30–5.

4 Bretschneider, *A Manual of Religion*, op. cit., p. 36.

5 Bretschneider, *Handbuch der Dogmatik der evangelisch-lutherischen Kirche*, vols. 1–2, 4th ed., Leipzig: Verlag von Johann Ambrosius Barth 1838 [1814], vol. 1, pp. 456–68 (*ASKB* 437–438).

6 Bretschneider, *Systematische Entwickelung aller in der Dogmatik verkommenden Begriffe*, 4th ed., Leipzig: Johann Ambrosius Barth 1841 (this appears in Kierkegaard's library in the first edition from 1805), pp. 338–95 (*ASKB* U 25).

7 Bretschneider, *Systematische Entwickelung*, op. cit., pp. 1–52; pp. 144–8.

8 *Magazin für Prediger*, vols. 1–8, Jena: Löffler 1803–16.

9 Isaak August Dorner, *History of Protestant Theology*, vols. 1–2, trans. by George Robson and Sophia Taylor, Edinburgh: T. & T. Clark 1871, vol. 2, pp. 326–7.

theologically moderate Kantians like Johann Heinrich Tieftrunk (1759–1837) only argued that there can be no truth in any putative revelation, including the Bible, except that which reason can independently corroborate.[10] The even more moderate Julius Wegscheider (1771–1849) rejected all supernaturalistic explanations of revelation, but continued to cherish Jesus as an expositor of the moral imperatives that can in principle be discovered by reason alone.[11] Jesus remains valuable as a stimulus to reflection on the moral law within and to the adoption of the categorical imperative as one's highest maxim.

Bretschneider did not align himself with these more radical Kantian rationalists, explicitly distancing himself from Wegscheider, and identified with more supernaturalistic yet still mildly Kantian theologians like Christoph Friedrich von Ammon (1766–1850). Bretschneider rejected the contention of the neologians and the stricter Kantians that reason cannot be supplemented by supernaturally communicated revelation and eschewed their rejection of all positive religion and its replacement by natural religion.[12] Rather, he espoused a middle course between rationalist "irreligion" and pietist superstition, accepting revelation in so far as it was congruent with reason.[13] Bretschneider proposed that it is reasonable to expect that revelation would contain elements not accessible to reason itself, supplementing it and expanding its scope.[14] The revealed truths can be seen to be not only consistent with reason, but also as logical extensions of the trajectory that reason had initiated. Bretschneider proposed that human cognitive limitations, particularly the epistemic damage done by sin, make a revelation by God logically conceivable and morally probable. For example, revelation furnishes the confidence that the forgiveness and freedom from sin for which reason yearns has indeed been made possible by God. For Bretschneider, the synthesizability of revelation and reason is grounded in the homogenous nature of the two, for they are both expressions of the same Logos. Thus Bretschneider can conclude that Christianity is the highest religion and that it comes from a supernatural source because it accords with the expectations and aspirations of reason. For Bretschneider, Christianity is not decisively proven by miracles or the fulfillment of prophecy, but is justified by the fact that its ideational content corresponds to ideas that reason suspected were true, but could not demonstrate.[15] With this nuanced justification of revelation, Bretschneider was confident that he had found a way to be both a champion of modern intellectual sensibilities and also an apologist for orthodox Christianity.

In developing this more appreciative view of revelation, Bretschneider borrowed themes from such earlier theologians as Gotthold Ephraim Lessing (1729–81) who argued that historical religions play a unique role in the education of the human race.

---

10 See Johann Tieftrunk, *Einzig möglicher Zweck Jesu aus dem Grundgesetz der Religionen entwickelt*, Berlin: Verlag der Königlichen Preussischen Akademie 1789.

11 See Julius Wegscheider, *Institutiones theologiae, christianae, dogmaticae: Scholis suis scripsit addita dogmatum singulorum historia et censura*, 6th ed., Halae: Gebauer 1829 [1815] (*ASKB* A I 27).

12 Bretschneider, *Handbuch der Dogmatik*, 4th ed., op. cit., vol. 1, pp. 1–6.; pp. 69–85.

13 Ibid., vol. 1, pp. 188–210.

14 Bretschneider, *Systematische Entwickelung*, 4th ed., op. cit., pp. 99–108; pp. 153–96.

15 Ibid., pp. 235–54.

Bretschneider agreed that revealed religion accommodates itself to the prevailing tastes, sensibilities, and thought-forms of a specific culture and historical period in order to make itself intelligible.[16] Consequently, revelation presents the conceptual truths of reason in a sensory, imagistic form suited to the religious infancy of the race. Revelation must be progressive, unfolding religious and moral ideas in more rationally adequate forms as human culture evolves. Bretschneider regarded this development of "positive" religion as the product of God's supernatural activity in the history of the human spirit. Religiously immature peoples may first adopt a religious conviction because it is endorsed by authority, and then later come to appreciate its intrinsic rationality. This slow pedagogy is necessary because human individuals and the species as a whole begin life as primarily sensory creatures, motivated by impulses, while their rational capacities are only gradually acquired.[17] Humanity is, however, perfectible and can evolve from the domination of sensory impulses to the free choice of following duty for its own sake. The maturation of the three central Kantian concepts of God, the law, and immortality can be discerned in the history of biblical religion, as these ideas struggled to express themselves in increasingly more adequate forms. The earlier phases of biblical religion functioned as a preparation for Christianity, the final and perfect revelation. For example, prior to the era of Jesus, the ideology of Jewish nationalism was necessary to foster a sense of corporate responsibility in the context of a parochial tribal culture. However, this ethnocentrism was only a transitory stage on the way to the Christian understanding of our more universal duties to humanity as a whole.

Bretschneider was a bit vague concerning exactly how God accomplishes this revelatory task. Most frequently he spoke of God's enlightenment of certain individuals, whose spiritual maturation was supernaturally accelerated beyond that of their cultural peers. At times, Bretschneider suggested that God has inspired specific persons, giving them an insight into religious ideas that natural human capacities could never attain.[18] In either case, revelation is a phenomenon in the religious consciousness of human beings, and not a dictation of divine words or a series of spectacular events in the natural world.

This focus on progressive revelation inspired Bretschneider's intense interest in the historical development of the central doctrines of the Christian churches. Bretschneider's doctrinal concerns were not unique to him. From about 1800, Franz Volkmar Reinhard, his early ecclesiastical patron, had promoted a renewed appreciation of Lutheran confessionalism. Like Reinhard, Bretschneider argued that the confessional tradition was necessary to combat what he regarded as the untrammeled subjectivism of resurgent pietism. At their best the doctrines of Protestantism were the historical garb of religious ideas acceptable to reason, a garb admirably suited to the evolution of Christian cultures. This positive assessment of the history of doctrine motivated Bretschneider to write several different expositions of this theological heritage. Bretschneider's numerous textbooks on theology always commenced with an appreciative description of the origins and history of each

16 Bretschneider, "Autobiography," op. cit., vol. 10, p. 256.

17 Bretschneider, *Handbuch der Dogmatik*, 4th ed., op. cit., vol. 1, pp. 822–30.

18 Bretschneider, *Systematische Entwickelung*, 4th ed., op. cit., pp. 301–15.

doctrine, and then proceeded to clarify their implicit ideational content, exposing their dependence on the conceptuality of their contemporary cultures. Finally, he would compare each doctrine to the teachings of Scripture and the dictates of reason in order to critique the culturally conditioned conceptualities in which they were expressed, and offer possible modifications of them more suited to modern modes of thought. In doing so, he tentatively articulated his own constructive and sometimes revisionist theological proposals.

The nature of Bretschneider's own theological vision is evident in his interpretation of certain core Christian doctrines. For example, according to Bretschneider, the doctrine of the Trinity in its developed form corroborates something that reason had dimly discerned: the fact that God is not only perfect existence (God the Father), but also perfect reason (God the Word), and perfect benevolence (God the Holy Spirit).[19] Similarly, the doctrine of original sin validates the common suspicion that human moral failings are universal and inevitable. Furthermore, the doctrine's focus on generational transmission supports reason's awareness of the deleterious power of heredity and culture.[20] The traditional teaching concerning sin's inevitability draws attention to the overwhelming influence of our sensory nature over our immature rational capacities in our early years.[21] The doctrine of the atonement, in the sense of God's resolve to enable human beings to overcome their unrighteousness, also meshes with reason's deepest tendencies, for it confirms the intimation that if God is truly good, and if God's creatures sin, then God would want to restore them to righteousness.[22] The doctrine of the incarnation's true meaning is that Jesus' love was the perfect embodiment of Kant's categorical imperative, highlighting the importance of obedience to the moral law as a divine command.[23] The venerable Lutheran doctrine concerning Jesus' state of humiliation, his surrender of divine glory, suggests that the moral law finds its ultimate completion in a life of self-sacrifice.[24] The doctrine of the distinction of the human and divine natures of Christ points to the fact that the sinlessness of Jesus must be regarded as the fruit of his genuinely human freedom, revealing the ideal of a human life free of sin.[25] Supporting the Antiochene school of Christology against the Alexandrians, Bretschneider insisted that Jesus did experience the conflict of the sensory and rational natures, although, of course, his sensory impulses did not master him or frustrate his development. Regarding the doctrine of justification, Bretschneider believed that Luther's rejection of merit corresponded to Kant's insistence that duty must be done for its own sake, and

19 Bretschneider, *Handbuch der Dogmatik*, 4th ed., op. cit., vol. 1, pp. 549–65; pp. 623–53; Bretschneider, *Systematische Entwickelung*, 4th ed., op. cit., pp. 395–434.

20 Ibid., pp. 515–48.

21 Bretschneider, *Handbuch der Dogmatik*, 4th ed., op. cit., vol. 2, pp. 79–95.

22 Ibid., pp. 296–345.

23 Ibid., pp. 300–4; Bretschneider, *Systematische Entwickelung*, 4th ed., op. cit., pp. 561–78.

24 Bretschneider, *Handbuch der Dogmatik*, 4th ed., op. cit., vol. 2, pp. 207–39; Bretschneider, *Systematische Entwickelung*, 4th ed., op. cit., pp. 578–82.

25 Bretschneider, *Handbuch der Dogmatik*, 4th ed., op. cit., vol. 2, pp. 183–207.

not for the prospect of any reward.[26] Moreover, the doctrine of justification gives humanity confidence that past sins do not destroy the possibility of future growth toward righteousness. In all these instances traditional theological teachings point to truths only vaguely suspected by unaided human reason.

Often in these expositions of historic doctrines Bretschneider would conclude that reason requires that certain traditional formulae be significantly modified. For example, the Augustinian doctrine of inherent depravity inadequately articulates the fact that humans sin because, morally speaking, they are undeveloped children who need to mature. Theologians should avoid both Augustine's deterministic view of the power of sin as well as Pelagius' unrealistic optimism about the potency of human freedom unaided by grace.[27] Similarly, inherited theories of the atonement are embedded in archaic notions of offended feudal honor and compensatory retribution, concepts that have been displaced by more enlightened understandings of justice and spiritual rehabilitation.

Bretschneider's doctrinal explorations and Kantian leanings informed many of his ecclesial activities, including his support of the union of Lutheran and Reformed churches that was occurring in several German states.[28] Like most theologians who had been at least somewhat influenced by the Enlightenment, Bretschneider concluded that differences in doctrine did not require sectarian division. The true church, the moral kingdom of God, is the totality of rational agents who have developed their moral capacities.[29] The plurality of historic church traditions does not negate the underlying moral unity of their members. Consequently, the toleration of confessional differences is absolutely imperative. Reason should highlight the common Christian core beneath the more superficial differences in doctrinal articulation. According to Bretschneider, many of these theological divergences are simply due to differences in cultural context, or to misguided attempts to be too precise about noumenal matters that defy exact conceptualization.

Bretschneider's mild rationalism also motivated him to champion civic freedoms that would give liberty of conscience a political basis. According to Bretschneider, the freedom to choose a religion was one of the distinctive contributions of Protestantism to the spiritual maturation of the human race. The human spirit, untrammeled by the constraints of authoritarian regimes and obscurantist traditions, should be capable of moral and spiritual self-regulation. Given his mildly Kantian proclivities, Bretschneider regarded the liberty of conscience as a crucial condition for the autonomous development of moral character.[30]

In his later years a series of polemical encounters with other theological movements further shaped and refined Bretschneider's theology. After the Napoleonic wars, influential theologians, preachers, and church leaders in Saxony and its neighboring territories pushed doctrinal confessionalism in a more conservative direction. Some

---

26 Ibid., pp. 490–521; Bretschneider, *Systematische Entwickelung*, 4th ed., op. cit., pp. 640–56.

27 Bretschneider, *Handbuch der Dogmatik*, 4th ed., op. cit., vol. 2, pp. 95–114.

28 Bretschneider, "Autobiography," op. cit., vol. 10, p. 258.

29 Bretschneider, *A Manual of Religion*, op. cit., pp. 78–81.

30 Ibid., p. 82.

were motivated by the fear of the dilution of distinctive Lutheran beliefs due to the state-mandated unions of the Lutheran and Reformed traditions. Some were influenced by the "awakening," the neo-pietist movement of the early nineteenth century which, unlike pietism's earlier seventeenth- and eighteenth-century expressions, was influenced both by Romanticism and idealism. The new variety of pietists emphasized intuition as the crucial medium for grasping sacred truths, a mode of knowledge that transcended the bounds of rationality. As their popularity grew, the leaders of the "awakening" and of neo-confessionalist movements began to attack the proponents of theological rationalism, many of whom, like Bretschneider, were upper-level bureaucrats in the territorial church establishments. The theological peace began to be disrupted when Martin Stephan (1777–1846), a rigidly orthodox demagogic minister, won the support of powerful Saxon political leaders like Detlef Count von Einsiedel (1773–1861). Most dramatically, Lutheran traditionalists accused Christoph Friedrich von Ammon, a rationalist who was also the Saxon church's titular head, of heresy. At this point Bretschneider, who was a friend of Ammon, felt obliged to defend the academic independence of theology against what he took to be retrogressive dogmatism. Bretschneider himself was attacked in print by August Hahn (1792–1863), a conservative theologian who had been called to teach at Leipzig, the very home of rationalism, and who proudly proclaimed that rationalism and Christianity were utterly incompatible. The controversy spread when in Jena, Karl August von Hase (1800–90), a well-known church historian, also launched attacks on theological rationalists of doubtful orthodoxy, including Bretschneider.

In opposition to the awakened and confessionalist parties, Bretschneider denounced the dangers of "mysticism" with increasing virulence. "Mystic" and "mystery" were terms used by the awakened faction to suggest an immediate and absolutely certain dimension of experience not accessible to the operations of reason, but nevertheless available to a more intuitive faculty.[31] Against this view Bretschneider argued that any religious proposition that could not be conceptualized or postulated by reason was cognitively empty, and therefore could not possibly be a candidate for belief, much less trust.[32] Without cognitive content, a religious experience of any sort would be impossible, for all experiences, including all religious experiences, are responses to some idea entertained by the knowing faculty.

This antipathy to immediate experience also motivated Bretschneider to critique the increasingly influential theology of Friedrich Schleiermacher. Bretschneider feared that Schleiermacher, like the troublesome pietists, based religion on an illusory immediate feeling, a feeling that Schleiermacher associated with self-consciousness. Against this view, Bretschneider argued that feeling is different from self-consciousness, and that Schleiermacher's collapse of the two led to Schleiermacher's misleading valorization of feeling as the most basic component of experience.[33] Accepting Schleiermacher's distinction of feeling, acting, and knowing,

---

31 Bretschneider, *Systematische Entwickelung*, 4th ed., op. cit., pp. 15–20.

32 Bretschneider, *Clementine oder die Frommen und Altgläubingen unsrer Tage*, Halle: C.A. Schwetschke 1841.

33 Bretschneider, *Handbuch der Dogmatik*, 4th ed., op. cit., vol. 1, pp. 95–115.

Bretschneider argued that the foundational element in this triad is knowledge, for an individual must receive an impression from an object in order to develop any intentional feelings regarding it. Consequently, some type of apprehension of God must be in an individual's consciousness in order for religious feelings to follow. Contrary to Schleiermacher, God is not immediately available through religious feelings, but rather is an inference of reason. Much of Bretschneider's antipathy to Schleiermacher's elevation of feeling was rooted in his anxiety that religion would be reduced to a type of natural instinct divorced from the appreciation of moral duty. Bretschneider also (probably mistakenly) suspected that Schleiermacher's identification of self-consciousness and feeling implied that the feeling of absolute dependence must be uninterrupted, and thereby contradicted humanity's ordinary experience of the extreme fluctuation of religious feelings. Bretschneider also worried that Schleiermacher's theology posited a necessary conflict between sensuous consciousness and religious consciousness, seeking to dissolve all experience of individuation into Jesus' absolute God-consciousness mediated by the Church.[34] According to Bretschneider, rational religion should regulate but not negate the sensuous life. Any unnatural otherworldliness should give way to a healthy sense of the centrality of a person's worldly vocation and moral duties.

With equal fervor Bretschneider combated the growing influence of speculative idealism in both its popular Hegelian and Schellingian forms.[35] He devoted particular energy to a critique of Philipp Marheineke's (1780–1846) comprehensive and seductive system. Against what he thought was idealism's confusion of subject and object, Bretschneider asserted that the distinction of subject and object is a primitive differentiation innate in consciousness.[36] Idealism had mistakenly imagined that the forms and categories of understanding could give knowledge of objects all by themselves, but, protested Bretschneider, these forms and categories are empty without intentional objects.[37] According to Bretschneider Hegel and Schelling attempted to dissolve the objective world either into the Absolute or into human subjectivity. To make matters worse, they and their followers misleadingly used Christian language to describe their metaphysical moves, pretending that their vain speculations presented the essence of Christianity in a more scientifically appropriate form. Their equation of speculative idealism with historic Christianity was an illicit and dangerous sleight of hand. Most damagingly for Bretschneider, both Hegel and Schelling failed to emphasize the moral teleology that is so integral to all Christian concepts. Consequently, the idealists should be dismissed as dangerous distorters of genuine historic Christianity.

---

34 Ibid., pp. 105–6; Bretschneider, *Systematische Entwickelung*, 4th ed., op. cit., p. 33; pp. 48–52; pp. 148–50; p. 163.

35 Bretschneider, *Handbuch der Dogmatik*, 4th ed., op. cit., vol. 1, pp. 85–93; pp. 115–41.

36 Ibid., pp. 115–24.

37 Bretschneider, *A Manual of Religion*, op. cit., pp. 8–31.

III. Kierkegaard's Use of Bretschneider

Bretschneider's own theological project was not a primary influence upon Kierkegaard's thought. Nevertheless, Bretschneider's work had an indirect impact upon Kierkegaard because of the extensive use that Kierkegaard made of Bretschneider's textbooks on doctrinal theology. Along with Karl August von Hase's more traditionally orthodox *Hutterus redivivus*[38] and August Hahn's biblically oriented *Lehrbuch des christlichen Glaubens*,[39] Bretschneider's overviews of the development of doctrine and compendia of doctrinal theology served as reference works providing much of Kierkegaard's information concerning the history of theology, doctrine, and the philosophy of religion. Since his student days Kierkegaard had been aware of Bretschneider as the author of *Lexicon manuale graeco-latinum in libros Novi Testamenti* which he used in his interpretations of New Testament passages, although he could be critical of Bretschneider's attempts to soften the strict demands of Jesus' message.[40] In 1836 he acquired Bretschneider's *Versuch der systematischen Entwickelung aller in der Dogmatik vorkommenden Begriffe* and sometime after 1838 he purchased Bretschneider's *Handbuch der Dogmatik*, which he owned in two different editions.

Kierkegaard's various expositions of theological topics often suggest that he relied upon Bretschneider's texts as reference works. This is most evident in Kierkegaard's treatment of doctrinal issues that had a complex and controversial history. For example, the discussion of original sin in *The Concept of Anxiety* employs technical terms such as "the head of the human race by nature, by generation, by covenant" (as a description of Adam) that echo the wording of Bretschneider's *Handbuch der Dogmatik*.[41] The references in the same book to the absence of sexuality in the resurrected state and to Christ's freedom from sexual temptation may also be based on Bretschneider's account.[42] Moreover, Vigilius' remarks about the guilt and debility of original sin reflect Bretschneider's elaboration of those topics.[43] Sometimes the probable influence of Bretschneider is less overt but also more pervasive. For example, the entire essay "The Gospel of Sufferings" in *Upbuilding Discourses in Various Spirits* is informed by somewhat technical Christological motifs typical of

---

38 Karl August von Hase, *Hutterus redivivus oder Dogmatik der evangelisch-lutherischen Kirche: Ein dogmatisches Repertorium für Studierende*, Leipzig: Sühring 1829 (this appears in Kierkegaard's Library in the 4th edition from 1839, *ASKB* 581).

39 August Hahn, *Lehrbuch des christlichen Glaubens*, Leipzig: Vogel 1828 (*ASKB* 535).

40 Kierkegaard's use of Bretschneider for exegetical purposes is evident in his treatment of Luke 14:26 in *SKS* 4, 164–5 / *FT* 72; Bretschneider, *Lexicon manuale graeco-latinum in libros Novi Testamenti*, 2nd ed., vols. 1–2, Lipsiae: Ioh. Ambr. Bahrdtium 1829 [1824], vol. 2, p. 87 (*ASKB* 73–74). See also *Pap.* I C 7, in *Pap.* XII, pp. 23–6. *SKS* 17, 145–57, CC:1. *SKS* 17, 195–7, CC:11. *SKS* 18, 361–71, KK:7.

41 *SKS* 4, 336–7 / *CA*, 29; Bretschneider, *Handbuch der Dogmatik*, 4th ed., op. cit., vol. 2, pp. 77–8.

42 *SKS* 4, 381–3 / *CA*, 78–80; Bretschneider, *Handbuch der Dogmatik*, 4th ed., op. cit., vol. 1, pp. 728–41.

43 *SKS* 4, 334–5 / *CA*, 26–7; Bretschneider, *Handbuch der Dogmatik*, 4th ed., op. cit., vol. 2, pp. 25–39; pp. 95–114.

Lutheranism concerning the distinction of the divine and human natures of Christ.[44] An elaborate exposition of these points is found in Bretschneider.[45] The same essay emphasizes the centrality of Christ's state of humiliation as distinguished from his state of exaltation, a theme that is discussed by Bretschneider with extreme technical precision.[46] In *For Self-Examination* and *Judge for Yourself!* Kierkegaard's treatment of the relationship of faith and works is rooted in a distinction of the three different uses of the law, a distinction that is developed in depth by Bretschneider.[47]

Bretschneider may have done more for Kierkegaard than merely provide doctrinal information. His own constructive theological proposals may have influenced Kierkegaard in more subtle ways. Most obviously, many of these ways were negative, in that Bretschneider provided Kierkegaard with numerous examples of how theology should not be done. Certainly Bretschneider's consistent desire to harmonize the spirit of modernity and the values of Christianity would have been anathema to Kierkegaard. Similarly, Bretschneider's identification of Christian love with the pursuit of civic duties would have been dismissed by Kierkegaard as a conceptual confusion. Kierkegaard's own emphasis of Christianity's offense to reason could not be harmonized with Bretschneider's deepest conviction that reason corroborates revelation. Bretschneider's claim that Jesus activates the innate moral archetype already resident in the human spirit ran counter to the basic thrust of *Philosophical Fragments*. Furthermore, Kierkegaard rejected Bretschneider's confidence in the efficacy of self-initiated repentance and preferred to stress the need for unmerited forgiveness and grace freely offered. Finally, Bretschneider's belief that history reveals the progressive spiritual maturation of the human race would have been in tension with Kierkegaard's theme of contemporaneity with Christ. Bretschneider, along with countless others who championed the synthesis of Christianity and the spirit of modernity, may have helped provoke Kierkegaard to develop some of his most distinctive themes.

In spite of the obvious points of conflict, Bretschneider may simultaneously have played a more positive role in Kierkegaard's development. Most importantly, Bretschneider may have been one of the vehicles that mediated to Kierkegaard an appreciation of the implications of Kant's ethics and philosophy of religion for theology. Of course, the extent of Kierkegaard's dependence upon Bretschneider for an awareness of Kantianism cannot be demonstrated. At most, Bretschneider was

---

44 Lee C. Barrett, "The Joy in the Cross: Kierkegaard's Appropriation of Lutheran Christology in *The Gospel of Sufferings*," in *Upbuilding Discourses in Various Spirits*, ed. by Robert Perkins, Macon, Georgia: Mercer University Press 2005 (*International Kierkegaard Commentary*, vol. 15), pp. 257–85.

45 Bretschneider, *Handbuch der Dogmatik*, 4th ed., op. cit., vol. 2, pp. 150–61.

46 *SKS* 8, 319–29, 353–5, 360, 377 / *UD* 217–28, 252–6, 263, 281; Bretschneider, *Handbuch der Dogmatik*, 4th ed., op. cit., vol. 2, pp. 207–39.

47 Ibid., pp. 489–521; Bretschneider, *Systematische Entwickelung*, 4th ed., op. cit., pp. 650–6. See Lee C. Barrett, "Faith, Works, and the Uses of the Law: Kierkegaard's Appropriation of Lutheran Doctrine," in *For Self-Examination and Judge for Yourself!*, ed. by Robert Perkins, Macon, Georgia: Mercer University Press 2002 (*International Kierkegaard Commentary*, vol. 21), pp. 77–109.

one source among many.[48] In any case, certain themes dear to Bretschneider have parallels in Kierkegaard's work. Bretschneider anticipated Kierkegaard's hostility to speculative metaphysical systems that claim to give objective knowledge of reality. Bretschneider also anticipated Kierkegaard's rejection of immediate religious intuition as the basic mode of Christian knowing. Both Bretschneider and Kierkegaard situated the meaningfulness of Christian discourse in subjectivity, favoring the realm of practical reason over that of theoretic reason, and regarded the struggle to live appropriately as the proper context for grasping Christian concepts. For both authors moral striving was central to the Christian life, although Kierkegaard had a deeper sense of the need for a qualitative transformation catalyzed by grace. Although Kierkegaard gave Christian practice a much broader scope than Kantian duty or civic virtue, both he and Bretschneider agreed that ethics demands rigorous adherence to the ideal. Moreover, Kierkegaard, like Bretschneider, emphasized the universality of the failure to perfectly actualize the ideal and in good Lutheran fashion lamented the seriousness of sin. Furthermore, Kierkegaard, like Bretschneider, resisted the theory that this sinfulness was necessitated by the race's biological descent from Adam and Eve. For both, the story of Adam functioned as a symbol of the fall of every individual. Finally, both made the theme of Christ as the prototype for the Christian life central to their understanding of the significance of Jesus. In all these instances Kierkegaard's concentration upon the ethical dimensions of religious pathos may at least have been reinforced by many of Bretschneider's proposals concerning the real significance of historic Christian doctrines.

---

48 Ronald Green, *Kierkegaard and Kant: The Hidden Debt*, Albany: SUNY 1992, pp. 1–31.

Bibliography

I. Bretschneider's Works in The Auction Catalogue *of Kierkegaard's Library*

Handbuch der Dogmatik der evangelisch-lutherischen Kirche oder Versuch einer beurtheilenden Darstellung der Grundsätze, welche diese Kirche in ihren symbolischen Schriften über die christliche Glaubenslehre ausgesprochen hat, vols. 1–2, 3rd ed., Leipzig: Johann Ambrosius Barth 1828 [1814] (*ASKB* A I 25–26).

Handbuch der Dogmatik der evangelisch-lutherischen Kirche oder Versuch einer beurtheilenden Darstellung der Grundsätze, welche diese Kirche in ihren symbolischen Schriften über die christliche Glaubenslehre ausgesprochen hat, mit Vergleichung der Glaubenslehre in den Bekenntnißschriften der reformirten Kirche, vols. 1–2, 4th ed., Leipzig: Verlag von Johann Ambrosius Barth 1838 [1814] (*ASKB* 437–438).

Lexicon manuale graeco-latinum in libros Novi Testamenti, vols. 1–2, 2nd ed., Lipsiae: Ioh. Ambr. Bahrdtium 1829 [1824] (*ASKB* 73–74).

Versuch einer systematischen Entwicklung aller in der Dogmatik vorkommenden Begriffe: nach den symbolischen Büchern der protestantisch-lutherischen Kirche; nebst der Literatur, vorzüglich der neuern über alle Theile der Dogmatik, Leipzig: Johann Ambrosius Barth 1805 (*ASKB* U 25).

II. Works in The Auction Catalogue *of Kierkegaard's Library that Discuss Bretschneider*

Baur, Ferdinand Christian, "Die Subjektivität in ihrer Negativität und Haltungslosigkeit bei Schott und Bretschneider," in his *Die christliche Lehre von der Versöhnung in ihrer geschichtlichen Entwicklung von der ältesten Zeit bis auf die neueste*, Tübingen: Osiander 1838, pp. 608–14 (*ASKB* 423).

Bruch, Johann Friedrich, *Die Lehre von den göttlichen Eigenschaften*, Hamburg: Friedrich Perthes 1842, p. 24n; p. 60n; p. 67n; p. 98; p. 101; p. 140n; p. 163n; p. 207n; p. 217n; p. 279n (*ASKB* 439).

Clausen, Henrik Nicolai, *Det Nye Testaments Hermeneutik*, Copenhagen: Jens Høstrup Schultz 1840, pp. 355–6 (*ASKB* 468).

Hahn, August (ed.), *Lehrbuch des christlichen Glaubens*, Leipzig: Friedrich Christian Wilhelm Vogel 1828, p. 4; p. 7; p. 45; p. 72; p. 272; p. 611 (*ASKB* 535).

Hase, Karl, *Hutterus redivivus oder Dogmatik der evangelisch-lutherischen Kirche: Ein dogmatisches Repertorium für Studierende*, 4th revised ed., Leipzig: Breitkopf und Härtel 1839, p. 16; p. 47; p. 71; p. 83; p. 130; p. 196 (*ASKB* 581).

Heiberg, Johan Ludvig, "Bretschneiders Tillæg til sit Forsvar for Rationalismen," *Kjøbenhavns flyvende Post*, 1830, 130, 29 October [pp. 526–7]; II, no. 131, 1 November [pp. 531–2]; III, no. 132, 3 November [p. 536] (see *ASKB* 1606–1607; U 55).

—— "Bretschneiders Forsvar for Rationalismen," *Kjøbenhavns flyvende Post*, 1830, I, no. 101, 23 August [p. 412]; II, no. 102, 25 August [pp. 415–6]; III, no. 103, 27 August [pp. 419–20]; IV, no. 104, 30 August [pp. 421–3]; V, no. 105, 1 September [p. 428]; VI, no. 107, 6 September [pp. 433–6]; VII, no. 108, 8 September [pp. 437–9]; VIII, no. 109, 10 September [pp. 443–4]; IX, no. 110, 13 September [pp. 446–7] (see *ASKB* 1606–1607; U 55).

Marheineke, Philipp, *Die Grundlehren der christlichen Dogmatik als Wissenschaft*, 2nd revised ed., Berlin: Duncker und Humblot 1827, p. xxvi; p. xxxi; p. xxxiii (*ASKB* 644).

Menzel, Wolfgang, *Die deutsche Literatur*, vols. 1–4, 2nd revised ed., Stuttgart: Hallberg'sche Verlagshandlung 1836, vol. 2, pp. 196ff. (*ASKB* U 79).

Møller, Jens, "Indhold af Dr. Bretschneiders Bog: Probabilia &c.," in *Nyt theologisk Bibliothek*, vols. 1–20, ed. by Jens Møller, Copenhagen: Andreas Seidelin 1821–32, vol. 5, pp. 284–345 (*ASKB* 336–345).

Mynster, Jakob Peter, *Blandede Skrivter*, vols. 1–3, Copenhagen: Den Gyldendalske Boghandlings Forlag 1852–53 [vols. 4–6, Copenhagen: Den Gyldendalske Boghandlings Forlag 1855–57], vol. 2, p. 99 (*ASKB* 358–363).

Rudelbach, Andreas Gottlieb, [Review of] "*Heinrich und Antonio, oder die Proselyten der römischen und der evangelischen Kirche*, von Dr. K.G. Bretschneider," *Theologisk Maanedsskrift*, ed. by Nikolaj Frederik Severin Grundtvig and Andreas Gottlieb Rudelbach, Copenhagen: Wahlske Boghandling, vol. 6, 1826, pp. 264–76 (*ASKB* 346–351).

—— [Review of] "*Apologie der neuern Theologie des evangelischen Deutschlands gegen ihren neuesten Ankläger (H.J. Rose)* von Dr. K.G. Bretschneider," *Theologisk Maanedsskrift*, op. cit., vol. 7, 1826, pp. 275–84.

Twesten, August Detlef Christian, *Vorlesungen über die Dogmatik der Evangelisch-Lutherischen Kirche: nach dem Compendium des Herrn Dr. W.M.L. de Wette*, vols. 1–2, 4th ed., Hamburg: Friedrich Perthes 1837–38, vol. 1, pp. 255–6 (vol. 1, 1838; vol. 2, 1837) (*ASKB* 849–849a).

Wolff, Oskar Ludwig Bernhard, *Handbuch deutscher Beredsamkeit enthaltend eine Uebersicht der Geschichte und Theorie der Redekunst, zugleich mit einer vollständigen Sammlung deutscher Reden jedes Zeitalters und jeder Gattung*, vols. 1–2, Leipzig: Carl B. Lorck 1845–46, vol. 1, pp. 325–35 (*ASKB* 250–251).

III. Secondary Literature on Kierkegaard's Relation to Bretschneider

Kloeden, W. von, "Bible Study," in *Kierkegaard's View of Christianity*, ed. by Niels Thulstrup and Marie Mikulová Thulstrup, Copenhagen: C.A. Reitzel 1978 (*Bibliotheca Kierkegaardiana*, vol. 1), pp. 16–38.

Thulstrup, Niels, "Kierkegaard og K.G. Bretschneider," in *Festskrift til Søren Holm*, ed. by Peter Kemp, Copenhagen: Nyt Nordisk Forlag Arnold Busck 1971, pp. 31–42.

—— "Theological and Philosophical Studies," in *Kierkegaard's View of Christianity*, ed. by Niels Thulstrup and Marie Mikulová Thulstrup, Copenhagen: C.A. Reitzel 1978 (*Bibliotheca Kierkegaardiana*, vol. 1), pp. 21–5; pp. 42–3.

Daub:

Kierkegaard's Paradoxical Appropriation of a Hegelian Sentry

Jon Stewart

Carl (or sometimes, Karl) Daub (1765–1836) is known today as little more than a footnote in the development of the right-Hegelian school. In this context he is often mentioned together with figures such as Philipp Marheineke (1780–1846), Karl Rosenkranz (1805–79) and Carl Friedrich Göschel (1784–1861). He was, however, a profoundly influential theologian in his own right and was recognized as such in his age. Indeed, in one account he is ranked together with Goethe (1749–1832), Hegel (1770–1831), Fichte (1762–1814) and Schleiermacher (1768–1834).[1] Daub authored a number of books which were significant for both the philosophical and the theological discussions of the day.

While it has long been apparent to some Kierkegaard scholars that Daub played an important role in the development of the young Kierkegaard's thought, very few studies have been devoted to exploring this connection.[2] In particular, while it is clear that Kierkegaard read some of Daub's works as a young student, it remains an open question whether that reading left any enduring mark on his thought. The present article hopes to establish the importance of Daub as a source for Kierkegaard's thought and to problematize this relationship in a way that points out possible directions for future research.

---

1 Karl Rosenkranz, *Erinnerungen an Karl Daub*, Berlin: Duncker und Humblot 1837, p. 40 (*ASKB* 743).

2 In fact, the only studies to date to treat it directly are Emanuel Hirsch's "Die Einführung in die Frage Glaube und Geschichte durch Karl Daub," in his *Kierkegaard-Studien*, vols. 1–2, Gütersloh: Bertelsmann 1933, vol. 2, pp. 93–105 [pp. 539–51] (reprinted, Vaduz, Liechtenstein: Toposverlag 1978. First published in *Studien des apologetischen Seminars in Wernigerode*, nos. 29, 31, 32, 36, 1930–33. The reprint retains the pagination of the first publication, giving the page numbers of the 1933 edition in square brackets. This convention will be followed here); and Niels Thulstrup's "Daub," in *Kierkegaard's Teachers*, ed. by Niels Thulstrup and Marie Mikulová Thulstrup, Copenhagen: C.A. Reitzel 1982 (*Bibliotheca Kierkegaardiana*, vol. 10), pp. 208–11.

I. Daub's Life and Works

Daub was born in humble circumstances in the German town of Cassel on 20 March 1765.[3] Apparently destined for the priesthood, he studied Hebrew from an early age. He attended the university at Marburg from 1786, where his main fields of study included theology and philosophy. This dual interest would characterize his intellectual activity throughout his life.

In 1791 he became instructor in Marburg, where he lectured on the fields of philosophy, philology and theology. During this time, he fell under the influence of Kant, who was his first philosophical passion. Inspired by the critical philosophy, he published in 1794 his *Predigten: nach kantischen Grundsätzen*.[4] His Kantian rationalism and skepticism made him suspect in some circles and led to him leaving Marburg to take an appointment in Hanau as professor of philosophy in 1794. This position only lasted a year since he received an appointment as *professor ordinarius* in 1795 at the distinguished Faculty of Theology at the University of Heidelberg. It was in Heidelberg that Daub came into his own as a scholar. He was to become an institution at the Faculty, remaining there as a defining figure until his death in 1836.

In 1801 he published his catechism, or *Lehrbuch der Katechetik*, as a textbook for his lectures.[5] A year later it appeared in a Danish translation.[6] This was also a work animated by an enthusiasm for Kant's philosophy. Daub was particularly interested in Kant's grounding of religion in morality, and the *Lehrbuch* attempts to incorporate many of Kant's moral principles. Thus, the focus of the work is on extracting the practical, ethical content of the Bible and church dogma.

Around 1805 Daub's philosophical interests started to change, and he soon abandoned Kant for the young Schelling, who at the time was taking the German philosophical world by storm. From 1805–11 he edited together with the philologist Friedrich Creuzer (1771–1858) six volumes of a journal under the simple title, *Studien*.[7] The articles in this work reflect a clear Schellingian orientation. Daub's contributions in this context were the lengthy essays, "Orthodoxie und Heterodoxie.

---

3 For Daub's life and works, see Ewald Stübinger, *Die Theologie Carl Daubs als Kritik der positionellen Theologie*, Frankfurt am Main et al.: Peter Lang 1993; Falk Wagner, *Die vergessene spekulative Theologie: zur Erinnerung an Carl Daub anläßlich seines 150. Todesjahres*, Zürich: Theologischer Verlag 1987; Ehrhard Pfeiffer, *Karl Daub und die Krisis der spekulativen Theologie*, Leipzig: A. Edlmann 1943; Ehrhard Pfeiffer, "Zur Erinnerung an Karl Daub," *Zeitschrift für Theologie und Kirche*, vol. 17, 1936, pp. 273–9; and Wilhelm Herrmann, *Die speculative Theologie in ihrer Entwicklung durch Daub*, Hamburg and Gotha: Perthes 1847.

4 Carl Daub, *Predigten: nach kantischen Grundsätzen*, Königsberg 1794.

5 Daub, *Lehrbuch der Katechetik: Zum Behuf seiner Vorlesungen*, Frankfurt am Mayn: August Hermann 1801.

6 Daub, *Lærebog i Kateketiken til Brug for sine Forelæsninger*, trans. by Andreas Krag Holm, Copenhagen: Thorings & Coldings Forlag 1802.

7 *Studien*, vols. 1–6, ed. by Carl Daub and Friedrich Creuzer, vol. 1, Frankfurt am Main: Mohr 1805, vols. 2–6, Heidelberg: Mohr und Zimmer 1806–11.

Ein Beitrag zur Lehre von den symbolischen Büchern"[8] and "Theologie und ihre Encyklopädie im Verhältnis zum akademischen Studium beider."[9]

Also during this period of his development, he penned the *Theologumena*,[10] and *Einleitung in das Studium der christlichen Dogmatik*.[11] In these works he attempts to carve out his own position between the poles of supernaturalism and rationalism. According to Daub, the goal is to come to knowledge of God, not through the Bible or the natural world, but through reason. While God is thus revealed in human reason itself, that reason, however, manifests itself in a number of different ways in various cultures and develops over time in historical peoples. As the culmination of this historical development, the Christian religion represents the most perfect manifestation of the divine revealed in reason. Daub thus attempts to interpret the Christian dogmas in terms of the rationality of Schelling's philosophical principles. According to Rosenkranz, the *Theologumena* represents "the true opposition to Kant's *Religion within the Limits of Reason Alone*."[12] Here he presumably has in mind Daub's criticism of the unknowability of God, which is one of the well-known results of Kant's critical philosophy.

Daub's two-volume *Judas Ischarioth, oder das Böse im Verhältnis zum Guten* from 1816–18 treats the age-old problem of evil in the Christian tradition.[13] The difficulty of explaining how evil can arise in a world created by a benevolent and all-powerful God leads Daub to declare evil to be a kind of incomprehensible, inexplicable, false "miracle." These evil miracles correspond to the true ones, which originate from divine goodness. While Thulstrup claims that this work was "[t]he first major result of [Daub's] studies and reflections under Hegel's influence,"[14] there is nothing to substantiate this claim. On the contrary, at the time it was regarded as a reactionary throwback to "papism" and medieval "barbarism."[15] Moreover, as Rosenkranz points out, already in Daub's previous work, the *Theologumena*, one finds a clear reflection of some aspects of Hegel's thought.[16]

Daub became Hegel's colleague when the latter was appointed to the University of Heidelberg in 1816. Daub, who happened to be the rector of the university at

---

8 Daub, "Orthodoxie und Heterodoxie. Ein Beitrag zur Lehre von den symbolischen Büchern," *Studien*, op. cit., vol. 1, 1805, pp. 104–73.

9 Daub, "Theologie und ihre Encyklopädie im Verhältnis zum akademischen Studium beider. Fragment einer Einleitung in die letztere," *Studien*, op. cit., vol. 2, 1806, pp. 1–69.

10 Daub, *Theologumena sive doctrinae de religione christiana ex natura Dei perspecta repetendae capita potiora*, Heidelberg: Mohr und Zimmer 1806.

11 Daub, *Einleitung in das Studium der christlichen Dogmatik aus dem Standpunkte der Religion*, Heidelberg: Mohr und Zimmer 1810.

12 Rosenkranz, *Erinnerungen an Karl Daub*, op. cit., p. 7.

13 Daub, *Judas Ischarioth, oder das Böse im Verhältnis zum Guten*, vols. 1–2, Heidelberg: Mohr und Winter 1816–18.

14 Thulstrup, "Daub," op. cit., pp. 208f.

15 This is reported by Karl Rosenkranz in his *Erinnerungen an Karl Daub*, op. cit., p. 12. It is repeated in the article on "Daub," in *Realencyklopädie für protestantische Theologie und Kirche*, vols. 1–24, ed. by Johann Jakob Herzog and Albert Hauck, 3rd ed., Leipzig: J.C. Hinrichs 1896–1913, vol. 4, p. 500.

16 Rosenkranz, *Erinnerungen an Karl Daub*, op. cit., p. 9.

the time, was instrumental in the appointment.[17] While Hegel was in Heidelberg, he had a collegial relation to Daub but not more.[18] Although Daub was actually older than Hegel, he abandoned Schelling and became one of Hegel's most loyal followers in the years to come, especially after Hegel left Heidelberg for Berlin in 1818. Following Hegel's departure, Daub is reported to have given lectures on Hegel's *Phenomenology of Spirit*.[19] Their exchange of letters during Hegel's Berlin period portrays a close friendship and collegiality.[20] So great was Hegel's confidence in Daub that he entrusted him with correcting the proofs of the second edition of the *Encyclopedia of the Philosophical Sciences* in 1827.[21]

In the same year the Berlin theologian and right-Hegelian Philipp Marheineke published his influential *Die Grundlehre der christlichen Dogmatik als Wissenschaft*, with a dedication to Daub.[22] Daub then subsequently wrote a book review of the work which appeared in the Hegelian journal, the *Jahrbücher für wissenschaftliche Kritik* in 1827–28.[23] This review was later used as the basis for an independent monograph under the title, *Die dogmatische Theologie jetziger Zeit oder die Selbstsucht in der Wissenschaft des Glaubens*.[24] This work represents Daub's undisputed main work

---

17 See Karl Rosenkranz, *Georg Wilhelm Friedrich Hegel's Leben*, Berlin: Duncker und Humblot 1844, pp. 296ff.; Günther Nicolin, *Hegel in Berichten seiner Zeitgenossen*, Hamburg: Felix Meiner 1970, p. 126.

18 See Rosenkranz, *Georg Wilhelm Friedrich Hegel's Leben*, op. cit., p. 300: "*Mit Daub war die Beziehung zwar eine geistig tiefe, allein persönlich eigentlich nicht intime. Sie kamen nicht so viel zusammen, als man vielleicht hätte erwarten sollen und sahen sich mehr nur bei allgemeinen Gelegenheiten.*"

19 Rosenkranz, *Erinnerungen an Karl Daub*, op. cit., p. 15.

20 See *Briefe von und an Hegel*, vols. 1–3, ed. by Johannes Hoffmeister, Hamburg: Meiner 1951–54, 3rd ed., 1969, vol. 2, letter 277, pp. 94–6; letter 279, pp. 103f.; letter 287, pp. 117f.; letter 291, p. 122; letter 298, pp. 129f.; letter 305, p. 137; letter 372, pp. 235f.; letter 387, pp. 261–4; letter 401, pp. 291f.; vol. 3, letter 506, p. 107; letter 519, pp. 124f.; letter 531, p. 149–52; letter 541, pp. 161f.; letter 543, pp. 163–5; letter 596, p. 252f.; letter 609, pp. 273–5; letter 615, pp. 279f. See also Friedhelm Nicolin, "Aus Hegels Briefwechsel mit Karl Daub," *Hegel-Studien*, vol. 17, 1982, pp. 45–52.

21 G.W.F. Hegel, *Encyclopädie der philosophischen Wissenschaften im Grundrisse*, 2nd ed., Heidelberg: August Oßwald 1827. See their correspondence on this as listed among the references in the previous footnote.

22 Philipp Marheineke, *Die Grundlehren der christlichen Dogmatik als Wissenschaft*, Berlin: Dunker und Humblot 1827 (*ASKB* 644): "Sr. Hochwürden dem Herrn Dr. Karl Daub, Großherzoglich Badische, Geheimen Kirchenrath, und Professor der Theologie an der Universität Heidelberg zur öffentlichen Bezeugung der gerechtesten Verehrung und Liebe und zur dankbaren Anerkennung seiner großen Verdienste um die speculative Theologie zugeeignet."

23 Daub, "*Die Grundlehren der christlichen Dogmatik als Wissenschaft* von Dr. Philipp Marheineke. Zweite völlig neu ausgearbeitete Auflage. Berlin, 1827," *Jahrbücher für wissenschaftliche Kritik*, Erster Artikel, nos. 211–8, 1827, columns 1684–1733; Zweiter Artikel, vol. 1, nos. 23–30, 1828, columns 186–228; vol. 2, nos. 25–32, 1828, columns 197–251.

24 Daub, *Die dogmatische Theologie jetziger Zeit oder die Selbstsucht in der Wissenschaft des Glaubens und seiner Artikel*, Heidelberg: J.C.B. Mohr 1833. See Daub's account here (in his "Vorrede" p. xiii) of the relation between this text and his review of Marheineke.

from this Hegelian period. It shows the clear influence of Hegel's *Phenomenology of Spirit*, which Daub had studied meticulously.

Daub died in Heidelberg on 22 November 1836. After his death, his friends, Marheineke and Theophor Wilhelm Dittenberger (1807–71), edited a seven-volume edition of his lectures, which was published from 1838–44.[25] This edition consists of Daub's *Lectures on Philosophical Anthropology*,[26] *Prolegomena to Dogmatics*,[27] *Prolegomena to Theological Morality and Principles of Ethics*,[28] *System of Theological Morality*,[29] and *System of Christian Dogmatics*.[30] During his lifetime, in 1834, there had already appeared an edition of his lectures, edited by Johann Christoph Kröger (1792–1874) under the title, *Darstellung und Beurtheilung der Hypothesen in Betreff der Willensfreiheit*.[31] This work was reviewed by Rosenkranz in the *Jahrbücher für wissenschaftliche Kritik* and subsequently reprinted in his recollections on Daub.[32]

In the last years of his life, Daub came to be recognized as one of the best-known advocates of speculative theology and right-Hegelianism, that is, the view that Hegel's philosophy of religion was consistent with orthodox Christianity. He is thus known for his attempts to reconcile speculative philosophy with theology by giving a speculative interpretation of key Christian dogmas in order to defend them against their critics. Due to his eclecticism and ability to change with the times philosophically, he was given the nickname "the Talleyrand of German philosophy,"[33] in reference to the great survivor of French politics and diplomacy, Charles Maurice de Talleyrand-Périgord (1754–1838), who played key roles in the *ancien régime*, the Napoleonic dictatorship and the Restoration.

Kierkegaard's interest in Daub is hardly surprising given that Daub was also a familiar figure to many Danish scholars at the time. During his trip to Germany, the Danish author and critic Peder Hjort (1793–1871) met Daub in Heidelberg in June of 1820. He secured from Daub a recommendation that he used to present

---

25 *Philosophische und theologische Vorlesungen*, vols. 1–7, ed. by Philipp Marheineke and Theophor Wilhelm Dittenberger, Berlin: Dunker und Humblot 1838–44 (*ASKB* 472–472g).

26 Daub, *Vorlesungen über die philosophische Anthropologie*, vol. 1, of *Philosophische und theologische Vorlesungen*, op. cit.

27 Daub, *Prolegomena zur Dogmatik und Kritik der Beweise für das Dasein Gottes*, vol. 2, of *Philosophische und theologische Vorlesungen*, op. cit.

28 Daub, *Prolegomena zur theologischen Moral und Prinzipien der Ethik*, vol. 3, of *Philosophische und theologische Vorlesungen*, op. cit.

29 Daub, *System der theologischen Moral*, Parts 1–2, vols. 4–5, of *Philosophische und theologische Vorlesungen*, op. cit.

30 Daub, *System der christlichen Dogmatik*, Parts 1–2, vols. 6–7, of *Philosophische und theologische Vorlesungen*, op. cit.

31 *Des Herrn Geheimen Kirchenraths und Professors, Dr. C. Daub Darstellung und Beurtheilung der Hypothesen in Betreff der Willensfreiheit. Mit Zustimmung des Verfassers aus dessen Vorlesungen herausgegeben*, ed. by J.C. Kröger, Altona: Hammerich 1834.

32 Rosenkranz, "C. Daub's *Darstellung und Beurtheilung der Hypothesen in Betreff der Willensfreiheit*," *Jahrbücher für wissenschaftliche Kritik* 1835, nos. 1–2, reprinted in *Erinnerungen an Karl Daub*, op. cit., pp. 39–55.

33 Rosenkranz, *Erinnerungen an Karl Daub*, op. cit., p. 3.

himself to Hegel in Berlin.[34] Similarly, the theologian, Hans Lassen Martensen (1808–84) and the jurist, Frederik Christian Bornemann (1810–61), met Daub in Heidelberg sometime presumably in 1835 during their trip through the German states.[35] It was not by accident that they met Hegel's sons, the historian Karl Hegel (1813–1901) and the government official Immanuel Hegel (1814–91) in Daub's home. Martensen clearly regarded Daub as a Hegelian pantheist at this late stage of his career. But there can be little doubt that Daub and Marheineke provided the models of speculative theology that Martensen would have so much success promoting when he returned to Denmark and began lecturing at the University of Copenhagen in 1837.

II. Kierkegaard's Use of Daub

The only books by Daub that Kierkegaard actually owned were the aforementioned seven-volume posthumous edition of his lectures, that is, *Philosophische und theologische Vorlesungen*. In addition to this work, Kierkegaard also had in his library a copy of Karl Rosenkranz's *Erinnerungen an Karl Daub*,[36] a work which was also available in Danish in the *Tidsskrift for udenlandsk theologisk Litteratur*.[37] However, there is, as we shall see, clear evidence that he made a careful study of other works by Daub. Indeed, there are several passages in both Kierkegaard's published works and in his journals and notebooks, which give evidence of a fairly extensive study of Daub's thought. Moreover, these passages are not limited to a particular period in Kierkegaard's life but rather span the entire period of the authorship.

A. Kierkegaard's Study of Daub's Article in the Journal DD

The *Journal DD*, which Kierkegaard started in May 1837, begins with a series of notes on articles from a number of Hegelian thinkers found in Bruno Bauer's (1809–82) *Zeitschrift für spekulative Theologie*.[38] One of these that particularly interested Kierkegaard was Daub's article, "Die Form der christlichen Dogmen- und Kirchen-

---

34 Morten Borup, *Peder Hjort*, Copenhagen: Rosenkilde og Bagger 1959, p. 76.

35 Hans Lassen Martensen, *Af mit Levnet*, vols. 1–3, Copenhagen: Gyldendal 1882–83, vol. 1, pp. 113–8.

36 Karl Rosenkranz, *Erinnerungen an Karl Daub*, op. cit.

37 Rosenkranz, "Erindringer om Karl Daub," *Tidsskrift for udenlandsk theologisk Litteratur*, vols. 1–20, ed. by Henrik Nikolai Clausen and Matthias Hagen Hohlenberg, Copenhagen: C.A. Reitzel 1833–52, vol. 5, 1837, pp. 534–62 (*ASKB* U 29).

38 In addition to Daub's article, Kierkegaard comments on Karl Rosenkranz's article, "Eine Parallele zur Religionsphilosophie," *Zeitschrift für spekulative Theologie*, vols. 1–3, ed. by Bruno Bauer, Berlin: Ferdinand Dümmler 1836–38, vol. 2, no. 1, 1837, pp. 1–31 (*ASKB* 354–357); J.E. Erdmann's "Ueber den Begriff des Sündenfalls und des Bösen," *Zeitschrift für spekulative Theologie*, op. cit., vol. 2, no. 1, 1837, pp. 192–214; and K.F. Göschel's "Der Pantheisumus und die Genesis," *Zeitschrift für spekulative Theologie*, op. cit., vol. 2, no. 1, 1837, pp. 184–91.

Historie."[39] This article addresses itself to the question of the significance of history for Christian doctrine. This was at the time a topical issue due to Strauss' *The Life of Jesus*, from 1835–36,[40] which had argued that a critical examination of the historical Jesus calls into question key points of dogma. Daub thus wishes to revisit the issue concerning what is at stake for Christian faith in a historical account, either of the life of Jesus or the history of the Church.

In the first entry of the journal, Kierkegaard explores Karl Rosenkranz's understanding of Jewish monotheism with the tautological statement, "God is God," from Rosenkranz's article, "Eine Parallele zur Religionsphilosophie."[41] Then in a marginal entry, perhaps added later, he makes reference to Daub's article as follows:

> Cf. Daub in the same journal vol. 2, issue 1, p. 135: "*Es ist nicht der Eine, als ein dreizeitiger Gott, oder: als der welcher (erstens) ist, der er (zweitens) war, und (drittens) seyn wird, der er ist, (wie ihn das Judenthum, dem Geschichts-Glauben den jenseitsgeschichtlichen unterordenend, und mit solcher Unterordnung sich selbst corrumpirend knechtisch verehrte) etc.*" [It is not the One, as a triple temporal God—he who (first) is, what he (second) was, and (third) will be, what he is—(whom Judaism slavishly worshipped by subordinating the transhistorical belief to the historical belief and by such subordination corrupting itself), etc.][42]

After this account of the divine in Judaism, Daub continues by contrasting this with the conception of the divine in Christianity:

> but rather the *One* as tri*une*, which the teaching of Jesus had revealed and which *Moses* and the *Prophets* had *prophesied* in relation to the founder of this faith and to the life of the founder, the *One* and tri*une*, which the teaching of Jesus—which made the life of Jesus the condition for its historical relation to mankind—revealed to mankind in and by the names, *Father, Son* and *Holy Ghost*, for mankind's faith and for its knowledge of faith.[43]

Here Daub makes a case for the dogma of the Trinity in contrast to Judaism. While the God of Judaism appears in three temporal dimensions, the God of Christianity is genuinely triune and consists of three persons. It is not clear if Kierkegaard refers to

---

39 Daub, "Die Form der christlichen Dogmen- und Kirchen-Historie," *Zeitschrift für spekulative Theologie*, op. cit., vol. 1, no. 1, 1836, pp. 1–60; vol. 1, no. 2, pp. 63–132; vol. 2, no. 1, 1837 pp. 88–161 (*ASKB* 354–357). For a treatment of this article and its relevance for Kierkegaard, see Emanuel Hirsch, "Die Einführung in die Frage Glaube und Geschichte durch Karl Daub," in his *Kierkegaard-Studien*, op. cit., vol. 2, pp. 93–105 [pp. 539–51].

40 David Friedrich Strauss, *Das Leben Jesu, kritisch bearbeitet*, vols. 1–2, Tübingen: Osiander 1835–36.

41 Rosenkranz, "Eine Parallele zur Religionsphilosophie," *Zeitschrift für spekulative Theologie*, op. cit., vol. 2, no. 1, 1837, p. 1.

42 *SKS* 17, 213, DD:1.c. Here Kierkegaard quotes from Daub's article in *Zeitschrift für spekulative Theologie*, op. cit., vol. 2, no. 1, p. 135.

43 Ibid.

Daub's account here since he agrees with it or simply because he finds it interesting and wishes to note it for later use.[44]

In the second entry in the journal, Kierkegaard refers to and quotes from a few pages earlier in Daub's article. He writes,

> There is a highly speculative and, re[garding] Daub's philosophical view, extremely interesting remark in the 3rd volume of Bauer's journal, p. 127. He has prior to this discussed the relationship between the natural and the historical sense, and shown the first to be a condition of the second, but now he explains how the individual can freely subordinate the second to the first (thereby history or freedom to nature, *completely*) or the first to the second (and thereby freedom over nature, in part), and adduces more precisely the consequences of subordinating the historical to the natural, saying that the subject thereby comes upon the idea: *an dem Vergangenen sei das anschaulich-Gewesene das Unvergängliche, am Gewesenen das Naturliche das Unverwesliche (das also nicht wie doch der Apostel lehrt "verweslich gesäet wird, und unverweslich auferstehe" sondern, indem es selbst das an sich Unverwesliche sei, nur bis zu seiner Wiederveranschaulichung den Schein des Verweslichen habe).* ["in what is the past the having-been for sense is the imperishable, and in what has been, the natural is the imperishable (and thus it does not hold true in this case that, as the apostle teaches, 'What is sown is perishable, what is raised imperishable,' but rather it has the appearance of the perishable only until it is perceived again since it is imperishable in itself)."][45]

Here by "the natural and the historical sense," Kierkegaard refers to Daub's foregoing discussion. In this article Daub begins by distinguishing the development of nature from that of history. While history displays a mechanical development of objects, history is the work of the freedom of the human subject in their actions and their interpretations. Later in his analysis, Daub treats these two terms in a dialectical fashion, which seems to be a part of what attracted Kierkegaard's attention to this passage. In other words, first, the historical is subordinated to the natural, and the results of this subordination are drawn out; and then, with an inversion, the natural is subordinated to the historical, and the results of this are drawn out.

In the passage immediately before the one quoted by Kierkegaard, Daub explains the dependence of the will on nature and history as follows:

> In this limitation the volition is reduced—since in it, in a mistaken manner, the historical sense conditions and *serves* the natural sense—to the desire of the past, if this volition in its remembrance is one that is pleasurable to sensation and imagination—and the desire is reduced to a longing for the past, which is in this way appreciated and popular, whereas in this limitation the longing is reduced to a demand for its return and temporal- and spatial-preserving presence. This demand, which is a *volition*, though in the form of a longing, has thus *the* equally necessary consequence that the intelligent subject substitutes

44 Here Hirsch takes Kierkegaard to be in agreement with Daub, interpreting this passage as an anticipation of Kierkegaard's understanding of the God in time. See Emanuel Hirsch, "Die Einführung in die Frage Glaube und Geschichte durch Karl Daub," in his *Kierkegaard-Studien*, op. cit., vol. 2, p. 102 [p. 548].

45 *SKS* 17, 213, DD:2. Kierkegaard quotes from Daub, "Die Form der christlichen Dogmen- und Kirchen-Historie," *Zeitschrift für spekulative Theologie*, op. cit, vol. 2, no. 1, 1836, p. 127.

> an act of imagination for an act of retrograde intuition since it can neither become nor be a directly intuitive one and merely conditions the representation of the past. Furthermore, this demand falls within the *intelligent* subject, which is only capable of mimicking the already formed principles of free movement and these movements themselves....[46]

The idea here seems to be that from our sense of history we obtain a desire or longing for the past. This natural emotion or desire is thus dependent on the fact that there was a past, which is continually the object of our thought and cognition. This longing then produces the desire to hold the past firmly for cognition by giving it a fixed form of thought so that it can be preserved. The importance of this idea for Kierkegaard becomes clear when one considers the account of the Incarnation in *Philosophical Fragments*. The individual believer relates to this event with feeling and emotion. This event of the past is constantly the object of reflection for the Christian. Its universal significance must be kept ever present in the mind of the believer.

Kierkegaard continues his reading of Daub's article in June of 1837. This time, he quotes from a passage considerably earlier in the article. Here he writes, "Daub (in Bauer's Journal, vol. 1, no. 2, p. 103) quite rightly observes that unbelief as well as doubt would be very well served by getting involved in a proof of the truth of biblical miracles."[47] Kierkegaard refers to the following passage in Daub's text:

> "Show me only," the doubter or unbeliever would like to say, "that any one fact, known as certain and true from good sources, would have been entirely impossible without a miracle happening previously or simultaneous with it—or let me myself only see or experience one miracle, then I would be prepared to believe everything that the Holy Scriptures report about prophesies and miracles."[48]

Here Daub presumably has in mind the then topical criticisms from skeptics like Strauss, who called into question the status of the reports of miracles in the gospels. Kierkegaard then quotes the following long passage in German from Daub's article, where "this demand" from the doubter is taken up:

> However, with this demand *freedom* in history is ignored—for if the miracle is to be believed, the certain and true fact shall *necessarily* be conditioned by it, as well as *necessity* in nature—for the miracle, a *free* act should be seen as if it were an event of *nature*, that is, it should be experienced; those present at the Ascension of the savior of the world *saw only* his removal from earth, but not the unconditional freedom, that is, the *power* of his removal. The truth which this miracle is, realizes itself and has its reality in the *power* but not in the fleeting and past sight of this movement. Thus, as long as they do not abandon the demand for a proof of the truth of miracles to be given from the standpoint of history or nature, both the doubter and the unbeliever prove that in miracles unconditional freedom has placed itself either under the law of causality (as in a *pragmatizing* theory of

---

46 Daub, "Die Form der christlichen Dogmen- und Kirchen-Historie," *Zeitschrift für spekulative Theologie*, op. cit., vol. 2, no. 1, 1836, pp. 126f.

47 *SKS* 17, 222, DD:12.

48 Daub, "Die Form der christlichen Dogmen- und Kirchen-Historie," *Zeitschrift für spekulative Theologie*, op. cit., vol. 1, no. 2, p. 103.

> history) or under sensuousness which miracles have in common with animality (as in a *merely empirical* theory of nature)...[49]

The main point of the response to the skeptic is that the true essence of miracles is the fact that they occur with freedom. However, this freedom is never something that can be straightforwardly seen or observed empirically either in the case of miracles or in any other event. It is thus absurd of the skeptic to demand empirical proof of something which by its very nature cannot be proven by empirical observation. Moreover, if a miracle could be explained in this way, then it would be subordinate to the normal laws of nature and thus would not be a free act. This recalls Kierkegaard's claim about the Incarnation in the *Fragments*, namely, that the fact of the Incarnation was not in itself an object of experience even for Christ's contemporaries. What they actually saw or witnessed was a humble man and not the Incarnation itself. Moreover, despite the topical claims about necessity in history, the Incarnation was a free act, which supersedes the laws of nature.

In the following entry in the *Journal DD*, dated 16 June 1837, Kierkegaard refers to yet another passage in Daub's article. Here he writes,

> Surely it's true what Daub says (Bauer's jour[nal]), that Christ's 3 statements contain his whole life story (Do you not know that I must be in my Father's house; I must work the works of him who sent me while it is day: the night is coming when no man can work; It is accomplished). Yet one must also not forget 3 others: He grew and waxed strong in spirit filled with wisdom Lk 2:40; He is tempted; My God, why hast thou forsaken me?[50]

Here Kierkegaard refers to the very beginning of the third installment of Daub's treatise, where he writes:

> The statement of *Jesus* to his parents: (in his first statement in the gospel) "Do you not know that I must be in my Father's house?" (Luke 2, v. 49), the other statement to his disciples: "We must work the works of him who sent me while it is day; night is coming when no one can work." (John 9, v. 4; cf. chap. 5, v. 17), and his statement to all humanity: "It is accomplished," (John 19, v. 30)—these three statements are just as many data, to which all the other data in the teachings he revealed refer, i.e., in the deeds he does, in the suffering he endures, and in the accounts of the gospel writers about him; and if only the relation of any of these other data to these aforementioned three statements as well as the relation of every fact that is either only indicated by every datum, or of every fact (concerning prophecy and miracles) that is described by every datum, is explored, then the form in its sublime unity with its content, undisturbed by any conflict, is recognized and the object (the life of *Jesus*, as the only one which is *just as* divine *as* human) of the history of the age is grasped.[51]

Kierkegaard refers to this account in Daub with approval, although he finds the list of statements incomplete and wishes to supplement it. Daub's point here is in part to indicate how at the time of the earliest Christianity, the most complex theological

49 Ibid., pp. 103f.

50 *SKS* 17, 223, DD:13.

51 Daub, "Die Form der christlichen Dogmen- und Kirchen-Historie," *Zeitschrift für spekulative Theologie*, op. cit., vol. 2, no. 1, p. 88f.

notions were expressed with the simplest of formulations. The task of current theological research is to get back to these simple original meanings.

It is difficult to discern a single thread that runs through all of these references. Thus, it is not easy to say in a word what exactly it was about Daub's article that Kierkegaard found so interesting. However, there can be no doubt that the general complex of issues that Daub addresses is one that would come to exercise Kierkegaard over the next several years, for example, the question of to what extent Christian faith depends on a veridical account of history. This recalls the main issue of *Philosophical Fragments*. Moreover, this article contains many methodological considerations relevant for the philosophy of history, which could potentially have been useful to Kierkegaard for studies such as *The Concept of Irony*.

B. Other References to Daub in the Journals and Notebooks

Apart from the references to Daub's article in the *Journal DD*, there are also numerous other scattered references to his works in several of Kierkegaard's journals and notebooks. These references have no recognizable thematic unity and thus will be treated in a straightforward chronological fashion.

In June 1837, in the *Journal FF*, Kierkegaard writes in a journal entry: "Daub's sentences are true labyrinths; one needs Ariadne's thread to read them—that is, love and inspiration."[52] As the commentators of *Søren Kierkegaards Skrifter* point out,[53] the dating of this comment clearly fits with Kierkegaard's reading of Daub's article "Die Form der christlichen Dogmen- und Kirchen-Historie" in May and June of 1837. As the foregoing section has indicated, there can be no doubt that Kierkegaard found a great degree of "inspiration" from the article. But it is clear that, like many readers, he found Daub's text rough going. In Strauss' account in his book *Charakteristiken und Kritiken*, he notes the difficulties that Marheineke had reading Daub's review of his book: he "had to read each sentence three times. The first time he understood nothing at all. The second time he understood a little. The third time he had still not understood it."[54] Thus, Kierkegaard was not alone with his complaint.

Kierkegaard was exposed to Daub in the lectures that he attended at the University of Copenhagen in Winter Semester of 1837–38,[55] given by Hans Lassen Martensen under the title "*Prolegomena ad dogmaticam speculativam*" or "Introduction to Speculative Dogmatics."[56] Martensen had only recently returned from his journey to Germany and Prussia and thus from his meeting with Daub. His lectures were

52 *SKS* 18, 87, FF:61 / *JP* 1, 619.

53 *SKS* K18, 133.

54 D.F. Strauss, "Schleiermacher und Daub, in ihrer Bedeutung für die Theologie unsrer Zeit," in his *Charakteristiken und Kritiken. Eine Sammlung zerstreuter Aufsätze aus den Gebieten der Theologie, Anthropologie und Aesthetik*, Leipzig: Wigand 1839, pp. 3–212; p. 125.

55 See Kim Ravn and Steen Tullberg, "Tekstredegørelse" to *Notesbog 4*, in *SKS* K19, p. 180. See also the commentary in *SKS* K19, pp. 186–7.

56 A complete list of Martensen's lectures can be found in Skat Arildsen, *Biskop Hans Lassen Martensen. Hans Liv, Udvikling og Arbejde*, Copenhagen: G.E.C. Gads Forlag 1932, pp. 156–8.

tremendously popular and created an instant sensation for Hegel's philosophy. Among his auditors was Søren Kierkegaard, who took notes to the lectures in his *Notebook 4*.[57] Kierkegaard's notes cover the first half of the course, in all ten lectures, from 15 November to 23 December 1837.[58] In the third lecture, from 22 November, Martensen refers twice to "Daub's last work,"[59] that is, *Die dogmatische Theologie jetziger Zeit oder die Selbstsucht in der Wissenschaft des Glaubens*,[60] which Rosenkranz had purportedly designated as a "phenomenology."[61] Here Martensen traces three stages of a phenomenology of Christian consciousness, the first of which is Catholicism and the second of which is the Reformation.

Daub also appears several times in the fourth lecture from 24 November. Here one reads,

> The spirit which we have in its first form in the apostolic inspiration (whereby it is strange that while the truth was only objective for the apostles, was, so to speak, palpable, they did not understand it; but only when it with spirit was subjectively carried over into consciousness—*Daub*—*Grundtvig*), later was the inspiration in the Church, in the Pope, in the Councils, etc....[62]

In a marginal note to this passage, one reads, "Therefore dogmatics assumes a wholly different relation in Catholicism than in Protestantism[;] there were several dogmaticians just as there were several popes and yet only one papacy, that is, *per successionem* (Daub) in Protestantism every new system had a new horizon."[63] Martensen continues, "(In the Middle Ages, the Church did not have spirit [*Aand*], but spirituality [*Geistlighed*]. *Daub*.)"[64] In these passages Martensen refers to the text by Daub that he mentioned in his previous lecture, *Die dogmatische Theologie jetziger Zeit oder die Selbstsucht in der Wissenschaft des Glaubens*.[65] The general point of these references to Daub seems to revolve around the issue of the way in which the individual consciousness appropriates divine inspiration and the way in which that inspiration is handed down from one person to another.

Some months later, in 1838, Kierkegaard writes in a marginal addition to the *Journal DD*: "I see that Daub in his now-published lectures on anthropology quite briefly makes a similar observation on why the anc.[ients] didn't have humor. Cf. p. 482."[66] This observation comes in the context of a number of entries in which Kierkegaard explores the concept of humor. Here Kierkegaard refers to Daub's

---

57 *SKS* 19, 125–43, Not4:3–12. See Niels Thulstrup, *Kierkegaard's Relation to Hegel*, trans. by George L. Stengren, Princeton: Princeton University Press 1980, p. 133.

58 See Kim Ravn and Steen Tullberg, "Tekstredegørelse" to *Notesbog 4*, in *SKS* K19, pp. 177–83.

59 *SKS* 19, 127, Not4:4 and 129, Not4:5.

60 Daub, *Die dogmatische Theologie jetziger Zeit*, op. cit.

61 This reference in Rosenkranz is unidentified in *SKS*.

62 *SKS* 19, 130, Not4:6.

63 *SKS* 19, 130, Not4:6a.

64 *SKS* 19, 130, Not4:6.

65 See *SKS* K19, 191, where the commentators refer to *Die dogmatische Theologie jetziger Zeit*, op. cit., p. 428.

66 *SKS* 17, 216, DD:6a.

lectures on philosophical anthropology in Marheineke's and Dittenberger's edition.[67] In these lectures humor is defined as follows: "The principle of humor is not a tendency, not to mention a passion, but rather it is the energy of reason and freedom in its independence from all passion, united with thoroughgoing understanding, acute power of judgment, lively fantasy, striking wit. The humorist has great knowledge of people..."[68] Daub explores how the humorist is able to rid himself of passions. Then comes the passage that Kierkegaard refers to, where Daub writes,

> Not every people has its humorists. In the literature of the Greeks and the Romans there are none; for satirists are not humorists. In the works of the *satirists* the finite is merely placed in opposition to the relative. The question of why the ancient world did not have the aesthetic way of thinking which we call humor could be the object of a scholarly investigation. Does it perhaps have its reason in the fact that the eternal light had still not risen then, as it has now in Christianity?[69]

It is unclear whether Kierkegaard agrees or disagrees with this statement. Given his interest in humor, he may well have simply been interested in noting different accounts and definitions of it for more careful consideration later.

In Summer Semester 1838 Martensen covered the first 59 paragraphs of his course on "Speculative Dogmatics," which would be continued the next semester (covering §§ 60–99).[70] Kierkegaard attended this course and took notes to the first 23 paragraphs in his *Journal KK*.[71] Another more detailed set of notes (covering both semesters) from a foreign hand is printed in the *Papirer* edition.[72] Daub appears here in § 2, where Martensen refers to his main works under the rubric: "The Literature of Speculative Dogmatics."[73] Here one reads, "Daub's *Theologumena* 1806 made an epoch, renewed speculation, set forth, among other things, speculative proofs for the existence of God. Daub *Einleitung in [das Studium] der Dogmatik* 1809, and *Die dogmat.[ische] Theologie jetziger Zeit*, criticism of the dogmatic systems 1833."[74] This passage only appears in the more detailed set of notes from the anonymous author and not in Kierkegaard's notes in *KK*. Daub is mentioned here simply as a part of a kind of narrative bibliography of the main works of the leading speculative theologians of the day. He is thus named along with Marheineke, the younger Fichte (1797–1879), Karl Philipp Fischer (1807–85), Franz von Baader (1765–1841), Anton Günther (1783–1863) and Franz Anton Staudenmaier (1800–56).

Daub appears again in § 4 in the anonymous set of notes: "Schleiermacher strictly distinguished between philosophy and religion: [this is] correct, but he overlooked

67 Daub, *Vorlesungen über die philosophische Anthropologie*, op. cit.

68 Ibid., p. 481.

69 Ibid., p. 482.

70 See Skat Arildsen, *Biskop Hans Lassen Martensen. Hans Liv, Udvikling og Arbejde*, Copenhagen: G.E.C. Gads Forlag 1932, p. 156; Niels W. Bruun and Finn Gredal Jensen, "Tekstredegørelse" to the *Journal KK*, in *SKS* K18, p. 479.

71 *SKS* 18, 374–86, KK:11.

72 *Pap.* II C 26–27 in *Pap.* XIII, pp. 3–43. *Pap.* II C 28 in *Pap.* XIII, pp. 44–116.

73 *Pap.* II C 26–27 in *Pap.* XIII, p. 7.

74 Ibid.

that there is a knowledge *in* religion prior to philosophy, that is, cognition *of* religion. Daub, Marhein[eke], Hegel are here served."[75] The point here, as is clear from what follows, is that the divine makes all knowledge possible by a kind of revelation. This knowledge precedes all other kinds of knowing, including philosophical knowing, and indeed makes it possible. Here again Daub is simply listed as an example of the speculative theologians who are known to defend this view (in contrast to Schleiermacher's position).

Daub also appears in Martensen's lecture course, "The History of More Recent Philosophy from Kant to Hegel," from Winter Semester 1838–39. While it is uncertain whether Kierkegaard attended these lectures in person, he was in possession of a set of lecture notes, written in a foreign hand, to this course; these notes were subsequently printed in the edition of Kierkegaard's *Papirer*.[76] In these lectures Martensen mentions Daub's *Theologumena*, once in his account of Schelling's system,[77] and once in his account of philosophy's relation to theology.[78] At the end of his lectures Martensen declares, "With the Hegelian philosophy, the history of dogma especially has won, especially with Daub. Before people treated the history of dogma as an aggregate of opinions."[79] With Hegel and Daub the goal is to see the Idea developing in the dogmas over the course of time. Dogma is thus more than a simple "aggregate of opinions" but rather a manifestation of the Idea in history.

While he was in Berlin in 1841–42, Kierkegaard had the opportunity to hear the lectures of Daub's friend and editor Philipp Marheineke. His notes to these lectures appear in *Notebook 9* and *Notebook 10*. The title of Marheineke's lectures was "Dogmatic Theology with Particular Reference to Daub's System."[80] In his discussion on the doctrine of the two states of Christ, Marheineke refers to Daub as follows: "According to Daub, the miracle is the unity of the historical and the dogmatic. The form of the miracle is human actions, its content is divine action."[81] In the posthumous edition of his *System der christlichen Dogmatik*,[82] which in part reproduces these lectures, Marheineke refers to Daub's *Einleitung in das Studium der christlichen Dogmatik* in this context.[83] This point takes up Daub's defense of miracles in his article treated in the previous section. As was seen there, Kierkegaard found his account sympathetic, and thus he was doubtless interested to hear Marheineke's view of it.

Daub also appears in the NB journals, which, as is well known, Kierkegaard kept during the second half of his authorship. In the *Journal NB* from 1846 one finds evidence of a study of Daub's posthumously published lectures with the title,

---

75 *Pap.* II C 26–27 in *Pap.* XIII, p. 11.

76 *Pap.* II C 25 in *Pap.* XII, pp. 281–331.

77 *Pap.* II C 25 in *Pap.* XII, p. 317.

78 *Pap.* II C 25 in *Pap.* XII, p. 330.

79 *Pap.* II C 25 in *Pap.* XII, p. 331.

80 *SKS* K19, 331.

81 *SKS* 19, 273, Not9:1.

82 *D. Philipp Marheineke's System der christlichen Dogmatik*, ed. by Stephan Matthies und Wilhelm Vatke, Berlin: Dunker und Humblot 1847, p. 326.

83 Daub, *Einleitung in das Studium der christlichen Dogmatik aus dem Standpunkte der Religion*, op. cit., p. 33.

System of Theological Morality.[84] Here he simply quotes the following passage with a reference to Daub's text:

> ...If freedom consisted in this wanting everything, then it would be impossible to think of any duty, any right, and obligation. If this is the opinion of the liberals of our day, then the definition is fitting for them as the ones who would rather want *everything* for themselves, while the servile only want *very much*.
>
> Cf. Daub's *Theological Morality. Collect[ed] Wri[tings]* vol. 4, p. 197.[85]

This comes from a discussion in Daub of the concept of obligation. His main point is that for wanting or desiring to make sense, they must have a determinate object. The idea of someone who wants everything is not just impracticable but straightforwardly incoherent. This would imply wanting contradictory things or things that are simply impossible. For Daub, the concept only makes sense when it is accompanied by a form of negation or limitation so that there is a finite sphere of things that are wanted. The political point here is that it is a mistaken conception of freedom to claim that it consists in the ability to want everything. Since this passage appears in his journal without any further commentary, it is impossible to know why Kierkegaard was interested in it. Given his interests in ethical and psychological questions of freedom, responsibility and desire, it is hardly surprising that considerations of this kind would capture his interest. It may well be that he simply wanted to note this passage for himself so that he could find it again when he returned to write on these topics.

In the next journal *NB2* from August 1847, Daub appears again. This time the reference is to his posthumously published lectures on philosophical anthropology. Kierkegaard writes,

> Daub speaks the truth and expresses it very well (in his *Philosophische Anthropologie*, Berlin: 1838; I, p. 25) when he says of the mob, "*dem Alles zur Lebensfrage wird, am Leben Alles und deßwegen am Rechte Nichts liegt*." [for whom everything is a life-question, only life is of consequence and right is of no consequence.][86]

In the passage in question, which Kierkegaard references directly here, Daub discusses the Enlightenment conception of natural rights. In this context, he talks about how people have grown accustomed to thinking that they have an inherent right to life, property, and so on. He analyzes this concept in a dialectical fashion. At first, there is the view that life is higher than law and rights. According to this opinion, rights and laws only exist to serve the end of life, or specifically, to make communal life possible. Laws must exist to prevent people from acting on immediate desires, which would be destructive to all social existence. In contrast to this is the view that these rights and laws stand higher than life itself and condition it. A person is only wholly human when he or she lives in harmony with a society governed by rules and laws. These laws thus constitute what it is to be a fully developed human

84 Daub, *System der theologischen Moral*, op. cit., Part 1, p. 197.

85 *SKS*, 20, 75, NB:91.

86 *SKS* 20, 192, NB2:130 / *JP* 1, 62.

being at all. According to this view, the loss of life is not as unfortunate as the loss of one's rights since this is what makes us human and makes life worth living.

In the passage quoted, Daub simply notes that the masses are not particularly interested in such abstract concepts like law and right. Thus, they advocate the first view, according to which life is higher than law. His point is that jurisprudence needs to make use of a certain insight into human psychology. It must realize that, for the mob, nothing is more important than life. However, for Daub, psychology, by contrast, must recognize that rights constitute a fully human life and must thus be incorporated into a complete psychological investigation of human beings.

Kierkegaard's quotation is confined to the account of the "mob" which only recognizes the validity of life and not rights or law. This can perhaps be understood in the context of his considerations of society and the social order, which appeared a year earlier in his *A Literary Review* of Thomasine Gyllembourg's (1773–1856) novel, *Two Ages*. He was, of course, also interested in the dynamic of "the mob" in connection with his journal polemic with *The Corsair*.

In the *Journal NB8* from 1848 Kierkegaard demonstrates a study of yet another text by Daub, namely, *Judas Ischariot*. He writes,

> One will get a deep insight into the state of Christianity in each age by seeing how it interprets Judas. Abraham of Santa Clara is naively convinced that he was the most villainous of all scoundrels, about whom one is to say only every conceivable evil—but does not have to explain him. Daub becomes too profoundly metaphysical.[87]

Here Kierkegaard seems not to have in mind any specific passage but rather to refer to Daub's general method of analysis. Here one can detect a slightly critical note. The idea seems to be that each generation interprets Judas in a way typical or characteristic of the age. Daub then interprets Judas metaphysically in a way that, for Kierkegaard, is typical of the overly metaphysical emphasis of the day. The implied criticism is then that this metaphysical approach misses the key point of this and other phenomena relevant for Christianity, which can only be properly understood existentially by the individual.

These various journal entries show a variety of different interests in and uses of Daub's texts. First, they show that Kierkegaard was exposed to different works by Daub in a number of different lecture courses that he attended by Martensen and Marheineke, two scholars closely related to Daub intellectually. Second, they also evidence an independent study of some of Daub's works long after his years as a student. This study shows that he returned to Daub's texts frequently and in different contexts. Thus, Daub was clearly not simply a passing intellectual phase for Kierkegaard. He seems to have had a genuine and enduring interest in Daub's theology.

---

87 *SKS* 21, 183, NB8:95 / *JP* 2, 2229. Kierkegaard also refers to Judas again a few entries later: *SKS* 21, 185f., NB8:99 / *JP* 3, 2497.

C. Kierkegaard's Interest in Daub's Account of Evil in the Journal NB15

Daub appears again in the *Journal NB15* from 1850. Here he is mentioned along with Hegel and Julius Müller (1801–78) in the context of the then topical issue of subjectivism or relativism, which Kierkegaard refers to with a term borrowed from Adolph Peter Adler (1812–69): "isolated subjectivity."[88] He writes,

> In this respect, too, I have not been understood at all. All the more profound thinkers (Hegel, Daub—and to name a less famous but very estimable one: Julius Müller et al.) are unanimous in locating evil in isolated subjectivity—objectivity is the saving factor. For a long time now this has been a catch-phrase; and every student knows, after all, that I am an isolated individuality—ergo, I am practically evil, "pure negativity, lacking earnestness, etc." O, abysmal confusion. No, the whole concept of objectivity, which has been made into the way of deliverance, is merely a feeding of the sickness, and the fact that it is lauded as restoration to health shows precisely how fundamentally irreligious the period is, for the way of deliverance is really a turning back to paganism.[89]

Kierkegaard refers to Hegel's criticism of the Romantics' various interpretations of subjectivism and relativism. With respect to Daub in this context, Kierkegaard seems to refer to *Judas Ischariot*, which, as noted, has the problem of evil as its main subject matter.

Daub appears again in the *Journal NB15*. Here reference is made to both Daub's *Judas Ischariot* and his *Darstellung und Beurtheilung der Hypothesen in Betreff der Willensfreiheit*.[90] Kierkegaard writes,

> There is an excellent little section on evil, on sin as the incomprehensible, the impenetrable, the world's secret—precisely because it is the groundless, an arbitrary discontinuity. I am also happy to see that he quotes Daub, who also explains it in *Judas Ischariot* this way and is not disinclined to place evil under a special definition of the miraculous, although he later abandoned this view and conceived of evil as the negative, for example in his book, *Hypotheser om den menneskelige Frihed*.[91]

Here Kierkegaard quotes from a note in Julius Müller's *Die christliche Lehre von der Sünde*, where Müller refers to Daub.[92] From his earlier reading, Kierkegaard is clearly already familiar with Daub's understanding of evil as something inconceivable and miraculous. This passage demonstrates an independent study of two of Daub's texts, which treat this issue.

---

88 Adolph Peter Adler, *Den isolerede Subjectivitet i dens vigtigste Skikkelser*, Copenhagen: Berlingske Bogtrykkeri 1840.

89 *SKS* 23, 49, NB15:71 / *JP* 4, 4555.

90 *Des Herrn Geheimen Kirchenraths und Professors, Dr. C. Daub Darstellung und Beurtheilung der Hypothesen in Betreff der Willensfreiheit*, op. cit.

91 *SKS* 23, 70, NB15:101 / *JP* 4, 4030.

92 Julius Müller, *Die christliche Lehre von der Sünde*, vols. 1–2, Breslau: Josef Max 1849, vol. 1, *Vom Wesen und Grunde der Sünde*, p. 460 (*ASKB* 689–690): "This inconceivability of evil is indicated with thorough earnestness especially in Daub's *Judas Ischarioth*."

D. Daub and the Image of the Sentry

Daub appears less frequently in Kierkegaard's published works than in his journals and notebooks. The first time Daub is directly mentioned by name in the published writings is in the "Preliminary Expectoration" in *Fear and Trembling*. There Johannes de silentio makes use of the image of a sentry at his post that he borrows from Daub. Kierkegaard continues to work with this image for many years to come. In *Fear and Trembling* it appears as follows:

> If everyone in my generation who does not wish to stop with faith is actually a person who has grasped the horror of life, has grasped the meaning of Daub's statement that a soldier standing alone with a loaded rifle at his post near a powder magazine on a stormy night thinks strange thoughts; if everyone who does not wish to stop with faith is actually a person who has the spiritual power to comprehend that the wish was an impossibility and then to take time to be alone with the thought…then what I am writing is the loftiest eulogy upon the generation by its most inferior member, who could make only the movement of resignation.[93]

In this passage Johannes de silentio critically examines what he takes to be a tendency typical of his age and typical of Hegelianism, namely, to regard faith as a transitional stage to something higher. Thus, according to Hegel's hierarchy, one should not stop with faith but rather proceed to speculation or philosophical cognition. Here, somewhat paradoxically, an image is borrowed from the Hegelian Daub in order to support the criticism. Johannes de silentio here explores the reasons why people are not satisfied with faith and want to go beyond it. In this context, Daub's image is mentioned in a positive manner as a reflection of a profound view of life which is consistent with Christian faith.

This passage has a forerunner in the *Journal JJ* from 1843 (the same year as the publication of *Fear and Trembling*), where Kierkegaard makes use of this same image from Daub, where he writes:

> One ought to be so developed esthetically that he is able to grasp ethical problems esthetically—otherwise it goes badly with the ethical. How many are able to do this? Daub says somewhere that when a soldier stands alone with a loaded rifle at his post near a powder magazine on a stormy night turbulent with thunder and lighting, he thinks thoughts others do not think. Quite possibly—if he is developed enough esthetically; quite possibly, if he is esthetically developed enough not to forget. How many people could be told about the ascetic who lived in solitude and drank only dew and rain and who, the moment he forsook solitude, got a taste of wine and took to drink—how many could hear this but find nothing more in it than curiosity? How many are there who feel the anxiety and trembling, who comprehend the ethical problem?[94]

This entry is entirely consistent with the passage from *Fear and Trembling*. Here Kierkegaard makes it explicit that he is using this image from Daub as an example of someone who has grasped the gravity of life or truly comprehended the ethical

---

93 *SKS* 4, 145 / *FT*, 50f.

94 *SKS* 19, 172, JJ:102 / *JP* 1, 899.

problem of existence. If this sort of person wishes to go beyond faith, then it is, for Kierkegaard, far less problematic and disdainful than the person who has not grasped this problem and wishes to go beyond faith for some trivial reason, such as to appear in fashion.

Finally, a closely related thought appears again in the first part of *Upbuilding Discourses in Various Spirits* from 1847, where Kierkegaard writes in the occasional discourse, known as "Purity of Heart is to Will One Thing":

> Recollection will be unable to remind him of the time when he sneaked along a devious path in order to avoid a decision, of the time when he gave the matter another turn in order to please people, of the time when he deserted his post in order to let the storm pass over, of the time when he yielded in order to find some relief in his awkward situation; of the time when he sought support and alliance with others—perhaps, as it is called, to work all the more for the victory of the good, that is to make his situation a bit less difficult in comparison with standing alone somewhat apprehensively, as in a midnight hour "with musket loaded at his dangerous post."[95]

While Daub's name does not appear here, it is clear that this passage builds on the two previous ones just quoted. Here the person is praised who does not shirk the difficulties of existence. The stormy night is thus understood as a metaphor for dealing with the existential challenges of life. Standing at one's post is then the symbol of the reflective individual who confronts these challenges in an authentic manner. While these three passages are all slightly different, it is clear that they belong to the same family or constellation of thought in Kierkegaard's mind.

At first glance, these allusions seem rather enigmatic since they do not actually refer to any of Daub's texts. Rather this image comes from an anecdote told by Karl Rosenkranz in his aforementioned memoirs about Daub, which Kierkegaard had in his library. Kierkegaard could also have read this anecdote in the Danish translation of Rosenkranz's text in the Danish periodical, *Tidsskrift for udenlandsk theologisk Litteratur*, to which he had a subscription.[96] Rosenkranz recounts a conversation he had with Daub, when Rosenkranz was complaining about the prospect of his future military service in Prussia. Then, Daub said to Rosenkranz that he should not complain about it, since it might have some unexpected advantages: "like a sentry at his lonely post at night, perhaps at a gunpowder magazine, one has thoughts that otherwise are altogether impossible."[97] There is no larger religious context to this passage in its original form. It seems simply to have caught Kierkegaard's eye, and he then proceeded to embroider it and develop it as a metaphor for authentic existence.

---

95 *SKS* 8, 202 / *UD*, 98.

96 See "Erindringer om Karl Daub," *Tidsskrift for udenlandsk theologisk Litteratur*, op. cit., vol. 5, 1837, pp. 534–62; p. 551. Cf. *SKS* K8, 246.

97 See Rosenkranz, *Erinnerungen an Karl Daub*, op. cit. p. 24f.

E. Daub and Understanding Life Backwards

At around the same time that Kierkegaard was reading Daub's article, he was writing his first book, *From the Papers of One Still Living*, which was ultimately published on 7 September 1838. In that work he refers directly to Daub as follows:

> There must come a moment, I say, when as Daub observes, life is understood backward through the idea....In analogy to this, individuals appear whose actual task lies behind them, but this does not help them to come into the right "backward" position for viewing life, since this task is placed rather like a hump on their own backs, and therefore they never actually come to see it or could never possibly become conscious of it in a spiritual sense....[98]

This is intended as part of Kierkegaard's criticism of Hans Christian Andersen for lacking a "life-view." The editors of *Søren Kierkegaards Skrifter* argue that this is not a reference to Daub at all but instead to Franz von Baader's *Vorlesungen über speculative Dogmatik.*[99] Indeed, in some sense the notion of understanding life or history "backward through the idea" is common to much of the thinking on the philosophy of history during the period of hegemony of German idealism. The idea is, however, found in Daub's aforementioned essay, "Die Form der christlichen Dogmen- und kirchen-Historie."[100] Daub's analysis there concerns the nature of historical actions. These actions are only correctly comprehended when they can be understood in terms of the goal which they serve. Thus, the task of the historian is then to determine or find the idea by means of which the past is understood. It is only grasped retrospectively by the historian, who has the opportunity to observe the various effects of the historical actions. Daub frequently refers to this grasping of the idea as an "act of divination" on the part of the historian.[101] Through this grasping of the idea, one makes the events of the past present.

In Kierkegaard's journals we also find allusions to the wider constellation of ideas of which this constitutes a part. For example, on 15 April 1838 he writes in the *Journal FF*, "Life can be interpreted only after it has been experienced, just as Christ did not begin to expound the Scriptures and show how they taught of him until his Resurrection."[102] Here Kierkegaard refers to the account in Luke 24 of how Jesus appears on the third day after the crucifixion and explains how what had taken place was in accordance with what the prophets had declared: "Then beginning with Moses and all the prophets, he interpreted to them the things about himself in all the scriptures."[103] The idea here obviously seems to be that the true meaning of these events is only clear after the fact. With this passage Kierkegaard seems to advocate a

---

98 *SKS* 1, 33 / *EPW*, 78.

99 Franz von Baader, *Vorlesungen über speculative Dogmatik*, no. 1, Stuttgart and Tübingen: Cotta 1828, p. 80 (*ASKB* 396). See *SKS* K1, 100.

100 Daub, "Die Form der christlichen Dogmen- und Kirchen-Historie," *Zeitschrift für spekulative Theologie*, op. cit., vol. 1, for example, p. 6.

101 Ibid., for example, p. 1; p. 5; p. 7.

102 *SKS* 18, 99, FF:122 / *JP* 1, 1025.

103 Luke 24:27. See *SKS* K18, 143.

retrospective understanding of history in line with Hegel's famous image of the Owl of Minerva.[104] However, it is clear that this is not his final word on the matter.

Five years later in a journal entry, Kierkegaard takes up this thought in the *Journal JJ*, where he writes,

> Philosophy is perfectly right in saying that life must be understood backwards. But then one forgets the other claim—that it must be lived forwards. The more one thinks through this claim, the more one concludes that life in temporality never becomes properly understandable, simply because never at any time does one get perfect repose to take a stance: backwards.[105]

With this famous passage Kierkegaard contrasts the purely philosophical approach to life, which puts a high premium on understanding, and the existential approach. The point is clearly that the "backwards" understanding, whatever its merits may be in philosophy, is not adequate for the existential demands of existence.

Daub is also mentioned by name in *Philosophical Fragments*, which is an understandable connection given the importance of the philosophy of history for both Daub and Johannes Climacus. The reference concerns precisely the question of understanding history retrospectively. It is an issue that will prove to be significant for Kierkegaard in different respects. In the difficult "Interlude" in the *Fragments*, Climacus writes,

> One who apprehends the past, a *historico-philosophus*, is therefore a prophet in reverse (Daub). That he is a prophet simply indicates that the basis of the certainty of the past is the uncertainty regarding it in the same sense as there is uncertainty regarding the future, the possibility (Leibniz—possible worlds), out of which it could not possibly *come forth* with necessity, *nam necessarium se ipso prius sit, necesse est* [for it is necessary that necessity precede itself].[106]

Here Climacus refers to the beginning of "Die Form der christlichen Dogmen- und Kirchen-Historie," where Daub describes in a Hegelian fashion the task of the historian as "recognizing in a divinatory manner the intransitory in the transitory, freedom in necessity, the eternal in the temporal."[107] Here one can see many echoes

---

104 *PR*, Preface, p. 23; *Jub.*, vol. 7, pp. 36f.: "As the *thought* of the world, it [sc. philosophy] appears only at a time when actuality has gone through its formative process and attained its completed state. This lesson of the concept is necessarily also apparent from history, namely that it is only when actuality has reached maturity that the ideal appears opposite the real and reconstructs this real world, which it has grasped in its substance, in the shape of an intellectual realm. When philosophy paints its gray in gray, a shape of life has grown old, and it cannot be rejuvenated, but only recognized, by the gray in gray of philosophy; the Owl of Minerva begins its flight only with the onset of dusk." *PR* = *Elements of the Philosophy of Right*, trans. by H.B. Nisbet, ed. by Allen Wood, Cambridge and New York: Cambridge University Press 1991. *Jub.* = Hegel's *Sämtliche Werke. Jubiläumsausgabe*, vols. 1–20, ed. by Hermann Glockner, Stuttgart: Friedrich Frommann Verlag 1928–41.

105 *SKS* 18, 194, JJ:167 / *JP* 1, 1030.

106 *SKS* 4, 279 / *PF*, 80.

107 Daub, "Die Form der christlichen Dogmen- und Kirchen-Historie," in *Zeitschrift für spekulative Theologie*, op. cit., vol. 1, p. 1.

of Kierkegaard's favorite paradoxical formulations to describe both human beings and the divine. Daub continues, "The act of looking backward [*Nachschauen*] is, like that of looking forward [*Vorausschauen*] an act of *divination*—thus it is equally, if not more, correct to say of the historian that he is a prophet of the *past*—the historical."[108] Kierkegaard here seems to be attracted to Daub's paradoxical idea that the historian, in the understanding and interpretation of the past, can be regarded as a prophet. This positive use of Daub can be taken as paradoxical at another level when one considers the general context of this passage in the *Fragments*. One of the main points of the "Interlude" is to refute the Hegelian idea of necessity in history. Here, however, reference is made to the Hegelian Daub to support the idea that the past is not necessary but contingent, and thus the historian can be regarded as a prophet of it.

III. Kierkegaard's Paradoxical Reception of Daub

In his foreword to Hermann Friedrich Wilhelm Hinrichs' (1794–1861) *Die Religion im inneren Verhältnisse zur Wissenschaft*,[109] from 1822, Hegel attempts to comfort the author regarding what he fears will be a hostile reception to the work given previous attempts to establish a speculative philosophy of religion. After criticizing what he takes to be the sorry state of philosophy, Hegel laments the fact that "the writings of Christian theologians like Daub and Marheineke, which still preserve Christian doctrine and the right and glory of thought,...suffer the meanest disparagement at the hands of shallow and ill-disposed critics."[110] Hegel refers to the incipient debates about the philosophy of religion, which would, after his death, lead to the split of the Hegelian schools into the right and left factions. The philosophy of religion was the primary battleground where the rights to the Hegelian heritage were contested.

While it cannot with justice be designated as either right or left Hegelian, Kierkegaard's thought belongs part and parcel to this intellectual world. He followed these debates closely and was well versed in the writings of most of its main representatives of both schools. While he was critical of left Hegelianism for rejecting Christianity, he saved his most violent criticism for the right Hegelians. In the Danish context he was locked in a virtually lifelong debate with Hans Lassen Martensen's version of speculative theology, which has often been identified as a straightforward right-Hegelian position. While there are clear signs that Martensen ultimately rejected some of the fundamental tenets of Hegel's speculative approach to religion, there can be no doubt that he was highly sympathetic to the overall project of a speculative interpretation of Christian dogma.

---

108 Ibid.

109 Hermann Friedrich Wilhelm Hinrichs, *Die Religion im inneren Verhältnisse zur Wissenschaft*, Heidelberg: Karl Groos 1822.

110 Hegel, "Vorwort" in Hinrichs, *Die Religion*, ibid., p. xxvii. Reprinted in *Jub.*, vol. 20, p. 27. (In English as "Foreword to Hinrichs' *Religion in Its Inner Relation to Science*" in *Miscellaneous Writings of G.W.F. Hegel*, ed. by Jon Stewart, Evanston: Northwestern University Press 2002, p. 352.)

What is striking in this general context is the fact that Kierkegaard nourished an unbending hatred for Martensen and constantly criticized what he regarded as Martensen's distortion and perversion of Christianity, while at the same time he showed a great openness and receptivity to Martensen's intellectual forerunners, the right Hegelians, Marheineke and Daub.[111] This is especially odd given that Kierkegaard was a first-hand witness to the way in which Martensen, in his lectures, actively tried to promote Daub's theology. This discrepancy is not easy to explain.

The image of the sentry at his post on a stormy night is poignant. While Martensen is consistently represented as a hypocrite and an inauthentic person who has compromised Christianity beyond repair by making it consistent with "objective thinking," Daub, by contrast, is hailed as an authentic person who stands like the sentry on a lonely night and confronts the deep problems of existence. While Martensen abandons his station as an individual confronted by these existential issues, Daub stands firm.

---

111 For an outstanding study of Kierkegaard's positive use of Marheineke, see Heiko Schulz's article in the present volume, "Marheineke: The Volatilization of Christian Doctrine," and his previous article, "Die spekulative Verflüchtigung des Christentums. Philipp Marheinekes System der christlichen Dogmatik und seine Rezeption bei Søren Kierkegaard," *Kierkegaard Studies. Yearbook*, 2003, pp. 20–47.

Bibliography

I. Daub's Works in The Auction Catalogue *of Kierkegaard's Library*

"Die Form der christlichen Dogmen- und Kirchen-Historie," in *Zeitschrift für spekulative Theologie*, vols. 1–3, ed. by Bruno Bauer, Berlin: Ferdinand Dümmler 1836–38, vol. 1, no. 1, 1836, pp. 1–60; vol. 1, no. 2, pp. 63–132; vol. 2, no. 1, 1837, pp. 88–161 (*ASKB* 354–357).

D. Carl Daub's Philosophische und theologische Vorlesungen, vols. 1–7, ed. by Philipp Marheineke and Theophor Wilhelm Dittenberger, Berlin: Duncker und Humblot 1838–44 (vol. 1, *Vorlesungen über die philosophische Anthropologie*; vol. 2, *Prolegomena zur Dogmatik und Kritik der Beweise für das Dasein Gottes*; vol. 3, *Prolegomena zur theologischen Moral und Prinzipien der Ethik*; vols. 4–5, *D. Carl Daub's System der theologischen Moral* [Parts 1–2]; vols. 6–7, *System der christlichen Dogmatik* [Parts 1–2]) (*ASKB* 472–472g).

II. Works in The Auction Catalogue *of Kierkegaard's Library that Discuss Daub*

Baader, Franz von, *Fermenta Cognitionis*, vols. 1–5, Berlin: Reimer 1822–24, vol. 3, 1823, p. 24; vol. 4, 1823, p. 24 (*ASKB* 394).

—— *Vorlesungen über speculative Dogmatik*, vol. 1, Stuttgart and Tübingen: Cotta'sche Buchhandlung 1828 (*ASKB* 396) [vols. 2–5, Münster: Theissing 1830–38], vol. 4, 1836, p. 6; p. 2; p. 105.

—— *Philosophische Schriften und Aufsätze*, vols. 1–2, Münster: Theissing 1831–32, vol. 1, p. 255; vol. 2, p. 23n; p. 64n; p. 215 (*ASKB* 400–401).

Baur, Ferdinand Christian, "Das rein spekulative oder metaphysische Moment in seiner Entwicklung in den Daub'schen Theologumena," in his *Die christliche Lehre von der Versöhnung in ihrer geschichtlichen Entwicklung von der ältesten Zeit bis auf die neueste*, Tübingen: Osiander 1838, pp. 696–703 (*ASKB* 423).

—— "Das Verhältnis des metaphysischen und historischen Moments bei Fichte und Daub," in his *Die christliche Lehre von der Versöhnung in ihrer geschichtlichen Entwicklung von der ältesten Zeit bis auf die neueste*, Tübingen: Osiander 1838, pp. 703–9 (*ASKB* 423).

Brøchner, Hans, *Nogle Bemærkninger om Daaben, foranledigede ved Professor Martensens Skrift: Den christelige Daab*, Copenhagen: P.G. Philipsens Forlag 1843, p. 25 (*ASKB* U 27).

Erdmann, Johann Eduard, *Vorlesungen über Glauben und Wissen als Einleitung in die Dogmatik und Religionsphilosophie*, Berlin: Duncker und Humblot 1837, p. 39; p. 271 (*ASKB* 479).

—— *Grundriss der Psychologie. Für Vorlesungen*, Leipzig: Fr. Chr. Vogel 1840, p. 55; p. 63; p. 65; p. 81; p. 88 (*ASKB* 481).

Hase, Karl, *Hutterus redivivus oder Dogmatik der evangelisch-lutherischen Kirche. Ein dogmatisches Repertorium für Studirende*, 4th revised ed., Leipzig: Breitkopf und Härtel 1839, p. 3; p. 55 (*ASKB* 581).

[Hegel, Georg Wilhelm Friedrich], *Georg Wilhelm Friedrich Hegel's vermischte Schriften*, vols. 1–2, ed. by Friedrich Förster and Ludwig Boumann, Berlin: Duncker und Humblot 1834–35 (vols. 16–7 in Georg Wilhelm Friedrich *Hegel's Werke. Vollständige Ausgabe*, ed. by Philipp Marheineke et al., Berlin: Duncker und Humblot 1832–45), vol. 2, p. 303; p. 483; p. 501 (*ASKB* 555–556).

Hotho, Heinrich Gustav, *Vorstudien für Leben und Kunst*, Stuttgart and Tübingen: Cotta'sche Buchhandlung 1835, p. 167 (*ASKB* 580).

Lechler, C., "Ueber die Aufgabe der Anthropologie mit besonderer Rücksicht auf den gegenwärtigen Stand der gesammten Philosophie," *Zeitschrift für Philosophie und spekulative Theologie*, vols. 1–16, ed. by Immanuel Hermann Fichte and Christian Hermann Weiße, Bonn et al.: Eduard Weber et al. 1837–46, vol. 15, 1846, pp. 282–93 and vol. 16, 1846, pp. 39–68 (*ASKB* 877–911).

M., "Nekrolog von Daub," *Zeitschrift für spekulative Theologie*, op. cit., vol. 2, no. 2, 1837, p. 488.

Martensen, Hans Lassen, *Den christelige Dogmatik*, Copenhagen: C.A. Reitzel 1849, pp. 12f.; p. 339n (*ASKB* 653).

Menzel, Wolfgang, *Die deutsche Literatur*, vols. 1–4, 2nd revised ed., Stuttgart: Hallberg'sche Verlagshandlung 1836, vol. 1, pp. 213ff. (*ASKB* U 79).

Müller, Julius, *Die christliche Lehre von der Sünde*, vols. 1–2, 3rd revised and enlarged ed., Breslau: Josef Max und Komp. 1849, vol. 1, pp. 559–65; vol. 2, pp. 236–7 (*ASKB* 689–690).

Mynster, Jakob Peter, *Blandede Skrivter*, vols. 1–3, Copenhagen: Den Gyldendalske Boghandlings Forlag 1852–53 [vols. 4–6, Copenhagen: Den Gyldendalske Boghandlings Forlag 1855–57], vol. 1, p. 65; p. 209n (*ASKB* 358–363).

Rauch, Friedrich August, *Vorlesungen über Goethe's Faust*, Büdingen: Heller 1830, p. 47n; p. 105n; p. 110n; p. 120n (*ASKB* 1800).

Romang, Johann Peter, *Ueber Willensfreiheit und Determinismus, mit sorgfältiger Rücksicht auf die sittlichen Dinge, die rechtliche Imputation und Strafe, und auf das Religiöse. Eine philosophische Abhandlung*, Bern: C.A. Jenni, Sohn 1835, p. 196n (*ASKB* 740).

Rosenkranz, Karl, *Encyclopädie der theologischen Wissenschaften*, Halle: C.A. Schwetschke und Sohn 1831, p. 324 (*ASKB* 35).

—— *Erinnerungen an Karl Daub*, Berlin: Duncker und Humblot 1837 (*ASKB* 743).

—— *Psychologie oder die Wissenschaft vom subjectiven Geist*, Königsberg: Bornträger 1837, p. 321 (*ASKB* 744).

—— "Daub's Anthropologie 1836," in his *Kritische Erläuterungen des Hegelschen Systems*, Königsberg: Bornträger 1840, pp. 138–49 (*ASKB* 745).

—— "Erindringer om Karl Daub," *Tidsskrift for udenlandsk theologisk Litteratur*, vols. 1–20, ed. by Henrik Nikolai Clausen and Matthias Hagen Hohlenberg, Copenhagen: C.A. Reitzel 1833–52, vol. 5, 1837, pp. 534–76 (*ASKB* U 29).

Rudelbach, Andreas, *De ethices principiis hucusque vulgo traditis, disquisito historico-philosophica, quæ systematum ethicorum secundum primas causas amplioris criseos introductionem continet*, Copenhagen: Hartv. Frid. Popp 1822, p. 97n (*ASKB* 750).

Wette, Wilhelm Martin Leberecht de, *Christliche Sittenlehre*, vols. 1–3, Berlin: G. Reimer 1819–23, vol. 1, p. 129n; p. 183n; p. 246n (*ASKB* U 110).

Zeuthen, Ludvig, *Om den christelige Tro i dens Betydning for Verdenshistorien. Et Forsøg*, Copenhagen: Gyldendalske Boghandlings Forlag 1838, p. 13n (*ASKB* 259).

III. Secondary Literature on Kierkegaard's Relation to Daub

Hirsch, Emanuel, "Die Einführung in die Frage Glaube und Geschichte durch Karl Daub," in his *Kierkegaard-Studien*, vols. 1–2, Gütersloh: Bertelsmann 1933, vol. 2, pp. 93–105 [pp. 539–51] (reprinted, Vaduz, Liechtenstein: Toposverlag 1978. First published in *Studien des apologetischen Seminars in Wernigerode*, nos. 29, 31, 32, 36, 1930–33. The reprint retains the pagination of the first publication, giving the page numbers of the 1933 edition in square brackets).

Leemans, Victor, *Sören Kierkegaard*, Antwerp and Amsterdam: Uitgeversmij. N.V. Standaard-Boekhandel 1956, see pp. 38–41.

Ruttenbeck, Walter, *Sören Kierkegaard. Der christliche Denker und sein Werk*, Aalen: Scientia Verlag 1979, see p. 76; p. 79; p. 173; p. 201.

Stewart, Jon, *Kierkegaard's Relations to Hegel Reconsidered*, New York and Cambridge: Cambridge University Press 2003, pp. 246–7.

Thulstrup, Niels, "Daub," in *Kierkegaard's Teachers*, ed. by Niels Thulstrup and Marie Mikulová Thulstrup, Copenhagen: C.A. Reitzel 1982 (*Bibliotheca Kierkegaardiana*, vol. 10), pp. 208–11.

—— *Kierkegaard's Relation to Hegel*, trans. by George L. Stengren, Princeton: Princeton University Press 1980; pp. 108–9; p. 155.

Erdmann:

Appropriation and Criticism, Error and Understanding

Stephan Bitter

Whoever deals with the Hegelian Johann Eduard Erdmann, also at some point stumbles upon Kierkegaard's encounter with him. But, by the same token, whoever deals with Kierkegaard, likewise soon comes across Erdmann. The contemporary relationship is still mirrored in this relationship today. While there seems to be no indication that Erdmann took notice of Kierkegaard, the younger thinker's interest in the philosopher and historian of religion, Erdmann, is well documented.

I. Erdmann's Biography

Johann Eduard Erdmann was born on 13 June 1805 in Wolmar, Livonia and died on 12 June 1892 in Halle.[1] He is known as a historian of philosophy, belonging to the so-called right wing of the Hegelian school.[2] His contributions to the philosophy of religion, specifically concerning the mediation of faith and knowledge, are generally forgotten today. In his lifetime, however, they enjoyed a considerable reception; and in fact, they represent, in addition to his work on the history of philosophy, the second lifelong topic for Erdmann, who was a follower of both Hegel and Schleiermacher.

---

1 Cf. Hermann Glockner, *Einführung in Johann Eduard Erdmanns Leben und Werke* (vol. 1 of Glockner's new edition of Erdmann's *Versuch einer wissenschaftlichen Darstellung der Geschichte der neuern Philosophie*), Stuttgart: Frommann 1932 (reprint Stuttgart-Bad Cannstatt: Frommann-Holzboog 1977); Hermann Glockner, "Ein deutsches Philosophenleben im 19. Jahrhundert. Johann Eduard Erdmann," in his *Kulturphilosophische Perspektiven*, Bonn: Bouvier 1968 (*Gesammelte Schriften*, vol. 4), pp. 391–565; Stephan Bitter, *Johann Eduard Erdmann. Kirchliche Predigt und philosophische Spekulation in der Entwicklung eines theologischen Hegelianers*, Rheinbach-Merzbach: CMZ Publisher 1994 (*Arbeiten zur Theologiegeschichte*, vol. 1).

2 His main works on the history of philosophy are *Versuch einer wissenschaftlichen Darstellung der Geschichte der neuern Philosophie*, vol. 1, Abtheilung 1, Riga: Frantzen 1834; vol. 1, Abtheilung 2 and vol. 2, Abtheilung 1, Leipzig, Riga, and Dorpat: Frantzen 1836–40; vol. 2, Abtheilung 2 vol. 3, Abtheilung 2, Leipzig: Vogel 1842–53; *Grundriss der Geschichte der Philosophie*, vols. 1–2, Berlin: Hertz 1866 (2nd ed., Berlin: Hertz 1869–70; 3th ed., Berlin: Hertz 1878; 4th ed., ed. posthumously by Benno Erdmann, Berlin: Hertz 1896).

The son of a Baltic pastor, Erdmann encountered the topic of faith and knowledge at an early stage. He delved into the works of Schleiermacher under the supervision of August Carlblom (1797–1877) in Dorpat.[3] His elder cousin, Julius Walter, first introduced him to the works of Carl Daub and then to those of Georg Wilhelm Friedrich Hegel.[4] After studying theology in Dorpat and Berlin, he became pastor in Wolmar in 1829. During his Berlin studies,[5] he came to regard Hegel as his mentor and never missed his lectures.[6] Then the young pastor wrote a philosophical dissertation for his doctoral degree at the University of Kiel. His treatise, which was based on his mentor's philosophy, was entitled *Quidnam sit discrimen philosophiam inter et theologiam* (1830).[7] The answer to the question posed by the title is that the means of cognition of both fields differ from each other solely with regard to form, but with regard to content, they converge due to the fact that they refer to a common truth.

Even as a preacher in Berlin and the Baltic provinces, the young philosopher tried to preserve the reconciliation of faith and knowledge by demonstrating to the educated elite the path from faith to speculation, by giving "an account of our faith."[8] It is unclear to what degree this was permissible in the eyes of the church. Even though he soon became an eminently respectable pastor of his established regional church, he still nourished the hope of one day becoming an academic instructor in philosophy.

He quit his position as pastor (although he had to face some criticism, he continued to work until old age as a preacher) and, in the spring of 1834, moved again to Berlin in order to write his *Habilitation* thesis in that city, which then as now was the scene of much academic nostalgia. He presented as his *Habilitation* the first volume of his *Versuch einer wissenschaftlichen Darstellung der Geschichte der neuern Philosophie*.

---

3 For Carlblom, cf. Johannes Frey, *Die Theologische Fakultät der Kaiserlichen Universität Dorpat-Jurjew*, Reval: Kluge 1905, pp. 195–7.

4 For Julius Walter, cf. Werner Gruehn, "Walter, Julius," in *Die Religion in Geschichte und Gegenwart. Handwörterbuch für Theologie und Religionswissenschaft*, vols. 1–6, 2nd ed., ed. by Hermann Gunkel and Leopold Zscharnack, Tübingen: Mohr 1927–32, vol. 5, cols. 1760f.

5 On this, cf. Julius Walter Jr. [anonymous], *Bischof Dr. Ferdinand Walter, weil. General-Superintendent von Livland. Seine Landtagspredigten und sein Lebenslauf*, Leipzig: Duncker und Humblot 1891, pp. 59–72.

6 Erdmann's postscripts are important for Hegel research (cf. on this Johann Eduard Erdmann, *Vorlesungen über akademisches Leben und Studium*, Leipzig: Geibel 1858, pp. 264f.). Cf. *G.W.Fr. Hegel. Vorlesungen über die Philosophie des Geistes Berlin 1827/1828. Nachgeschrieben von Johann Eduard Erdmann und Ferdinand Walter*, ed. by Franz Hespe and Burkhard Tuschling, Hamburg: Meiner 1994.

7 Only the handwritten draft of his work remains preserved, cf. the sketch in Stephan Bitter, *Johann Eduard Erdmann*, op. cit., pp. 143–5.

8 Cf. Erdmann, *Rechenschaft von unserm Glauben. Reihe von Predigten, theils in Wolmar in Livland, theils in Berlin gehalten*, Riga and Dorpat: Frantzen 1835.

Erdmann's *Vorlesungen über Glauben und Wissen als Einleitung in die Dogmatik und Religionsphilosophie*,[9] which Kierkegaard thoroughly studied, dates from his first Berlin lecture in the Winter Semester 1834–35. When he was appointed in the Winter Semester 1836–37 in Halle, he held this lecture once again and supplemented it with relevant articles on the philosophy of religion. Three of these will be outlined here since Kierkegaard refers to them.

In Halle, Erdmann enjoyed for decades a highly respected career both as an academic and in university politics. Later, famous theologians, such as Albrecht Ritschl (1822–89), ranked among his students. Influential colleagues such as Martin Kähler (1835–1912) also attended his lectures. Erdmann attracted only Kuno Fischer (1824–1907), the later Heidelberg philosopher and historian of philosophy, as an immediate follower.

Not only within the Hegelian school did Erdmann find thorough readers, such as Bruno Bauer (1809–82),[10] Ludwig Feuerbach (1804–72), and Carl Ludwig Michelet (1801–93), but beyond it as well in Germany's vast academic and ecclesiastical circles.[11]

II. Kierkegaard and Erdmann

In Copenhagen, Søren Kierkegaard regularly took notice of Erdmann's publications during the decades of his own literary activity, as the auction catalogue of his library shows.[12] The series of Erdmann's writings which Kierkegaard owned ranges from *Vorlesungen über Glauben und Wissen* from the year 1837 to Erdmann's *Psychologische Briefe*, the first edition of which was published in 1852.

Among the writings which Kierkegaard himself published, only his dissertation, *The Concept of Irony* (1841), contains references to Erdmann. But entries in his journals and notebooks[13] show that many of Kierkegaard's fundamental insights, which had far-reaching implications for his later work, were inspired by an examination, during his student years, of Erdmann, especially his *Vorlesungen über Glauben und Wissen als Einleitung in die Dogmatik und Religionsphilosophie* (1837). Niels Thulstrup claims that Erdmann's book was "one of the quite few more recent books in the field of philosophy of religion, which he read completely through."[14] There was apparently a certain *kairos* for Kierkegaard—who then was 24 years old—studying the young professor's publications, which at that time were hot

9 Erdmann, *Vorlesungen über Glauben und Wissen als Einleitung in die Dogmatik und Religionsphilosophie*, Berlin: Duncker und Humblot 1837.

10 Cf. bibliography, second section.

11 Cf. Bitter, *Johann Eduard Erdmann*, op. cit., pp. 297–300.

12 Cf. bibliography, first section.

13 As to the nomenclature, cf. Hermann Deuser's proposal in his essay "'Philosophie und Christentum lassen sich doch niemals vereinen.' Kierkegaards theologische Ambivalenzen im Journal AA/BB (1835–1837)," in *Kierkegaard Studies. Yearbook*, 2003, pp. 1–19, see especially p. 1.

14 Cf. Niels Thulstrup, "Kierkegaards Kenntnis der philosophischen und theologischen Tradition," *Theologische Zeitschrift*, no. 35, 1979, pp. 351–62; p. 359.

off the press. We do not have any evidence that Kierkegaard read Erdmann's later writings on philosophy of religion.

Emanuel Hirsch was the first to suggest the importance of Kierkegaard's concern with Erdmann.[15] Hirsch points out that Kierkegaard read Erdmann before reading Hegel himself, and that Kierkegaard's judgments on Hegelian philosophy are substantially due to this early reading of Erdmann on his own terms.[16] The question of the consequences of Kierkegaard's concern with Erdmann for the important topic of "Kierkegaard and Hegel"[17] has until now eclipsed the question of the specifics of Kierkegaard's examination of Erdmann on his own terms.[18] In the following, it will be obvious that Kierkegaard's hermeneutical processes of the year 1837 deserve an inspection in more detail.

At first (in section III), I will give a survey of the sources, then (in section IV) I will outline the content of Erdmann's *Vorlesungen über Glauben und Wissen*; I will then add (in section V) an account of Kierkegaard's treatment of Erdmann's *Vorlesungen* in his papers and journals, and in doing so, also analyze a single mistaken, but significant, effort of Kierkegaard to understand Erdmann's line of thought. The conclusion (in section VI) will sum up the interpretations of Kierkegaard's examination of Erdmann.

III. The Sources

(1) Kierkegaard's notes on Erdmann's *Vorlesungen über Glauben und Wissen als Einleitung in die Dogmatik und Religionsphilosophie* (1837) date from fall and winter 1837 and can be found in his journals and notebooks. With the exception of the mere excerpts and summaries, these notes appear in volume II of the old *Papirer* edition, published by P. A. Heiberg and V. Kuhr.[19] Most of the texts are also available in

---

15 Emanuel Hirsch, *Kierkegaard-Studien*, vols. 1–2, Gütersloh: Bertelsmann 1933, vol. 2, pp. 84–93 [pp. 530–9] (reprinted, Vaduz, Liechtenstein: Toposverlag 1978. First published in *Studien des apologetischen Seminars in Wernigerode*, nos. 29, 31, 32, 36, 1930–33. The reprint retains the pagination of the first publication, giving the page numbers of the 1933 edition in square brackets. This convention will be followed here).

16 Cf. Thulstrup, *Kierkegaards Verhältnis zu Hegel und zum spekulativen Idealismus 1835–1846. Historisch-analytische Untersuchung*, Stuttgart et al.: Kohlhammer 1972, pp. 96–105; Bitter, *Johann Eduard Erdmann*, op. cit., pp. 174.

17 As to this, see Richard Kroner, "Kierkegaards Hegelverständnis," in *Kant-Studien*, vol. 46, 1954–55, pp. 19–27; Michael Theunissen, "Die Dialektik der Offenbarung. Zur Auseinandersetzung Schellings und Kierkegaards mit der Religionsphilosophie Hegels," in *Philosophisches Jahrbuch*, vol. 72, 1964–65, pp. 134–60; Heiko Schulz, "Kierkegaard über Hegel. Umrisse einer kritisch-polemischen Aneignung," *Kierkegaardiana*, vol. 21, 2000, pp. 152–87; and now Jon Stewart's grand monograph, *Kierkegaard's Relations to Hegel Reconsidered*, Cambridge and New York: Cambridge University Press 2003.

18 Thulstrup: "*Entscheidend ist, daß Erdmann sich als Rechtshegelianer versteht und daß er von seinem Leser, dem Studenten Kierkegaard, so verstanden worden ist.*" (Thulstrup, "Kierkegaards Kenntnis der philosophischen und theologischen Tradition," op. cit., p. 102).

19 When I dealt with Kierkegaard's reception of Erdmann for the first time in the Winter Semester of 1979–80, Prof. Dr. Henning Schröer (1931–2002), Hans Jørgen Lundager Jensen

Howard V. and Edna H. Hong's selection, entitled *Journals and Papers*, where they are arranged not chronologically, but systematically. Kierkegaard's complete notes on the *Vorlesungen über Glauben und Wissen*, including the excerpts, translations, and reflections, which have been omitted in the *Papirer* and *Journals and Papers*, are now available in the new Danish edition, *Søren Kierkegaards Skrifter*, that is, *SKS* 19, pp. 145–69 (*Notesbog 4*);[20] in addition, the editors' commentaries in *SKS* K 19, pp. 204–17 should be consulted.[21]

I will focus on Kierkegaard's adoption of Erdmann's *Vorlesungen* in the journals in the fall and winter of 1837. But I will also list Kierkegaard's other references to Erdmann just below, referring to them marginally.

(2) Kierkegaard's individual references to Erdmann's essays on the philosophy of religion can be found in the journal and notebooks. He refers specifically to Erdmann's "Pantheismus die Grundlage der Religion," in *Zeitschrift für spekulative Theologie*, vol. 1, no. 2, 1836, pp. 133–57,[22] and his "Ueber den Begriff des Sündenfalls und des Bösen. Ein Versuch," in *Zeitschrift für spekulative Theologie*, vol. 2, no. 2, 1837, pp. 192–214.[23]

(3) In his journals and notebooks, Kierkegaard also refers to Erdmann's writings on the history of philosophy. In this context he refers specifically to Erdmann's *Versuch einer wissenschaftlichen Darstellung der Geschichte der neuern Philosophie*, volume 1, Abtheilung 1: "Darstellung und Kritik der Philosophie des Cartesius, nebst einer Einleitung in die Geschichte der neuern Philosophie," Riga: Frantzen 1834; volume 1, Abtheilung 2: "Malebranche, Spinoza und die Skeptiker und Mystiker des siebzehnten Jahrhunderts. Darstellung und Kritik ihrer Systeme," Leipzig: Frantzen 1836; volume 2, Abtheilung 1: "Die Entwicklung des Empirismus und Materialismus in der Zeit zwischen Locke und Kant," Leipzig: Vogel 1840; volume 2, Abtheilung 2: "Leibnitz und die Entwicklung des Idealismus vor Kant," Leipzig: Vogel 1842,[24] and Erdmann's edition of God. *Guil. Leibnitii*

---

and Lars Larsen from Århus, then students at the university of Bonn, translated the *Pap.* and *SV* texts for me. I gratefully acknowledge this; the translations from that time still constitute my basis.

20 The texts, which are synoptically listed below in (partly conjecturable) chronological order, can be found in *SKS* and *JP*: *SKS* 19, 145–8, Not4:13–9 / *JP* 5, 5271. *SKS* 19, 148, Not4:20 / *JP* 5, 5272. *SKS* 17, 248, DD:81 / *JP* 5, 5274. *SKS* 19, 149–54, Not4:21–7 / *JP* 5, 5273. *SKS* 19, 151f., Not4:25.1 / *JP* 2, 1972. *SKS* 19, 154f., Not4:28f. / *JP* 5, 5278. *SKS* 19, 155–62, Not4:30–40 / *JP* 5, 5278. *SKS* 19, 163–5, Not4:41–41.d / *JP* 2, 2250. *SKS* 19, 164f., Not4:41.b / *JP* 5, 5278. *SKS* 19, 165f., Not4:42 / *JP* 2, 2251. *SKS* 19, 167, Not4:43 / *JP* 1, 772. *SKS* 19, 167, Not4:44 / *JP* 2, 2252. *SKS* 19, 168f., Not4:45 / *JP* 5, 5283.

21 I sincerely thank Prof. Dr. Jon Stewart for copies from *JP*, *SKS*, and *SKS* K; further, I thank him and Prof. Dr. Heiko Schulz for their bibliographical help.

22 *SKS* 17, 219, DD:9. Cf. Kierkegaard, *Die Tagebücher*, vols. 1–5, trans. and ed. by Hayo Gerdes, Düsseldorf and Köln: E. Diederichs 1962–74; vol. 1, 1962, p. 131 (as to this, cf. note 359) (1837).

23 *SKS* 17, 219, DD:8–8a / *JP* 4, 3998.

24 *SKS* 19, 385, Not13:5 / *JP* 5, 5579. This is merely a *pro forma* allusion.

Opera philosophica quae exstant latina gallica germanica omnia. Edita recognovit e temporum rationibus disposita pluribus ineditis auxit introductione critica atque indicibus instruxit, pars I et II, Berlin: Eichler 1840.[25]

(4) Individual references to Erdmann can also be found in the dissertation, *On the Concept of Irony* (1841). Here Kierkegaard refers to Erdmann's *Vorlesungen über Glauben und Wissen als Einleitung in die Dogmatik und Religionsphilosophie* (1837),[26] and his essay "Ueber Widersprüche unter den christlichen Glaubenslehren," in *Zeitschrift für spekulative Theologie*, vol. 3, no. 1, 1837, pp. 1–48.[27]

(5) Also in *Johannes Climacuss, or De Omnibus dubitandum est* (probably written in 1842–43),[28] Kierkegaard recalls Erdmann's essay, "Über Widersprüche unter den christlichen Glaubenslehren," in *Zeitschrift für spekulative Theologie*, vol. 3, no. 1, 1837, pp. 1–48.

IV. Erdmann's Vorlesungen über Glauben und Wissen

Erdmann's *Vorlesungen über Glauben und Wissen als Einleitung in die Dogmatik und Religionsphilosophie* (1837) appeared at the beginning of his academic career. In his Introduction, Erdmann himself describes the context, with regard to the philosophy of religion, to which they and his individual essays on philosophy of religion belong.[29] The book presents material from the lecture which Erdmann, then just promoted to professor—three years after Hegel's death and only months after Schleiermacher's death—gave in Winter Semester 1834–35 in Berlin. After giving these lectures once again in 1837 in Halle, he had them printed in a slightly revised version.[30]

After some "introductory considerations" (lectures 1 and 2, pp. 1–21), the *Vorlesungen* demonstrate, in Hegel's spirit, the reconciliation of faith and knowledge by discussing "faith" (lectures 3 to 15, pp. 22–138) and "knowledge" (lectures 16–28, pp. 139–276) in two analogous parts and describing a circular movement, by

---

25 *SKS* 18, 150, JJ:24 / *JP* 3, 2361. *SKS* 18, 153, JJ:37 / *JP* 3, 2362. *SKS* 19, 394, Not13:26.a / *JP* 5, 5597, undated. These, too, are merely *pro forma* allusions.

26 *SKS* 1, 324 / *CI*, 289.

27 *SKS* 1, 155–7 / *CI*, 102–3.

28 *Pap.* IV B 1 p. 137 / *JC*, 154. *Pap.* V B 39 / *JC*, 176. As to the dating, cf. Søren Kierkegaard, *Gesammelte Werke*, vols. 1–26, trans. and ed. by Emanuel Hirsch et al., Düsseldorf, Köln: E. Diederichs 1950–69, Abteilung 10, 1960, p. xi.

29 Erdmann, *Grundriss der Geschichte der Philosophie*, vols. 1–2, Berlin: Hertz 1866, vol. 2, Appendix: "Die deutsche Philosophie seit Hegel's Tode," pp. 618–798. Cf. the facsimile reprint of this appendix of the Berlin edition 1896 with Hermann Lübbe's introduction, Stuttgart-Bad Cannstatt: Frommann-Holzboog 1964.

30 Erdmann, *Vorlesungen über Glauben und Wissen*, op. cit., p. viii.

which consciousness develops from "naive faith" on a path through several stages of dialectical movement,[31] to "speculative knowledge."[32]

The individual chapters are arranged such that after the necessary deduction of a stage of consciousness has been given, the corresponding actual form of this stage of mind is sought "in reality" and described.

The path begins with "naive faith" (lectures 3 and 4, pp. 22–45), which, in its simple blessedness, knows that God and human beings are one. This unity is not indifference but identity, for faith knows that disunion preceded the unity. Its blessedness is immediate and at the same time mediated. It knows the unity between God and humans as a unity of reconciliation.

This knowledge will drift beyond the beginning. However, Erdmann believes that he is justified in assigning the character of "immediacy" to "naive faith" as a "beginning." At this stage, religion is still the unreflective, childlike consciousness of being reconciled with God. This parallel to the "nature of childhood" is limited insofar as the unreflective consciousness of the child, in its pagan serenity, does not have any recollection of a preceding reconciliation, and therefore does not know the inner restlessness, which drives the recollecting consciousness beyond this stage which lacks reflection.

Although religion appears at this stage in the subjective sense as "the subject's state of mind," it is nevertheless "the religious truth as doctrine of religion" in the objective sense. While religion in subjective shape often occurs only transiently and with unreflective people, its objective shape is always represented in the doctrine of the Church, which, as such, knows no reflection and thus no doubt.

The historical character of religious truth cannot be alienating nor can the contradictory content of the dogmas, for truth must appear to immediate religiosity in the shape of temporal facts which contradict and neutralize each other, and thus impart a truth, which, at this stage of consciousness, can appear in no other way than in a deficient dual shape which must rectify itself. We must note that here some additions have been made *vis-à-vis* the lectures given in 1834 in view of David Friedrich Strauss' work, *The Life of Jesus*, which was published in 1835–36.[33]

---

31 Cf. Johannes Climacus' "ladder of paradise." *Pap*. IV B 1 p. 105 / *JC*, 118.

32 As to the following, cf. my analysis, *Johann Eduard Erdmann*, op. cit., pp. 157–80.

33 Cf. Erdmann's reference to Strauss, pp. 36ff. Erdmann continues these considerations in his essay "Ueber Widersprüche unter den christlichen Glaubenslehren," *Zeitschrift für Spekulative Theologie*, vols. 1–3, ed. by Bruno Bauer, Berlin: Dümmler 1836–38, vol. 3, no. 1, 1837, pp. 1–48 (*ASKB* 354–357), which Kierkegaard quotes in his dissertation. The essay develops the following scheme of stages of consciousness: feeling [*Gefühl*], perception [*Anschauung*], representation [*Vorstellung*]. This scheme is developed in order to show that the contradictions within the Christian traditions are not opposed to their speculative tendency, that is the reconciliation of faith and knowledge. Driven beyond the primordial feeling, intelligence contradictorily finds *vis-à-vis* itself the subject-matter, which is in principle its own, as something external, it acts as an observer and is driven beyond this unsatisfactory stage through the (latter's) inner dialectics. It thus arrives at the stage of representation, in which the active moment of intelligence and its referentiality to something purported are linked together. One can only envisage what has already been purported in one's recollection; and yet, one should rightly ask: should one envisage anything! Representation does not yet

The at first "intransitive" faith of the subject, in spite of its naïveté, has moments of doubt, turns to a comparative consciousness and transforms itself, by means of reflection, into an active "faith in something believed." It thereby enters into the tension of the subject, which will determine the further course of the development of consciousness.

"Reflected faith" (lectures 5 to 8, pp. 45–73) notices that the "I" stands opposite blessedness, that is, identity is lost. Without recalling the caveat which asserted a difference between childlike consciousness and religious naïveté, Erdmann, however, retrospectively presupposes now the stage of consciousness of a child in order to distinguish it from the child's awakening as an abandoning of naïveté.

Consciousness, which stands opposite the unity between God and mankind, blessedness and truth, now passes, in the tension between object and subject, through different stages of preliminary situations. If it turns the positive into truth, this would be the stage of "dogmatism" (this stage in fact stands for the orthodoxy of the seventeenth and eighteenth centuries). Dogmatism does not believe in truth as history but *because* it is history. If here the positive stood negatively against being posited by the "I," then such a consciousness would result in dogmatic superstition.

This must result in a dialectical shift; the "I," the slave of the object, gets the upper hand either through the shift of superstition into magic or through the shift of dogmatism into doubt. Since the "I" posits the truth of the object, religious doubt, if it is also certain, arises. After regarding childhood in terms of naive faith, Erdmann states that adolescence is the stage of development of the "I" to which doubt in particular belongs.

"Doubt" (lectures 9 to 12, pp. 74–112) is a necessary point of transit. It must take place just as boyhood must take place. Erdmann dispenses with a further proof so that here the development of the religious consciousness coincides with that of consciousness generally.

Thus, with a dialectical turn, dogmatism leads to doubt and, moreover, to the fact that the "I" does not know any other law than that of being identical with itself. This is, as Erdmann defines it, the point of view of "religious irony." If the ironic consciousness needs the object in order to ironize about it, the consciousness, in a shift, enters into a new one-sidedness, namely, knowing only itself as true and repudiating every objective content. Erdmann calls this stage "disbelief." Only the unreal chimera appears as truth since it is characteristic of all free-thinking, examples of which can readily be found, for instance, in the French Revolution. Although disbelief appears to be entirely free, it is, however, dependent on the negation of the object, so that here too truth lies in the opposite of the "I," and disbelief proves to

---

mean conceiving; if I have the formula of a parabola, I have conceived it; as long as I envisage it, I just know it as a trajectory. Representation still has its subject-matter in the coexistence of contents which contradict each other, it is still bound to sensations. Truth still appears distorted because it is supposed to appear to all persons, even those who do not get beyond the stage of consciousness of idea. It appears in a series of facts which contradict each other, but which successively rectify and neutralize each other, for example, in myth. Faith still namely juxtaposes opposed terms, only conceptual thinking is assigned the task of sublating the contradictions.

be related to superstition. Since the shift between the "I" and the object continues infinitely, the opposite must be conceived as unity.

Thus, the contradiction appears to be inherent at this stage of consciousness, and Erdmann is not afraid of calling the "content of the infinite progress" the "religious drive" or "religious restlessness." The dialectics of the progress so far demonstrates that both sides (object and subject) have equal rights; the religious drive aims at equilibrium and unification, at an elimination of the opposition.

Within religion, consciousness hereby attains the point of view of "mysticism" (lectures 13–15, pp. 102–38). As union of object and subject, mysticism bears a resemblance to the stage of naive faith but differs from it in the violence of its unification of both sides. In church history, examples of the mystical point of view can be found starting from Dionysius the Areopagite to Ernst Wilhelm Hengstenberg (1802–69) or Hermann Olshausen (1796–1839).

An organic connection would emerge, if the object were to become a necessary being, and the "I" were to act speculatively; this, however, is not the case here. Consciousness does not forget the violence of the unification. Thus, the opposition of two groups arises: some entirely in truth, and the others entirely in untruth. We hereby reach the point of view which Erdmann calls the "mystic separatism" or "religious enthusiasm." Erdmann names as an exemplary exponent of this point of view Gottfried Daniel Krummacher (1774–1837) from his own day.

While Erdmann avoided the concept of "feeling" as a designation for the "naive faith" at the beginning of the evolution of consciousness and, instead, spoke of a "state of mind," he nonetheless uses it here at this much later stage of consciousness. Here, where what is at issue is religious enthusiasm, a violent unification of the object and the subject, and their becoming ensnared in the onesidedness of an extreme, Erdmann assigns "the immediacy of feeling" to the religious point of view. This immediacy is *toto coelo* different from the immediacy of faith, which Erdmann places at the beginning of the development. Later, Erdmann looked for an equivalent at the beginning of the formation of consciousness and assigned a pre-religious stage to it.[34]

---

[34] For instance, in his essay, "Pantheismus die Grundlage der Religion," *Zeitschrift für spekulative Theologie*, op. cit., vol. 1, no. 2, 1836, pp. 133–57. The essay, which Erdmann published in Bruno Bauer's periodical, who at that time was still close to him, was written between the Berlin lecture *Über Glauben und Wissen* and this lecture's final publication. It supplements what has been stated in the printed lectures about the proximity between Schleiermacher's theology of the "feeling of absolute dependence" and pantheism. Transcending his *Vorlesungen*, Erdmann strives to allot feeling a place of its own within the sequence of the stages of consciousness and locates it at a stage which precedes religion, namely, the passive feeling which pantheism erroneously conceives as religion. In it, substance and subject are still conjoined to one another; the subjects here are only "nonessential, vanishing modifications" of the substance. Religion, however, begins only where the subject stands opposite the substance. Another essay ("Ueber den Begriff des Sündenfalls und des Bösen. Ein Versuch," *Zeitschrift für spekulative Theologie*, op. cit., vol. 2, no. 2, 1837, pp. 192–214) explains that religion is the "consciousness of difference"; it presupposes a disruption as a point of transit which consciousness has had to pass through; in the story of the Fall of man

If that which accords with feeling is true, then everything is true, Erdmann further says. For everything can be felt. Feeling is a vessel for any possible content, and therefore nothing which accords with the feeling of everything is true.[35] Thus, the mystical separatism, in spite of its elevation to universality, does not get beyond the inner contradiction of mysticism. The universality attained here is the arbitrary sum, the "universality of reflection," but not yet necessary universality, the "universality of the concept." The restlessness of consciousness seeks not a violent, but an organic unification of subject and object. It seeks the real universality, which is identical with the substance of the individual. But the "I" that is at the same time subjective and objective, is reason or "the I that is sublated toward thinking."

The point of view now reached tries to recognize reason in everything, that is, to recognize itself. Erdmann traces this recognition in the second part of his lectures ("knowledge," lectures 16–28, pp. 139–276), following his "preliminary remarks" (lecture 16; pp. 139–51) through three stages of "empirical knowledge" (lectures 17–20, pp. 151–86), three stages of "critical knowledge" (lectures 21–4, pp. 187–228) and ultimately, three stages of "speculative knowledge" (lectures 25–8, pp. 234–76).

In his "preliminary remarks," Erdmann gives an account of the transition of the "I" of faith to the universal consciousness of knowledge: the question of the universal in self-awareness is synonymous with that of the particular, in which self-conscious human beings differ from all other creatures (p. 141). Among the stages of "critical knowledge," Erdmann even assigns a place to naturalism, about which it is said correctly that it "does not content itself with ignoring or doubting the reality of an actual, supernatural revelation, but even denies the possibility of it" (p. 193). In naturalism, reason displays its force *a priori* by "laying down laws as the conditions by which alone the content of religious doctrine can be true" (p. 197).

We will now pass over this step and cast another glance at Erdmann's definition of the last stages of consciousness, which belong to "speculative knowledge" and thereby go beyond the described *aporia*. To some degree, Erdmann explains, knowledge at all its stages has already moved beyond the mere opposition of the objective and the subjective. But up to now reason has not yet dealt with the unity of the objective and the subjective, as such. Through the stages of critical knowledge, reason is driven by the self-contradiction, through which it, on the one hand, turns knowledge into something subjective but, on the other hand, claims something objective, that is, the unrecognizability of truth, is driven beyond the critical point of view as well. Rationalism and supernaturalism appear as shapes of a "theology

---

(Genesis 3), a reminiscence of this point of transit has been preserved; the Fall of man is to be conceived as a progress inasmuch as it is the condition of the religious consciousness.

35 In his essay, "Ueber Widersprüche unter den christlichen Glaubenslehren," *Zeitschrift für spekulative Theologie*, op. cit., vol. 3, no. 1, 1837, pp. 1–48, he says, critical of Schleiermacher, that it is after all a joke if he puts in his doctrine of faith that feeling be mistaken, for it lacks the possibility of this in the same manner as the mute lacks the possibility of a speech defect (p. 11). (Cf. Friedrich Schleiermacher, *Der christliche Glaube nach den Grundsätzen der evangelischen Kirche im Zusammenhang dargestellt*, 3rd printing, Berlin: G. Reimer 1835, § 7.)

of non-knowledge" (p. 211),[36] at which consciousness cannot stop. This happens in such a way that reason becomes "practical" and, as such, proceeds independently of the object. In the field of religion, religious truth now does not appear as a matter of knowledge but of "willing."

Even this point of view of reason—that is, the "practical idealism" defended by Johann Gottlieb Fichte—suffers from an inner contradiction: reason is split into a theoretical and a practical dimension. Subject and object are joined with one another, but this identity does not exist, but is yet to be realized. This contradiction creates the "infinite progress of being realized." It aims at a true identity of object and subject, one not merely to be realized, but one that really exists. If this identity is attained, it is no longer a matter of willing but of immediate perception. Now the object is viewed as the existing substance of the perceiving subject, which itself, however, appears as a moment or as an accident in that substance.

On the one hand, this is the point of view of the "perception of the absolute," while on the other hand, it is, in its more subjective form, the "theology of the feeling of absolute dependency." The first point of view was held by the later J.G. Fichte, and the second by Schleiermacher.[37] It is not unjustified to reproach Schleiermacher for pantheism, for, following Spinoza, he understands God as the sole substance. While the identity of the objective and the subjective get their rights here, their difference does not. Here the non-being and the being of truth still stand opposite one another, while reason corresponds to the postulation lying in it and recognizes truth in its becoming. The truth of becoming is recognized if its law, its concept, is recognized. Reason, recognizing the concept, produces and perceives. Its activity is now conceptual or speculative recognition. At this last shape of knowledge, its previous stages are sublated. Erdmann names Schelling and Hegel as the fathers of speculative philosophy of religion, and as exponents of speculative dogmatics, he names Carl Daub, Philipp Marheineke and Karl Rosenkranz.

With "speculative knowledge," Erdmann claims, the end of the development, which began with "naive faith," is reached. The result returns to the beginning. While faith knew the identity of God and Man as mediated identity, which occurred after sin, speculative theology asserts the identity of the subject with God and differs from pantheism due to the fact that it acknowledges its simultaneous difference. The correspondence between the beginning and the end of the development demonstrates that through the attainment of this stage of consciousness, the wheel of development has actually turned full circle.

V. Erdmann's Vorlesungen über Glauben und Wissen *in Kierkegaard's Journals and Notebooks*

Kierkegaard studied Erdmann's book intensely. He read and wrote at the same time. He made excerpts of it while he was reading; he summarized the text, continued the

---

36 Erdmann defines supernaturalism as "dogmatism...forced into the point of view of non-knowledge" (p. 216), and rationalism as "nihilism...forced into the point of view of non-knowledge" (p. 219).

37 Erdmann explicates this in more detail in his essay on pantheism, see above.

line of thought and criticized the work. We will here examine in detail the notes in his journals and notebooks.

(A) At first, we will examine Kierkegaard's excerpts and adaptions or critical references to particular topics. Kierkegaard excerpts particularly extensive passages without commenting on them, for example, from the eighth lecture (pp. 70f., 73).[38] He points with approbation to definitions of individual concepts which he finds particularly successful, for example, Erdmann's concept of "religious irony" (tenth lecture),[39] or his definition of the concept of "mysticism" in Erdmann's 13th lecture (p. 104).[40] He welcomes and quotes one of Erdmann's analyses of the history of ideas, namely, his account of Schleiermacher's theology in his 27th lecture, pp. 251, 253, 266.[41] He criticizes Erdmann's analyses of the history of philosophy, for example, his distinction between Kant's "practical idealism" and that of Fichte in his 25 lecture (pp. 238–241).[42] He points out some minor discrepancies, for example, in the 16th lecture (pp. 149ff.), noting that it is odd that Erdmann adopts the word "faith" here "in an almost vulgar sense," whereas he previously intended to adopt it (cf. third lecture, p. 30) "only in a certain historical sense."[43]

(B) Other entries differ from these excerpts and notes. In these Kierkegaard critically analyzes the "transition" that Erdmann's book attempts to establish between the conceptional deduction and the "proofs in reality" as well as that between "faith" and "knowledge."

In a Socratic manner he takes up Erdmann's considerations and gives them such a pointed formulation that they appear to be questionable. The first entry commenting

38 *SKS* 19, 148, Not4:20–20.1.

39 *SKS* 17, 248, DD:81. Cf. Markus Kleinert, "Leere und Fülle. Möglichkeiten der Läuterung bei Hegel und Kierkegaard," *Kierkegaard Studies. Yearbook*, 2003, pp. 168–88, see p. 181.

40 *SKS* 19, 151f., Not4:25.1 / *JP* 2, 1972. In his work *The Concept of Irony*, Kierkegaard, in defining "abeyance" and the "duality," of the mythical, recalls Erdmann's essay "Ueber Widersprüche unter den christlichen Glaubenslehren," *Zeitschrift für spekulative Theologie*, op. cit., vol. 3, no. 1, 1837, pp. 1–48, and his deduction of myth from a series of contradictory facts without, however, retracing Erdmann's dialectical stages of consciousness. He uses Erdmann in a critical and eclectic manner. Wherever Erdmann assumes dialectical restlessness, Kierkegaard allows fantasy to look and rest, "weary of the dialectical work" (*SKS* 1, 154 / *CI*, 101).

41 *SKS* 19, Not4:45. Cf. Kierkegaard as to Erdmann's essay on pantheism: "That pantheism constitutes a surmounted factor in religion, is the foundation for it, seems now to be acknowledged, and hereby also the error in Schleiermacher's definition of religion as remaining in pantheism" (*SKS* 17, 219, DD:9 / *JP* 4, 3849). However, it appears to him that Erdmann's speculative interpretation of Genesis 3 in his essay "Ueber den Begriff des Sündenfalls und des Bösen. Ein Versuch," *Zeitschrift für spekulative Theologie*, op. cit., vol. 2, no. 2, 1837, pp. 192–214, is not defensible. Kierkegaard asks about the real meaning of Genesis 3:22 ("Behold, the man [Adam] has become like one of us etc.") and notes in the margin: "See I John 3:2, where likeness is the result." (*SKS* 17, 219, DD:8–8.a / *JP* 4, 3998).

42 *SKS* 19, 168f., Not4:45.

43 *SKS* 19, 154f., Not4:28f.

on the excerpts is of this kind. Erdmann claimed in his eighth lecture (pp. 71f.) that it was difficult to explain the dialectical shift between thesis and antithesis to a philosophically untrained person, but that there were everyday experiences which facilitate understanding this. Kierkegaard absorbs the account of Erdmann's critical hermeneutical consideration into his own concept of "the incommensurability of life." He adds to this his main objection against Erdmann, who endeavors to demonstrate the respective correspondences in the phenomena of religious and theological reality for the different stages of consciousness: "As the reason that it is so difficult to get people to perceive this dialectical movement and that they imagine it to be much easier by means of the phenomenal analogies Erdmann names that such a transition seems to involve the incommensurability of life."[44] Kierkegaard already includes his criticism of Erdmann in the account and concludes that the "incommensurability of life" is "inaccessible to the abstract dialectic developing through the thought-knots of necessity."[45] Erdmann himself appears as the one who should have noticed the impossibility of his undertaking. Kierkegaard can symbiotically put his own argument into the mouth of the person whom he criticizes.[46]

Kierkegaard criticizes the inconsistency of Erdmann's philosophical deduction. He criticizes the transition of the subject in the first part of the lectures to the subject-object-schema in its second part (16th lecture). "The first part of the book ["faith"] seems," he writes, "to stand up far better than the second"[47] ("knowledge") and indicates once more how profitable his reading of Erdmann is. But now the person disappears and in his place appears a mere subject-object schema;[48] the preceding analysis does not justify this. Kierkegaard concludes his entry by saying that it may well be true that reason is universal self-consciousness, but the fact that man has reason does not constitute man's *differentia specifica vis-à-vis* the rest of creation, as Erdmann claims.[49]

Kierkegaard criticizes Erdmann (19th lecture) for disregarding the "historical side of Christianity."[50] If he seeks in experience affirmations of the conceptually deduced hypotheses, then this implies the abandonment of what is particular about Christian consciousness. For this has already primarily been based on experience and tradition so that these concepts cannot be deduced by later subordination to a general categorization.[51]

---

44 *SKS* 19, 148, Not4:20 / *JP* 5, 5272.

45 Ibid.

46 *SKS* 19, 148, Not4:20 / *JP* 5, 5272.

47 *SKS* 19, 163, Not4:41 / *JP* 2, 2250.

48 *SKS* 4, 318 / *CA*, 10f.

49 Erdmann, *Vorlesungen über Glauben und Wissen*, op. cit., p. 141.

50 *SKS* 19, 163, Not4:41 / *JP* 2, 2250.

51 *SKS* 19, 163–5, Not4:41–41.d. In the face of the problem posed by Erdmann, Kierkegaard finds himself stimulated to consider if there could be another manner in which reason and history correspond. Hypothesis and "accident," he notes in an additional remark (*SKS* 19, 164–5, Not4:41.b), ought to be "related" to each other, related like Adam and Eve: "Adam finds his Eve." Cf. Kierkegaard later in *On the Concept of Irony*: Thinking behaves "erotically," "not heroically" *vis-à-vis* the historical phenomenon (*SKS* 1, 71 / *CI*, 9).

While Kierkegaard makes his fundamental criticism about disregarding Christianity's specific focus on history against Erdmann only as a bare assertion, he in turn intends to show elsewhere that Erdmann (also with reference to the 19th lecture), under the constraints of his basic intent to account for correspondences between speculation and historical reality, becomes entangled in a vicious circle. He projects what he is looking for onto reality and produces mere caricatures. Kierkegaard concludes, "In general the plunging chasm between abstract deduction and the historical actuality is this: even though it can be shown that the necessity of thought lays down a certain element of thought, it still does not at all show its historical actuality."[52] The crucial point of his criticism, however, is an *externum* in principle. Reminiscent of Anselm, Kierkegaard, contrary to all speculative mediation between reason and history, adds trenchantly: "*Cur deus homo*?"[53] For him, the basic condition of Christian history is beyond speculative construction.

(C) Finally, a significant misunderstanding reflected in Kierkegaard's entries at the end of November and the beginning of December 1837 will be analyzed.[54]

After his critical considerations concerning the "transition" between the two parts of the book ("faith" and "knowledge") and, so to speak, between the two sides of the book (speculation and historical reality), which have just been discussed, Kierkegaard comes to the 21st lecture, which opens the second section ("critical knowledge") and deals with the critically acting reason and its shape in naturalism. "But here is a new difficulty,"[55] Kierkegaard notes at the beginning of the entry. At first he points out Erdmann's merit of saying of reason that it is "*making* an experiment"; but employing "this kind of thinking particularly in the realm of Christianity" leads him "onto most dangerous ground."[56] Here a "border conflict"[57] takes place, for Christian experience cannot be subsumed under an *a priori* judgment.

Kierkegaard however, then interrupts his considerations, stopping at a point where there is an apparent lack of clarity in Erdmann's book. Kierkegaard observes that the spheres of speculation and experience are not clearly distinguished, for Erdmann writes (p. 189): "Reason, thus, will be able to calm down insofar as any religious content proves to be true through inner experience."[58] In fact, Erdmann wrote just the opposite: "If we employ it in the realm we are concerned with, reason will thus *not* be able to calm down insofar as any religious content proves to be true through inner experience."[59] Due to a simple lapse in Kierkegaard's transcription, a

---

52 *SKS* 19, 164, Not4:41 / *JP* 2, 2250.

53 Ibid.

54 *SKS* 19, 165–7, Not4:42–4.

55 *SKS* 19, 165, Not4:42 / *JP* 2, 2251.

56 *SKS* 19, 166, Not4:42 / *JP* 2, 2251.

57 Ibid.

58 Ibid.: "*So wird also die Vernunft sich damit beruhigen können, daß irgend ein religiöser Inhalt durch die innere Erfahrung sich als wahr zeigt.*"

59 Erdmann, *Vorlesungen über Glauben und Wissen*, op. cit., p. 189: "*Machen wir die Anwendung auf dasjenige Gebiet, mit dem wir es zu thun haben, so wird also die Vernunft sich nicht damit beruhigen können, daß irgend ein religiöser Inhalt durch die innere Erfahrung sich als wahr zeigt....*"

contrary statement arose, which Kierkegaard actually presupposes in what follows. Therefore it is not about a *lapsus calami*, where the correct statement is actually assumed. An *aberratio oculi* led to the assumption of a mistaken statement, and this is the starting point of Kierkegaard's misunderstanding.

Until now, Kierkegaard's error has not attracted attention. P.A. Heiberg and V. Kuhr apparently failed to notice it. The editors of the English Kierkegaard edition, Howard V. Hong and Edna H. Hong, translate the erroneous text into English without comment, and even the editors of the grand new Kierkegaard edition, *Søren Kierkegaards Skrifter*, repeat the mistaken quotation without any elucidating hint.[60]

It seems as if Hirsch too assumed that Kierkegaard transcribed correctly but, not wrongly, hesitated for a moment. He, however, holds that the problem was solved in so far as the interpretation of supernaturalism—which Erdmann, however, does not discuss until later—became his key to understanding the issue.

While Erdmann judged supernaturalism to be "dogmatism…forced into the point of view of non-knowledge,"[61] Kierkegaard, by contrast, notes, "but therefore the supernaturalist maintains also that there must be a complete change in consciousness, that a development must begin from the very beginning and be just as eternal in idea as the first."[62] Hirsch holds that Kierkegaard concedes "that forcing supernaturalism into Kantian non-knowledge, as historical supernaturalism did," is wrong. But stumbling across Erdmann's alleged indistinct demarcation between reason *a priori* and Christian experience paved the way for a judgment of his true intention, a deepened and positive judgment which deviates from his wholly critical assessment of supernaturalism and goes beyond the opposition between thinking *a priori* and religious consciousness. According to this, Erdmann would have helped a deeper understanding of supernaturalism to come to power than can be found in his own works.[63]

Hirsch welcomes the result of such a consensus emphatically in an account which Niels Thulstrup said went clearly beyond Kierkegaard's statement.[64] Hirsch writes,

> Kierkegaard apparently considers faith a new wonderful consciousness, indeed a consciousness which implies everything genuinely human: faith is just as eternal in the idea, just as it implies knowledge as the first immediate consciousness….Thereby we [!] had been given the riddle of the *a priori*, which, in the becoming of the personality, remains preserved by the disruption and has been resolved: rebirth is at the same time the reawakening of the human.[65]

---

60 Cf. *SKS* K 19, 215.

61 Erdmann, *Vorlesungen über Glauben und Wissen*, op. cit., p. 216.

62 *SKS* 19, 167, Not4:44 / *JP* 2, 2252.

63 The assumption of Kierkegaard's fertile misunderstanding continues from Hirsch to Niels Thulstrup and further right up to the present; see Andrew J. Burgess, "Caricatures and the Comic in the Early Journals," *Kierkegaard Studies.Yearbook*, 2003, pp. 125–42; p.132, n. 28.

64 Thulstrup, "Kierkegaards Kenntnis der philosophischen und theologischen Tradition," op. cit., p. 104.

65 Hirsch, *Kierkegaard-Studien*, op. cit. vol. 2, pp. 89f. [pp. 535f.].

May we assume that focusing on this *telos* has hampered the interpretation of Erdmann and Kierkegaard? To begin with, as already mentioned, Erdmann does not write what Kierkegaard transcribes and what apparently Hirsch also assumes. Further, it is impossible to see how the lines from Kierkegaard's very error lead to the interpretation of supernaturalism, as Hirsch understands it.

Erdmann's treatment of naturalism,[66] rather, already added to Kierkegaard's amazement about the indistinct boundary between reason and inner experience, between hypotheses *a priori* and empirical evidence. Following immediately his statement about the lack of clarity in the relationship between the two fields, Kierkegaard notes, "But when Erdmann characterizes naturalism in this way, as he properly does, the whole position seems to take on an eccentricity whereby it lies beyond the scope designated by faith and knowledge, if faith is to be understood in the purely historical, Christian way."[67] How does this square with the talk of the self-chosen limit of reason? This remains an open question for Kierkegaard.

Kierkegaard begins his next entry by saying that he now believes that he understands what Erdmann means in saying "that the eccentricity of the later position is conditioned by its transition to the essentially speculative, whereby its very presupposition (faith) is drawn along within the doubt; consequently one discovers within the immediate an element which now constrains the later position as a tendency in the totality to doubt its own presupposition."[68]

Far from finding in the supernaturalism a solution to the riddle which was given by Erdmann, Kierkegaard, returning to the path of speculation, and presumably in accordance with Erdmann's logic, projects the coexistence of faith and doubt back onto the beginning of the entire development of consciousness. There, in the questionable initial definition of faith, Kierkegaard finds the solution to the riddle by supposing that Erdmann conceives the beginning as an immediacy, which is not just that of faith on its own, but which already carries in it the germ of the eccentricity of *a priori* reason *vis-à-vis* faith.[69]

Kierkegaard is confirmed in his assumption that Erdmann, in the entire development of consciousness, follows a process which moves vaguely between Christian and universal consciousness. However, on account of his erroneous presupposition about the text, he is actually on the wrong track and misses Erdmann's point regarding the understanding of the beginning of the development of the religious consciousness, which is so important for him. Erdmann tried to define the beginning more precisely by analyzing Schleiermacher's understanding of feeling and religion in order to distinguish what is distinctly Christian from an immediacy, in which there would be

---

66 Ibid., pp. 87ff. [pp. 533ff.].

67 *SKS* 19, 165f., Not4:42 / *JP* 2, 2251.

68 *SKS* 19, 167, Not4:43.

69 Did the critical considerations, which were already made in 1836 *vis-à-vis* Philipp Konrad Marheineke, prepare this inference? For Marheineke, see Heiko Schulz, "Die spekulative Verflüchtigung des Christentums. Philipp Marheinekes System der christlichen Dogmatik und seine Rezeption bei Søren Kierkegaard," *Kierkegaard Studies. Yearbook*, 2003, pp. 20–47, see pp. 44f. Even at the beginning of 1837, Kierkegaard lamented that "the philosophers" had "faith" become "the immediate consciousness" (*SKS* 17, 199f., CC:12). Cf. *SKS* 4, 161 / *FT*, 69 and *SKS* 4, 318 / *CA*, 10.

space for something other than the naive faith in the reconciliation, which has come about.[70]

The beginning was "the most difficult," Bruno Bauer said.[71] It became the *shibboleth* of Kierkegaard and speculative theology.

VI. Appropriation and Criticism

Even though Hirsch and Thulstrup examined Kierkegaard's preoccupation with Erdmann mainly from the perspective of Kierkegaard's criticism of Hegel and its soundness with regard to his knowledge of Hegel, which had been imparted first by Erdmann and other Hegelians, nonetheless this preoccupation in any case displays such richness in both form and content that a renewed investigation appeared to be reasonable.

His appropriation ranges from an excerpt to an antithesis, from a quotation to a symbiotic rewording, from adaptation to critical dissociation, from immanent criticism to the justification of his own positions. This appropriation consists in understanding, misunderstanding, and formation of opinion. If one condenses from it not only the criticism of the Hegelian, one gains insight into a remarkable process of interpretation, which is of importance for understanding both sides.

Kierkegaard defends the "incommensurability of life." We can see that this key concept in Kierkegaard is inspired by Erdmann's considerations of the difficulty of mediating between life and concept. Kierkegaard even formulates his own ideas in such a way as if he were able to take this important concept virtually out of Erdmann's mouth.

Kierkegaard defends the impossibility of capturing the subject by means of conceptual deduction. We have seen how his response results from an encounter with Erdmann's transition between the definition of the subject as individuality and as reason.

Kierkegaard turns against the volatilization of Christianity by arguing that the Christian tradition is left out in the determination of the beginning of the religious development in the stages of consciousness. He becomes aware that Erdmann has emptied the history of religious consciousness and turned it into a history of universal consciousness.

What is characteristic about Erdmann's lectures was his consistent search for an analogy between deduction and reality. In this, his endeavor shows unintentionally

---

70 In connection with a discussion of the relationship between immediacy and doubt, Johannes Climacus still recalls this effort by Erdmann. Cf. *Pap.* IV B 1, p. 146n. / *JC*, 167n.

71 Bruno Bauer, "*Vorlesungen über Glauben und Wissen als Einleitung in die Dogmatik und Religionsphilosophie*, von Dr. Joh. Ed. Erdmann, 1837," *Zeitschrift für spekulative Theologie*, op. cit., vol. 3, no. 1, 1837, pp. 253–61, see pp. 259f. Kierkegaard received the periodical, see bibliography II.

"the *pudendum* of Hegelian philosophy," Emanuel Hirsch writes.[72] Niels Thulstrup holds that this specific point is to be disregarded as a *signum* of autonomy.[73]

However, the strong point of the book, and possibly what attracted Kierkegaard, is in this specific point. Especially Erdmann's double effort for making conceptional dialectics and for presenting, in a differentiated manner, the phenomena which correspond to it in the abundance of reality, appears to have stimulated Kierkegaard to discussion and clarification.

He hardly would have praised, with Bruno Bauer, "the clearness and accuracy," through which Erdmann "accounts for the logical categories in the manifold relations of reality and relations of consciousness,"[74] but in spite of his criticism of principle and methodology of Erdmann's bridging deduction and empiricism, he finds himself stimulated by Erdmann's dialectical hermeneutics, for example, through the latter's definitions of irony, mysticism and myth, and the critical concept of the "incommensurability of life" arises straightforwardly from taking up questions which Erdmann himself had posed.

By contrast, Erdmann was actually, in his own way, on the trail of the "incommensurability of life"—in fact, soon much more manifestly than at that *kairos* when Kierkegaard opened the *Vorlesungen über Glauben und Wissen*. Erdmann later called these lectures "an immature product."[75] In fact, they occupy an intermediary position in the development of his thought on religious philosophy. His dissertation had still worked with the assumption that the common content could be gained on occasion of the reconciliation between faith and knowledge by simply subtracting the form of faith. Though the *Vorlesungen* still presuppose this possibility, they already follow a much longer path. They not only subtract but also go far afield in order to gain reality for conceptional deduction. Later, Erdmann transcends even this. He arrives at the conclusion that "it is erroneous to ascribe the same content to religion and philosophy if both are different from each other in view of their form, and that therefore, there can be only a feigned peace between the two, if it has that error as an essential part.[76]

Erdmann has made explicit such an undivided historical understanding not only philosophically.[77] In his sermons, one can also demonstrate an increasing openness toward the historicity of the biblical *kerygma* as well as of the presence of Ecclesiastes.[78]

On the one hand, one can say by way of conclusion that Kierkegaard's insights, which he formulated in his examination of Erdmann, point to his later work. The texts

---

72 Hirsch, *Kierkegaard-Studien*, op. cit., vol. 2, p. 87 [p. 533].

73 Thulstrup, "Kierkegaards Kenntnis der philosophischen und theologischen Tradition," op. cit., p. 102.

74 Bauer, *Vorlesungen über Glauben und Wissen*, op. cit., p. 255.

75 Erdmann, *Grundriss der Geschichte der Philosophie*, op. cit., vol. 2, p. 648.

76 Erdmann, *Vermischte Aufsätze*, Leipzig: Vogel 1846, p. v. Cf. already Erdmann, "Ueber Widersprüche unter den christlichen Glaubenslehren," *Zeitschrift für spekulative Theologie*, op. cit., vol. 3, no. 1, 1837, pp. 20f.

77 Erdmann, "Phänomenologie des religiösen Bewußtseyns," in *Vermischte Aufsätze*, Leipzig: Vogel 1846.

78 Cf. Bitter, *Johann Eduard Erdmann*, op. cit., pp. 61–138.

have the character of a primitive understanding. The reading of Erdmann apparently served to orient Kierkegaard and form his opinion at an important *kairos*,[79] and the structure of his reception gives the impression of experiencing *in statu nascendi* his acquisition of new formulations such as that of the "incommensurability of life."[80] One cannot say to what extent the early judgments on imparting faith and knowledge in speculative theology, which have been expressed here, are entitled to temporal priority *vis-à-vis* other matter-of-factly related texts, until the topic "Kierkegaard and his contemporaries" is further illuminated. This is also true for the question (which has been intially answered by Hirsch and Thulstrup): what impact does Kierkegaard's reception of Erdmann have for his discussion of Hegel himself?

On the other hand, Kierkegaard's perception of Erdmann's writings, in so far as it may be related to the views of other Hegelians, while—like Erdmann's own development—eluding their schematization into right- and left-wing factions, is an indication of the fact that the traditional accounts of the Hegelian school, which are still oriented to the contemporary self-assessment with regard to the grouping of the school and its internal perspective, require revision.[81]

---

79 Cf. Thulstrup: "Reading Erdmann's book...sharpened Kierkegaard's sense for the problems and aroused his criticism" (in his "Kierkegaards Kenntnis der philosophischen und theologischen Tradition," op. cit., pp. 351–62, see p. 359).

80 As to Kierkegaard's "epigrammatical" way of speaking, see Wilhelm Anz, *Kierkegaard und der deutsche Idealismus*, Tübingen: Mohr 1956 (*Sammlung gemeinverständlicher Vorträge und Schriften aus dem Gebiet der Theologie und Religionsgeschichte*, vols. 210–1), pp. 6–9.

81 David Friedrich Strauss, *Streitschriften zur Vertheidigung meiner Schrift über das Leben Jesu und zur Charakteristik der gegenwärtigen Theologie*, vol. 1, nos. 1–3, Tübingen: Osiander 1837 (reprinted, Hildesheim: Olms 1980), no. 3, p. 95.

Bibliography

I. Erdmann's Works in The Auction Catalogue *of Kierkegaard's Library*

"Pantheismus die Grundlage der Religion," *Zeitschrift für spekulative Theologie*, vols. 1–3, ed. by Bruno Bauer, Berlin: Dümmler 1836–38, vol. 1, no. 2, 1836, pp. 133–157 (*ASKB* 354–357).

"Schriften über die ewige Persönlichkeit des Menschen," *Zeitschrift für spekulative Theologie*, op. cit., vol. 1, no. 1, 1836, pp. 205–46.

"Ueber den Begriff des Sündenfalls und des Bösen. Ein Versuch," *Zeitschrift für spekulative Theologie*, op. cit., vol. 2, no. 2, 1837, pp. 192–214.

"Ueber Widersprüche unter den christlichen Glaubenslehren," *Zeitschrift für spekulative Theologie*, op. cit., vol. 3, no. 1, 1837, pp. 1–48.

Vorlesungen über Glauben und Wissen als Einleitung in die Dogmatik und Religionsphilosophie, Berlin: Duncker und Humblot 1837 (*ASKB* 479).

Leib und Seele nach ihrem Begriff und ihrem Verhältnis zu einander. Ein Beitrag zur Begründung der philosophischen Anthropologie, Halle: C.A. Schwetschke & Sohn 1837 (*ASKB* 480).

Grundriss der Psychologie für Vorlesungen. Für Vorlesungen, Leipzig: Vogel 1840 (*ASKB* 481).

Natur oder Schöpfung? Eine Frage an die Naturphilosophie und Religionsphilosophie, Leipzig: Vogel 1840 (*ASKB* 482).

Grundriss der Logik und Metaphysik. Für Vorlesungen, Halle: Lippert 1841 (*ASKB* 483).

Psychologische Briefe, Leipzig: Geibel 1852 (*ASKB* 484).

[ed.] *Vorlesungen über Religionsphilosophie gehalten von Dr. Joh. Gust. Friedr. Billroth*, ed. by Johann Eduard Erdmann, Leipzig: Vogel 1837 (*ASKB* 428).

[ed.] [Leibniz, Gottfried Wilhelm], *God. Guil. Leibnitii Opera philosophica quae exstant latina gallica germanica omnia. Edita recognovit e temporum rationibus disposita pluribus ineditis auxit introductione critica atque indicibus instruxit*, vols. 1–2, ed. by Johann Eduard Erdmann, Berlin: Eichler 1840 (*ASKB* 620).

II. Works in The Auction Catalogue *of Kierkegaard's Library that Discuss Erdmann*

Bauer, Bruno, "*Vorlesungen über Glauben und Wissen als Einleitung in die Dogmatik und Religionsphilosophie*, von Dr. Joh. Ed. Erdmann, außerord. Prof. der Phil. an der Univers. zu Halle. Berlin, Duncker und Humblot. 1837. X. 276," *Zeitschrift für spekulative Theologie*, op. cit., vol. 3, no. 1, 1837, pp. 253–61.

Chalybäus, Heinrich Moritz, [Review of] "*Vorlesungen über Glauben und Wissen, als Einleitung in die Dogmatik und Religionsphilosophie*, gehalten und auf den Wunsch seiner Zuhörer herausgegeben von Dr. Joh. Ed. Erdmann, außerord. Prof. v. Phil. an d. Univ. zu Halle. Berlin, Verl. v. Duncker und Humblot. 1837. gr. 8," *Zeitschrift für Philosophie und spekulative Theologie*, vols. 1–16, ed. by Immanuel Hermann Fichte and Christian Hermann Weiße, Bonn et al.: Eduard Weber et al. 1837–46, vol. 2, 1838, pp. 138–53 (*ASKB* 877–911).

—— [Review of] "Natur- und Geistesphilosophie. In Bezug auf: Dr. Joh. Ed. Erdmann: *Leib und Seele nach ihrem Begriff und ihrem Verhältniß zu einander. Ein Beitrag zur Begründung der philosophischen Anthropologie*. Halle 1837. und K. Rosenkranz, *Psychologie oder die Wissenschaft vom subjektiven Geist*. Königsberg 1837," *Zeitschrift für Philosophie und spekulative Theologie*, op. cit., vol. 3, 1839, pp. 160–95.

Frauenstädt, Julius, *Briefe über die Schopenhauer'sche Philosophie*, Leipzig: F.A. Brockhaus 1854 (*ASKB* 515).

Helfferich, Adolph, *Die christliche Mystik in ihrer Entwickelung und in ihren Denkmalen*, vols. 1–2, Gotha: Friedrich Parthes 1842, vol. 1, p. 22n; pp. 27–8 (*ASKB* 571–572).

Michelet, Carl Ludwig, *Geschichte der letzten Systeme der Philosophie in Deutschland von Kant bis Hegel*, vols. 1–2, Berlin: Duncker und Humblot 1837–38, vol. 2, 1838 (*ASKB* 679).

Mynster, Jakob Peter, *Blandede Skrivter*, vols. 1–3, Copenhagen: Den Gyldendalske Boghandlings Forlag 1852–53 [vols. 4–6, Copenhagen: Den Gyldendalske Boghandlings Forlag 1855–57], vol. 1, p. 209n; p. 225n (*ASKB* 358–363).

Trendelenburg, Adolf, *Logische Untersuchungen*, vols. 1–2, Berlin: G. Bethge 1840, vol. 1, p. 41n; p. 42n (*ASKB* 843).

—— *Die logische Frage in Hegel's System. Zwei Streitschriften*, Leipzig: F.A. Brockhaus 1843, pp. 19–20 (*ASKB* 846).

Weiße, Christian Hermann, "Die philosophische Literatur der Gegenwart. Die monadologischen Systeme," *Zeitschrift für Philosophie und spekulative Theologie*, op. cit., vol. 7, 1841, pp. 255–304.

—— "Die philosophische Literatur der Gegenwart. [Review of among others] J.G. Erdmann, *Grundriß Logik und Metaphysik, für Vorlesungen*; Halle 1841—Derselbe, *Natur und Schöpfung? Eine Frage an die Naturphilosophie und Religionsphilosophie*; Leipzig 1840…," *Zeitschrift für Philosophie und spekulative Theologie*, op. cit., vol. 8, 1841, pp. 231–70.

III. Secondary Literature on Kierkegaard's Relation to Erdmann

Bitter, Stephan, *Johann Eduard Erdmann. Kirchliche Predigt und philosophische Spekulation in der Entwicklung eines theologischen Hegelianers*, Rheinbach-Merzbach: CMZ Publisher 1994 (*Arbeiten zur Theologiegeschichte*, vol. 1), pp. 172–76.

Hirsch, Emanuel, "Die Auseinandersetzung mit Erdmanns Hegelianismus und der Begriff des Humoristischen," in his *Kierkegaard-Studien*, vols. 1–2, Gütersloh: Bertelsmann 1933, vol. 2, pp. 84–93 [pp. 530–9] (reprinted, Vaduz, Liechtenstein: Toposverlag 1978. First published in *Studien des apologetischen Seminars in Wernigerode*, nos. 29, 31, 32, 36, 1930–33. The reprint retains the pagination of the first publication, giving the page numbers of the 1933 edition in square brackets).

Leemans, Victor, *Sören Kierkegaard*, Antwerp and Amsterdam: Uitgeversmij. N.V. Standaard-Boekhandel 1956, see pp. 38–41.

—— "Kierkegaards Kenntnis der philosophischen und theologischen Tradition," *Theologische Zeitschrift*, vol. 35, 1979, pp. 351–62.

Thulstrup, Niels, "Kierkegaard and Erdmann's Lectures on *Faith and Knowledge*," in his *Kierkegaard's Relation to Hegel*, trans. by George L. Stengren, Princeton, New Jersey: Princeton University Press 1980, pp. 116–27.

Günther:
Kierkegaard's Use of an Austrian Catholic Theologian

Christoph Kronabel and Jon Stewart

The Austrian Catholic theologian Anton Günther (1783–1863) remains one of the great unexplored sources in Kierkegaard's authorship. Although Kierkegaard owned several of Günther's works and all evidence indicates that he read them carefully, there has been to date no detailed study of this relation.

I. Günther's Life and Works

Günther was born on 17 November 1783 in Lindenau, a small town in Bohemia.[1] He came from undistinguished family origins. He attended secondary school in Leitmeritz and studied philosophy and law at the University of Prague under, among others, Bernhard Bolzano (1781–1848). After completing his studies, he came to Vienna in 1810 where he gained employment as a private tutor for a noble family. During this time Günther made the acquaintance of Clemens Maria Hofbauer (1751–1820), whom he made his spiritual guide. He developed an interest in religion and, at the age of 34, decided to embark on a study of theology both in Vienna and in Raab in Hungary. In 1821 he was ordained and went to Poland in 1822, where he attended a Jesuit novitiate for two years. Günther's health suffered in Poland, and after some conflicts with the Jesuits there, he returned to Vienna in 1824, where he led the existence of a private scholar until the end of his life. There he actively continued his studies in philosophy and theology. One of the main targets of his criticism was the pantheistic systems of the day as expounded by Hegelianism. They seemed to him to exclude the Christian *creatio ex nihilo* from the "parliament of philosophy."

---

1 For Günther's life and works, see Peter Knoodt, *Anton Günther, Eine Biographie*, vols. 1–2, Vienna: Braumüller 1881; Eduard Winter, *Die geistige Entwicklung Anton Günthers und seiner Schule*, Paderborn: Schöningh 1931; Joseph Pritz, *Glauben und Wissen bei Anton Günther. Eine Einführung in sein Leben und Werk mit einer Auswahl aus seinen Schriften*, Vienna: Herder 1963, pp. 15–67; Johann Reikerstorfer, "Anton Günther (1783–1863) und seine Schule," in *Christliche Philosophie im katholischen Denken des 19. und 20. Jahrhunderts*, vols. 1–3, ed. by Emerich Coreth SJ, Walter M. Neidl, and Georg Pfligersdorffer, Graz: Styria 1987, vol. 1, pp. 266–84.

In addition to his writing activity, he worked as a tutor and as a chaplain at the court church. He was supported financially by an annual grant from a nobleman.

Günther soon became the spiritual focus for many enlightened Christians, who, like him, were searching for a form of mediation between Christianity and philosophy, especially that of German idealism. That Günther enjoyed great respect in the philosophical community is evidenced by the fact that he was offered the position in Munich as the successor of Schelling, which he, however, turned down.

The Güntherians courageously represented an anti-Josephian spiritual direction in Austria and, after 1848, were the leading proponents of the movements of ecclesiastical freedom and the Restoration there. When the revolution broke out, many of the religious groups such as the Redemptorists withdrew from Vienna. By contrast, Günther's followers remained and played an active role in organizing the clergy in the absence of the Archbishop, who had also fled. Günther's friend Johann Emanuel Veith (1787–1876) played a pivotal role through his sermons at this time. The Güntherians thus followed the revolutionary trend by demanding a constitutional monarchy. They also hoped to seize the opportunity to help the church break free of the state. They wished to introduce ecclesiastical reforms, including allowing the laity to play a more active role in the decisions of the church. Similarly, they advocated freedom of speech, press and association and, with a view to the grounding of faith, demanded freedom of thought in the Church, which, however, met with little understanding from the Church hierarchy.

In their political activism, the Güntherians created the Catholic Union, an organization run by the laity. Further, they published two journals: *Wiener Kirchenzeitung* and *Aufwärts!*. They played a leading role in the local politics in Vienna. When the revolution was over and the Archbishop was restored, the Güntherians were repressed. In the 1850s the Güntherian movement was actively suppressed to the advantage of the ultramontane movement. This marked a clear move to the right, and the new order placed the power clearly in the hands of the clergy. Günther's academic followers were driven from their positions, and in 1857 his teachings were officially condemned. Günther died in Vienna on 24 February 1863.

From a scholarly point of view, Günther's attack on Hegelian pantheism was something that clearly left its stamp on his contemporaries. It is conceivable that this aspect of his thinking was what initially awakened Kierkegaard's interest. Günther was anxious to warn against the misconceptions in Hegel's philosophy of religion, which, to his mind, led away from true Christianity. He sought instead to restore the fundamental doctrines of Christianity, such as the Creation (a new determination of the God–world relation on the basis of the "*creatio ex nihilo*"), the Incarnation and the Trinity, and to rescue them from, among others, Hegel's speculative interpretation.

II. Günther's Works in Kierkegaard's Library

Günther was a prolific writer. Six of his ten main works are registered in Kierkegaard's library. The first of these is his *Vorschule zur spekulativen Theologie des positiven Christenthums*, the book with which Günther founded his school.[2] It is his maiden work and the only one to see a second, expanded printing (in 1846–48). Kierkegaard's library contains the first edition from 1828–29. The first volume treats the doctrine of Creation, and the second that of the Incarnation. In these two volumes the groundwork for the entire breadth of Günther's thematic spectrum is laid. It is an attempt at a scholarly grounding of the facts of faith, an ideal reconstruction of Christianity as a world-historical fact. Günther presents his thoughts—in a manner sometimes reminiscent of Jean Paul—in a correspondence between Peregrinus Niger, the "much loved, sincere, loyal uncle and parson of Kirchfels"[3] and his "most obedient, most indebted, restless, but not infidel, nephew Thomas Wendeling."[4]

Kierkegaard also owned a copy of Günther's *Peregrin's Gastmahl. Eine Idylle in eilf Octaven aus dem deutschen wissenschaftlichen Volksleben* from 1830.[5] After the *Vorschule* this is Günther's second work. In this book a handful of scholars meet in the hermitage of Peregrinus Niger for a cozy banquet at which they discuss the traditionalism of Joseph De Maistre (1753–1821), Félicité Robert de Lamennais (1782–1854), GioacchinoVentura (1792–1861) and Vicomte de Bonald (1754–1840) as well as their "German parrots."[6]

Kierkegaard also had a copy of Günther's *Süd- und Nordlichter am Horizonte speculativer Theologie* from 1832.[7] In this work Günther presents the letters of two Protestant pastors, David d'Herlice and Christian Franke, who discuss the Catholic truths of faith. In the letters the pastors take positions against the rationalism of the age. Theological questions concerning redemption and hypostatic union are mentioned, and dualism is presented as the true point of orientation and remedy for the current problems in both philosophy and theology.

Kierkegaard also owned Günther's *Der letzte Symboliker* from 1834.[8] Here the familiar Protestant pastors, David Herlicius and Christian Franke, debate the "newest affairs of the day in the field of German theology."[9] This work represents an attempt to "contribute to the mediation of the confessional opposition"[10] concerning the conflict between the Catholic Johann Adam Möhler (1796–1838), on the one side, and his critic, the Protestant and Hegel-follower Ferdinand Christian Baur (1792–1860), on the other side.

---

2 Anton Günther, *Vorschule zur spekulativen Theologie des positiven Christenthums*, vols. 1–2, Vienna: Wallishausser 1828–29 (*ASKB* 869–870).

3 Ibid., "Briefanreden," vol. 1, p. 8; p. 25; p. 107; vol. 2, p. 1; p. 46; p. 135.

4 Ibid., "Briefunterschriften," vol. 1, p. 12; vol. 2, p. 152; p. 205.

5 Günther, *Peregrin's Gastmahl. Eine Idylle in eilf Octaven aus dem deutschen wissenschaftlichen Volksleben*, Vienna: Mechitaristen 1830 (*ASKB* 1672).

6 Ibid., p. 287.

7 Günther, *Süd- und Nordlichter am Horizonte spekulativer Theologie*, Vienna: Mechitaristen 1832 (*ASKB* 520).

8 Günther, *Der letzte Symboliker. Eine durch die symbolischen Werke Doctor J. A. Möhler's und Doctor F. C. Baur's veranlaßte Schrift, in Briefen*, Vienna: Wallishausser 1834 (*ASKB* 521).

9 Ibid., p. v.

10 Ibid., p. iii.

Moreover, Kierkegaard also owned a copy of Günther's *Die Juste-Milieus in der deutschen Philosophie gegenwärtiger Zeit* from 1838.[11] In this work Günther wanted to make up for the lack of a systematic account of his dualism. The book criticizes the various false attempts at mediation between unequal opposites such as that between freedom and necessity as well as monism (which he refers to as the *Alleinheitslehre*) and monadism (which he refers to as the *Allvielheitslehre*). He does not, however, manage to sketch a detailed theory of dualism. Resigned, Günther, at the end of *Juste-Milieus*, concludes that he has not gotten past a "historical introduction to a theory of thought."[12]

A further work of Günther found in Kierkegaard's library is *Euristheus und Heracles. Meta-logische Kritiken und Meditationen*.[13] This work, published in 1843, concerns the emancipation of spirit from the snares of the concept. Herakles, as servant of the Idea, works in the service of his weak master, Euristheus, the representative of the Concept. These considerations are designated as "metalogical" insofar as not the *logical* but the *metalogical*, the ideal thinking, is able to grasp the essence of things. Finally Kierkegaard could read a handful of essays by Günther in the *Zeitschrift für Philosophie und spekulative Theologie*.[14] This was a leading journal at the time edited by the younger Fichte (1797–1879) and Christian Hermann Weiße (1801–66).

III. Kierkegaard's Use of Günther's Works

Kierkegaard refers a handful of times to Günther in his corpus. For whatever reason, however, Günther is never mentioned explicitly in Kierkegaard's published works. By contrast, he appears in a number of the journals and notebooks that Kierkegaard kept throughout his life.

Kierkegaard first refers to Günther in the *Journal AA*. In the main text of one of the famous Gilleleje entries, Kierkegaard writes,

> From this spot I have seen the sea ruffled by a soft breeze, seen it play with the pebbles; from here I have seen its surface transformed into a massive snowstorm and heard the bass voice of the gale begin to sing falsetto; here it is as though I had seen the world's emergence and destruction—a sight that truly enjoins silence. But to what purpose that word which is so often profaned? How often do we not encounter those sentimental blondes who, like nymphs in white gowns, behold such things with armed eyes, and then burst out in "silent admiration"?[15]

---

[11] Günther, *Die Juste-Milieus in der deutschen Philosophie gegenwärtiger Zeit*, Vienna: Beck 1838 (*ASKB* 522).

[12] Ibid., p. 418.

[13] Günther, *Euristheus und Heracles. Meta-logische Kritiken und Meditationen*, Vienna: Beck 1843 (*ASKB* 523).

[14] *Zeitschrift für Philosophie und spekulative Theologie*, vols. 1–16, ed. by Immanuel Hermann Fichte and Christian Hermann Weiße, Bonn et al.: Eduard Weber at al. 1837–46 (*ASKB* 877–911).

[15] *SKS* 17, 15, AA:6 / *JP* 5, 5099.

In a footnote to this passage, he writes the following referring to the "sentimental blondes": "Something Gynther said of them on another occasion is also true: 'People who come with eyes armed but also with hearts armored.'"[16] Here Kierkegaard refers to Günther's *Vorschule zur spekulativen Theologie des positiven Christenthums*, where Günther writes,

> If Providence today would introduce spirits into the field of art, which would let the great epic of the world of spirits and of human beings reflect now in the magic of the light and its sounds, now in the magic of the sound and its colors, so that *Klopstock* would be blinded and the blind *Milton* would lose his hearing, then you will see the staring world standing before these creations no differently than you catch a glimpse of the world of shadows of our art lovers before the *night* of a *Coreggio,* and before the *morning of the Resurrection* of an *Andray*—with protected eyes but also with armored heart, which is not accessible to any shimmer of faith or love from that world.[17]

In his reference to this passage, Kierkegaard misunderstands Günther in a way that is atypical for him since the misunderstanding proceeds in a manner diametrically opposed to his epistemological approach. For Günther, it is not intuition that is productive but rather the investigative understanding and reason penetrated by the idea. The literary form of letters which Günther uses to express his thoughts is what makes this kind of misunderstanding possible. Günther here appeals to the statements of his nephew and continues then as follows after the passage just quoted: "Be assured that our age will never reach for anything with the arm of the will before it has failed to be achieved and grasped with the arm of the understanding. The age lies in this and no other birth pains; and that is the reason why those researchers...are the sole true midwives."[18] What Günther is trying to express here is the primacy of the understanding above all other epistemological approaches. Science overarches art and not the other way around, as, for example, in Schiller, whose poem, "Die Künstler," Günther quotes in this context.[19]

In a long entry, also from the *Journal AA*, which mentions, among others, Schleiermacher and Schelling, Kierkegaard writes referring to the system of the younger Fichte,

> What this system really captures in time (true, Fichte speaks in one place of "*besondere Zeit*" which is supposed to get him beyond Schelling, but it stops there) is not the Christian doctrine of time—of the Devil's fall from the eternal and therefore man's in time, not satisfaction in time, not faith (only the immediate consciousness). Fichte has to that extent made an advance in going beyond Hegel's abstraction to intuition.[20]

In a footnote to the first sentence Kierkegaard refers to Günther as follows:

---

16 *SKS* 17, 15n, AA:6 / *JP* 5, 5099.

17 Günther, *Vorschule*, op. cit., vol. 2, p. 308.

18 Ibid.

19 Ibid., p. 309.

20 *SKS* 17, 41, AA:22 / *JP* 2, 1190.

> There must surely be something corresponding to this in F. Baader, where, for example, on behalf of humankind, he declines the honor of being the first discoverer of sin and rants against Kant's radical evil—here, too, belongs Günther's theory of hereditary sin conditioned by the evolution of the race; Adam and Eve were not conscious of gender difference before the Fall.[21]

Kierkegaard correctly categorizes Günther's theory of hereditary sin. Günther too turns against Kant's view from *Religion within the Limits of Reason Alone* that human beings are by nature evil. Günther sketches a highly differentiated picture, penetrated with greater speculative force, of the Fall and the human race, which does not bear exclusively features of corruption. In his *oeuvre*, he stated his views on these issues several times, especially in the second volume of the *Vorschule zur spekulativen Theologie des positiven Christenthums*,[22] in *Süd- und Nordlichter am Horizonte spekulativer Theologie*,[23] and in *Der letzte Symboliker*.[24] All of these works were available to Kierkegaard, who evidently made a careful study of them. In contrast to Kant and Augustine, Günther does not regard evil in its possibility as identical with the fact of created being as such. To be able to be sinful and to be created are, for him, not synonymous statements.[25] And sins, like the hereditary sin, are not connected with sexuality in such a manner that sexuality is to be understood in an exclusively pejorative manner.[26] Rather, sexuality, the procreation of human beings, the continuation of humanity into the future, according to Günther, already contains within itself the character of redemption. Günther sees himself led to this view through a close look at the Holy Scriptures:

> "On the day that you should eat from it [sc. the tree of knowledge]," says the word of God, "You will die!" And look then! God seems to have broken his word for the first time in Paradise. Not only did the original couple live on after the catastrophe, but they even produced a race of human beings...and, moreover, with the consciousness of possessing a will as *liberum arbitrium*, a gift, which Adam did not know he had before the Fall.[27]

Günther draws the conclusion from this that the idea of redemption is already present here: "Could the continuation of humanity not in this way already be regarded as a retroactive effect of the future redemption in the promise?"[28] He interprets the voice of conscience as an indication of this. The voice of conscience is a "surviving remainder from the original bond and association between God and the fallen creature."[29] The

21 *SKS* 17, 41n, AA:22 / *JP* 2, 1190.

22 See especially the first seven letters, pp. 1–152.

23 Here Günther discusses above all Augustine's "*massa damnata*": pp. 114ff.; pp. 152ff.; pp. 181ff.; and pp. 207ff. He regards this kind of characterization of the human race after the Fall as "too dark" (see *Süd- und Nordlichter*, op. cit., p.192).

24 See especially pp. 1–76; pp. 304ff.; and pp. 317–42.

25 Cf. Günther, *Vorschule*, op. cit., vol. 2, pp. 64ff.

26 See, for example, Günther, *Der letzte Symboliker*, op. cit., pp. 68ff.

27 Günther, *Der letzte Symboliker*, op. cit., p. 51. Cf. also *Süd- und Nordlichter*, op. cit., pp. 192ff.

28 Günther, *Süd- und Nordlichter*, op. cit., p. 193.

29 Ibid.

Holy Scripture also seems to support him in this supposition since it "earlier, when it speaks of the first offspring of Eve, mentions the promise that the offspring of the woman will tread on the head of the serpent. Is not the continuation of the race a condition for the appearance of the one who will tread on the serpent?"[30]

The actual continued existence of Adam and his actual propagation in his descendents must

> ...be placed...under a law of mercy, if the actual, living race is to be thought without contradiction as coming from Adam (who has himself died). But if the one doomed to death still lives and continues to live in his descendents, in short, has history, then he cannot have life and history as a sinner and fallen person, but rather as redeemed and righteous.[31]

Thus, Günther sees a far-reaching parallel between Adam and Christ:

> Our race exists only by the original merit of a second progenitor in the person of Christ, for the original blame of the first progenitor in the person of Adam....Just as the actual race is not possible without a redeemer, so also vice versa the actual redeemer (the historical Christ) cannot exist with the race; in short the race and its redeemer are inseparable elements; likewise, the second Adam, as priest and redeemer, since he sacrificed his life for his race according to the will of God, cannot be separated from the first Adam as the one to be redeemed. Thus, where the first progenitor finds his representation in the race, there (as a result of the inseparability) the second progenitor as redeemer will also find it.[32]

Günther distinguishes his position decisively from that of Kant and Augustine.[33] He treats Augustine at some length in his work, *Süd- und Nordlichter am Horizonte spekulativer Theologie*. As noted above, the book consists of a fictional correspondence between the reformed priest David d'Herlice and the Protestant pastor Christian Franke; while d'Herlice argues against Augustine's doctrine of hereditary sin and predestination,[34] Franke wishes to reformulate it.[35] Kierkegaard seems to refer to Franke's defense of Augustine's doctrine of hereditary sin, where Franke interprets Augustine's view based on the late scholastic concept of "humanity" as the universal:

> With this presupposition he now claims that *all human beings* had sinned in Adam and Eve and would have contracted a sin, because the *whole human nature* had then been

30 Günther, *Süd- und Nordlichter*, op. cit., pp. 192f.; Cf. also *Der letzte Symboliker*, op. cit., p. 71.

31 *Der letzte Symboliker*, op. cit., p. 58.

32 Ibid., pp. 304; Cf. also *Süd- und Nordlichter*, op. cit., pp. 194f.: the fact that Adam continued to exist as a human being after the Fall "he has Christ to thank for, his spiritual progenitor in this relation." The personal blame of the old Adam can only "become a historical or hereditary blame for a real race."

33 Cf., for example, *Vorschule*, op. cit., vol. 2, pp. 64ff.; *Der letzte Symboliker*, op. cit., pp. 53ff.; especially also *Süd- und Nordlichter*, op. cit., pp. 114ff.; pp. 180ff.

34 Ibid., pp. 114ff.

35 Ibid., pp. 180ff.

present in them—just as our theologian of natural philosophy claims the same thing with new words when he says: It is not the individual but rather the race which had sinned in Adam and Eve.[36]

Günther writes further:

> Man since the Fall is certainly *free to be evil*, but not *free to be good. Adam* certainly had *complete* freedom in Paradise, through which he could will and do *both good and evil*; but through the Fall the entire human *nature* is radically *changed,* and with it also the *freedom of the will weakened.* The fallen human beings still have freedom but in a completely different sense. Namely, they do *only* evil and do so out of their *own* impulse and free will, therefore not out of compulsion; they have lost, by contrast, the *complete* freedom which contains the ability to do the good.[37]

At the end of the aforementioned entry in Kierkegaard's *Journal AA*, one reads, "And thus the question of why God created the world can arise, which the old dogmaticians also considered since there is a revelation; but Fichte *et al.* naturally can never get beyond the universally human immediacy: consciousness."[38] In the midst of such nuanced and acute speculations about the Creation, human freedom and man's abandonment of God in sin, then the question arises about why God created the world at all. Kierkegaard contrasts the answer of the "old dogmaticians" with that of "Fichte *et al.*" The old dogmatics gives its answer in the context of the Revelation: "*Creatio est revelatio Dei universalis et primitiva, qua rerum universitatem ad summum bonum communicandum ex aeterno amore suo esse voluit*" (Creation is the universal and original revelation of God, whereby he in his eternal love wished that everything should serve to communicate to the highest good).[39] In contrast to this, the philosophy of German idealism rejects the idea of placing the creation in a thought relation to the revelation of God. No one has ever managed to say a comprehensible word about the creation from nothing, claimed the elder Fichte. For Schelling, the creation *ex nihilo* was the cross of the understanding. The younger Fichte and many of his contemporaries agreed with this view. The basis for this is their view that God needs the world for the purpose of the completion of his perfection. Correspondingly, there was before the creation of the world no personality of the Absolute, no self-consciousness of God, as traditional Christianity would have it in the inner-trinitarian event as *manifestatio dei ad intra.*

With this issue we find ourselves at the very center of the entire Güntherian speculation. Here he seeks nothing less than a new founding of theology with the declared goal of "creating a seat and a voice for the idea of Creation in the

36 Günther, *Süd- und Nordlichter*, op. cit., p. 186.

37 Ibid., p. 188.

38 *SKS* 17, 42, AA:22 / *JP* 2, 1190, p. 40.

39 *Hutterus redivivus oder Dogmatik der evangelisch-lutherischen Kirche: Ein dogmatisches Repertorium für Studierende*, ed. by Karl Hase, 4th ed., Leipzig: Sühring 1839 [1829], § 61, p. 151 (*ASKB* 581); Cf. also § 60 "Begriff, Ursache und Zweck der Schöpfung," in August Hahn, *Lehrbuch des christlichen Glaubens*, Leipzig: Vogel 1828, pp. 265–83, especially Remark 4 "Zweck der Schöpfung," pp. 271–6, where several older dogmaticians are discussed (*ASKB* 535).

parliament of philosophy, from which it has been wholly excluded since Fichte and Schelling."[40] For Günther it is clear that it must be maintained that God had self-consciousness and personality before the creation of the world. Only in this way can the pantheism of then contemporary philosophy be avoided. Only in this way does God maintain his dignity of independence from the world and its development. The loss of the premundane personality of the Absolute leads to the loss of the basic doctrines of Christianity: "first, the doctrine of sin as a free action of human beings and the doctrine of the redemption of sin as the free act of God and human beings, but also the doctrine of the creation of the world as a free act of God."[41] Günther was concerned with these issues and this basic view throughout his entire life. Accordingly, one can find in his works harsh debates with the younger Fichte and his associates. Throughout his life Günther had in Fichte a bitter antipode to his Christian, dualistic system. The available literature provides an eloquent testimony of this. In all, four longer monographs in Günther's works characterize these debates.[42] Three of these four works are also found in Kierkegaard's library.

According to Fichte, God as redeemer of the world has three persons, that is, not as creator of the world and certainly not prior to or without any creation of the world. To be sure, Günther agrees with Fichte's criticism of Hegel with respect to the personality of God and declares, so to speak, his solidarity with Fichte in developing a Christian philosophy in negation of Hegel. However, insofar as Fichte's program leads to various kinds of mediation between pantheism and theism, Günther is no longer able to remain in agreement. For the results of his thought stand in opposition to this program and, moreover, place Günther in the position to unmask Fichte's thought as itself pantheistic.[43] In the becoming of the world God, to be sure, does not achieve consciousness, since this comes to him *a priori*, but rather self-consciousness. Accordingly, without and prior to the becoming of the world, God is related to God in the world as a lower consciousness to a higher one. But then "the world is immediately a moment in the self-perfection of the divine, as the

---

40 Günther, "Fingerzeige. Aus dem Archiv des altkatholischen Bischofs in Bonn," printed as "Anhang," Eduard Winter, *Das positive Vernunftkriterium. Eine historisch-kritische Studie zu der philosophisch-dogmatischen Spekulation Anton Günthers*, Warnsdorf: Opitz 1928, pp. 71f., here p. 72. The "Fingerzeige" refers to the result of a meeting of the Güntherians with Günther himself in Rodaun near Vienna. They enclosed with the letter a note from Günther to Knoodt dated 1 August 1854 and received "die Weisungen für Knoodt, aber auch für Baltzer in Bezug auf die Weiterverteidigung Günthers in Rom" (p. 88).

41 Günther, *Lydia. Philosophisches Tagebuch, als Seitenstück zu A. Ruge's "Akademie,"* vols. 1–5, Vienna: Braumüller 1849–54, vol. 1, p. 94. Cf. Anton Günther and Johann Heinrich Pabst, *Janusköpfe. Zur Philosophie und Theologie*, Vienna: Wallishausser 1834, pp. x–xiii (*ASKB* 524).

42 Günther, *Vorschule*, op. cit; Günther, *Janusköpfe*, op. cit. (see Beilage "Sendschreiben an I. Hermann Fichte"); *Thomas a Scrupulis. Zur Transfiguration der Persönlichkeits-Pantheismen neuester Zeit*, Vienna: Wallishausser 1835 (Fichte was the occasion and reason for this work; of the seven chapters, four are dedicated exclusively to Fichte.); Günther, *Euristheus und Heracles*, op. cit.

43 Cf. also Kronabel, *Die Aufhebung der Begriffsphilosophie. Anton Günther und der Pantheismus*, Freiburg: Karl Alber 1989, pp. 92–107.

essential form of the divine, that is, a moment in the personality itself."[44] Thus, only the relation of the finite and the Absolute can be completely developed; however, the question of the motivation for the creation cannot be explained by deducing the original relation.

Kierkegaard thus shares the analytic diagnosis with Günther: Fichte's God, in his premundane determination, does not manage to make it beyond consciousness. This passage in Kierkegaard reveals again that he attentively studied Günther. However, he does not identify with Günther's synthetic construction. Otherwise, we would certainly be given a constructive hint about this direction of thought, which is, however, missing. For Kierkegaard, what is interesting in Günther's works, in any case, seems to be the fact that Günther, while remaining on the foundation of traditional Christianity, nonetheless moves to the conceptual heights of the philosophical avant-garde.

In the *Journal DD*, in a long entry on the doctrine of original sin, Kierkegaard refers to Günther as follows: "Or does not original sin consistently condition the doctrine of the Church—for otherwise what is hereditary would have no influence upon the given in society—or are individuals emancipated and the concept of the Church abolished? In this respect I believe Günther has something under the doctrine of works."[45] Here Kierkegaard refers presumably to the 7th and 13th letter in Günther's *Vorschule zur spekulativen Theologie des positiven Christenthums*.[46] It is surprising that Kierkegaard in this passage does not embark on a deeper analysis of the matter in Günther. This is true especially given the fact that in one of his main works, namely, *The Concept of Anxiety*, Kierkegaard explicitly treats this issue.

In the *Journal EE* from 1839 Kierkegaard refers to another of Günther's works as follows: "The latest work by Günther (*Die Juste-Milieus in der deutschen Philosophie gegenwärtiger Zeit*) has such a felicitous title that I have become so infatuated and preoccupied with it that I pause at the title and almost do not get the book read."[47] Here it is obviously Günther's formulation which has caught Kierkegaard's eye and not anything particular about his theology. In a somewhat cryptic entry Kierkegaard writes,

> About eternal damnation
> *Eternal, continuous development* (*contrad. in adjecto*) the eternal as the opposite of time, not an infinite succession of moments in time.
> Children who die early—
> Pagans—
> See Gynther, II, p. 118 bottom.[48]

44 Günther, *Thomas a Scrupulis*, op. cit., pp. 99f.; p. 137.

45 *SKS* 17, 229, DD:27 / *JP* 4, 3393.

46 Günther, *Vorschule*, op. cit., vol. 2 ("Die Incarnationstheorie"), pp. 135–52, especially pp. 146–9; pp. 306–52, especially pp. 312–5; and pp. 325–45. Cf. also the fifth and sixth letter, "Die Lehre von der Kirche" in Günther, *Der letzte Symboliker*, op. cit., p. 177; pp. 213–27.

47 *SKS* 18, 11, EE:14 / *JP* 3, 3271.

48 *Pap.* II A 630 / *JP* 5, 5276.

Here Kierkegaard refers to *Vorschule zur spekulativen Theologie des positiven Christenthums*.[49] In the context quoted, Günther distinguishes between empirical and pure time. Both are related to the world of human beings and spirits, where man is conceived as the synthesis of spirit and nature. Empirical time can be negated, while pure time cannot. In pure time there is no becoming. Günther can be taken into account only in a superficial manner in the service of Kierkegaard's assumption that eternity cannot be grasped as an eternally long time but rather must be characterized as a qualitative difference in time. He distinguishes between time here at the level of the realm of spirits and the human world, and then in the respective processes of being and appearance. There takes place in man, as synthesis of nature and spirit, a development by means of procreation, insofar as it is the blood of the life of nature. However, there takes place no development by means of procreation insofar as "Spirit does not stand *vis-à-vis* spirit in a sexual relation."[50]

In the *Journal NB 12*, Kierkegaard reproaches the Danish theologian Hans Lassen Martensen (1808–84) for not making use of Günther: "It is characteristic of Martensen that he never quotes the younger Fichte, Baader, Günther, but constantly quotes Schleiermacher, whom he corrects. This means that he directly capitalizes upon what has appeared since Schleiermacher and also profits by correcting Schleiermacher."[51] This passage is clearly a part of Kierkegaard's ongoing attempts to demonstrate that Martensen is an unoriginal thinker. The point here is that Martensen has made use of Günther and others without adequately acknowledging his debt to them. He then attempts to appear novel in his overt criticisms of Schleiermacher. The justice of Kierkegaard's criticism of Martensen cannot be evaluated here, but this passage does indicate clearly that Günther was regarded as standard reading by Danish theologians at the time.

IV. Critical Evaluation

In Kierkegaard's time Anton Günther was one of the most influential theologians in Europe. Given this, it is hardly surprising that there are several works from Günther's pen in Kierkegaard's library. In addition, Günther and Kierkegaard often share the same intention at various points of departure, for example, their views on the doctrine of Incarnation or their critical disposition towards Hegel. As noted above, the declared goal of Günther was to create for the Christian idea of a *creatio ex nihilo* "a seat and voice...in the parliament of philosophy, from which it has been wholly excluded since Fichte and Schelling."[52] In this regard Günther must have awakened the curiosity of Kierkegaard. This was the case for many philosophers of the day with a Christian orientation, who acknowledged Günther's work with great gratitude. What is amazing at first glance is that the effect of Günther cannot

49 Günther, *Vorschule*, op. cit., vol. 2, p. 118.

50 Ibid., p. 117.

51 *SKS* 22, 167, NB12:47 / *JP* 6, 6460.

52 Günther, "Fingerzeige," op. cit., in Winter, *Das positive Vernunftkriterium*, op. cit., pp. 71f., here p. 72.

be traced in any of Kierkegaard's published works. In none of them does he refer to Günther directly.

However, a closer examination of the works by Günther, which are found in Kierkegaard's library, reveals the first indication of this influence. This reveals a genuine interest on Kierkegaard's part but by no means a great enthusiasm or zeal. Some of Günther's main works are missing, which would not have been the case had Kierkegaard been a convinced zealot or follower of Günther's views. Particularly striking is the absence of the five volumes of his *Lydia. Philosophisches Tagebuch.*[53] Also lacking is the work, *Thomas a Scrupulis*[54] as well as the second, largely expanded edition from 1848 of the *Vorschule*. This work contains more or less the foundation of all of Günther's thought.[55]

It seems that Kierkegaard only made use of Günther in the manner of a quarryman. And in this quarrying there are no large conceptual blocks of thought but rather only accidental pebbles, which Kierkegaard could make use of in an associative manner. The standard is always his own thought and not Günther's system or train of thought. Kierkegaard thus "uses" Günther in an associative and not a systematic manner. Günther's central concerns are never mentioned, at least in the direct quotations. Among these one might mention above all the relation of God–world, and its significance for the critical discussion with German idealism, especially Hegel, as well as Günther's doctrine of Incarnation. In the direct quotations Kierkegaard does not really do justice to Günther. The themes mentioned by Kierkegaard are not Günther's main concern but are only marginal. For this reason it is also appropriate that these sporadic and discontinuous quotations occasionally are to be found in the footnotes. Here they function as an associative and decorative support for Kierkegaard's argumentation, so to speak, as his auxiliary troops. Indeed, Günther's thoughts in their main lines with their argumentative strength would certainly also be able to function as a champion for many of Kierkegaard's main themes. At first glance it is, however, not clear whether and to what degree Kierkegaard integrated the Güntherian ideas into his philosophy and theology.

The more precise reasons for this must remain the object of future investigation. Here there is only room for speculation. Certainly, one important reason Kierkegaard perceived Günther as an amicably disposed contemporary is his manner of presentation. This was often criticized and regarded as damaging for Günther's influence.

> Many people who wish to familiarize themselves with his works end up putting them aside unread since they do not like his manner of writing. Why in *Süd- und Nordlichtern* does he put the Catholic faith into the mouth of a Protestant pastor and why in general does he write such that one does not really know what the author himself thinks? — This will

---

53 Günther, *Lydia. Philosophisches Tagebuch, als Seitenstück zu A. Ruge's "Akademie,"* vols. 1–5, Vienna: Braumüller 1849–54.

54 Günther, *Thomas a Scrupulis. Zur Transfiguration der Persönlichkeits-Pantheismen neuester Zeit*, Vienna: Wallishausser 1835.

55 Günther's works, *Lentigos und Peregrins Briefwechsel*, Vienna: Braumüller 1857, and *Anti-Savarese*, ed. by Peter Knoodt, Vienna: Braumüller 1883, only appeared after Kierkegaard's death.

> always be the case for the uninitiated: but in order to be initiated into these works, they would have to work through them. Thus in brief! — Put aside, dear friend, this manner of writing and choose the usual form of philosophical exposition! I say this because you will win much more influence on the reading public.[56]

These are the words of the Catholic critic of Hegel, Franz Anton Staudenmaier (1800–56).

The suspicion remains that, alongside the direct quotations from Günther's works, some of his central thoughts can be found indirectly integrated in Kierkegaard's *oeuvre*. Günther's criticism of Hegel could certainly have challenged Kierkegaard to the extent that he integrated it into his own work. Günther's dualism of spirit and nature and the, for Günther, mistaken separation of the consciousness of nature as spirit could well have had an influence on Kierkegaard's criticism of Hegel. Günther's characterization of the inner-trinitarian event, the *manifestatio ad intra* as a "contradiction," which in the one substance emerges in three forms, and the "contraposition" of the Creation, the *manifestatio ad extra*, which in the three substances finds itself again in a single form, recalls in its structure Hegel's *Encyclopaedia*, with its trinitarian sphere of universality, which ends in "one-sided subjectivity," and the "overarching subjectivity," in the individual, in which the mundane events find their completion. To what degree such a conception could have had an influence, positive or negative, on Kierkegaard requires a more detailed investigation. To be sure, both thinkers deserve such an investigation.

---

56 Quoted from *Anton Günther. Eine Biographie*, op. cit., vol. 1, p. 289; Cf. also Johann Eduard Erdmann, *Grundriß der Geschichte der Philosophie*, Berlin: Hertz 1866, p. 638, where Erdmann finds terrifying the way in which Günther, "at the same time recalling Jean Paul, Hamann and Baader, but outdoing all three, treats everything in a humorous manner, which even goes down to the very title of his works."

Bibliography

I. Günther's Works in The Auction Catalogue *of Kierkegaard's Library*

Süd- und Nordlichter am Horizonte spekulativer Theologie. Fragment eines evangelischen Briefwechsels, Vienna: Mechitaristen 1832 (*ASKB* 520).

Der letzte Symboliker. Eine durch die symbolischen Werke Doctor J. A. Möhler's und Doctor F. C. Baur's veranlaßte Schrift, in Briefen, Vienna: Wallishausser 1834 (*ASKB* 521).

Die Juste-Milieus in der deutschen Philosophie gegenwärtiger Zeit, Vienna: Beck 1838 (*ASKB* 522).

Euristheus und Heracles. Meta-logische Kritiken und Meditationen, Vienna: Beck 1843 (*ASKB* 523).

Vorschule zur speculativen Theologie des positiven Christenthums. In Briefen, vols. 1–2, Vienna: Wallishausser 1828–29 (*ASKB* 869–870).

[Review of] "*Die Apologetik als wissenschaftliche Nachweisung der Göttlichkeit des Christenthums in seiner Erscheinung*, dargestellt von Dr. Joh. Seb. v. Drey, ordentl. Professor der kathol. theolog. Facultät in Tübingen. Erster Band: *Philosophie der Offenbarung*. Mainz, bei Fl. Kupferberg 1838. Erster Artikel," *Zeitschrift für Philosophie und spekulative Theologie*, vols. 1–16, ed. by Immanuel Hermann Fichte and Christian Hermann Weiße, Bonn et al.: Eduard Weber at al. 1837–46, vol. 2, 1838, pp. 289–336; Zweiter Artikel, vol. 4, 1839, pp. 132–65; Dritter Artikel, vol. 5, 1840, pp. 276–312; Vierter und letzter Artikel, vol. 6, 1840, pp. 104–49 (*ASKB* 877–911).

"Ueber Atheism im metaphysischen Systemen," *Zeitschrift für Philosophie und spekulative Theologie*, op. cit., vol. 3, 1839, pp. 312–31.

"Andeutungen über das wissenschaftliche Verhältniß der Naturkunde zur Theologie," *Zeitschrift für Philosophie und spekulative Theologie*, op. cit., vol. 7, 1841, pp. 80–102 and pp. 157–72.

[Review of] "K.F.E. Trahndorff, *wie kann der Supranaturalismus sein Recht gegen Hegels Religionsphilosophie behaupten? eine Lebens- und Gewissensfrage an unsre Zeit*; Berlin, bei Fr. Hentze 1840," *Zeitschrift für Philosophie und spekulative Theologie*, op. cit., vol. 8, 1841, pp. 131–54 and pp. 271–308.

Peregrin's Gastmahl. Eine Idylle in eilf Octaven aus dem deutschen wissenschaftlichen Volksleben, Vienna: Mechitaristen 1830 (*ASKB* 1672).

Günther, Anton and Johann Heinrich Pabst, *Janusköpfe. Zur Philosophie und Theologie*, Vienna: Wallishausser 1834 (*ASKB* 524).

II. Works in The Auction Catalogue *of Kierkegaard's Library that Discuss Günther*

Erdmann, Johann Eduard, *Vorlesungen über Glauben und Wissen als Einleitung in die Dogmatik und Religionsphilosophie*, Berlin: Duncker und Humblot 1837, p. 272 (*ASKB* 479).

Fichte, Immanuel Hermann, *Grundzüge zum Systeme der Philosophie*, vols. 1–2, Heidelberg: I.C.B. Mohr 1833–36, vol. 2, p. 522 (*ASKB* 502–503).

—— *Die Idee der Persönlichkeit und der individuellen Fortdauer*, Elberfeld: Büschler'sche Verlagsbuchhandlung und Buchdruckerei 1834, pp. 82–6 (*ASKB* 505).

Hagen, Johan Frederik, *Ægteskabet. Betragtet fra et ethisk-historiskt Standpunct*, Copenhagen: Wahlske Boghandels Forlag 1845, p. 10 (*ASKB* 534).

Helfferich, Adolph, *Die christliche Mystik in ihrer Entwickelung und in ihren Denkmalen*, vols. 1–2, Gotha: Friedrich Perthes 1842, vol. 1, p. 448; p. 461 (*ASKB* 571–572).

Martensen, Hans Lassen, "Betragtninger over Ideen af Faust. Med Hensyn paa Lenaus *Faust*," *Perseus*, vols. 1–2, ed. by Johan Ludvig Heiberg, Copenhagen: C.A. Reitzel 1837–38, vol. 1, pp. 91–164, see p. 114n (*ASKB* 569).

Menzel, Wolfgang, *Die deutsche Literatur*, vols. 1–4, 2nd revised ed., Stuttgart: Hallberg'sche Verlagshandlung 1836, vol. 3, pp. 245ff. (*ASKB* U 79).

Rosenkranz, Karl, "Günther's und Pabst's katholische Polemik gegen Hegel 1831," in his *Kritische Erläuterungen des Hegelschen Systems*, Königsberg: Bornträger 1840, pp. 286–309 (*ASKB* 745).

Weiße, Christian Hermann, *Die Idee der Gottheit. Eine philosophische Abhandlung. Als wissenschaftliche Grundlegung zur Philosophie der Religion*, Dresden: Grimmer'sche Buchhandlung 1833, p. 256n (*ASKB* 866).

III. Secondary Literature on Kierkegaard's Relation to Günther

Thulstrup, Niels, *Kierkegaard's Relation to Hegel*, trans. by George L. Stengren, Princeton: Princeton University Press 1980, p. 106; p. 177.

Marheineke:
The Volatilization of Christian Doctrine

Heiko Schulz

On 31 October 1841, the freshly graduated Master of Philosophy, Søren Kierkegaard, wrote in a letter from Berlin to his friend, Emil Boesen, in Copenhagen: "I have begun to attend lectures. I heard one by Marheineke with which I was quite pleased, for although it did not contain anything new, it was very nice to hear much of that which one is accustomed to seeing in print. Schelling has not yet begun."[1] The biographical background to this brief statement is probably commonplace: on 25 October, that is, just after the defense of his master's thesis, *The Concept of Irony*, and just two weeks after the end of his engagement fiasco, Kierkegaard had sailed with the postal ship from Copenhagen to Berlin, where he stayed until 6 March 1842. The purpose of the stay was, on one hand, to work on *Either/Or* and, on the other hand, to attend the lectures of Schelling, who in 1840 had been hired as professor in Berlin in order "to wipe out the dragon seed of Hegelian pantheism" in German philosophy.[2]

The passage cited above, along with other epistolary evidence,[3] shows that Kierkegaard took the opportunity of his stay—in the "only place in Germany worth visiting for scholarly reasons"[4]—to attend three further courses offered by more or less famous contemporaries, namely the Hegelian Karl Werder, the Norwegian Romantic and Schellingian natural philosopher Heinrich Steffens, and the aforementioned theologian Philipp K. Marheineke.[5] In what follows, the focus will be exclusively on the last of these three.

---

1 *B&A*, vol. 1, p. 71 / *LD*, Letter 49, p. 90.

2 *SKS* K19, 421.

3 See, for example, *B&A*, vol. 1, pp. 83f. / *LD*, Letter 55, pp. 106f.

4 *B&A*, vol. 1, p. 85 / *LD*, Letter 55, p. 108.

5 As is documented in the Berlin course catalogue of Winter Semester 1841–42, Kierkegaard would also have had the opportunity there to meet numerous other academic celebrities in person: among the theologians, for example, Hengstenberg, Neander and Twesten, among the philosophers, for example, Gabler, Michelet and Trendelenburg.

I.

Born in Hildesheim in 1780, Marheineke was among the most internationally renowned German theologians after Schleiermacher's death in 1834.[6] First, a professor ordinarius in philosophy in Erlangen (1805), he was appointed in 1807 as extraordinarius, in 1809 as professor ordinarius in systematic and practical theology in Heidelberg. There he became the topic of much discussion through his *Christliche Symbolik*[7] in three volumes (1810–13).[8] In 1811, he accepted an appointment to the newly founded Friedrich-Wilhelms-Universität in Berlin, where he worked alongside Schleiermacher, Martin Leberecht de Wette and August Neander. With regard to his research and area of specialization, at least until 1819, when he gave up the field to the benefit of Neander, he was especially active as a church historian, to which his four-volume *Geschichte der teutschen Reformation* bears special witness.[9] During the Berlin years, a successive shift in Marheineke's interest to the field of Christian dogmatics and the history of dogma can be observed. The first fruits of this shift are *Die Grundlehren der christlichen Dogmatik*, which appeared in 1819.[10] This work still displays the influence of Schelling and Carl Daub, a colleague from Heidelberg whom Marheineke greatly esteemed throughout his entire career.[11]

A decisive theological and philosophical change occurred with Hegel's appointment to a professorship in Berlin in 1818. Both the personal contact to Hegel and the intensive study of his works motivated Marheineke to rework his dogmatics, which then appeared again in 1827 under the—in fact more than slightly modified[12]—title *Die Grundlehren der christlichen Dogmatik als Wissenschaft*.[13] The agenda he followed in this work was that of a reconciliation of Christian theology with philosophy, of faith and knowledge, of religious ideas and abstract understanding via speculative thought—a program to which Marheineke remained true until his death

---

6 My biographical sketch draws on the information provided by the editors of Marheineke's posthumous lectures; see *D. Philipp Marheineke's System der theologischen Moral*, ed. by St. Matthies and W. Vatke, Berlin: Duncker und Humblot 1847 (vol. 1 in *D. Philipp Marheineke's theologische Vorlesungen*, ed. by St. Matthies and W. Vatke, Berlin: Duncker und Humblot, 1847–19, vols. 1–4) (hereafter *V1*), pp. ix–xxiv.

7 Philipp Marheineke, *Christliche Symbolik oder historischkritische und dogmatischkomparative Darstellung des katholischen, lutherischen, reformierten und socianischen Lehrbegriffs*, Heidelberg: Mohr und Zimmer 1810–13.

8 For the bibliographical information, I have made use of *V1*, pp. xi–xxii; see also Rupprecht's exhaustive bibliography in Eva-Maria Rupprecht, *Kritikvergessene Spekulation. Das Religions- und Theologieverständnis der spekulativen Theologie Philipp Konrad Marheinekes*, Frankfurt am Main, New York: Peter Lang 1993, pp. 323–9.

9 Marheineke, *Geschichte der teutschen Reformation*, vols. 1–2, Berlin: Duncker und Humblot 1816 (2nd ed., 1831), vols. 3–4, 1831–34.

10 Marheineke, *Die Grundlehren der christlichen Dogmatik*, Berlin: Dümmler 1819.

11 See the editors' remarks in *V1*, p. xix.

12 Regarding this, see Karl Barth, *Die protestantische Theologie im 19. Jahrhundert. Ihre Vorgeschichte und ihre Geschichte*, 4th ed., Zürich: Theologischer Verlag 1981, pp. 445f.

13 Marheineke, *Die Grundlehren der christlichen Dogmatik als Wissenschaft*, 2nd ed., Berlin: Duncker und Humblot 1827.

in 1846. In numerous writings and lectures, he tirelessly tried to win recognition for this project, albeit with varying degrees of success.

His various efforts are evidenced not only by four posthumous lecture volumes (1847–49),[14] edited by his students, Conrad Stephan Matthies and Wilhelm Vatke, but also by the *Einleitung in die öffentlichen Vorlesungen über die Bedeutung der Hegelschen Philosophie in der christlichen Theologie* (1842)[15] and his later work, *Zur Kritik der Schellingschen Offenbarungsphilosophie* (1843).[16] There can be no doubt that it is precisely this, that is, in the parlance of his own time, "right-Hegelian" dogmatician, whom Kierkegaard is interested in, as he sets out to examine his own preconception of Marheineke (which up until then had only been formed by reading his books) by first-hand experience in his lectures.

II.

It is obvious that Kierkegaard was well prepared for this undertaking; by this time, he had already familiarized himself with *Die Grundlehren* in the new edition from 1827 and with Marheineke's propaedeutical *Lehrbuch des christlichen Glaubens und Lebens* from 1823.[17] He had also acquainted himself with Marheineke's

---

14 It was originally planned (in addition to vol. 1, *Christliche Moral*; vol. 2, *Christliche Dogmatik*; vol. 3, *Christliche Symbolik*; vol. 4, *Christliche Dogmengeschichte*) to publish a fifth volume, which was to contain Marheineke's lectures on practical theology: see *V1*, p. v.

15 *Einleitung in die öffentlichen Vorlesungen über die Bedeutung der Hegelschen Philosophie in der christlichen Theologie*, Frankfurt am Main: Minerva 1983 [1842]. See further Marheineke's introductions in the first (1832: pp. xi–xvi) and second edition (1840: pp. v–x) of vol. 11 of *Hegel's Werke* (vols. 1–18, Berlin: Duncker und Humblot 1832–45), which he himself edited containing the first part of Hegel's posthumous *Vorlesungen über die Philosophie der Religion*.

16 Marheineke, *Zur Kritik der Schellingschen Offenbarungsphilosophie. Schluß der öffentlichen Vorlesungen über die Bedeutung der Hegelschen Philosophie in der christlichen Theologie*, Berlin: Enslin 1843 (*ASKB* 647).

17 Marheineke, *Lærebog i christelig Tro og Levnet for tænkende Christne*, trans. by M. Mørch Hansen, Copenhagen: P.G. Philipsen 1842 [originally as *Lehrbuch des christlichen Glaubens und Lebens: zum Gebrauch in den oberen Klassen an den Gymnasien und für die reifere Jugend überhaupt*, Berlin: Nicolai 1823]. Kierkegaard owned both works, the latter in the Danish translation from 1842 *and* in the second German edition (see *ASKB* 644, 646 and 257). According to the editor of the *Papirer*, he refers—for example, in *Pap.* VII–2 B 235, p. 97 / *BA*, 55—to both. See also *Pap.* I C 25–6, in *Pap.* XII, pp. 131–2 as excerpts of *Die Grundlehren der christlichen Dogmatik als Wissenschaft*, op. cit. Already as a student, in 1831, Kierkegaard had quoted excerpts from, and otherwise referred to, vol. 1 of Marheineke's *Geschichte der teutschen Reformation*, op. cit.—especially to passages dealing with Luther's life and works (see *Pap.* I C 1, in *Pap.* XII, pp. 3–16). Later, in writing *The Concept of Anxiety*, Marheineke's *Zur Kritik der Schellingschen Offenbarungsphilosophie*, op. cit., had his special attention (*ASKB* 647) (see *SKS* 4, 364 / *CA*, 59). Aside from the works already mentioned, Kierkegaard owned (a) the aforementioned posthumous edition of Daub's lectures in seven volumes (*ASKB* 472–472g); (b) the aforementioned edition of Hegel's works for which Marheineke was partly responsible (*ASKB* 549–565; *ASKB* 1384–1386); (c) the *Institutiones symbolicae*, 3rd ed., Berlin: Voss 1830 (*ASKB* 645); finally and as the only secondary source

work indirectly. As early as Kierkegaard's time as a student at the University of Copenhagen, Henrik Nikolai Clausen (1793–1877) had made sporadic reference to his colleague in Berlin in his course on dogmatics in 1833–34.[18] Hans Lassen Martensen must also have referred to Marheineke and to his *Die Grundlehren* in his two-semester lecture course on speculative dogmatics in 1838–39.[19] And since the 1841–42 lectures, at least in method, intent and outline, if not in delivery, must have borne certain specific resemblances to the dogmatics of 1827, Kierkegaard's statement that it contained "nothing new" hardly seems surprising.

This is the case, however, only if it is assumed, with the editors of the *Papirer*,[20] that the comment concerns Marheineke's lecture on *Die christliche Dogmatik, mit Rücksicht auf Daubs System*, which Kierkegaard attended in the winter of 1841–42. For in the same period Marheineke also held another lecture, *Die christliche Dogmengeschichte*.[21] The problem is that Kierkegaard does not mention anywhere which lecture he actually attended.[22] Contrary to the *communis opinio*, the current editors of *Søren Kierkegaards Skrifter* assert that it is in fact the latter lecture course.[23] As evidence, they draw on three observations.[24] First of all, Kierkegaard's notes correspond (even to the point of the exact wording) to Marheineke's lectures in volume two of the posthumously published *System der christlichen Dogmatik*. Secondly, both sources, each under the title, "Die kirchliche Vorstellung," contain a series of paragraphs with a decidedly historical profile. Thirdly, neither of the texts addresses "Daub's system."

The correctness of all three observations notwithstanding, they do not, in my opinion, lead to the conclusion they are meant to support. *Pro primo*, Kierkegaard explicitly explains (in the epistle to Boesen quoted above) that he was satisfied to hear "nothing new" in Marheineke's lectures, but rather that which he was accustomed to see in print already. At this point in time, however, no history of Christian dogmatics

---

(d) J. Görres, *Die Triarier H. Leo, P. Marheinecke* [sic!], *K. Bruno*, Regensburg: Verlag von G. Joseph Manz 1838 (*ASKB* 533).

18 *SKS* 19, 7–85, Not1. *SKS* 19, 30; 57f. Since these passages contain Kierkegaard's marginal notes, they may possibly originate from as late as 1839 or 1840 (*SKS* K19, 10).

19 *SKS* 18, 374–386, KK:11. See, for example, Martensen's suggested reading on speculative dogmatics found in a third party's lecture notes, in which (aside from Hegel, Daub, Baader et al.) the second edition of Marheineke's *Die Grundlehren* is also listed: *Pap.* II C 26–27, in *Pap.* XIII, p. 7; p. 11.

20 See their introduction to *Pap.* III C 26, in *Pap.* XIII, p. 197; further Niels Thulstrup, *Kierkegaards Verhältnis zu Hegel und zum spekulativen Idealismus 1835–1846. Historisch-analytische Untersuchung*, Stuttgart: Kohlhammer 1972, p. 221.

21 *SKS* K19, 331.

22 Both would have been chronologically possible. For, as can be gleaned from the *Verzeichnis der Vorlesungen, welche von der Friedrich-Wilhelms-Universität zu Berlin im Winterhalbenjahre 1841–42 vom 11. October an gehalten werden* (available in the archives of the Humboldt University, Berlin), neither of Marheineke's two lectures overlaps one or more of those lecture courses which Kierkegaard attended in this semester (Schelling, Steffens, Werder).

23 Ibid., p. 328; p. 331.

24 Ibid., pp. 331f.

by Marheineke was available in print, but only his *Die Grundlehren* (in the two versions from 1819 and 1827). Furthermore, it appears *a priori* improbable that Kierkegaard, whose interest was doubtless focused on Marheineke as a Hegelian dogmatist, should have attended his historical lecture course in Berlin, especially when at the same time he had the opportunity to attend his dogmatics lectures.

A third observation, though, is decisive: if the editors were correct, then what was published posthumously by Matthies and Vatke in 1847 under the title, *System der christlichen Dogmatik*, would originally, that is, in its lecture form, have borne the title, *Christliche Dogmengeschichte*. However, such a significant alteration by the editors of Marheineke's unpublished work seems wildly unlikely; nor is there any indication of such an alteration in the foreword to their edition.[25] Furthermore, this suggestion ignores the fact that with volume four of the posthumous lectures Marheineke's *Dogmengeschichte* is already existent in printed form.[26] And in fact Kierkegaard's notes do *not* correspond to this work.[27] Thus, either we deduce from the available text of Kierkegaard's notes which of Marheineke's lectures he actually attended, in which case it cannot have been the history of Christian dogmatics; or we assume that it is in fact this very course, in which case our assumption lacks textual evidence. I conclude that in all probability Kierkegaard attended Marheineke's course on dogmatics in Berlin, that is, the course which corresponds to the text which was published posthumously in 1847 under the title *System der christlichen Dogmatik*.

Nevertheless, how is the explicit reference to "Daub's system" in the lecture of 1841–42 to be explained under this presupposition—especially when, as a closer examination reveals, Kierkegaard's notes on the lecture in fact only once refer explicitly to Daub?[28] A possible answer would draw on Kierkegaard's rhapsodic note taking.[29] But this escape route is already blocked since the published version

---

[25] The editors apparently relied on the "letzte Form der Ausarbeitung" (*V1*, p. vii) of the lectures. As here, though, in comparison to the then still existing earlier versions, "oft Veränderungen, Tilgungen, Zusätze," (ibid.) were added by Marheineke's hand, the final editing required a "*Vergleichung treu nachgeschriebener Hefte, durch welche denn auch hin und wieder dem Zusammenhange und leichteren Verständnisse nachgeholfen ist*," (ibid.). In other words, the editors attempted to reconstruct (a) out of the last hand lectures, as well as with the help of (b) the students' lecture notes a publishable version of each text. They claim, however, "*Marheinekes Werk nach Inhalt und Form ohne fremde Zuthat dem Publicum zu übergeben*," (ibid.). Under these prerequisites, an alteration of a lecture's title on their own authority seems more than improbable.

[26] *D. Philipp Marheineke's christliche Dogmengeschichte*, ed. by St. Matthies and W. Vatke, Berlin 1849 (vol. 4 in *Ph. Marheineke's theologische Vorlesungen*, ed. by St. Matthies and W. Vatke, op. cit.) (hereafter *V4*).

[27] Even a superficial glance at the table of contents of the historical lecture (*V4*, pp. vf.) confirms that—despite a basic analogy in the trinitaric structure—it diverges considerably from both the dogmatic system of 1847 and the dogmatic lecture of 1841.

[28] *SKS* 19, 273, Not9:1. See *D. Philipp Marheineke's System der christlichen Dogmatik*, ed. by St. Matthies and W. Vatke, Berlin: Duncker und Humblot 1847 (vol. 2 in *Ph. Marheineke's theologische Vorlesungen*, ed. by St. Matthies and W. Vatke, op. cit.) (hereafter: *V2*), p. 326.

[29] A fact to which even a superficial glance at the table of contents of Kierkegaard's notes (*Pap.* III C 26, in *Pap.* xiii, p. 198) in comparison to the system of 1847 already bears witness: see *V2*, pp. v–x.

of the text also contains only three explicit Daub references.[30] The real reason, then, must be sought elsewhere. One thing, though, is for certain: the expression "Daub's system," as the editors of the *Papirer* already correctly conjecture,[31] refers to the Heidelberg theologian's *System der christlichen Dogmatik*, the first part of which Marheineke had published in 1841, that is, in the very same year that he lectured on his own dogmatic system "taking Daub's system into account."[32] We also have to bear in mind that Daub's system itself had been drafted in an attempt to deal with the second edition of Marheineke's *Die Grundlehren* and that Daub even held his own lectures on that "Compendium"[33] of his younger colleague.[34] In this context, Marheineke reports that for Daub the use of the former's instruction book only had

> ...the goal of giving to the auditors a guide by means of which they could in general orient themselves in the material to be treated. The lecture followed precisely the external order of the textbook, with respect to the sequence of the paragraphs, the Biblical passages, etc. With regard to the rest, the lecture was developed wholly independently and on its own.[35]

Marheineke indicates that due to the close methodological drawing upon the draft, on the one hand, and to the technically independent further development of its content, on the other, a new edition of his long out-of-print *Lehrbuch* seemed henceforth superfluous.[36] This was not the only reason why he wished for the time being to step back and restrict himself to oral instruction.[37] Marheineke notes this in March 1841, a good half year before he began the program just mentioned, namely of presenting his dogmatic reflections orally, that is, in the form of a lecture.

In my opinion, the "account of Daub's system," with which this lecture is conceived, refers to nothing other than that "independence and autonomy" with which

---

30 *V2*, p. 62; p. 315; p. 326.

31 *Pap.* III C 26, in *Pap.* XIII, p. 197.

32 The second part appeared in 1844, the complete edition of the lectures (vols. 1–7) 1838–44 in Berlin. For an interpretation of Daub's theology in general, see Ewald Stübinger, *Die spekulative Theologie Carl Daubs als Kritik der positionellen Theologie*, Frankfurt am Main, New York: Peter Lang 1993; further Falk Wagner, *Die vergessene spekulative Theologie. Zur Erinnerung an Karl Daub anläßlich seines 150. Todestages* (*Theologische Studien*, vol. 133), Zürich: Theologischer Verlag 1987. The bibliographical overview is found ibid., p. 7 (Wagner erroneously presumes eight instead of seven volumes: part I and II/1 of the *System der theologischen Moral* were bound together in one volume, however).

33 Daub, *System der christlichen Dogmatik*, vol. 2 (1844) in *Philosophische und theologische Vorlesungen*, vols. 1–7, ed. by [Philipp] Marheineke and [Theophor Wilhelm] Dittenberger, Berlin: Duncker und Humblot 1838–44, p. 141 (*ASKB* 472–472g).

34 "Vorrede" in *C. Daub's System der christlichen Dogmatik*, vol. 6 (1841), in *Philosophische und theologische Vorlesungen*, ibid. (hereafter *VR*), p. x. Furthermore, Daub deemed the second edition of the *Grundlehren* worthy of a lengthy review; see his "Ph.K. Marheineke, *Die Grundlehren der christlichen Dogmatik als Wissenschaft* (1827)" (*Jahrbücher für wissenschaftliche Kritik*, vol. 2, 1827, pp. 1684–1728; pp. 1729–33; continued in vol. 1, 1828, pp. 118ff. and in 2, 1828, pp. 197–251).

35 *VR*, p. x.

36 Ibid., pp. xf.

37 Ibid., p. xii.

Daub had developed and modified Marheineke's views. Although his dogmatics may be "uncommonly similar"[38] to that of Daub at its core, its independent modifications include in some parts palpable criticism of his former pupil's claims. He then takes account of this criticism by attempting, in his lecture of 1841, to resolve those flaws in *Die Grundlehren* of 1827 to which he admits, and thus to do justice to the criticism of his Heidelberg teacher and colleague.[39] Given that Marheineke was wont regularly to rework and alter his lecture manuscripts,[40] the conjecture seems hardly far-fetched that he should have simply dropped any reference to Daub in the later versions, according to the current focus or developmental stage of his dogmatic reflections.[41] This would explain, in any case, why any reference to Daub in the posthumously published system of 1847 is missing.

III.

The focus of the conference which originally served as the occasion for writing the present article was Kierkegaard's journals and notebooks from 1833–46;[42] my own text is supposed to be an inventory of Kierkegaard's reception of Marheineke, and in particular of his dogmatics. That the one has to do with the other, and to what extent, has hitherto only been demonstrated on the basis of some philological and historical evidence, leading to the conclusion that those passages from Kierkegaard's

---

38 Horst Stephan, *Geschichte der evangelischen Theologie seit dem Deutschen Idealismus*, Berlin: Töpelmann 1938, p. 75.

39 As evidence for this, just one example: Daub criticizes Marheineke's use of the expression *Offenbarsein in Gott* in the first paragraph of the second, christological part of his *Die Grundlehren der christlichen Dogmatik als Wissenschaft*, op. cit., pp. 123ff. As it indicates "a becoming" (see Daub, *System der christlichen Dogmatik*, op. cit., vol. 2, p. 140), "*kraft dessen das Dunkle in's Klare gesetzt, das Ungewisse in's Gewisse verwandelt werde*" (ibid.). This, however, may in his opinion at most be said of man, but not of God. Daub himself speaks of an eternal "*Sichselbstoffenbarsein Gottes*" (ibid.) in his identity of essence and being instead. Marheineke takes on the same term in the corresponding passage of his lecture of 1841 (*SKS* 19, 249, Not9:1; as a parallel *V2*, p. 128).

40 *vi*, p. v; p. vii.

41 Thulstrup's supposition goes in a similar direction: he draws from the reference to Daub what is in my opinion a quite plausible conclusion, namely that the lecture presents "in der Formulierung ein Zwischenstadium...zwischen der stark umgearbeiteten 2. Ausgabe des Werkes *Die Grundlehren der christlichen Dogmatik*, die in recht knapper Form gehalten war, und der besseren, posthum erschienenen Darstellung *System der christlichen Dogmatik* (1847)" (*Kierkegaards Verhältnis zu Hegel*, op. cit., p. 221). As a paradigmatic text reference *SKS* 19, 301, Not10:9 shall suffice: Here Kierkegaard adds under III the heading *Friheden* (Freedom). A paragraph with this title is missing in the *System* of 1847 (see ibid., the corresponding paragraph *Von der Rechtfertigung*: *V2*, pp. 470–88), but not in *Die Grundlehren der christlichen Dogmatik als Wissenschaft* of 1827, where it appears—exactly as in the lecture of 1841—as a third main part in the second paragraph of part III (see *Die Grundlehren der christlichen Dogmatik als Wissenschaft*, op. cit., pp. 302–19). With this outline the lecture is therefore still rooted in *Die Grundlehren der christlichen Dogmatik als Wissenschaft*, and thus presents an intermediary stage between this and the final version of 1847.

42 *SKS* vols. 17–19.

Notebooks 9 and *10*, which contain his notes on the Marheineke lectures of 1841–42,[43] with great probability recount his lecture course on dogmatics—that very course which two of his students published posthumously in 1847 under the title *System der christlichen Dogmatik*. If this purely philological and historical inventory is to be incorporated into a more sufficient context of the history of reception, then we are faced *de re* as well as methodologically with the following alternatives: on the one hand, we can insert Kierkegaard's notes as one stone in a mosaic among others into the cluster of Marheineke references found implicitly and explicitly in his journals and notebooks between 1833 and 1846 in order, on this basis, to reconstruct at least the outlines of a coherent picture of Kierkegaard's view of the former.

On the other hand, a contribution to Marheineke research in a stricter sense would also be possible. As the editors of *Søren Kierkegaards Skrifter* have meticulously demonstrated, Kierkegaard's notes yield not only astounding parallels over longer passages, but also, at least in the final parts, significant differences to the version published in 1847.[44] And since these notes are the only source available for comparison,[45] they could also, at least indirectly, be made fruitful for Marheineke research in a stricter sense. In what follows I must restrict myself to the former aspect, not only due to the thematic focus of my article but also because, in attending to the latter, substantial results might only be hoped for, if, on the one hand, Marheineke's unpublished works could be examined for purposes of a literary–critical or material comparison and if, on the other hand, all three sources, that is, the unpublished works, the system of 1847 and *Die Grundlehren* of 1827, would be compared. However, I must refrain from this here since the required unpublished works are unavailable, and since the task, even if the basis of sources were sufficient for its execution, would require a separate enquiry.[46]

Now, if one distinguishes *explicit* references (that is, material and/or nominal ones) from *implicit* (that is, purely material) references, and furthermore *direct* (that

---

43 *SKS* 19, 247–77, Not9:2. *SKS* 19, 288–301, Not10:8–9.

44 *SKS* 19, especially pp. 297–301, Not10:9; also *SKS* K19, especially pp. 409ff.

45 According to the library staff of the Humboldt University (Berlin) an archive for the preservation of Marheineke's posthumous works and lecture manuscripts does not exist.

46 Two additional circumstances make such an enquiry appear not only almost impossible, but also dispensible: *firstly,* most of the divergences on the last pages of Kierkegaard's notes (see *SKS* 19, 297–301) from the 1847 version are not pertinent to the actual issue, but rather brief and insignificant addenda or clarifications. More substantial additions appear only in three places: on one hand, in the context of an explanation of the predestination problem (*SKS* 19, 298. 22–32, Not10:9); on the other hand, in connection with an analysis of the subjective prerequisites of conversion (*SKS* 19, 299.36–300.6, Not10:9); and finally in the context of a dogmatical account of sanctification, in which Marheineke inserts a paragraph on the concept of the holy (*SKS* 19, 300.24–39). *Secondly*, it is plain to see that those passages, where the lecture actually diverges from the 1847 version, do *not* reflect Marheineke's recourse to Daub's *System*. For these divergences pertain with no exception to the concluding third part of the dogmatics, specifically to the doctrine of grace. However, Daub's system, as has been pointed out already, remained a torso: the concluding third part, which, among other things, would have developed the doctrine of grace, was never written, or at least never published or delivered as a lecture (see *VR*, p. x).

is, originating from Kierkegaard himself) from *indirect* references (that is, those mediated through third parties in Kierkegaard's work) to Marheineke's person and work, an examination of the sources yields the following results. (A) *Explicitly and directly*, Marheineke is only once referred to in Kierkegaard's pseudonymous works.[47] Excepting a reasonably small number of citations,[48] excerpts,[49] and the aforementioned lecture notes,[50] the same goes for the journals: even here Marheineke's name is only mentioned once.[51] Finally, both of the explicit Marheineke references in the letters[52] are also to the lectures of 1841–42. (B) *Explicit and indirect* references are only to be found in Clausen[53] and Martensen.[54] (C) *Implicit and direct* allusions prove naturally somewhat more difficult to localize. Worthy of mention are, among some more or less unambiguous instances in the pseudonymous works, a passage about the erroneous interpretation of faith;[55] a further series of materially central passages which criticize the "volatilization"[56] of the Christian doctrine through (right-) Hegelianism;[57] a further note from the journals[58] anticipating the aforementioned passage from the treatise on anxiety, as well as two similar passages which can be read as an implicit criticism of Marheineke's concept of revelation.[59] (D) The *implicit and indirect* references can be ignored here as irrelevant since they

---

47 *SKS* 4, 364 / *CA*, 59: on Marheineke's *Zur Kritik der Schellingschen Offenbarungsphilosophie*, op. cit., pp. 46f. See *V2*, p. 2.

48 *Pap.* I C 26, in *Pap.* XII, pp. 131–2: on *Die Grundlehren der christlichen Dogmatik als Wissenschaft*, op. cit., p. 4.

49 *Pap.* I C 1, in Pap XII, pp. 3–16: on *Die Grundlehren der christlichen Dogmatik als Wissenschaft*, op. cit. *Pap.* I C 25, in *Pap.* XII, pp. 131–2 / *JP* 5, 5065: on *Geschichte der teutschen Reformation*, op. cit., vol. 1.

50 *SKS* 19, 249–77, Not9:1 and *SKS* 19, 288–301, Not10:8–9: on the lecture of 1841–42.

51 *SKS* 19, 246, Not8:52–53 / *JP* 3, 3285: probably also about the aforementioned lecture.

52 *B&A*, vol. 1, p. 71 / *LD*, Letter 49, p. 90. *B&A*, vol. 1, p. 83 / *LD*, Letter 55, p. 106.

53 *SKS* 19, 30, Not1:6 and *SKS* 19, 57–8, Not1:7; *SKS* 19, 384–91, Not13:2–23; *SKS* 19, 227ff., Not8; *SKS* 19, 209f., Not7:9–19: on *Die Grundlehren der christlichen Dogmatik als Wissenschaft*, op. cit.

54 *Pap.* II C 26–7, in *Pap.* XIII, p. 7 and p. 11: on *Die Grundlehren der christlichen Dogmatik als Wissenschaft*, op. cit. summarily or as bibliographical reference.

55 *SKS* 4, 318 / *CA*, 10: on *Die Grundlehren der christlichen Dogmatik als Wissenschaft*, op. cit., pp. 48f.

56 "*Forflygtigelse*" and "*forflygtige*" are Kierkegaard's own terms; the Hong edition, which I am following here, translates "volatilization" and "volatilize" throughout (see the following references).

57 See, for example, *SKS* 4, 318f., 341 / *CA*, 10f., 35. *SKS* 7, 199, 521, 526 / *CUP1*, 217, 573, 579.

58 *Pap.* I A 273 / *JP* 2, 1096.

59 Analogously to *SKS* 19, 246, Not8:52–3. See *Pap.* VII–2 B 235, p. 97 / *BA*, 55: probably about *Lehrbuch des christlichen Glaubens und Lebens*, op. cit., p. 69; pp. 89f.; see also *Die Grundlehren der christlichen Dogmatik als Wissenschaft*, op. cit., pp. xviiiff.; pp. 15ff.; pp. 125f.; further *Pap.* VI– 2 B 235, p. 206 / *BA*, 119: on *Zur Kritik der Schellingschen Offenbarungsphilosophie*, op. cit., pp. 9ff.; pp. 21f.

contribute nothing to an account of the *Kierkegaardian* reception of Marheineke.[60] Seen schematically, this overview yields the following picture:

	explicit	**implicit**
direct	1. *Pseudonymous works:* *SKS* 4, 364 / *CA*, 59 [1844]	1. *Pseudonymous works*, e.g.: *SKS* 4, 318f., 341 / *CA*, 10f., 35 [1844] *SKS* 7, 199, 521, 526 / *CUP1*, 217, 573, 579 [1846]
	2. *Journals and notebooks*: *Pap.* I C 1, in *Pap.* XII, pp. 3–16 [1831–32] *Pap.* I C 25, in *Pap.* XII, pp. 131–2 / *JP* 5, 5065 [1834–35] *Pap.* I C 26, in *Pap.* XII, pp. 131–2 [1834–35] *SKS* 19, 249–77, Not9:1; *SKS* 19, 288–301, Not10:8–9 [1841–42] *SKS* 19, 246, Not8:52–3 / *JP* 3, 3285 [1841]	2. *Journals and notebooks*, e.g.: *Pap.* I A 273 / *JP* 2, 1096 [1836] *Pap.* VII–2 B 235, pp. 97f. / *BA*, 55 [1846–47] *Pap.* VII–2 B 235, p. 206 / *BA*, 119 [1846–47]
	3. *Letters:* *B&A*, vol. 1, pp. 71f. and pp. 83f. / *LD*, Letter 49, p. 90, and Letter 55, p. 106 [1841]	3. *Letters*:
indirect	1. *Pseudonymous works*:	[irrelevant]
	2. *Journals and notebooks:* *SKS* 19, 30, Not1:6 [1833–34] *SKS* 19, 57f., Not1:7 [1833–34 or 1839–40] *Pap.* II C 26–27, in *Pap.* XIII, p. 7; p. 11) [1838–39]	[irrelevant]

60 The following quotation from Martensen's lecture on speculative dogmatics from 1838 may serve as a paradigmatic example of a material reflection of Marheineke's revelation–theological accentuation of the trinitarian idea (see, for example, *V2*, pp. 410–18, especially pp. 416ff.): "*Da Gud...som Fader, Søn og Aand ikke blot har aabenbaret sin Villie men sit Væsen, staar Gud gjennem denne sin væsentlige Aabenbaring ikke blot i Relation til Verden, men ogsaa i uendelig Relation til sig selv*" (*SKS* 18, 382, KK:11).

Even a superficial perusal of these passages yields five peculiarities of Kierkegaard's reception of Marheineke. *First*, it is concentrated in the time-period from 1831 to 1846, that is, roughly from Kierkegaard's university studies until the temporary end of his pseudonymous writings. *Second*, in its portrayal and judgment of Marheineke from the early journal notes[61] to the late allusions in the *Book on Adler*,[62] the profile of this reception displays a hardly surprising continuity. There are, in other words, no grave breaks or changes in Kierkegaard's reading of Marheineke. *Third*, he sees the Berlin theologian, especially on the basis of his writings during and following the 1820s,[63] as a paradigmatic right-wing Hegelian, that is, as a representative of that school of Hegelian theologians who answer affirmatively to the question debated so fervently after the master's death in 1831 of whether the contents of the Christian religion, or its biblical foundation, require and/or admit of a transformation into the form of speculative thinking.[64] *Fourth*, the tendency of his references to Marheineke, implicit or explicit, is thoroughly critical—although it must be added that Kierkegaard aims much more numerous and vehement attacks at Martensen's variant of speculative theology than that of his Berlin colleague.[65] *Fifth* and finally, from the point of view of typology of reception, we can classify Kierkegaard's treatment of Marheineke as a borderline case between unproductive and productive reception.[66] A reception is unproductive, if and only if, although author A has evidently been taken note of by author B (be it ever so sporadically or briefly), this reception leaves no or only marginal (explicit and/or implicit) traces in B's writings.[67] A genuinely productive reception is distinguished by the central role that author A's work takes

61 *Pap.* I A 273 / *JP* 2, 1096.

62 See, for example, *Pap.* VII–2 B 235, p. 206 / *BA*, 119.

63 Here especially *Die Grundlehren der christlichen Dogmatik als Wissenschaft*, op. cit., and the *Lehrbuch des christlichen Glaubens und Lebens*, op. cit.

64 See Horst Stuke, "Hegelianismus," in *Historisches Wörterbuch der Philosophie*, vols. 1–12, ed. by Joachim Ritter et al., Basel et al.: Schwabe 1971–2004, vol. 3, 1974, p. 1028. The question may still remain whether Marheineke claimed, or would have claimed, the Straussian label "right-Hegelian" (ibid.) for himself (see, for example, Marheineke's *Einleitung in die öffentlichen Vorlesungen*, op. cit., p. 27); what is meant by it reflects Marheineke's self-understanding in any case (see, for example, *V2*, pp. 17f.; pp. 20f.; p. 24; *Einleitung in die öffentlichen Vorlesungen*, op. cit., p. 12; p. 14; pp. 37f.; p. 53). Insofar as Kierkegaard's assessment appears quite justified here, it also corresponds to the classification of other contemporaries: see, for example, Hans Lassen Martensen, *Af mit Levnet*, vols. 1–3, Copenhagen: Gyldendalske Boghandels Forlag 1882, vol. 1, pp. 95f.

65 A glance at the quantity and polemic tendency of the argument with Martensen, which was mainly carried out in the journals, may suffice here as evidence: see the references under the heading "Martensen" in Niels Jørgen Cappelørn's *Papirer* index (*Pap.* XV, pp. 226–30) as well as the individual passages listed there. See also Hermann Brandt, *Gotteserkenntnis und Weltentfremdung. Der Weg der spekulativen Theologie Hans Lassen Martensens*, Göttingen: Vandenhoeck & Ruprecht 1971, pp. 240–7.

66 This typology of reception is further explained in Heiko Schulz, "Die theologische Rezeption Kierkegaards in Deutschland und Dänemark. Notizen zu einer historischen Typologie," *Kierkegaard Studies. Yearbook*, 1999, pp. 220–44.

67 Such traces can be of the affirmative or (as is the case in Kierkegaard's reception of Marheineke) of the critical sort.

on in author B's work *vis-à-vis* type, content and genesis, even when traces of the former are only recognizable in isolated passages of the latter. Thus, on the one hand, the relative infrequency of unambiguous references and allusions in Kierkegaard's reception of Marheineke suggests more the unproductive variety. However, since, on the other hand, Kierkegaard profiles the Christian-theoretical corrective function of his pseudonymous work to a great extent against the negative backdrop of Hegelian speculation; and since, finally, Marheineke's writings contain a whole series of central concepts, theses and thought structures to which parallels are found in the *corpus Kierkegaardianum* (be they critical or laudatory),[68] one may rightly be able to speak of productive reception, or at least of substantial material reflection, even if a direct dependence in individual cases may prove difficult to demonstrate.[69]

---

68 I cite a number of select passages, to which in my opinion material parallels in Kierkegaard's thought and/or in that of his pseudonyms can be found: *Einleitung in die öffentlichen Vorlesungen*, op. cit., pp. 28f.; p. 43 (the contemptibility of those who assert *man müsse weiter gehen, über Hegel hinausgehen* (ibid., p. 43)); *V2*, p. 40; p. 236; p. 295; p. 296; p. 313; p. 315; p. 317 (Marheineke's anthropologically, hamartiologically and christologically accentuated concepts of the "universal man" versus the "absolute individual"); *V2*, pp. 50f. (Judaism as *Religion des Diesseits*); *V2*, pp. 81ff. (the threefold movement of religious–historical development from paganism to Judaism to Christianity); *V2*, pp. 181f.; p. 188 (the impossibility of tracing man back genetically to something extra- or prehuman); *V2*, p. 194; p. 213 (the state of innocence as the expression of both the greatest perfection and imperfection); *V2*, pp. 204ff.; p. 239 (the impermissibility of separating Adam from the context of humanity in its entirety); *V2*, p. 223 (the loss of innocence as an ambivalent, namely equally guilty and innocent, process); *V2*, p. 325 (God's powerlessness as the expression and proof of his omnipotence); *V2*, p. 436 (creation as completed first in and with Christ); *V2*, p. 454 (feeling as *die erste Erscheinungsweise, die noch in sich verschlossene Knospe der Religion*); *V2*, p. 484 (the new life of the justified sinner as a state in which the sins of his former life are *als Schmerz...aufgehoben*); *V2*, p. 537 (together with the *Bewußtseyn überhaupt kommt der Mensch auch zu dem seiner Freiheit*); *V2*, p. 553 (Christianity as "true humanity"); *V2*, p. 578 (the human spirit, in its *natürliche[m] Daseyn, in der Concretion mit einem Leibe ist Seele*, that is subjective spirit or self-consciousness); *V2*, p. 590 (as a unity of freedom and necessity the "self is spirit").

69 That Kierkegaard otherwise had a certain respect for Marheineke as a theologian can be concluded from the fact that of the four lecture courses which he attended in winter 1841–42, with the exception of Schelling's (*SKS* 19, 305–67, Not11), he only took notes more or less continuously and completely to Marheineke's. As to Werder's lecture, only sporadic notes have surfaced so far (*SKS* 19, 245, Not8:50–51. *SKS* 19, 278–82, Not9:2–9), whereas no notes at all exist on Steffens' lecture (See *LD*, Letter 55, pp. 106f.). Singularly enough, in Kierkegaard's epistulary portrayal of the person and presentation of those whom, or whose lectures, he heard in Berlin, only Marheineke escapes any mention whatsoever (see ibid.). One reason could be that the letter in question is directed to Sibbern, and Kierkegaard may have assumed that, as a philosopher, he would only be interested in the three philosophers, but not in the dogmatician Marheineke. A surprisingly sympathetic portrayal of Marheineke's person and presentation in Berlin is delivered by Friedrich Engels who attended the *Vorlesungen über die Bedeutung der Hegelschen Philosophie in der christlichen Theologie* (see *Einleitung in die öffentlichen Vorlesungen*, op. cit. as published version of the introductory lecture) in May 1842, that is, at a time, when Kierkegaard was already back in Copenhagen: see Engels' report in *Rheinische Zeitung*, 130 (10 May 1842). Regarding Marheineke's significance as a person

IV.

Let us now turn our attention to the critical core of Kierkegaard's Marheineke reception. The central objection against his dogmatics as well as against right Hegelianism in general is that they perform a "volatilization" of central Christian dogmatical concepts and theorems. A central example is hereafter discussed in greater detail, namely in that form which Kierkegaard gave it with reference to Marheineke's lecture in an already mentioned journal entry from 1841: "The doctrine of revelation as presented by Marheincke [sic!] in his *Dogmatik* serves to illuminate the philosophic volatilization of Christian doctrinal concepts....The doctrine of the image of God according to Marheincke's [sic!] lecture is also such a volatilization."[70] The entry was probably written in early December 1841, therefore in Berlin.[71] At this point in time Kierkegaard had attended and taken notes on those parts of the lecture which had as their topic the (here, so-called mediated) revelation of God as well as—in the second part of this superordinate theme—the doctrine of man in the image of God.[72] Now, since Kierkegaard *firstly* was only able to attend and take notes to one part of Marheineke's doctrine of revelation;[73] since *secondly* an entire series of later attacks on right Hegelianism focus on this very topic;[74] and since *thirdly* the thought of revelation occupies a central role in Marheineke's dogmatics, it behoves us not only to address this in its own right, but also to locate it in the outline of the entire system.

---

and as an academic teacher, see also Martensen's portrayal, in Hans Lassen Martensen, *Af mit Levnet*, op. cit., vol. 1, pp. 85ff.

70 *SKS* 19, 246, Not8:52–53 / *JP* 3, 3285. Kierkegaard is not the only one who formulates his accusation in such a way. Thus Rudolf Schmidt, a contemporary author equally inspired by Kierkegaard and Rasmus Nielsen, writes in retrospect: "*Den Hegelske Theologi [that is, speculative theology] forflygtede paa sin vis...Kjendsgerningerne og gjorde Aabenbaringens enfoldige Fremstilling til Symboler for den immanente Logiks abstrakteste Kategorier*." (Rudolf Schmidt, *Grundtvig og den tyske Orthodoxi*, Copenhagen: F.H. Eibes 1883, p. 100; here quoted from Carl Henrik Koch, *En flue på Hegels udødelige næse eller om Adolph Peter Adler og om Søren Kierkegaards forhold til ham*, Copenhagen: C.A. Reitzels Forlag 1990, p. 125.)

71 This is at least circumstantially suggested by the fact that it follows two entries dated 1 and 6 December: see *SKS* 19, 245, Not8:50–51 / *JP* 1, 257 and *JP* 2, 1592.

72 *SKS* 19, 250–5, Not9:1; also *V2*, pp. 140–96. These temporal and material parallels as well as Kierkegaard's twofold use of the word "lecture" [*Foredrag* or *foredrage*] lead us to conjecture that he is here in fact referring to Marheineke's *Vorlesung*, and not to his already *published* dogmatics, that is, *Die Grundlehren der christlichen Dogmatik als Wissenschaft* from 1827. If this is correct, however, it can, in connection with the fact that his note pertains explicitly to dogmatics and not to its history, count in support of my aforementioned hypothesis that Kierkegaard visited and took notes to Marheineke's dogmatics lecture in the winter of 1841–42, and not his history of the Christian dogma.

73 See the previous paragraph on the so-called immediate revelation: *V2*, pp. 112–40; as a comparison see *SKS* 19, 249f, Not9:1; *V2*, p. 126 corresponds to the beginning of Kierkegaard's notes (looking back on ibid., p. 125).

74 See, for example, *Pap.* VII–2 B 235, pp. 97; pp. 206ff. / *BA*, 55, 119f. *Pap.* VII–2 B 266.23.

Marheineke's dogmatics in its mature form of the 1840s is based in its outline on *Die Grundlehren* of 1819 and 1827. As such, it offers a dialectic of the Christian dogma, whose architectonic principle is trinitarian[75]—similar to the example of the portrayal of Christianity in Hegel's philosophy of religion in the edition edited by Marheineke.[76] Consistently enough, the trinity is not only materially explicated—namely in the concluding third part, the doctrine of "God the Spirit" qua pneumatology[77]—but also at the beginning of the entire work in its formal or genuinely principle–theoretical function.[78] Directly after the introduction, which determines the standpoint, element and motion of dogmatics as a speculative science mediated via a biblical–ecclesiastical conception,[79] the material dogmatics unfolds itself according to the well-known dialectical scheme in three parts (Of God, Of God the Son, Of God the Spirit),[80] each of which is subdivided into three headings,[81] though these too—at least in part—are divided into three main sections. Within each of these main sections, the dialectical scheme dominates again. In all of them the dogma is shown, raised to the height of the speculative "concept" (*Begriff*), as the

---

75 This trinitarian structure is no longer recognisable in Kierkegaard's notes; it is merely suggested in the heading of the final main part to which he took notes, "III. Læren om Aanden" (*SKS* 19, 293, Not10:8–9. *SKS* 19, 293–301, Not10:8–9; in comparison: *V2*, pp. 389–593).

76 See Emanuel Hirsch, *Geschichte der neuern evangelischen Theologie im Zusammenhang mit den allgemeinen Bewegungen des europäischen Denkens*, vols. 1–5, 4th ed., Gütersloh: G. Mohn 1968, vol. 5, p. 367.

77 See *V2*, pp. 389–593.

78 See *V2*, pp. 25f. This consistent trinitarian structure, with which Marheineke became a paragon in nineteenth-century theology, left its mark also on Martensen (see his *Den christelige Dogmatik*, Copenhagen: C.A. Reitzel 1849), although he, in contrast to his predecessor, shifts the materially dogmatic development of the doctrine of the Trinity from pneumatology into the doctrine of God (see ibid., pp. 123–36; also Brandt, *Gotteserkenntnis und Weltentfremdung*, op. cit., pp. 143f.; Hirsch, *Geschichte der neuern evangelischen Theologie*, op. cit., vol. 5, p. 367). Daub, too, took on Marheineke's specifications, though the third part of his system, that is, the pneumatology, remained unfulfilled (*System der christlichen Dogmatik*, op. cit., vol. 2; *VR*, p. x).

79 Ibid., pp. 1–26.

80 That Marheineke entitles the first part of his dogmatics "Von Gott" ("Of God"), and not, following ecclesiastical convention, "Von Gott, dem Vater" ("Of God the Father"), is without a doubt determined by that dialectical schematism upon which the system in its entirety is founded: for the concept of the Father already implies that moment of reciprocal relationality which, according to Marheineke, corresponds to the subject-, or the becoming-for-itself of God's substantiality, and hence, for him, can only be spoken of in part two ("Von Gott, dem Sohn"; "Of God the Son"). Daub has already noted that a theologically as well as philosophically unsolved problem is hidden behind this decision—here with regard to *Die Grundlehren der christlichen Dogmatik als Wissenschaft* of 1827, on which he had held his own lectures (*VR*, p. x): see C. Daub, *System der christlichen Dogmatik*, op. cit., vol. 1, p. 137. Hence, Daub prefers to leave the first part of his dogmatic system, in contrast to the second ("Vom Sohne Gottes"; "Of the Son of God"), entirely without a heading—an alternative which seems hardly less problematic.

81 Part 1: Wesen Gottes / Sein Gottes / Eigenschaften Gottes; Part 2: Unmittelbare Offenbarung (= Sohn) / Mittelbare Offenbarung (= Schöpfung, Erhaltung, Vorsehung) / Gottmensch; Part 3: Trinität / Gnadenwirkungen des Geistes / Reich Gottes.

reconciling "epitome of all antitheses"[82] in the biblical as well as in the (history of the) ecclesiastical "idea" (*Vorstellung*).[83] Thus, according to Marheineke, dogmatics as science "cannot and will not be only Christian faith but rather the self-knowing, self-conceiving faith, and thereby a knowledge, a grasping of faith and its collective context."[84]

However, to make faith and its content transparent for itself at the height of speculative thinking is, for Marheineke, tantamount to reaching the absolute self-certainty of divine revelation in the medium of such thinking. To this extent his entire dogmatics—at least in the versions of 1827 and 1847[85]—is nothing but a theology of revelation with speculative intentions, structured in a consistently trinitarian fashion.[86] The speculative accent falls firstly upon the concept of revelation itself: the term neither denotes—and in the broader, still not specifically religious sense—any

---

82 *V2*, p. 18; pp. 5ff.

83 Analogously to Marheineke's threefold structure, Daub's *Prolegomena*—also edited by the former—distinguishes an introduction to dogmatics from the standpoint of the Bible, of religion (not of the Church!) and of speculation; see Carl Daub, *Prolegomena zur Dogmatik*, vol. 2 (1839) *Philosophische und theologische Vorlesungen*, op. cit., pp. ixff. On the relation of concept and idea in Marheineke, see further *V2*, p. 18; p. 134 and p. 566; *Einleitung in die öffentlichen Vorlesungen*, op. cit., pp. 55ff. Marheineke profiles his attempt of a speculative synthesis of all doctrinal antipodes over great lengths in the treatment of the "self-misunderstood friends"—that is, supernanaturalism and rationalism (see *V2*, pp. 11f.)—on the one hand, the "'self-misunderstood enemies'" of the Christian dogma, that is, the left Hegelians (Feuerbachians and especially Straussians) on the other hand (see ibid., pp. 9ff.). See also *Einleitung in die öffentlichen Vorlesungen*, op. cit., pp. 15–26; pp. 26–50.

84 *V2*, pp. 17f.; p. 2. regarding Marheineke's concept of faith. See further: ibid., p. 2; p. 14; p. 57; p. 383. That he did not really carry out his program of a speculative reconstruction and justification of the entire Christian dogma, but on the contrary merely practiced a kind of pseudo-speculation for the sake of a mere accomodation of the biblical–ecclesiastical tradition, orthodox conventions of language and of rationalist theology is an often repeated objection in recent Marheineke scholarship: see Falk Wagner, "Der Gedanke der Persönlichkeit Gottes bei Ph. Marheineke," *Neue Zeitschrift für Systematische Theologie und Religionsphilosophie*, vol. 30, 1968, pp. 44–88; also Rupprecht, *Kritikvergessene Spekulation*, op. cit. (especially, pp. 219–23 and pp. 311–21) and Samuel M. Powell, "Philipp Konrad Marheineke," unpublished manuscript, especially p. 3; p. 19; pp. 24f.

85 Due to my decision for a methodic and material orientation toward Kierkegaard's central "volatilization" argument, insofar as it is articulated and founded in relation to Marheineke's dogmatics of 1841, I shall restrict myself here to the latter's *System* of 1847, and to the parallel texts in *SKS* vol. 19 as a reference source. A subtle interpretation of the idea of revelation in Marheineke's *Die Grundlehren* of 1827 is offered by Powell (see his "Philipp Konrad Marheineke," especially pp. 7f. and pp. 16–9); See also Rupprecht, *Kritikvergessene Spekulation*, op. cit., pp. 250–68.

86 On the meaning and function of the term revelation in Marheineke: *V2*, p. 2; p. 25; p. 112; pp. 128ff.; pp. 151ff.; p. 156; pp. 183ff.; p. 186; p. 188; p. 414; pp. 417f. It is indubitably this revelation–theological approach which made Marheineke's dogmatics (more specifically, their earlier versions from 1819 and 1827) seem so attractive to Barth: see his *Die protestantische Theologie im 19. Jahrhundert*, op. cit., pp. 444ff.; in this regard also Wolfhart Pannenberg, *Problemgeschichte der neueren evangelischen Theologie in Deutschland. Von Schleiermacher bis zu Barth und Tillich*, Göttingen: Vandenhoeck & Ruprecht 1997, p. 248; p. 258.

(regarding its source and content) *supernatural communication from God to man* nor stands—in a narrower sense—for each and every divine *self*-communication. In the dialectical "*Aufhebung*" of this second sense it must rather be understood speculatively, that is, as a "*self*-revelation of God."[87] In a properly Hegelian manner, God has to be conceived of not only as the source but also as the addressee and the medium of the revelatory process. Marheineke spells out this process in a genuinely trinitarian fashion: God is the identity of identity and difference, of substantiality and subjectivity, of being and thought, of object and subject, of eternity and time, of necessity and freedom—and this is, theologically speaking, made possible by the begetting of the Son and made real by virtue of love, that is through the Spirit as the "bond of unity,"[88] by which the Father eternally reveals himself to himself.[89]

Seen in the light of the general Protestant conviction that the trinitarian *opera ad extra sunt indivisa*,[90] the corresponding thesis, according to which the Son[91] and the Spirit[92] also function as principles of *creation*, can hardly come as a surprise. However, in Marheineke's work, this thesis takes on an important role, with regard to both a speculative and a revelation–theoretical perspective—and only for this reason is it worthy of mention at this point. *Pro primo*, it shall be made clear in this way that creation is actually understood as a (specifically mediated)[93] form of revelation, not the other way around with revelation being regarded as a purely concomitant phenomenon or as a purely instrumental end of creation—more generally speaking, as part of the "economical" dimension of the Trinity. God reveals himself not also and *inter alia* through his creation, so that it might already have its own theological significance apart from and independent of this revelation. The status of the divine act of creation, rather, is that of a mere medium of divine self-revelation. To this extent the thought of creation becomes functionalized in Marheineke's thought. Secondly, however, a genuine speculative functional determination of the Trinity in its economical dimension is closely connected with this move. For the *mediated* form of revelation is unthinkable without the *immediate* self-revelation of the Father in the Son.[94] In other words: "If God is not revealed to Himself, then He cannot be revealed to a world."[95] But in all dialectical consistency, the opposite must obviously also be the case: "Only through that which is posited for itself as world and other, as God, is the thing positing revealed as what it is in itself"[96]—namely as absolute self-knowledge and self-willing in the "spiritually" mediated unity of Father and Son.[97]

87 *V2*, p. 128 (my emphasis); see *SKS* 19, 249, Not9:1.

88 *V2*, p. 417.

89 *V2*, pp. 25f.; p. 134; pp. 415–8. On the relation of revelation and generation (*Zeugung*), see ibid., pp. 135f.

90 Ibid., p. 153.

91 Ibid., p. 155.

92 Ibid., p. 417.

93 Ibid., p. 25; p. 112; p. 140.

94 Ibid., p. 25; pp. 112f.

95 Ibid., p. 156.

96 Ibid.

97 The logically stricter "only" is my own addition. As far as I see, it does full justice to Marheineke's own intentions, as other relevant passages confirm; see, for example,

At this very point the concept of man, made in the image of God, and thus anthropology, comes into focus, namely in the sense of understanding a necessary condition for the possibility of the genesis and the plausibility of the speculative project as a whole. Unlike the rest of creation, in which God is supposed to be revealed as in his own Other, man possesses, by virtue of his intellectual endowment, that is, according to his own spiritual essence, the capacity for the speculative insight, that is, understanding *that* God reveals Himself in such a way. The positive significance of being made in the image of God consequently lies in the idea that man—and man alone—is the "finite spirit in the *infinite*,"[98] that is, a potentially self-transparent manifestation of God's presence in the world. Here alone can the ground of all being *as such* also come to actuality in the grounded, so that—mediated through the ontological *tertium comparationis* of spirit[99]—the "similarity of man to God is at the same time the similarity of God to man,"[100] or is at least destined to reveal itself as such.[101] This means not only that without God's self-communication man can know nothing about him;[102] vice versa, and with *speculative* consistency even God, without his own givenness for himself by virtue of the Spirit, as it becomes manifest in the human mind, could not achieve absolute identity, that is, be fully revealed to himself. At least at the level of the "revealed or absolute religion,"[103] that is, at the level of Christianity, human knowledge is thus no longer "this human knowledge... but it is divine knowledge, which places itself in human knowledge, and which...is the consciousness of the divine being beyond itself...and thereby knowledge in and from God or his spirit."[104]

---

ibid., pp. 133f. (my emphasis): "*Gott vernimmt, erkennt, liebt sich als Gott* nur *in dem ihm Andern...Sieht man von diesem Gedanken...ab, und bleibt man nur und allein bei Gott als der absoluten Substanz stehen, so steht, daß Gott sich offenbar sey,...gar nicht zu erkennen.*" See also ibid., p. 25; p. 137; p. 141; p. 151; pp. 153–8. That Marheineke sometimes wavers on this point may be read as further evidence that the aforementioned objection of inconsistency is correct. I give preference to the genuinely speculative reading, only because it seems to be the one that Kierkegaard follows throughout.

98 Ibid., p. 185 (my emphasis). Kierkegaard's notes repeat this formulation word for word: see *SKS* 19, 254f., Not9:1. Perhaps he alludes to it in his journal comment as well (*SKS* 19, 246, Not8:52–53 / *JP* 3, 3285: "the logical proposition that the finite is the infinite")—although in the same passage he refers to the explanation that Werder had given for it: namely "that the stress is on the last word" (ibid.). As to this, see also *SKS* 19, 245, Not8:50–51 / *JP* 1, 257 and *JP* 2, 1592.

99 Ibid., p. 418.

100 Ibid.

101 Marheineke emphazises, however, that this counts only for Christ in the sense of *homoousia* (essential identity), for man, by contrast, only in the sense of an essential similarity, that is, *homoiousia*. See ibid., pp. 182f.

102 Ibid.

103 Ibid., p. 417.

104 Ibid.

V.

Kierkegaard's verdict of "volatilization" merely repeats here in the context of the Marheineke's doctrine of revelation a fundamental objection raised elsewhere against Hegel himself, and in its radicalized form against the "speculative theology of mediation"[105] that most right-wing Hegelians subscribe to, in general: this kind of theology defends Christianity by betraying it. And it betrays it by systematically "volatilizing" its dogmatical content and foundation or, as Kierkegaard puts it elsewhere, by "explaining it away."[106] Far from openly denying the truth of Christianity, speculation, on the contrary, rushes to its defense, without noticing that what it purports to be defending ceases to be true Christianity, precisely in and through the very form of its defense. Without wanting to contest the fact and dogmatic necessity of revelation, but, on the contrary, by trying to demonstrate its speculative truth, such false theology champions its cause in a way which unintentionally belies the goal. It is precisely this unexpected (and at the same time, potentially comical) result which also proves, according to Kierkegaard, that speculation "hobbles first on one leg then on the other."[107] Its volatilization of the Christian dogma amounts to a fundamental and, subjectively speaking, superstitious inconsistency. For correctly understood, there remain all but two alternatives for the speculative philosopher: *either* ceasing to believe *or* parting with speculation.[108]

When one wishes to specify this alternative by applying it to the doctrine of revelation, it is natural to begin with its latter part, that is, with the assertion that the genuinely Christian use of this term necessitates the rejection of speculation. First, we need to keep in mind that Kierkegaard, where he uses the term "revelation" (*Aabenbaring*) in a religious context, distinguishes a weaker (A) from a stricter sense (B).[109] The term "revelation" in the general religious sense refers to any divine act of self-communication—an act, mind you, which, as such, is conceived of *a priori* as being salvific by nature. This definition serves as the basis for the concept of revelation in its stricter religious sense also, as it is used (only) in Christianity. Here it is claimed that the act of divine self-communication has gained its final and religiously unsurpassable form in God's incarnation for the purpose of saving a sinful world.[110]

---

105 As to this label, see Pannenberg, *Problemgeschichte der neueren evangelischen Theologie*, op. cit., p. 256.

106 *Pap.* VII–2 B 235, p. 189 / *BA*, 103.

107 See 1 Kings 18:21.

108 I have tried to spell out this alternative in greater detail in Heiko Schulz, "Kierkegaard über Hegel. Umrisse einer polemischen Rezeption," *Kierkegaardiana*, vol. 21, 2000, pp. 152–78, especially pp. 165–8.

109 See, for example, *SKS* 7, 195 / *CUP1*, 213.

110 See, for example, *SKS* 4, 226 / *PF*, 17. *SKS* 4, 428 / *CA*, 127 (the Hong translation has "disclosure" here). Strangely enough, terms like "*Aabenbaring*," "*aabenbare*" and so on ("revelation," "reveal," "disclosure," "disclose") play a rather subordinate role in both of the pseudonymous texts: see, for instance, *SKS* 4, 220, 236, 239, 242 / *PF*, 11, 30, 33, 45. *SKS* 4, 424f., 427ff. / *CA*, 123f., 126ff. Concerning (a) Kierkegaard's understanding of revelation in general, (b) his distinction between a wider and a stricter sense of the term, see also: *SKS*

Thus understood, the actuality of a revelatory communication is paradoxically qualified in at least four respects. (A) The *subject* of the revelation is paradoxically qualified, in that through and for the sake of the communication it is or becomes what it cannot be according to its own essence (as the eternal and divine): temporal and human. (B) The *addressee* or recipient of the revelation is qualified paradoxically, namely as that which in and through the process of understanding, the communicated message becomes what, according to his own prior identity (as a sinner), he can neither be nor become: saved and reborn in the image of God. (C) The *content* of the revelation is qualified paradoxically, both with regard to (A)—that is, christologically (with the keyword being "God-man")—and to (B)—that is, anthropologically (with the keyword being "justified sinner"). (B) Finally, the *process* of the revelation is also qualified paradoxically since its subject, by way of communicating its message to the recipient, simultaneously has to constitute the conditions of its being properly received and understood by the latter (via faith).

Certain ontological as well as epistemological implications are closely connected with the assertion of the facticity of such a paradoxically qualified revelatory event. Ontologically crucial is the fact that in and through the act of *understanding* the divine message, the *reality* of its content, is at once constituted. In other words, to understand the salvific message, as such, is tantamount to actually *being* saved—and vice versa.[111] Regarded epistemologically, the paradoxical accent of revelation leads to the conclusion that God can—nota bene, *extra fidem*—not also and *inter alia*

7, 41, 195, 223f., 393 / *CUP1*, 35, 213, 245f., 432. *SKS* 18, 205, JJ:203–6 / *JP* 2, 1335. *SKS* 18, 331, KK:2 / *JP* 3, 3262. *Pap.* VII–2 B 235, p. 134 (see 249.27); p. 136; pp. 189–209 / *BA*, 275f., 277f., 102–22. *Pap.* VII–2 B 266.23. *SKS* 21, 50, NB6:66–9 / *JP* 2, 1957. *Pap.* X–3 A 626 / *JP* 3, 3110. Within the research literature, the following titles are to be compared, in particular: Torsten Bohlin, *Kierkegaards dogmatische Anschauung in ihrem geschichtlichen Zusammenhange*, Gütersloh: Bertelsmann 1927, Chapter 7; Arnold B. Come, *Kierkegaard as Theologian. Recovering my Self*, Montreal: McGill-Queen's University Press 1997, pp. 19–24; Steven M. Emmanuel, *Kierkegaard and the Concept of Revelation*, Albany: State University of New York Press 1996, Chapters 2, 4 and 7; C. Stephen Evans, *Passionate Reason. Making Sense of Kierkegaard's Philosophical Fragments*, Bloomington: Indiana University Press 1992, pp. 73–7; Valter Lindström, *Stadiernas Teologi. En Kierkegaard-Studie*, Lund: C.W.K. Gleerup 1943, Chapter 3.

111 Therefore the facticity of revelation, by being possible alone through divine action, and in this sense only eschatologically possible, is, to cite Richard Swinburne loosely, *eo ipso* "ontologically efficacious." (See his *The Evolution of the Soul*, Oxford: Oxford University Press 1986, p. 38.) To show that and to what extent faith can be a necessary and/or sufficient condition for constituting reality—at least for constituting the reality of what is believed—has, under the keyword "*ontologische Macht des Bewußtseins*" ("ontological power of consciousness") been my main intention in Heiko Schulz, *Theorie des Glaubens*, Tübingen: J.C.B. Mohr 2001 (especially pp. 353ff.; in detail § 19). See also Heiko Schulz, "To Believe is to Be. Reflections on Kierkegaard's Phenomenology of (Un-)Freedom in the *The Sickness unto Death*," *Kierkegaard-Studies. Yearbook*, 1996, pp. 164–85 (here I try to spell out a similar idea with regard to Kierkegaard's account of the relation between faith and being, or faith and reality).

but rather *per se* be known only in potentially offensive ambiguity, that is, only as present in absence, as visible in invisibility, as revealed in hiddenness and so on.[112]

Summing up, we may illustrate the inconsistency of speculative theology according to Kierkegaard with the following syllogism: (1) The appropriation of a divine revelation in the medium of speculative thought is impossible. (2) Incarnation is an expression of divine revelation. (3) Ergo, the appropriation of incarnation in the medium of speculative thought is impossible. From Kierkegaard's perspective, Hegelian theology holds fast to the second premise, but denies the first. In Christian terms, however, it would either have to accept both premises—and thus give up speculative theology's fundamental claim—or deny both premises and in so doing give up the claim of standing in, as Marheineke puts it, "the demonstrable agreement with Christianity."[113] In fact, however, it comes up short on both sides: it volatilizes the paradoxical implications of the Christian concept of revelation, which, as such, imply a compelling "either-or" between faith and reason, in favor of an ambivalent "both-and," which in its consequence leads to a "neither-nor."

Kierkegaard also investigates this inconsistency *categorically*, namely aesthetically and logically. As we have seen, Hegelian theology reduces the Christian concept of revelation to a modification of human consciousness in its progressive transition to the level of speculative thought. The "qualitative concept of a revelation" is thus volatilized to the point at which it merely describes a "change of subjectivity."[114] Now, since, on the one hand, dogmatic science is, according to Marheineke, to be regarded as the only conceivable place for a divine self-revelation to become manifest and since, on the other hand, not every human being is, in his opinion, granted the prerequisites to raise himself to the height of scientific thinking,[115] the conditions for the possibility of receiving such a revelation become a question of genius and talent. Hence revelation is erroneously converted from a strictly religious and anthropologically universal category into a mere *aesthetic* category.[116]

Additionally, speculation itself, by reinterpreting logically central christological (for example, incarnation) and anthropological (for example, rebirth) categories, obscures what must be Christianly seen as an unavoidable break with the immanence of philosophical thought, and thereby makes itself guilty of a fatal mixing of categories. In Marheineke's work this flaw becomes obvious not only in the misunderstanding of faith as a form of (first) immediacy;[117] but it is also and primarily evident in the

---

112 Strictly speaking the paradoxical implications of the Christian idea of revelation only accentuate more sharply that essential correlation between revelation and mystery—subjectively speaking: between revelation and suffering—which is already constitutive for the weaker, that is, universally religious understanding of the term: see *SKS* 7, 195, 223f., 393 / *CUP1*, 213, 245f., 432. *Pap.* X–3 A 626 / *JP* 3, 3110.

113 *Einleitung in die öffentlichen Vorlesungen*, op. cit., p. 14.

114 *Pap.* VII–2 B 235, p. 206 / *BA*, 119.

115 See, for example, *V2*, pp. 14ff.; p. 403; *Einleitung in die öffentlichen Vorlesungen*, op. cit., pp. 44f.

116 *Pap.* VII–2 B 235, pp. 136f.; pp. 138ff. / *BA*, 277f.

117 *SKS* 4, 318 / *CA*, p. 10: on *Die Grundlehren der christlichen Dogmatik als Wissenschaft*, op. cit., pp. 48f.; also *Pap.* I A 273 / *JP* 2, 1096.

speculative claim that God's "*An-sich*" (in itself) necessarily becomes "*Für sich*" (for itself) by virtue of the eternal begetting of the Son;[118] and it is finally obvious in the accompanying anthropological view of human innocence as immediacy,[119] which, as such, is to be thought of as always already having passed over into some self-mediated form that is equally lacking and is capable of a reconciling reflection of the absolute.[120] In these and other cases, what is from Kierkegaard's perspective a paradoxical, that is, speculatively unassimilatable dogmatic phenomenon is wrongly treated as speculatively logical, with the result that revelation appears as always already reconciled with reason, the temporal with the eternal, the finite with the infinite, the contingent with the necessary, innocence with sin, faith with knowledge, and so on. In this very way, though, theological Hegelianism speculatively "volatilizes" basic Christian ideas and concepts.[121]

---

118 See, for example, *V2*, pp. 25; p. 112; pp. 128–40.

119 Ibid., p. 186; also *SKS* 4, 341 / *CA*, 35.

120 *V2*, pp. 186f.; pp. 191ff.; pp. 195f. Kierkegaard's subsequent response to a corresponding thesis of Julius Schaller in a journal entry from 1838 could hence also be directed at Marheineke: If "every contrast between God and man is abrogated in this way, it shows that the contrast was a purely logical contrast and that the contrast within the sphere of religious-moral views (sin, etc.) is not touched, for the simple reason that it has not been reached" (*SKS* 18, 331, KK:2 / *JP* 3, 3263; see also *SKS* 18, 331, KK:2 / *JP* 3, 3262).

121 Accordingly, Kierkegaard uses the concept of volatilization with two objections in mind: *pro primo* with that of a *mixing of categories*, for example, of logic and dogmatics (see, for example, *SKS* 4, 318 / *CA*, 10), metaphysics and dogmatics (see, for example, *SKS* 7, 526 / *CUP1*, 579), aesthetics and dogmatics (see, for example, *Pap.* VII–2 B 235, p. 206 / *BA*, 119), aesthetics and ethics (see, for example, *SKS* 2, 145f. / *EO1*, 146), metaphysics and ethics (see, for example, *SKS* 7, 117f. / *CUP1*, 122), ethics and dogmatics (see, for example, *SKS* 7, 243 / *CUP1*, 267f.) and so on; secondly—and on the basis of the first aspect—with the objection of an *inappropriately restrictive use of the term "immediacy"* in mind. Thus, for instance, Kierkegaard holds that every (sc. religious) faith is a form of immediacy, but not every—but only the post- or transreflexive—form of immediacy is faith (see, for example, *SKS* 20, 363, NB4:159 / *JP* 2, 1123, p. 12; also *SKS* 4, 318 / *CA*, 10). Now, his core accusation against speculative theology lies not so much in the fact that it employs the concept of immediacy for dogmatical purposes *at all*; it consists, rather, in a too restrictive *logical* use of this category *within* dogmatics. Logic *begins* as such "with something produced by the subtlest abstraction, namely, what is most elusive [*det...Flygtigste*]: the immediate" (*SKS* 4, 318 / *CA*, 10). As such it is fully justified to declare the immediate as always already mediated—namely via language, that is by virtue of *speaking* of it, as such. Indeed, the (logical) immediate is as fleeting and elusive as the passing scent of a flower, which as such cannot be spoken of without already transforming it into another, something already passed by and as such merely remembered in the medium of abstract language and thought. Hence to "volatilize" the dogmatic concept of faith does not mean to interpret it as a form of immediacy *at all*, but rather to misunderstand it as something immediate in the logical sense (that is, as an immediate analogous to the flower's scent or, "in an emotional-intellectual sense," to "the atmosphere we breathe" (*Pap.* I A 273 / *JP* 2, 1096)). Thus, in Kierkegaard's opinion the conclusion seems all too rash that dogmatics, as is the case with logic, *begins* with immediacy—with an immediacy in the *logical* sense—so that we are entitled to draw the further conclusion that such an immediacy (interpreted, for instance, as innocence) is always already mediated by way of speaking and thinking.

Finally, if one recalls Marheineke's dialectical intertwining of revelation theology and anthropology, it is worth mentioning that we are in fact dealing with correlative aspects of one and the same fundamental objection, which is raised in Kierkegaard's journal entry from 1841.[122] For the volatilization of the concept of revelation in Marheineke goes hand in hand with that of the concept of the image of God. The latter is dialectically functionalized in the service of the former and vice versa. Just as the paradoxical beginning of the eternal in time, in the sense of the world-historically decisive moment of revelation in incarnation, is speculatively volatilized in Marheineke's dogmatics, so too the individual decisive moment of faith, by virtue of the sinner's rebirth, paradoxically restores him as God's image, or more precisely lets the latter come to be "in the moment."[123] Yet, if this is true, then both the *Philosophical Fragments* and the *The Concept of Anxiety* can be read as two aspects of one and the same overall project, the execution of which had already been envisaged by Kierkegaard with those words in the note of 1841, in which he reminds himself that "all this" (namely, Marheineke's own twofold volatilization of the Christian concepts of revelation and *imago dei*) "must be gone through meticulously in order, if possible, to bring clarity into the confusion."[124] Conversely, the journal entry proves to be the seed of the christological–anthropological double project carried out in his two pseudonymous works of 1844.

When one judges Kierkegaard's Marheineke reception as a whole (inasmuch as it can be traced back to his encounter with the latter's lectures of 1841–42), it seems evident that the Berlin theologian is first and foremost seen critically, by being accused of betraying a fundamental Protestant insight. According to this insight, invoking a revelation *nolens volens* entails the admission of (the real possibility of) a paradoxical fact—a fact that, as paradoxical, proves speculatively unassimilatable and only dogmatically legitimate. In this sense, one may, by using the obvious *contradictio in adjecto* as an ironic point, call Kierkegaard a left Hegelian *ad maiorem dei gloriam*. In order to steer safely between Scylla and Charybdis, that is, between an unbelieving left- and a superstitious right-wing Hegelianism, he sees himself forced to orient the interpretation of Christianity toward the mark in the sea which is the paradox,[125] and thus to save faith from going under in the cliffs and abysses of the age of reflection. However, one may wish to assess the originality and persuasiveness of this strategy from a systematic point of view. Historically it can hardly be denied that in comparison to the other two options of post-Hegelian reason in relation to Christianity, it seems little more than a late and certainly unintentional reflection of that very choice, with which David Hume had already confronted his contemporaries a century before Kierkegaard: either unbelief or superstition or—retreat into mysticism.[126]

Translated by Alan Duncan

---

122 *SKS* 19, 246, Not8:52–3 / *JP* 3, 3285.

123 *SKS* 4, 228f. / *PF*, 20f.

124 *SKS* 19, 246, Not8:52–3 / *JP* 3, 3285.

125 *SKS* 11, 206 / *SUD*, 93.

126 See David Hume, *Dialogues Concerning Natural Religion*, in *Writings on Religion*, ed. by Anthony Flew, La Salle: Open Court 1992, pp. 185–292 (here p. 219; p. 262).

Bibliography

I. *Marheineke's Works in* The Auction Catalogue *of Kierkegaard's Library*

Lehrbuch des christlichen Glaubens und Lebens für denkende Christen und zum Gebrauch in den oberen Klassen an den Gymnasien, 2nd revised ed., Berlin: Nicolai 1836 (*ASKB* 257).

"Ueber christliche Kirchenverfassung. Bruchstück aus der praktischen Theologie," *Zeitschrift für spekulative Theologie*, vols. 1–3, ed. by Bruno Bauer, Berlin: Dümmler 1836–38, vol. 1, no. 1, 1836, pp. 182–202 (*ASKB* 354–357).

"Ankündigung der zweiten, verbesserten Auflage von dem *Lehrbuch des christlichen Glaubens und Lebens* für denkende Christen und zum Gebrauch in den oberen Klassen an den Gymnasien," *Zeitschrift für spekulative Theologie*, op. cit., vol. 1, no. 1, 1836, pp. 249–66.

"Uebersichtliche Einleitung in die praktische Theologie," *Zeitschrift für spekulative Theologie*, op. cit., vol. 2, no. 1, 1837, pp. 162–91.

Die Grundlehren der christlichen Dogmatik als Wissenschaft, 2nd revised ed., Berlin: Duncker und Humblot 1827 (*ASKB* 644).

Institutiones symbolicae, 3rd ed., Berlin: Voss 1830 (*ASKB* 645).

Lærebog i christelig Tro og Levnet, trans. by M. Mørch Hansen, Copenhagen: P.G. Philipsen 1842 (*ASKB* 646).

Zur Kritik der Schellingschen Offenbarungsphilosophie. Schluß der öffentlichen Vorlesungen über die Bedeutung der Hegelschen Philosophie in der christlichen Theologie, Berlin: Enslin 1843 (*ASKB* 647).

[ed.] *D. Carl Daub's Philosophische und theologische Vorlesungen*, ed. by Philipp Marheineke and Theophor Wilhelm Dittenberger, vols. 1–7, Berlin: Duncker und Humblot 1838–44 (vol. 1, *Vorlesungen über die philosophische Anthropologie*; vol. 2, *Prolegomena zur Dogmatik und Kritik der Beweise für das Dasein Gottes*; vol. 3, *Prolegomena zur theologischen Moral und Prinzipien der Ethik*; vols. 4–5, *D. Carl Daub's System der theologischen Moral* [Parts 1–2]; vols. 6–7, *System der christlichen Dogmatik* [Parts 1–2]) (*ASKB* 472–472g).

[ed.] *Georg Wilhelm Friedrich Hegel's Vorlesungen über die Philosophie der Religion*, vols. 1–2, ed. by Philipp Marheineke, 2nd revised ed., Berlin: Duncker und Humblot 1840 (vols. 11–2 in *Georg Wilhelm Friedrich Hegel's Werke. Vollständige Ausgabe*, ed. by Philipp Marheineke et al., Berlin: Duncker und Humblot 1832–45), Berlin: Duncker und Humblot 1840 (*ASKB* 564–565).

"Kirkens Reform ved Staten" [1844], *Tidsskrift for udenlandsk theologisk Litteratur*, vols. 1–20, ed. by Henrik Nikolai Clausen and Matthias Hagen Hohlenberg, Copenhagen: C.A. Reitzel 1833–52, vol. 12, 1844, pp. 342–404 (*ASKB* U 29).

II. Works in The Auction Catalogue *of Kierkegaard's Library that Discuss Marheineke*

Baader, Franz von, *Vorlesungen, gehalten an der Königlich-Bayerischen Ludwig-Maximilians-Hochschule über religiöse Philosophie im Gegensatze der irreligiösen, älterer und neuer Zeit*, vol. 1, *Einleitender Theil oder vom Erkennen überhaupt*, Munich: Giel 1827, p. 41; p. 65; p. 90 (*ASKB* 395).

—— *Philosophische Schriften und Aufsätze*, vols. 1–2, Münster: Theissing 1831–32, vol. 1, p. 260; p. 265 (*ASKB* 400–401).

Baur, Ferdinand Christian, *Die christliche Lehre von der Versöhnung in ihrer geschichtlichen Entwicklung von der ältesten Zeit bis auf die neueste*, Tübingen: Osiander 1838, pp. 718–22 (*ASKB* 423).

Biedermann, A. Emanuel, *Die freie Theologie oder Philosophie und Christenthum in Streit und Frieden*, Tübingen: Ludwig Friedrich Fues. 1844, p. 106; p. 192n (*ASKB* U 20).

Brøchner, Hans, *Nogle Bemærkninger om Daaben, foranledigede ved Professor Martensens Skrift: Den christelige Daab*, Copenhagen: P.G. Philipsens Forlag 1843, p. 21; pp. 25f. (*ASKB* U 27).

Bruch, Johann Friedrich, *Die Lehre von den göttlichen Eigenschaften*, Hamburg: Friedrich Perthes 1842, p. 25n; p. 38n; p. 107n; p. 108n (*ASKB* 439).

Erdmann, Johann Eduard, *Vorlesungen über Glauben und Wissen als Einleitung in die Dogmatik und Religionsphilosophie*, Berlin: Duncker und Humblot 1837, p. 271 (*ASKB* 479).

Fichte, Immanuel Hermann, *System der Ethik*, vols. 1–2.1, Leipzig: Dyk 1850–51 (*ASKB* 510–511), vol. 2.2, Leipzig: Dyk 1853 (*ASKB* 504), vol. 2.2, p. 442n.

Görres, J., *Die Triarier H. Leo, P. Marheinecke, K. Bruno*, Regensburg: Verlag von G. Joseph Manz 1838 (*ASKB* 533).

Hahn, August (ed.), *Lehrbuch des christlichen Glaubens*, Leipzig: Friedrich Christian Wilhelm Vogel 1828, p. 8; p. 288; p. 407 (*ASKB* 535).

Hase, Karl, *Kirkehistorie. Lærebog nærmest for akademiske Forelæsninger*, trans. by C. Winther and T. Schorn, Copenhagen: C.A. Reitzel 1837, p. 11; p. 406 (*ASKB* 160–166).

—— *Hutterus redivivus oder Dogmatik der evangelisch-lutherischen Kirche. Ein dogmatisches Repertorium für Studirende*, 4th revised ed., Leipzig: Breitkopf und Härtel 1839, p. 3; p. 53; p. 101; p. 133; p. 239; p. 249; p. 262 (*ASKB* 581).

Martensen, Hans Lassen, *Den christelige Dogmatik*, Copenhagen: C.A. Reitzel 1849, p. 136 (*ASKB* 653).

Menzel, Wolfgang, *Die deutsche Literatur*, vols. 1–4, 2nd revised ed., Stuttgart: Hallberg'sche Verlagshandlung 1836, vol. 1, pp. 197ff. (*ASKB* U 79).

Mynster, Jakob Peter, *Blandede Skrivter*, vols. 1–3, Copenhagen: Den Gyldendalske Boghandlings Forlag 1852–53 [vols. 4–6, Copenhagen: Den Gyldendalske Boghandlings Forlag 1855–57], vol. 1, p. 20; p. 463; vol. 2, p. 139; p. 141 (*ASKB* 358–363).

Nielsen, Rasmus, *Forelæsningsparagrapher til Kirkehistoriens Philosophie. Et Schema for Tilhørere*, Copenhagen: P.G. Philipsens Forlag 1843, p. 92 (*ASKB* 698).

—— *Dr. H. Martensens Dogmatiske Oplysninger belyste*, Copenhagen: C.A. Reitzel 1850, pp. 17ff.; p. 29; p. 54 (*ASKB* 703).

Romang, Johann Peter, *Ueber Willensfreiheit und Determinismus, mit sorgfältiger Rücksicht auf die sittlichen Dinge, die rechtliche Imputation und Strafe, und auf das Religiöse. Eine philosophische Abhandlung*, Bern: C.A. Jenni, Sohn 1835, p. 301n (*ASKB* 740).

Rosenkranz, Karl, *Erinnerungen an Karl Daub*, Berlin: Duncker und Humblot 1837, p. 7; p. 11; p. 16; p. 20; pp. 44f. (*ASKB* 743).

—— *Psychologie oder die Wissenschaft vom subjectiven Geist*, Königsberg: Bornträger 1837, p. 241 (*ASKB* 744).

—— "Marheineke's kirchliche Religionsphilosophie 1836," in his *Kritische Erläuterungen des Hegelschen Systems*, Königsberg: Bornträger 1840, pp. 260–7 (*ASKB* 745).

Rudelbach, Andreas G., *Om Psalme-Literaturen og Psalmebogs-Sagen, Historisk-kritiske Undersøgelser*, vol. 1, Copenhagen: C.G. Iversen 1854, p. 191 (vol. 2, 1856) (*ASKB* 193).

Stilling, Peter Michael, *Om den indbildte Forsoning af Tro og—Viden med særligt Hensyn til Prof. Martensens "christelige Dogmatik." Kritisk-polemisk Afhandling*, Copenhagen: C.A. Reitzel 1850, p. 12n; p. 66 (*ASKB* 802).

Strauß, David Friedrich, *Fremstilling af den christelige Troeslære i dens historiske Udvikling og i dens Kamp med den moderne Videnskab*, vols. 1–2, trans. by Hans Brøchner, Copenhagen: Forlagt af H.C. Klein 1842–43, p. 21 (*ASKB* 803–804).

Trendelenburg, Adolf, *Die logische Frage in Hegel's System: Zwei Streitschriften*, Leipzig: F.A. Brockhaus 1843, pp. 37ff. (*ASKB* 846).

Twesten, August Detlef Christian, *Vorlesungen über die Dogmatik der Evangelisch-Lutherischen Kirche: nach dem Compendium des Herrn Dr. W.M.L. de Wette*, vols. 1–2, 4th ed., Hamburg: Friedrich Perthes 1837–38, vol. 1, pp. 250–2 (vol. 1, 1838; vol. 2, 1837) (*ASKB* 849–849a).

Usteri, Leonhard, *Udvikling af det Paulinske Lærebegreb i dets Forhold til det Ny Testamentes bibelske Dogmatik. Et exegetisk-dogmatisk Forsøg*, trans. by W.J.J. Boethe, Copenhagen: Philipsen 1839 (*ASKB* 850).

Wolff, Oskar Ludwig Bernhard, *Handbuch deutscher Beredsamkeit enthaltend eine Uebersicht der Geschichte und Theorie der Redekunst, zugleich mit einer vollständigen Sammlung deutscher Reden jedes Zeitalters und jeder Gattung*, vols. 1–2, Leipzig: Carl B. Lorck 1845–46, vol. 1, pp. 383–95 (*ASKB* 250–251).

III. Secondary Literature on Kierkegaard's Relation to Marheineke

Munster, H.A. van, "Marheineke, Martensen, Schleiermacher," *Søren Aabye Kierkegaard*, Den Haag: Lannoo 1963, pp. 109–17.

Schulz, Heiko, "Die spekulative Verflüchtigung des Christentums. Philipp Marheinekes System der christlichen Dogmatik und seine Rezeption bei Søren Kierkegaard," *Kierkegaard Studies. Yearbook*, 2003, pp. 20–47.

Suances Marcos, Manuel, *Sören Kierkegaard*, vols. 1–2, Madrid: Universidad Nacional de Educación a Distanca 1997, vol. 2 (*Trayectoria de su pensamiento filosófico*), pp. 39–45.

Thulstrup, Niels, "Marheineke's Lectures on Dogmatic Theology," in his *Kierkegaard's Relation to Hegel*, trans. by George L. Stengren, Princeton: Princeton University Press 1980, pp. 265–7.

Torralba Roselló, Francesc, "La Teología Dogmática de Marheineke," in his *Amor y diferencia. El Misterio de Dios en Kierkegaard*, Barcelona: PPU, Promociones y Publicaciones Universitarias 1993, pp. 304–7.

Julius Müller:
Parallels in the Doctrines of Sin and Freedom in Kierkegaard and Müller

Christine Axt-Piscalar

Julius Müller was a famous nineteenth-century theologian who initially taught at Halle University and made a name for himself especially as dogmatist and scholarly defender of the Protestant Union. Müller's reputation as dogmatist is based upon his chief work, *The Christian Doctrine of Sin*. It represents the classic outline of the Protestant doctrine of sin in German-speaking theology of the nineteenth century. Kierkegaard knew Müller's monograph, which had grown to two volumes in its second edition;[1] he dealt with the first one-volume edition[2] both critically and approvingly within the scope of his own works regarding the problem of human sin. We will later go into more detail regarding Kierkegaard's demonstrable references to Müller. However, it would be a mistake to attempt to comprehend Kierkegaard's reception of Müller's thinking solely based on the handwritten notes which discuss Müller directly. It is no secret to anyone who has studied Müller's doctrine of sin as a whole that there are points of overlap between Kierkegaard and him as regards both their fundamental opposition to contemporary speculative theology and philosophy and the emphasis on and exposition of the topic of sin. And whoever follows Müller's own career from a grammar school pupil to a student of jurisprudence and later, to a theologian, receives, in addition, the impression that—in a similar, however, not so extreme way as with Kierkegaard—the experience of individual sin and guilt and the struggle for the firm ground of individual existence shaped Müller's path to theology decisively.

I. Julius Müller: Life and Works

Julius Müller was born the second son of a field preacher in Brieg in Silesia (present-day Poland) on 10 April 1801.[3] At his parents' request, he began to study law at

1 Julius Müller, *Die christliche Lehre von der Sünde*, 2nd ed., vols. 1–2, Breslau: Josef Max 1844.

2 Müller, *Die christliche Lehre von der Sünde*, Breslau: Josef Max 1839.

3 Cf. David Hupfeld, "Julius Müller," in *Realenzyklopädie für protestantische Theologie und Kirche*, vols. 1–18, ed. by Johann Jakob Herzog and Albert Hauck, 2nd ed., Leipzig: Hinrichs 1877–88, vol. 10, pp. 343–56; Leopold Schultze, *D. Julius Müller. Mittheilungen*

Breslau University in 1819, but he felt a "deep inward need," which, despite his achievements, he could not satisfy with his law studies. Müller moved to Göttingen in 1820 and there experienced his first religious awakening which prompted him to begin his studies of theology in 1821. He recognized that "whatever urged me on" was "in principle nothing but earthly pride and earthly vanity"; further, he praised divine grace for having in a timely way "saved him from the labyrinth of a merely mundane activity and making a pure, childish, heartfelt belief become strong in him."[4] Nonetheless, the young student Müller felt that he was still unable to achieve a firmly established certainty of faith or a real peace in God. Again and again, he was seized by profound crises of faith which were further intensified by his studies of theology and later of philosophy. In his religious mind as well as in his thinking, he was increasingly repelled by the rationalistically saturated spirit of Göttingen's Faculty of Theology. He turned away from theology and, with passion, towards philosophy. He studied the contemporary systems, especially those of idealism, above all that of Schelling. Müller was constantly distressed by deep doubts which rose almost to "complete insanity as regards all faith"; "the most unhappy and desperate moods recurred."[5]

While he could lay aside rationalistic theology as non-existential, his preoccupation with speculative thinking led him to the experience of the nothingness of his own being, an experience which influenced Müller strongly and would later always determine his struggle against speculation. Müller bears vivid witness to this experience in a letter:

> You cannot know and believe it if you did not experience it, if you did not once search for your salvation in this doctrine with all your heart and soul; how terrible and annihilating the Absolute is, conceptualized as the absolute unity of all oppositions, of thinking and being so that all that is opposite as regards the Absolute as the only true Being, is merely void. I was the unhappiest human being; all my faith being annihilated by the most rigorous proof dwindled down to nothing...my own individual being was merely void to me, absolutely indifferent; it did not matter to me if I existed at all or not.[6]

During this stage of an acute crisis of faith, the theologian August Tholuck (1799–1877) became, as it were, the mundane savior for Müller. In a dedication, Müller addresses Tholuck thus:

> When the Lord's call had made me a theologian, and I yet again was overwhelmed by doubts and conflicts during my detailed study of theology and particularly of philosophy, there a...friend's advice led me to you. You called my attention at that time to the moral

aus seinem Leben, Bremen: C.E. Müller 1879; Martin Kähler, *D. Julius Müller, der Hallische Dogmatiker Gestorben 27. September 1878*, Halle: Fricke 1878; Joachim Mehlhausen, "Julius Müller," in *Theologische Realenzyklopädie*, vols. 1–36, ed. by Gerhard Müller, Berlin and New York: Walter de Gruyter 1977–2004, vol. 23, 1994, pp. 394–9.

4 Cited from Hupfeld, "Julius Müller," op. cit., p. 344.

5 Hupfeld, "Julius Müller," op. cit., p. 345.

6 Müller's letter to Tholuck dated 26 November 1822, cited from Leopold Witte, *Das Leben D. Friedrich August Gotttreu Tholuck's*, vols. 1–2, Bielefeld et al.: Velhagen & Klasing 1884–86, vol. 1, p. 205.

> spirit of Christianity and aroused the confidence in me again that the beatific truth can be found in the Protestant faith and nowhere else.[7]

By the "moral spirit of Christianity," Müller means the individual and unjustifiable experience of sin and guilt which can find reconciliation solely in the unconditional personal faith in Jesus Christ. Through Tholuck he obtained, as he himself stressed retrospectively, the insight that everything in Christianity "refers to the great opposition of sin and deliverance and that it is impossible to truly understand the real nature of Christianity—deliverance—as long as sin has not been soundly recognized."[8] Through this conviction, which mirrored his own religious experience, Müller had achieved the fixed point of his scholarly theological thinking. Starting from it, he was passionately engaged in the contemporary theological and philosophical debates later as an academic teacher.

At first, however, his study led him to Berlin, following Tholuck's advice, where he studied with Tholuck and also August Neander (1789–1850). He came under the influence of the revivalist Berlin circles which were shaped by the figures of Hans Ernst Baron von Kottwitz (1757–1843) and Samuel Elsner. Müller was hoping to obtain work as a pastor. He took the parochial exams and was elected to a rectorate in Silesia. Here, he opposed the institution of the Protestant Union decreed by the Prussian state because with such an approach he believed the state would encroach upon the freedom of the Church in what were purely ecclesiastical matters. Müller's stubborn objection enraged the Ministry of Church Affairs in Berlin. Müller managed to get out of the conflict gracefully by accepting an appointment as university preacher in Göttingen in 1830. His impact in Göttingen was, however, only limited.

This changed when, in 1834, Müller was appointed to the *Lehrstuhl* for Dogmatics in Marburg. During the Marburg period, the first volume of his *Doctrine of Sin* was produced, which in 1839 was published in Breslau, with the title, *The Christian Doctrine of Sin.* The first volume (*About the Nature and Cause of Sin. A Theological Study*) was published in a revised edition, together with the second volume published in 1844. This second edition of *Doctrine of Sin*, in two volumes, was the authoritative edition, and was highly influential in contemporary theology. It was printed in a total of six editions in the nineteenth century. The third edition was translated into English as well.[9]

When the opportunity of appointing Müller to a vacant professorship in Halle arose, his friends Tholuck and Neander spared no effort to bring about Müller's appointment by recommending him to the department in Halle. Conversely, the Hegelians, through vocal opposition, attempted to prevent Müller's appointment in favor of Ferdinand Christian Baur (1792–1860). Müller emerged as an influential

---

7 From Müller's dedication of his *Dogmatische Abhandlungen*, Bremen: C.Ed. Müller 1870, to August Tholuck.

8 Preface of the first edition of *Die christliche Lehre von der Sünde*, vols. 1–2, printed in the 1858 edition (4th ed., Breslau: Josef Max), p. iii. Müller's doctrine of sin is cited in the following according to this 4th edition from 1858.

9 *The Christian Doctrine of Sin*, trans. from the original German, of the third improved and enlarged edition, by William Pulsford, Edinburgh: T. & T. Clark 1852 (*Clark's Foreign Theological Library*, vol. 27).

critic of Hegelian philosophy and speculative theology. He regarded it to be a fundamental apostasy from the core teachings of Christianity and set forth this conviction aggressively in the contemporary debates.

Notwithstanding the strong resistance against him, Müller was appointed to Halle where he taught alongside Tholuck for almost 20 years, from 1836 to 1856. He contributed considerably to the fact that Halle, once a stronghold of rationalism, turned into a significant center of revivalist theology which attracted a multitude of students. Moreover, the change of the perception of the sovereign government of the Church which accompanied Friedrich Wilhelm IV's accession to the throne, as well as a personal contact with the government minister Eichhorn (1799–1856), resulted in a clear easing of tension in the relationship of the Prussian state to Müller. He was even appointed councillor of the consistory and in this role, furnished numerous opinions for the minister. Under these new circumstances, Müller became a supporter of the Protestant Union which he defended with dedication both at the level of the Church and in scholarly articles.[10] In 1856, Müller suffered a stroke, after which his activity as a writer was very limited. He died on 27 September 1878 in Halle.

II. Müller's The Christian Doctrine of Sin

There can be no doubt that Müller's *Doctrine of Sin* had an influence on Kierkegaard's considerations about sin as he set them forth primarily in *The Concept of Anxiety* and *The Sickness unto Death*. In this regard, Emanuel Hirsch judged that Kierkegaard "regarded Müller's doctrine of sin very highly and learnt from it for his fight against Hegel."[11] Admittedly, Hirsch gave no references to support this opinion, nor did he give any explanations about the actual content of the influence. I have myself brought out some of the parallels between Müller's and Kierkegaard's thinking in my book, *Ohnmächtige Freiheit* and will initially fall back here on these considerations.[12] They refer to the points of overlap between Kierkegaard and Müller with regard to the basic intention of their thinking in view of the phenomenon of sin as well as the frontal position taken up by both in it, particularly *vis-à-vis* speculative theology and philosophy but also *vis-à-vis* Schleiermacher's conception and, last but not least, *vis-à-vis* traditional ecclesiastical hamartiology.[13] We will not go into detail about the explicit remarks which Kierkegaard made about Müller until later.

---

[10] Müller, *Die Evangelische Union, ihr Wesen und göttliches Recht*, Berlin: Wiegandt und Grieben 1854.

[11] Emanuel Hirsch, *Geschichte der neuern Evangelischen Theologie im Zusammenhang mit den allgemeinen Bewegungen des europäischen Denkens*, vols. 1–5, Gütersloh: G. Mohn 1964, vol. 5, p. 393.

[12] Christine Axt-Piscalar, *Ohnmächtige Freiheit. Studien zum Verhältnis von Subjektivität und Sünde bei August Tholuck, Julius Müller, Sören Kierkegaard und Friedrich Schleiermacher*, Tübingen: J.C.B. Mohr (P. Siebeck) 1996, pp. 26–173; see also Hans-Peter Willi, *Unbegreifliche Sünde. "Die christliche Lehre von der Sünde" als Theorie der Freiheit bei Julius Müller*, Berlin and New York: Walter de Gruyter 2003.

[13] See also Stanley Russell's excellent comparison of both thinkers, "Two Nineteenth Century Theologies of Sin—Julius Müller and Soren Kierkegaard," *Scottish Journal of Theology*, vol. 40, 1987, pp. 231–48.

In the course of his personal theological development, Müller became a resolute opponent of speculative philosophy and theology. The fundamental arguments of his criticism of speculative thinking refer to the relativization of evil and sin, which he sees as the result of the logico-dialectical derivation of all being from the Absolute. Here evil, according to Müller, is conceived solely as a moment to be sublated in the process of the self-unfolding of Spirit. Moreover, speculative thinking leads, for Müller, to a levelling out of the meaning of the individual before God, which, in his view, results from the non-personal determination of God as the Absolute.[14]

In doing so, Müller anticipates, as it were, an argument of the later personalist philosophy.[15] Starting from the phenomenon "that human self-consciousness does not have the principle of its essence and existence in itself, but *in Another One*"[16] because it cannot justify itself in its being and its being-as-it-is through itself, Müller next puts forward the argument that this "Other One" is neither merely nature nor merely other persons but, first and foremost, the divine self-consciousness. It is the personal God in relation to whom human self-consciousness becomes aware of itself as being constituted as an unmistakeable self. *Vis-à-vis* the absolute Thou, it experiences itself as this concrete self, as, to say it with Kierkegaard, an individual. This is precisely the foundation of the religion of *ethical*–religious character, which is how he characterizes the Christian religion. For "Religion is community with God; but there is no real community with the Absolute which in itself is no self, and thus no Thou for our prayer; love which calls for personality, according to the strictness of its concept, in its object as well as in its subject loses all meaning here."[17]

Therefore, Müller vehemently insists upon the concept of the personal God *vis-à-vis* the pantheistic speculation of the Absolute. The speculative doctrine of God, according to Müller, cannot distinguish between God and the world sufficiently and thereby undermines both the moral–religious relationship regarded as a relationship of a self to an other and the freedom of the finite subject. We need not go into Müller's theistic doctrine of God here any further.[18] The interest guiding Müller in this should, however, have become apparent.

For Müller, the abyss of the consciousness of sin and guilt is undermined by speculation inasmuch as it attempts to deduce evil from the Absolute and define it as the solely negative. The meaning of the individual comes off badly by being the victim of the process of the self-unfolding of the Absolute in the course of history. Together with both sin and guilt, what is idiosyncratic of Christianity gets lost. For Christianity is, at its core, a religion of salvation; and whoever relativizes sin and guilt cannot comprehend the meaning of the historical Savior and thus, that of historical epiphany. The consciousness of sin and guilt as well as the experience of faith, however, bring the individual in his irreplaceable particularity before

---

14 See Müller, *Die christliche Lehre von der Sünde*, 1844, op. cit., vol. 1, pp. iv ff.; ibid., vol. 1, pp. 6f.

15 This is correctly noted by Russell, "Two Nineteenth Century Theologies of Sin," op. cit., p. 233.

16 Müller, *Die christliche Lehre von der Sünde*, 1844, op. cit., vol. 1, p. 102.

17 Ibid., vol. 2, p. 150.

18 See Axt-Piscalar, *Ohnmächtige Freiheit*, op. cit., pp. 62ff.; pp. 124ff.

himself by bringing him before God. In speculation, however, the individual is reduced to a mere moment in the self-unfolding of the Absolute. Müller's struggle against speculation is based upon his interest in the meaning of the individual, in religion as a relationship between the self and the other, and ultimately in the freedom of the finite subject. Therefore, Müller accuses the speculative thinkers of underdetermining finite freedom. Starting from this, Müller's doctrine of sin aims at a conception of finite freedom according to which freedom as unconditional represents the root of evil.

These are the crucial points of Müller's antispeculative criticism. From this it is clear that, for Müller, the struggle for the truth of Christianity proves itself in the struggle for the doctrine of sin. The doctrine of sin turns into antispeculative apologetics as such.[19] And yet, it is not just Hegel and the Hegelians whom Müller opposes. It is also Schleiermacher whom he regards as not free from pantheistic tendencies and whom he also blames for diminishing the role of sin. For, according to Müller's conviction, Schleiermacher also gives sin a place in the natural development of the individual and thus comprehends it as a transitory moment necessary for it. Through this criticism of Schleiermacher, Müller influenced the theological debate of his time considerably and determined the judgment of Schleiermacher's theology at this point in a manner that continued far beyond his time.[20]

Martin Kähler correctly summarizes as follows Müller's basic position in his dispute about contemporary pantheism, which, for Müller, had always been a dispute about the meaning of the individual and its freedom:

> Why did Julius Müller stress this individual person so strongly? It was the struggle against pantheism as a matter of principle, which he early took up so strongly and consciously that made him Schleiermacher's opponent and insensitive to him already as a youth. Speculative pantheism, he said, succeeded in making pantheism the bias of all intellectuals. He had experienced that this pantheism, which is always speculatively traced back to the Absolute, destroyed every value of personality, every form of individuality, and therefore also inevitably the history and meaning of the historical Christ, of the historical epiphany; therefore, he vowed war on pantheism and waged war on it as long as the sharp sword of his mind remained unshattered.[21]

Kähler's judgment also makes plain that Müller's thinking emphasizes, together with the meaning of sin and guilt, the historicity of the Savior and the epiphany, which he regards as volatilized in speculation to the mere idea of reconciliation.[22]

---

19 Ibid., pp. 26–35.

20 As to Müller's criticism of Schleiermacher, see *Die christliche Lehre von der Sünde*, 1844, op. cit., vol. 2, pp. 238ff.; 424ff.; also vol. 1, pp. 55ff.

21 Martin Kähler, *Geschichte der protestantischen Dogmatik im 19. Jahrhundert*, 2nd ed., Wuppertal: Brockhaus 1989, op. cit., p. 136.

22 This constitutes the core idea of Müller's treatise, "Untersuchung der Frage, ob der Sohn Gottes Mensch geworden sein würde, wenn das menschliche Geschlecht ohne Sünde geblieben wäre," *Deutsche Zeitschrift für christliche Wissenschaft und christliches Leben*, vol. 1, 1850, pp. 314–28 and pp. 333–41. Modified and expanded reprint in Julius Müller, *Dogmatische Abhandlungen*, Bremen: C. Ed. Müller 1870, pp. 66–126.

For Müller, it is the consciousness of guilt in which the inevitable force of sin becomes manifest for the individual.[23] It ascribes sin to the sinner as his personal misdeed and as his guilt and, as such, is an inescapable "force over man"; for "it is not that man has got this consciousness, but it has got him."[24] Ascribing guilt based on the consciousness of guilt makes the individual the sole originator of sin.

Starting from this phenomenology of the consciousness of guilt, Müller attempts to conceive the possibility for sin. Since the consciousness of guilt declares the individual the sole originator of sin, an *absolutely free* act, according to the principle of causality, must be presupposed as the cause of sin. It must be posited in order to explain the consciousness of guilt which ascribes sin as guilt to the sinner and unveils him as the *sole* originator of sin. An act, unconditional as such, however, cannot be perceived under empirical conditions, where the individual is placed in the context which conditions him with another and others. Therefore, Müller presupposes a "self-determination beyond time" of the individual in which he determines himself from the state of innocence to evil.[25]

The function of Müller's thesis of a self-determination to evil beyond time is obvious. It is supposed to justify the consciousness of guilt. It is supposed to conceive the sole responsibility of the subject for sin which "falls" from the innocent primordial state of creature into sin. Moreover, it is supposed to explain in detail the fact that sin could not be anticipated. For according to this view, every individual comes into the world as a sinner because of a free choice of evil made beyond time. This primordial sin determines subsequently his empirical existence from the outset and continuously. He is responsible for it, and it is his guilt because it arose from his acting freely.

Müller thereby focuses the doctrine of sin very strongly on the individual self-determination to evil. The guilt of sin, as it expresses itself in the consciousness of guilt, can be explained only as a fall of each individual from the innocent primordial state to evil by means of free self-determination. Müller sees taken up in this self-determination the traditional doctrine of the original sin which he criticizes in its classical form.[26] It is not, as this doctrine presents it, the *one* Adam who brought the power of sin into and over the world and thus into each man. Rather it is *each person for himself* who has determined himself from the state of innocence to sin. For if it were the *one* Adam with whom sin comes into the world for all mankind, then the guilt of sin could not be asserted actually for the individual.

By focusing on the act of freedom of each individual which constitutes (his) guilt, Müller incurred the reproach that his understanding of sin disregards the

---

23 For Müller's phenomenology of the consciousness of guilt, see *Die christliche Lehre von der Sünde*, 1844, op. cit., vol. 1, pp. 258ff.

24 Ibid., p. 284.

25 See Müller, *Die christliche Lehre von der Sünde*, 1844, op. cit., vol. 2, pp. 91ff. and vol. 2, pp. 188ff.; for this, see Axt-Piscalar, *Ohnmächtige Freiheit*, op. cit., pp. 96–113.

26 For Müller's criticism, see *Die christliche Lehre von der Sünde*, 1844, op. cit., vol. 2, pp. 410–85, section "Die kirchliche Lehre von der Erbsünde," where Müller concludes "that the dogma of the original sin in the form created by our prior theology cannot be sustained" (vol. 2, p. 460).

fact that the individual is connected with the history of the human race.[27] Müller attempts to take up this aspect by dealing with a specific characteristic of sin in the individual through his historical position within the development of the human race and its connection with its particular surroundings. He does not deny the biblical assumption of a primal human couple and the factual nature of its Fall (into sin). He concedes—if only for exegetical reasons—an influence which originates from primal men and their sin which determines their offspring. The ascription of sin to the individual, however, cannot be explained by this, according to Müller.[28]

But how does it come to such a self-decision to evil? What forms the potential for sin in the individual? The potential for sin lies in the freedom of the creature because only in this way can the sole responsibility of the individual for his sin be conceptualized. In doing so, Müller distinguishes two kinds of freedom. *Real* freedom takes place in the correspondence between human will and the Good, the divine law. *Formal* freedom, by contrast, is the capability of determining oneself through oneself to both good and evil. It is the capability of acting also in a different manner. This capability of freedom of acting also in a different manner in principle appertains to the creature in the primordial state; it must attain to that real freedom, as the determination of man through self-determination first and foremost.[29]

In the primordial state, the creature finds itself, *vis-à-vis* the divine law, in the potential for determining itself through itself to the acceptance or denial of the divine law as life-determining base. The freedom in the primordial state is no freedom consolidated in good; it is not yet real freedom. It rather has the potential in itself to deviate from the divine law inasmuch as it is the capability in principle of acting in a different manner. Sin now takes place in the deviation from the divine law, qua free self-determination. This deviation is, according to Müller, based on the "selfishness"[30] of the individual. But as such, the deviation from the divine law being posited by freedom cannot be derived from any necessity; rather it is contingent as such. It originates from the mere potential for acting (in any manner at all). Sin comes into the world through itself. "It is the hubris of evil to be, in its own way, *causa*

---

27 This is the criticism of Isaak August Dorner (1809–89), who reproaches Müller for conceiving the consciousness of sin merely as personal–individual consciousness of guilt whereby "the extent of the consciousness of guilt is reduced." See Isaak August Dorner, *System der christlichen Glaubenslehre*, vols. 1–2, 2nd printing, Berlin: Hertz 1886 [1879–81], vol. 2, pp. 153 and pp. 161f. Müller himself quotes Dorner's judgment from his review of Müller's hamartiology in which he reproaches him for his concept of a "personal consciousness conceived atomistically." Cited from Müller, *Die christliche Lehre von der Sünde*, 1844, op. cit., vol. 2, p. 547. Kierkegaard comments on this point and agrees with Müller. As to this, see below.

28 For "*Müllers kritische Transformation der traditionellen Erbsündenlehre*," see the corresponding section in Axt-Piscalar, *Ohnmächtige Freiheit*, op. cit., pp. 113–24.

29 As to Müller's doctrine of freedom, see especially *Die christliche Lehre von der Sünde*, 1844, op. cit., vol. 2, pp. 6–36.

30 See Müller, *Die christliche Lehre von der Sünde*, 1844, op. cit., vol. 1, pp. 173ff.

sui like God, to start from itself as such, to presuppose only itself."[31] Therefore, sin cannot be derived and is unconceivable in its cause.[32]

III. Points of Overlap in Müller's and Kierkegaard's Theory of Sin

We have explored the main ideas of Müller's doctrine of sin in some detail. The parallels with Kierkegaard are obvious to the expert on his doctrine of sin. Needless to say, Müller did not achieve nearly the existential force of expression in view of the experience of sin as Kierkegaard did in *The Concept of Anxiety* and *The Sickness unto Death*. Focusing on sin under the phenomenon of anxiety and under the phenomenon of despair respectively, and thereby conceiving it existentially, is Kierkegaard's great merit. Müller, as Kierkegaard states, is in fact no existential thinker compared to himself. Above all, Müller understands the idea of sin as a transgression from the divine law. Thus, he accepts a moral restriction of the understanding of sin, whereas from the outset Kierkegaard unfolds a phenomenology of sin which is disposed more broadly and more profoundly with respect to anthropological and psychological aspects. This difference in the way of dealing with the phenomenon of sin, however, cannot hide the common grounds in the fundamental decisions which both of them make in regard to the general conception of sin as well as in their dispute with speculation.

First and foremost, there is a correspondence between Kierkegaard and Müller in their basic view of the essence of Christianity. For both of them, Christianity can be understood only if one holds to the mutual unity of the consciousness of sin and deliverance; from there, one conceives the fundamental meaning of the historical Savior and of the historicity of the epiphany. Kierkegaard emphasizes the necessity of this:

> That this is the case is something that orthodox dogmatics and orthodoxy on the whole have always contended, and they have rejected as pantheistic any definition of sin that made it out to be something merely negative—weakness, sensuousness, finitude, ignorance, etc. Orthodoxy has perceived very correctly that the battle must be fought here...here it is a matter of holding back; orthodoxy has correctly perceived that when sin is defined negatively, all Christianity is flabby and spineless.[33]

This is the reason why both of them agree upon their opposition to speculation. Kierkegaard's criticism of it can be read as a direct appropriation of Müller's arguments. He criticizes the speculative view "that the negative is the evil"[34] because it entails that it ends up as a moment to be merely sublated in the dialectical process of the Spirit. "The negative, then, is immanent in the movement, is something vanishing, is that which is annulled."[35] And also his criticism of Schleiermacher is quite similar

---

31 Müller, *Die christliche Lehre von der Sünde*, 1844, op. cit., vol. 2, p. 229.

32 As to Müller's explications of the inconceivability of sin, see especially *Die christliche Lehre von der Sünde*, 1844, op. cit., vol. 2, pp. 232ff.

33 *SKS* 11, 209 / *SUD*, 96.

34 *SKS* 4, 321 / *CA*, 13.

35 *SKS* 4, 321 / *CA*, 13.

to Müller's. Like Müller, Kierkegaard is convinced that Schleiermacher's thinking is determined by the "Spinozian being"[36] and cannot conceive sin radically enough.[37]

In addition, there is also the meaning and function which both of them assert for the consciousness of sin. As with Müller, so also in Kierkegaard's conception, it is the consciousness of sin which burdens the subject in its absolute responsibility and concerns the individual in its concrete individuality. "The earnestness of sin is its actuality in the single individual, be it you or I."[38] In this respect, they both criticize the traditional doctrine of the primordial state and fall of the primal human couple and the continued effect of sin in the human race with the argument that it cannot justify the individual's sin because guilt and personal responsibility are mutually dependent.[39] Further, both of them hold the conception of a primordial state for each individual and a fall for each individual,[40] and, in addition, both of them attempt to connect the idea of the historicity of the primal human couple to the influence, starting from his sin, on the characteristic nature of the sinfulness in his offspring.[41] Therefore, "every individual is both himself and the race."[42]

That is why one may state that there is a significant correspondence between Kierkegaard and Müller in the focus in which their doctrine of sin appears. In addition, Müller is also interested in the meaning of the concrete individual in the religious relationship. This virtually constitutes the core of his dispute with the speculative concept of the Absolute. He sees what is specific to the Christian religion in its—

---

36 *SKS* 23, 58, NB15:83 / *JP* 4, 3852.

37 As to the relationship between Kierkegaard's and Schleiermacher's doctrines of sin, see Axt-Piscalar, *Ohnmächtige Freiheit*, op. cit., pp. 174–219, and further my article "Das Selbst in der Selbstverstrickung. Eine vergleichende Betrachtung zu Schleiermachers und Kierkegaards Sündenlehre," *Kierkegaard Studies. Yearbook*, 2004, pp. 452–72.

38 *SKS* 11, 231 / *SUD*, 120.

39 Cf. *CA*, Chapter I, § 1. Cf. also *SKS* 4, 352 / *CA*, 47 where Kierkegaard emphasizes that his view of the first sin "does not deny the propagation of sinfulness through generation, or, in other words, that sinfulness has its history through generation. Yet it is said only that sinfulness moves in quantitative categories, whereas sin constantly enters by the qualitative leap of the individual."

40 Regarding Kierkegaard, this is true at least for *The Concept of Anxiety*. Cf. *SKS* 4, 342 / *CA*, 35: "Just as Adam lost innocence by guilt, so every man loses it in the same way." *SKS* 4, 337 / *CA*, 31: "Through the first sin, sin came into the world. Precisely in the same way it is true of every subsequent man's first sin, that through it sin comes into the world." In my opinion, Kierkegaard does not hold this conception of a primordial state and fall for each individual. It rather begins with the fact that we realize ourselves at all times as selves, and find ourselves at all times in despair. For this interpretation, see Axt-Piscalar, *Ohnmächtige Freiheit*, op. cit., pp. 159–73; pp. 206ff., and my article "Das Selbst in der Selbstverstrickung," op. cit.

41 *SKS* 4, 343f. / *CA*, 37f.: "The race has its history, within which sinfulness continues to have its quantitative determinability, but innocence is always lost only by the qualitative leap of the individual. It is no doubt true that this sinfulness, which is the progression of the race, may express itself as a greater or lesser disposition in the particular individual who by his act assumes it, but this is a more or less, a quantitative determination, which does not constitute the concept of guilt."

42 *SKS* 4, 338 / *CA*, 31.

as Müller says—moral–religious character in contrast to the mystical–religious character. Also in relation to this interest, points of overlap between Kierkegaard's emphasis on the ethical–religious dimension of human existence and Müller's concern can be ascertained.

IV. Kierkegaard's Direct References to Müller's Doctrine of Sin

The traceable remarks in which Kierkegaard refers directly to Müller's concept of sin are to be distinguished from the correspondences in their fundamental understanding of the doctrine of sin and are now to be considered separately. None of them can be found in Kierkegaard's principal texts regarding the doctrine of sin nor in his other writings but solely in his journals and notebooks.[43] The first of these notes dates from winter 1841–42. During his stay in Berlin, Kierkegaard attended a lecture by Heinrich Steffens as well as Philipp Konrad Marheineke's lectures on dogmatics. In Kierkegaard's notes to Marheineke's course, a review of Julius Müller is mentioned, which was published in *Theologische Studien und Kritiken*.[44] Against the speculative derivation of the world from God, Kierkegaard approvingly takes up Müller's basic thesis that the creation of the world is based on divine freedom and does not necessarily emanate from the divine will.[45]

No further notes about Julius Müller can be found until the period from 6 January to 5 March 1850. In Kierkegaard's library, there was the third edition of Müller's two-volume *Doctrine of Sin* published in 1849, which he quoted from. But he also quoted from the first edition published in 1839. This might suggest that Kierkegaard purchased the first edition of Müller's *Doctrine of Sin* during his stay in Berlin. Then, however, it is hardly imaginable that Kierkegaard would not have studied it at all, especially since he himself worked on the topic of sin during the following years.[46]

---

43 In the appendix to his work, Hans-Peter Willi recently published a list of all quotations, translated by Tim Hagemann (op. cit., pp. 422–33), but without interpreting them with regard to their relationship towards Müller. We will rely on them in the following.

44 See Müller's review of "C.H. Weiße's, C.F. Göschel's und I.H. Fichte's Schriften und Rezensionen, die Lehre von der Unsterblichkeit betreffend," *Theologische Studien und Kritiken*, no. 3, 1835, pp. 703–94.

45 *SKS* 18, 374–86, KK:11.

46 As to this, see Willi's considerations, op. cit., pp. 420ff. Willi considers this probable: "The page references noted by Kierkegaard himself not only allow one to reach conclusions about his precise and diligent reading (among others, annotations are also quoted), but also about the circumstances of his reading. Kierkegaard read the first three books of the *Doctrine of Sin* in the first edition from 1839, and that happened already before 1849, the year of the publication of the third edition (probably even before 1844). For if Kierkegaard had not begun with the reading of the *Doctrine of Sin* until 1849, he would hardly have fallen back on the volume of the first edition which had been surpassed by the new edition; further, one can hardly assume that in 1849–50, he had read the first three books of the *Doctrine of Sin* in the first edition, in order to continue then the reading of the fourth book in the middle of the second volume of the third edition. In 1850, the reading of the first edition must date back a fairly long time. If these assumptions are correct, then Kierkegaard had only read the fourth and fifth books of the third edition published in 1849...and he did so right after the

In Kierkegaard's handwritten notes regarding Julius Müller, the following can be observed: Kierkegaard is full of admiration for Müller. He regards him as a "very estimable (thinker)"[47] who is accustomed to a "far deeper perception"[48] of sin than others are. However, he finds Müller lacking in a real "μεταβασις εις αλλο γενος."[49] Thereby, Kierkegaard emphasizes the consistent conception of the existential dimension of the experience of sin and salvation. It is true, according to Kierkegaard, that Julius Müller is a profound thinker but no real "existential thinker."[50] Kierkegaard's insistence on the meaning of the individual stands in close connection with this criticism of the existential approach to sin and salvation which Müller is lacking. In his view neither the speculative (thinkers) nor Müller give a satisfactory account of it.[51] In contrast, Kierkegaard says decidedly: "we must pass all the way through 'to the single individual'—face to face with God."[52] The individual as individual, however, is, according to Kierkegaard,[53] not yet conceived by understanding sin as subjectivity fixed on itself as is the case in speculative thinking and, according to his view, also in Müller's understanding of sin as selfishness. Müller's criticism of Hegel's understanding of sin as "abstract subjectivity, arbitrariness, the encroachment of the individual on the Absolute—that is, as egoism" applies to Müller himself, Kierkegaard says. As to the determination of sin as "egoism," Müller is still close to Hegel.[54]

In this context, Kierkegaard criticizes Müller's doctrine of salvation for the same thing as Hegel. Müller also emphasized salvation too strongly as "objectivity" and in doing so, underdetermined the idea of God as "the infinitely compelling

---

publication of the work." This would mean that Kierkegaard read the explications of the third edition only in view of Müller's transformation of the traditional doctrine of the original sin; whereas he read all further fundamental views in Müller's doctrine of sin in any case before 1849, but probably already before 1844, and in turn, this would mean before *The Concept of Anxiety* was published. Why should Kierkegaard not consult a book regarding the doctrine of sin for his own considerations about sin, a book which he knew was a central contribution of German-speaking theology and that he possibly had already purchased in Berlin? Against the background of this result, our explications regarding the common grounds between Kierkegaard and Müller take on even more importance. For in this case, Kierkegaard, in connection with the elaboration of his principal writings on the doctrine of sin, would already have read Müller's conception, which has a lot to commend it. If one, by contrast, assumes that Kierkegaard worked on his doctrine of sin completely independently of Müller, then the parallel, in terms of their doctrines, is striking, and we would have to assume that both of them came to these independently of each other. This is the view of Stanley Russell, "Two Nineteenth Century Theologies of Sin," op. cit., p. 240, who, however, does not take into account that Kierkegaard also quotes from the first edition of Müller's *Doctrine of Sin*.

47 *SKS* 23, 49, NB15:71 / *JP* 4, 4555.

48 *SKS* 23, 49, NB15:71.a / *JP* 4, 4556; see *SKS* 23, 114, NB16:32 / *JP* 2, 1531.

49 *SKS* 23, 114, NB16:32 / *JP* 2, 1531.

50 *SKS* 23, 114, NB16:32 / *JP* 2, 1531.

51 *SKS* 23, 49, NB15:71 / *JP* 4, 4555, and especially *SKS* 23, 51f., NB15:75 / *JP* 1, 73.

52 *SKS* 23, 49, NB15:71 / *JP* 4, 4555.

53 Ibid.

54 *SKS* 23, 63, NB15:91 / *JP* 2, 1614.

subjectivity."[55] Kierkegaard therefore reproaches Müller for not going far enough in his criticism of Hegel and for not recognizing that Hegel's conception of God is a mere abstraction; he "does not come to God, the subjective in the absolute sense, or to the truth—that ultimately the single individual is really higher than the universal, namely, the single individual in his God-relationship."[56]

By contrast, Kierkegaard calls it an "excellent little section"[57] when Müller insists on the fact that sin cannot be derived from its potential and when he considers sin as the "groundless."[58] Kierkegaard also compliments Müller on his remarks on the multiplying energy of evil as an excellent "answer to the explanation that sin is weakness."[59]

Moreover, he emphasizes Müller's understanding of freedom positively, that is to say that "freedom cannot be regarded indiscriminately as a capacity for good and for evil, for then evil is really also a good. Nor can one say that the basis of evil is the misuse of the will, for the very misuse of the will is precisely the evil."[60] In doing so, Kierkegaard does not go into the details of Müller's doctrine of freedom and his distinction between real and formal freedom.

Furthermore, Kierkegaard refers approvingly to Müller's criticism of the original sin, arguing that sin, guilt, and personal responsibility are correlative concepts and that the "original sin" has to be understood as that from which "actual sins necessarily come."[61] He defends Müller's understanding of the primordial sin against Dorner's reproach of atomism, for, according to Kierkegaard, *individuum* does not mean anything else but ατομον.[62] In this context, Kierkegaard notices that Müller also wrestles with the character of guilt of the original sin as "a composite of qualitatively heterogeneous categories. To 'inherit' is a category of nature. 'Guilt' is an ethical category of spirit."[63] He also makes a case for Müller against Richard Rothe's criticism that Müller's consciousness of guilt is exaggerated, although Kierkegaard again qualifies this, saying Müller "does not make it qualitatively ethical enough."[64]

Kierkegaard criticizes Müller for his idea of the Fall beyond time. Müller has "invented" the theory "that original sin (*peccatum originale*) is traceable to a timeless fall before the lives of all men in time."[65] According to Kierkegaard, this is no solution but only a shift of emphasis to another level. For the problem consists, to put it with Johannes Climacus, in the question how "an eternal blessedness or unblessedness is decided in time by a relation to something historical."[66] This, for its part, cannot be conceptualized but must be believed. Yet, he concedes to Müller

55 *SKS* 23, 49, NB15:71 / *JP* 4, 4555.
56 *SKS* 23, 63, NB15:91 / *JP* 2, 1614.
57 *SKS* 23, 70f., NB15:101 / *JP* 4, 4030.
58 *SKS* 23, 71, NB15:101.d / *JP* 4, 4031.
59 *SKS* 23, 50, NB15:73 / *JP* 4, 4028.
60 *SKS* 23, 71, NB15:102 / *JP* 2, 1262.
61 *SKS* 23, 100, NB16:5 / *JP* 4, 4034.
62 *SKS* 23, 103, NB16:12 / *JP* 2, 2023.
63 *SKS* 23, 103f., NB16:13 / *JP* 2, 1530.
64 *SKS* 23, 114, NB16:32 / *JP* 2, 1531.
65 *SKS* 23, 116f., NB16:33 / *JP* 3, 3093.
66 Ibid.

that "a man's choice becomes his fate,"[67] that is to say, the first sin is the sin which determines the entire existence of man.

How should we judge these statements by Kierkegaard? First, one might state that Kierkegaard surely brings out those moments in Müller's doctrine of sin which are specific to Müller's conception and which are, one might say, of importance for Kierkegaard's own thinking, too. Kierkegaard agrees with Müller's claim that sin cannot be derived and its nature cannot be conceived, which both take as a central argument against speculation.[68] For Müller's view of a force gathering momentum which pertains to evil, Kierkegaard in *The Concept of Anxiety* and *The Sickness unto Death* unfolds an emphatic phenomenology.

Kierkegaard also sees correctly that Müller looks for a conception of freedom which means no mere capability of indifference[69] as well as no abstract capability of choice and which does not yet presuppose what he attempts to justify first of all: freedom already destined for abuse.[70] For Kierkegaard, both the criticism of the idea of freedom as the capability of indifference and the criticism of an idea of freedom which already presupposes a sinfulness of the will in order to be able to explain sin, constitute the starting point of his own conception of freedom as the unconditional cause of sin. With it, Kierkegaard attempts to conceive freedom as the fulfillment of self-positing by which the individual falls into sin.[71]

Moreover, Kierkegaard sees that in the concept of original sin, what is at issue is conceiving of it as the cause of the actual sins which constantly has an effect. This is the meaning of Kierkegaard's idea that the first sin is not the first sin numerically but just the primordial sin as the cause which has an effect on all actual sins. "That the *first* sin signifies something different from *a* sin (i.e., a sin like many others), something different from *one* sin (i.e., no. 1 in relation to no. 2), is quite obvious. The first sin constitutes the nature of the quality: the first sin is the sin."[72] In addition, Kierkegaard shares Müller's criticism of the traditional doctrine of the original sin insofar as it cannot justify the guilt of the individual; he defends the "atomism" connected with Müller's transformation of the doctrine of the original sin, that is, the concentration on the individual. Consequently, he conceives the relationship

---

67 *SKS* 23, 130, NB16:49 / *JP* 2, 1263.

68 Cf. particularly *SKS* 11, 209ff. / *SUD*, 96ff. and, regarding Kierkegaard's idea of a "leap" of freedom into sin, particularly *SKS* 4, 338, 344, 388 / *CA*, 32, 37, 85.

69 It is known that, for Kierkegaard, the definition of freedom as capability of indifference is a "nuisance for thought," *SKS* 4, 355 / *CA*, 49, cf. *SKS* 4, 413ff. / *CA*, 111ff. For him, too, freedom is no capability of choice; "...freedom's possibility is not the ability to choose the good or the evil. Such thoughtlessness is no more in the interest of Scriptures than in the interest of thought." *SKS* 4, 354 / *CA*, 49.

70 This, too, is Kierkegaard's central argument against all attempts to explain sin from the "selfishness" or the *concupiscentia*, respectively: these already presuppose what is to be explained first and foremost (see especially *SKS* 4, 346f., 381, 382 / *CA*, 40, 77f., 79).

71 This is the thesis for the interpretation of Kierkegaard's conception of freedom in *The Concept of Anxiety* and *The Sickness unto Death*, which was developed in more detail in Axt-Piscalar, *Ohnmächtige Freiheit*, op. cit.

72 *SKS* 4, 336 / *CA*, 30.

between original sin and the sin of the (human) race in a way that is in complete accordance with Müller.[73]

Moreover, Kierkegaard agrees with Müller's view of the original sin in that it determines the existence of man as the cause which constantly has an effect, and, in this respect, man's choice becomes his destiny. Sin is a force which determines the existence of man.

Now, concerning Kierkegaard's criticism of Müller's insufficient grasp of the existential dimension of human existence before God which "does not make it qualitatively ethical enough,"[74] one may grant Kierkegaard this criticism, but at the same time, one must concede that Müller also attempts to capture this dimension in his doctrine of sin and that it even constitutes the motivation of his thinking. This is evident from Müller's personal development, and it appears in his criticism of speculation. The motifs that are here on Müller's mind—the central significance of the concrete individual, the understanding of religion as an I-Thou-relationship towards God, the emphasis of the moral–religious character of Christian religion, the assertion of the freedom of the individual which is based on God—all these are motifs which Müller shares with Kierkegaard, although the latter has without question developed them, as concepts, more consistently and with greater existential verve.

It is not surprising that Kierkegaard attacks Müller's unique idea of an extratemporal self-determination of each individual to evil. But while Kierkegaard shares the fundamental views of the doctrine of sin with Müller, while disagreeing with the presupposition of an extratemporal self-determination conceived by Müller himself as the sole conclusion which is consistent and meets the requirements of a justification of absolute sin in the individual, the really exciting question is how Kierkegaard himself attempts to give a "solution" to this problem under the same premises. For it is known that Kierkegaard, at least in *The Concept of Anxiety*, makes use of the concept of the "first" sin in order to assert a primordial state and fall for each individual. Admittedly, he attempts to supply "intermediate terms"[75] in order to conceive the possibility of sin from anxiety—intermediary relations which are superior to Müller's not only because of their existential dimension but also because of their stronger (conceptual) difference in view of the concept of freedom—although even here, the proximity between Vigilius Haufniensis and Müller in their conceptions of freedom should not be overlooked.[76] In order to be able to conceive the guilt of sin, Vigilius Haufniensis also thinks that a primordial state of being created is to be assumed, from which each individual "falls" into sin. But then the question is how such a primordial state can be conceptualized in more detail. A detailed discussion of this, however, would lead even more strongly to an analysis of Kierkegaard's own doctrine of sin; however, this is not the place to explore this. What mattered here was to indicate the points of overlap between Kierkegaard and Müller in the development of the doctrine of sin, which are of a genuinely conceptual nature and not merely limited to a few references.

---

73 Kierkegaard, however, rejects the concept of a self-determination to evil beyond time.

74 *SKS* 23, 114, NB16:32 / *JP* 2, 1531.

75 *SKS* 4, 354, 379 / *CA*, 49, 75.

76 See Axt-Piscalar, *Ohnmächtige Freiheit*, op. cit., pp. 148ff.

Bibliography

I. Müller's Works in The Auction Catalogue *of Kierkegaard's Library*

Die christliche Lehre von der Sünde, vols. 1–2, 3rd revised and enlarged ed., Breslau: Josef Max 1849 (*ASKB* 689-690).

"Bemærkninger angaaende den hegelske Philosophies Forhold til den christelige Tro," *Tidsskrift for udenlandsk theologisk Litteratur*, vols. 1–20, ed. by Henrik Nikolai Clausen and Matthias Hagen Hohlenberg, Copenhagen: C.A. Reitzel 1833–52, vol. 2, 1834, pp. 85–106 (*ASKB* U 29).

"Den christelige Lære om Synden…Første Bind. 1839," *Tidsskrift for udenlandsk theologisk Litteratur*, op. cit., vol. 7, 1839, pp. 653–724.

"Den christelige Lære om Synden…2 Dele. 1844," *Tidsskrift for udenlandsk theologisk Litteratur*, op. cit., vol. 13, 1845, pp. 189–271.

"De nærmeste Opgaver for den protestantiske Kirkeforfatnings-Uddannelse," *Tidsskrift for udenlandsk theologisk Litteratur*, op. cit., vol. 13, 1845, pp. 500–50.

"Den første preussiske General-Synode og de kirkelige Bekjendelser," *Tidsskrift for udenlandsk theologisk Litteratur*, op. cit., vol. 15, 1847, pp. 491–586.

II. Works in The Auction Catalogue *of Kierkegaard's Library that Discuss Müller*

Beck, Frederik, *Begrebet Mythus eller den religiøse Aands Form*, Copenhagen: P.G. Philipsen 1842, p. 27 (*ASKB* 424).

Bruch, Johann Friedrich, *Die Lehre von den göttlichen Eigenschaften*, Hamburg: Friedrich Perthes 1842, p. 262n; p. 263n; p. 264n (*ASKB* 439).

Martensen, Hans Lassen, *Den christelige Dogmatik*, Copenhagen: C.A. Reitzel 1849, p. 194n (*ASKB* 653).

Mynster, Jakob Peter, *Blandede Skrivter*, vols. 1–3, Copenhagen: Den Gyldendalske Boghandlings Forlag 1852–53 (vols. 4–6, Copenhagen: Den Gyldendalske Boghandlings Forlag 1855–57), vol. 2, p. 106 (*ASKB* 358–363).

III. Secondary Literature on Kierkegaard's Relation to Müller

Axt-Piscalar, Christine, *Ohnmächtige Freiheit. Studien zum Verhältnis von Subjektivität und Sünde bei August Tholuck, Julius Müller, Sören Kierkegaard und Friedrich Schleiermacher*, Tübingen: J.C.B. Mohr (P. Siebeck) 1996, pp. 26–173.

Russell, Stanley H., "Two Nineteenth Century Theologies of Sin—Julius Müller and Soren Kierkegaard," *Scottish Journal of Theology*, vol. 40, 1987, pp. 231–48.

Willi, Hans-Peter, *Unbegreifliche Sünde. "Die christliche Lehre von der Sünde" als Theorie der Freiheit bei Julius Müller*, Berlin and New York: Walter de Gruyter 2003.

Rosenkranz:

Traces of Hegelian Psychology and Theology in Kierkegaard

Heiko Schulz

I.

Johann Karl (sometimes Carl) Friedrich Rosenkranz was born in Magdeburg on 23 April 1805, as the son of a tax official. He studied theology, philosophy and German philology in Berlin, Halle and Heidelberg, where he came under the influence of Karl Daub (1765–1836) and where he later received his doctorate. In 1828, he was appointed *Privatdozent* in Halle, where he had submitted a thesis on Spinoza; soon afterwards he became professor "extraordinarius." Although initially unimpressed by Hegel—occasionally attending his lectures in Berlin—he began reading his works more intensively in Halle and from 1831 participated actively in the Hegelian circle there. Having received a professorship in Berlin, he became friends with Hegel himself and even attended his birthday celebration a few weeks before Hegel's death. In 1833 Rosenkranz became professor "ordinarius" of philosophy at the University of Königsberg (then Prussia) as the successor of Johann Friedrich Herbart (1776–1841). Apart from a brief political career in Berlin during the revolutionary crisis of 1848–49, he remained in Königsberg, where he died on 14 June 1879.

Rosenkranz's vast opus comprises over 40 monographs in addition to countless articles. These works make substantial contributions to a variety of fields, such as logic, metaphysics, aesthetics, psychology, theology, pedagogy, biography, literary history, political and social theory.[1] With very few exceptions, however, none of his major works has enjoyed an extensive reception. Nor have they been reprinted—most of them simply fell into oblivion after the heyday of Hegelianism in the second half of the nineteenth century.[2]

---

1 For an almost exhaustive bibliography of the sources (together with a biographical sketch and useful secondary material) see Klaus-Gunther Wesseling, "Rosenkranz, Johann Karl [Carl] Friedrich," in *Biographisch-Bibliographisches Kirchenlexikon*, vols. 1–14, ed. by Traugott Bautz, Herzberg: Bautz 1995, vol. 8, pp. 673–80. I quote a number of titles that I believe to be pertinent for Kierkegaard's reception of Rosenkranz and/or characteristic of the latter's theological or philosophical thought *per se*. (I am particularly indebted here and in the following to cand.theol. Mareike Reinwald for her invaluable bibliographical support.)

2 A fact that is further illuminated by the rather scanty secondary literature on Rosenkranz. For a general introduction and/or a survey of his theological or philosophical views, see,

That things were quite different in Kierkegaard's day, is plain to see. Although occasionally accused of being a mere epigone, Rosenkranz was at the time considered and respected generally as one of the more original, in any case one of the most productive and stylistically accessible, Hegel-adepts among contemporary German philosophers. Ever striving to mediate between the more extreme claims of the right Hegelians (for example, Erdmann, Gabler, Marheineke, Michelet) and the left Hegelians (for example, Feuerbach, Strauss, Vatke, Ruge), he was, according to the Straussian label, considered the main representative of the "center"[3]—trying as such to do justice both to Hegel's own views and to their apparently contradictory applications within the two opposing groups of the master's followers.[4] Even in

---

for instance: Friedrich W. Graf, *Kritik und Pseudospekulation. David Friedrich Strauß als Dogmatiker im Kontext der positionellen Theologie seiner Zeit*, Munich: Christian Kaiser 1982, especially pp. 132–58; pp. 171–8; and pp. 206–11; Richard Jonas, *Karl Rosenkranz*, Leipzig: Weicher 1906; Werner Jung, "Rosenkranz, Karl," in *Metzler Philosophen Lexikon. Von den Vorsokratikern bis zu den Neuen Philosophen*, ed. by Bernd Lutz, 3rd ed., Stuttgart and Weimar: Metzler 2003, pp. 610f.; Ferdinand Lassalle, *Die Hegelsche und Rosenkranzsche Logik und die Grundlagen der Hegelschen Geschichtsphilosophie im Hegelschen System*, Leipzig: Wilhelm Heims 1927; Joachim Mehlhausen, *Dialektik, Selbstbewußtsein und Offenbarung. Die Grundlagen der spekulativen Orthodoxie Bruno Bauers in ihrem Zusammenhang mit der Geschichte der theologischen Hegelschule dargestellt*, Ph.D. Thesis, University of Bonn 1965; Erwin Metzke, *K. Rosenkranz und Hegel. Ein Beitrag zur Geschichte der Philosophie des sogenannten Hegelianismus im 19. Jahrhundert*, Leipzig: Wilhelm Heims 1929; Willy Moog, *Hegel und die Hegelsche Schule*, Munich: Ernst Reinhardt 1930; Richard Quäbicker, *Karl Rosenkranz. Eine Studie zur Geschichte der Hegelschen Philosophie*, Leipzig: Koschny 1879; Hans-Martin Saß, *Untersuchungen zur Religionsphilosophie in der Hegelschule 1830–1850*, Ph.D. Thesis, University of Münster 1963, pp. 157–65; John E. Toews, *Hegelianism. The Path towards Dialectical Humanism*, Cambridge: Cambridge University Press 1980, pp. 155–64; Falk Wagner, "Zur Pseudoproduktivität von Mißverständnissen in der Hegel-Schule. Der Gedanke der Persönlichkeit Gottes bei Karl Rosenkranz und K.L. Michelet," *Neue Zeitschrift für Systematische Theologie und Religionsphilosophie*, vol. 12, 1970, pp. 313–37. Rosenkranz's aesthetics have received wider and also more recent attention; see, for instance: Olaf Briese, "'Biedermeierliche Vermittlung. Karl Rosenkranz' 'Ästhetik des Hässlichen,'" in *Konkurrenzen: philosophische Kultur in Deutschland 1830–1850. Porträts und Profile*, Würzburg: Königshausen & Neumann 1998, pp. 54–64; Holger Funk, *Die Ästhetik des Hässlichen. Zur Schwierigkeit kategorialer Bestimmungen in der Kunstphilosophie des deutschen Idealismus und Spätidealismus*, Berlin: Agora 1983; Werner Jung, *Schöner Schein der Häßlichkeit oder Häßlichkeit des schönen Scheins. Ästhetik und Geschichtsphilosophie im 19. Jahrhundert*, Frankfurt am Main: Athenäum 1987, especially pp. 187–244; Dagmar Mirbach, "Johann Karl Friedrich Rosenkranz," in *Ästhetik und Kunstphilosophie. Von der Antike bis zur Gegenwart in Einzeldarstellungen*, ed. by J. Nida-Rümelin and M. Betzler, Stuttgart: Kröner 1998, pp. 669–73.

3 David F. Strauß, *Streitschriften zur Verteidigung meiner Schrift über das Leben Jesu und zur Charakteristik der gegenwärtigen Theologie*, Tübingen: Osiander 1837; part 3, Tübingen 1837, pp. 95ff.; pp. 120ff.; and p. 126.

4 As to a basic account of Hegelianism and its varieties in nineteenth-century thought, see Robert Stern and Nicholas Walker, "Hegelianism," in *Routledge Encyclopedia of Philosophy*, vols. 1–10, ed. by Edward Craig, London and New York: Routledge 1998, vol. 3, pp. 280–302; see also Horst Stuke, "Hegelianismus," in *Historisches Wörterbuch der*

retrospect Strauss' judgment seems essentially correct: not only with regard to the contemporary *theological* debate (where the compatibility of Hegel's thought with Christianity was the main point at issue), but also with respect to Rosenkranz's efforts to compromise in *philosophy* (where he tried to reconcile central views of Kant and Hegel[5]) and in *politics* (where he advocated a constitutional monarchy, while at the same time defending the freedom of the press and vigorously attacking the repressive policies of the Prussian administration[6]).

II.

Kierkegaard did not read or know many of Rosenkranz's books or articles.[7] The ones that he actually worked with, however, left (at least in part) a lasting impression on

---

Philosophie, vols. 1–12, ed. by Jochim Ritter et al., Basel et al.: Schwabe 1971–2004, vol. 3, 1974, pp. 1026–30. *Encyklopädie der theologischen Wissenschaften* may be read as the primary reflection of Rosenkranz's own assessment of Hegelianism in the 1830s.

5 In fact, Rosenkranz edited Kant's works: *Immanuel Kant's sämmtliche Werke*, vols. 1–12, ed. by Karl Rosenkranz and F.W. Schubert, Leipzig: Voss 1838–42.

6 For a brief survey of Rosenkranz's political views in relation to Hegel see: Jon Stewart, *Kierkegaard's Relations to Hegel Reconsidered*, New York and Cambridge: Cambridge University Press 2003, pp. 48f.

7 Nor did his library contain any book-length studies on Rosenkranz—there may not have been many at his time, anyway (the most infamous was probably a harsh polemic against the former's psychology written by Franz Exner, *Die Psychologie der Hegelschen Schule*, Leipzig: Fleischer 1842). However, Kierkegaard possessed numerous volumes of the *Zeitschrift für Philosophie und spekulative Theologie*, vol. 1–16, ed. by Immanuel Hermann Fichte and Christian Hermann Weiße, Bonn et al.: Eduard Weber 1837–46 (*ASKB* 877–911), which contain several articles on Rosenkranz. For instance: H.M. Chalybäus, "Natur- und Geistesphilosophie," *Zeitschrift für Philosophie und spekulative Theologie*, op. cit., vol. 3, 1839, pp. 160–95; I.H. Fichte, "Zu Hegels Charakteristik, mit Rücksicht auf 'G.W.Fr. Hegels Leben, beschrieben von Karl Rosenkranz 1844,'" *Zeitschrift für Philosophie und spekulative Theologie*, op. cit., vol. 8, 1844, pp. 295–311. It also seems quite likely that at least some of the contemporary accounts of post-Kantian philosophy and/or speculative theology that were in Kierkegaard's possession contain sporadic passages or even whole paragraphs on Rosenkranz. Since most of these were not accessible to me, I could not check them, however. I am thinking here, in particular, of respective works by authors such as Franz von Baader (*ASKB* 396, 416), Heinrich Moritz Chalybäus (*ASKB* 461), the younger Fichte (*ASKB* 506, 509), Günther (*ASKB* 520, 522, 524), Arnold Ruge (*ASKB* 753), Gotfried Jakob Schaller (*ASKB* 758), Franz Anton Staudenmaier (*ASKB* 789), Heinrich Steffens (*ASKB* 797–798), Peter Michael Stilling (*ASKB* 801), Christian Hermann Weiße (*ASKB* 866) and Johann Ulrich Wirth (*ASKB* 876). Books which I could actually look at and which do refer to Rosenkranz are, among others: Carl Ludwig Michelet, *Geschichte der letzten Systeme der Philosophie in Deutschland von Kant bis Hegel*, vols. 1–2, Hildesheim: Georg Olms Verlag 1967 [reprint of the original edition, Berlin: Duncker und Humblot 1837–38, which Kierkegaard possessed: *ASKB* 678–679]; see vol. 2, 1838, p. 613; p. 633; p. 648; pp. 657f.; pp. 659f.; pp. 662ff.; pp. 679f.; further D.F. Strauß, *Die christliche Glaubenslehre in ihrer geschichtlichen Entwicklung und im Kampfe mit der modernen Wissenschaft*, vols. 1–2, Darmstadt: Wissenschaftliche Buchgesellschaft 1973 [reprint of the original edition

him, as will soon become clear. The first time that he stumbled upon the latter's name may have been in May 1837, as a journal entry witnesses.[8] Kierkegaard had obviously just received or read the first number of the second volume of Bruno Bauer's *Zeitschrift für spekulative Theologie*, which contains a long article by Rosenkranz—an article that will eventually turn out to be of crucial importance for Kierkegaard's view of the relation between Pagan, Jewish and Christian religion.[9] Before hearing his name again in Martensen's lectures on speculative dogmatics,[10] Kierkegaard had presumably already purchased Rosenkranz's *Encyklopädie der theologischen Wissenschaft* (*ASKB* 35), for he quotes the book in a notebook entry from summer 1837.[11] During his first stay in Berlin, he then bought the *Kritische Erläuterungen* (*ASKB* 745) and used it while working on *Either/Or*, Part Two.[12] In April 1843 Kierkegaard acquired Rosenkranz's *Schelling* study (*ASKB* 766)[13]—a book that would prove to be of major importance for a number of passages in *The Concept of Anxiety*. In addition to these, there are two further works by Rosenkranz—both from 1837—that were part of Kierkegaard's library;[14] however, we do not know, when he acquired them.[15]

Tübingen: Osiander and Stuttgart: Köhler 1840–41, whose Danish translation Kierkegaard possessed, see *ASKB* 803–804]; see vol. 1, p. 2; pp. 245ff.; and p. 505; vol. 2, pp. 212ff. and p. 221.

8 *SKS* 17, 213, DD:1 / *JP* 2, 2211.

9 See Rosenkranz, "Eine Parallele zur Religionsphilosophie," *Zeitschrift für spekulative Theologie*, vols. 1–3, ed. by Bruno Bauer, Berlin: Dümmler 1836–38, vol. 2, 1837, pp. 1–31 (*ASKB* 354–357). Kierkegaard obviously belonged to the subscribers of the journal, since he possessed all three volumes that were published.

10 *SKS* 19, Not4:4.

11 *SKS* 17, 234, DD:36.a. Later in November 1838 we find him taking long notes and making excerpts from the book (see *SKS* 18, KK:4–KK:4.k), perhaps in order to prepare for his theological exams.

12 See Tonny Aagaard Olesen, "Kierkegaards Schelling. Eine historische Einführung," in *Kierkegaard und Schelling. Freiheit, Angst und Wirklichkeit*, ed. by Jochem Hennigfeld and Jon Stewart, Berlin and New York: De Gruyter 2003, pp. 1–102; p. 63 (note 206). *Pap.* III B 41.9 shows that Kierkegaard read and/or used Rosenkranz's book while working on *Either/Or*, Part Two.

13 See the editors' explanations to *Pap.* IV A 185 (*SKS* 18, 200, JJ:187 / *JP* 2, 1604).

14 Namely *Psychologie oder die Wissenschaft vom subjectiven Geist*, Königsberg: Bornträger 1837 (*ASKB* 744) and *Erinnerungen an Karl Daub*, Berlin: Duncker und Humblot 1837 (*ASKB* 743). Although it seems likely for different reasons (which I will mention later) that Kierkegaard did not read the former before working on *The Concept of Anxiety*, it seems equally likely that he purchased the book much earlier: for when he starts working on his own psychological treatise he quotes and refers to the first edition of *Psychologie oder die Wissenschaft vom subjectiven Geist* throughout; however, since 1843 a second, extended and emended edition was already available: see Rosenkranz, *Psychologie oder die Wissenschaft vom subjectiven Geist*, 2nd amended ed., Königsberg: Bornträger 1843 (a third edition appeared 20 years later).

15 The same goes for Rosenkranz's edition of Hegel's *Philosophische Propädeutik*, Berlin: Duncker und Humblot 1840 (*ASKB* 560).

On a surface level it seems quite unproblematic to assess the extent and significance of Kierkegaard's reception of Rosenkranz—which is a non-reciprocal reception, anyway.[16] For, on the one hand, not only the *direct* and *explicit*, but also (at least some of) the *direct* and *implicit* references to the latter's work are relatively easy to identify within the Kierkegaardian corpus.[17] And, on the other hand, these references are not very numerous. However, if we dig a little deeper, there is, in my opinion, more to be said—both with respect to a number of formal and material reflections or repercussions of Rosenkranzian themes and ideas in Kierkegaard. Without, for the time being, differentiating between both levels of the history of reception, I will, in order preliminarily to orient the reader, give a schematical overview that comprises what I take to be (most of) all of the pertinent references:

	explicit	**implicit**
direct	1. *Pseudonymous Works:* *SKS* 1, 134 / *CI*, 75 (source unknown; maybe Rosenkranz's review of Schleiermacher's *Glaubenslehre*, in: *Jahrbücher für wissenschaftliche Kritik* 2, 1831, p. 949) *SKS* 4, 337 / *CA*, 30 (allusion to *Psychologie oder die Wissenschaft vom subjectiven Geist*, p. 332 or *Schelling. Vorlesungen, gehalten im Sommer 1842 an der Universität zu Königsberg*, pp. xxiii–xxx, and 179–82) *SKS* 4, 447f. / *CA*, 147ff. (on *Psychologie oder die Wissenschaft vom subjectiven Geist*, pp. 320ff., pp. 209ff., and pp. 157–62)	1. *Pseudonymous Works:* *SKS* 4, 235–8 / *PF*, 29–32 (probably a reflection of "Eine Parallele zur Religionsphilosophie," especially p. 1) *SKS* 4, 322 / *CA*, 14 (maybe a reflection of *Psychologie oder die Wissenschaft vom subjectiven Geist*, pp. 11f.) *SKS* 4, 331 / *CA*, 23 (probably allusion to the title of *Psychologie oder die Wissenschaft vom subjectiven Geist*) *SKS* 4, 356 / *CA*, 51 (a reflection of *Psychologie oder die Wissenschaft vom subjectiven Geist*, p. 133)* *SV1* 11, 235 / *SUD*, 126 (maybe a reflection of "Eine Parallele zur Religionsphilosophie," especially p. 1)

* That Kierkegaard freely draws on Rosenkranz here has hitherto gone unnoticed (see *SKS* K4, 418). However, it seems that the latter's own report refers to yet another (still unidentified) source; see *Psychologie oder die Wissenschaft vom subjectiven Geist*, p. 133: "*Wenn man seinen Namen vergißt, wie jener Hofrath, der in einer fremden Stadt so viel Visiten machte, daß er zuletzt den Lohnbedienten fragte, wie er selbst denn eigentlich heiße, so ist ein solches sich Abhandenkommen Verrücktheit.*"

[16] There is no evidence whatsoever that Rosenkranz ever took notice of his Danish contemporary—no evidence at least within the limits of those sources that I had the opportunity to check.

[17] As to the distinction between explicit/implicit versus direct/indirect reception, see my article on Kierkegaard and Marheineke in the present volume.

	explicit	implicit
direct	2. *Journals and Notebooks*: *SKS* 17, 213, DD:1 / *JP* 2, 2211 (on "Eine Parallele zur Religionsphilosophie," especially p. 1) *SKS* 17, 219–20, DD:10 / *JP* 5, 5222 (paraphrase of "Eine Parallele zur Religionsphilosophie," pp. 1–31) *SKS* 17, 234, DD:36 (quotation from *Encyklopädie der theologischen Wissenschaften*, p. 73) *SKS* 18, 343–52, KK:4–KK:4.k / *JP* 3, 2747 [abbreviated] (numerous excerpts from E) *Pap.* III B 41.9 (on *Kritische Erläuterungen des Hegel'schen Systems*, pp. 308f.) *SKS* 18, 172, JJ:102 / *JP* 1, 899 (on *Erinnerungen an Karl Daub*, pp. 24f) *SKS* 19, 406, Not13:41 / *JP* 2, 1596 (reference to Rosenkranz's edition of Hegel's *Philosophische Propädeutik*, Berlin 1840, p. 93) *Pap.* V B 53.2 (maybe allusion to *Psychologie oder die Wissenschaft vom subjectiven Geist*, p. 332) *Pap.* V B 53.18 (on *Schelling. Vorlesungen, gehalten im Sommer 1842 an der Universität zu Königsberg*, pp. 303f. and pp. 308ff.) *Pap.* V B 67 and V B 69 / *JP* 3, 3795 (on *Psychologie oder die Wissenschaft vom subjectiven Geist*, pp. 320ff. and pp. 157–62)	2. *Journals and Notebooks:* *SKS* 18, 200, JJ:187 / *JP* 2, 1604 (maybe allusion to *Schelling. Vorlesungen, gehalten im Sommer 1842 an der Universität zu Königsberg*, p. 187) *Pap.* V B 14, p. 71 (maybe allusion to *Kritische Erläuterungen des Hegel'schen Systems*, p. 11 or pp. 155ff.) *Pap.* V B 53.9 / *JP* 3, 3557 (allusion to *Psychologie oder die Wissenschaft vom subjectiven Geist*, p. 96 and p. 331) *Pap.* V B 55.17 (maybe a reflection of *Schelling. Vorlesungen, gehalten im Sommer 1842 an der Universität zu Königsberg*, pp. 259f.) *Pap.* V B 60, p. 134 (allusion to *Psychologie oder die Wissenschaft vom subjectiven Geist*, p. 334) *Pap.* V B 72.10 (a reflection of *Schelling. Vorlesungen, gehalten im Sommer 1842 an der Universität zu Königsberg*, p. 303) *Pap.* V B 150.25 (allusion to *Georg Wilhelm Friedrich Hegel's Leben*, pp. 296ff. and pp. 315ff.)

indirect	1. *Pseudonymous Works*	[irrelevant]
	2. *Journals and Notebooks:* *SKS* 19, 126–7, Not4:4 (a Martensen reference to Rosenkranz; source unknown)	[irrelevant]

Surveying these references, we may at first note a few striking, if more or less superficial features of Kierkegaard's reception of Rosenkranz, inasmuch as the former's writings bear witness to them.

(1) Signs of *indirect* reception are (with the exception of *SKS* 19, 126–7, Not4:4) fully absent from the Kierkegaardian corpus. Thus, it seems safe to conclude that his knowledge of and reference to Rosenkranz are to a large extent based on a first-hand acquaintance with the latter's works.

(2) Since most of the pertinent references (be they explicit or implicit) draw upon works of the German philosopher, which Kierkegaard himself possessed,[18] the former conclusion is not only corroborated, but at the same time specified: Kierkegaard's knowledge of and interest in Rosenkranz is restricted to a selection of (philosophical, theological, psychological) facets of the latter's authorship, which not by accident find expression precisely in those writings, which are part of the former's private library. In other words, Rosenkranz, the literary critic, the political, historical and pedagogical thinker is not only absent from Kierkegaard's library, but he is simply of no importance for him.[19]

(3) In terms of a purely quantitative ranking, we may note, first of all, that references to Rosenkranz appear exclusively in the pseudonymous works and the journals, but not—at least, as far as I can tell—in the edifying corpus or in the letters. With regard to pertinent passages and entries in the former parts of Kierkegaard's authorship, *Psychologie oder die Wissenschaft vom subjectiven Geist* comes in first with nine references (five in the published works, four in the journals and notebooks), followed by *Schelling. Vorlesungen, gehalten im Sommer 1842 an der Universität zu Königsberg* (one in the published works, five in the journals), "Eine Parallele zur Religionsphilosophie" (two in the published works, two in the journals), *Encyklopädie der theologischen Wissenschaften* (one reference in the published works and in the journals, respectively) and finally *Kritische Erläuterungen des Hegel'schen Systems*

18 Exceptions: *SKS* 1, 134 *CI*, 75; *Pap.* V B 150.25. Maybe in the latter case Kierkegaard does not refer to a passage in *Georg Wilhelm Friedrich Hegel's Leben*, Berlin: Duncker und Humblot 1844 (pp. 296ff. or pp. 315ff.), but rather to something he read in the abbreviated Danish translation of it, which was published in *Tidsskrift for udenlandsk theologisk Litteratur*, vols. 1–20, ed. by Henrik Nikolai Clausen and Matthias Hagen Hohlenberg, Copenhagen: C.A. Reitzel 1833–52, vol. 12, 1844, pp. 511–36 (see *SKS* K4, 396f.).

19 This conclusion may prove rash upon closer inspection, of course. For it may as well have forced itself upon me, simply because I restricted my investigation to the works mentioned above.

(also one reference in the published works and journals, respectively[20]). All other sources are quoted or alluded to only once: *Erinnerungen an Karl Daub* (journals), *Georg Wilhelm Friedrich Hegel's Leben* (journals), Rosenkranz's review of Schleiermacher's *Glaubenslehre* (works), and finally the former's edition of Hegel's *Propädeutik* (journals).

(4) A qualitative ranking goes hand in hand with this statistical result. Not surprisingly the single references turn out, without exception, to be just scattered remarks, made in passing and having no deeper or more far-reaching systematic impact. By contrast, both the frequency and the way of referring to *Psychologie oder die Wissenschaft vom subjectiven Geist, Schelling. Vorlesungen, gehalten im Sommer 1842 an der Universität zu Königsberg* and "Eine Parallele zur Religionsphilosophie" bear witness to the fact that Kierkegaard not only read these works carefully, but that they also left a more substantial impression on him. The *Encyklopädie der theologischen Wissenschaften* may be regarded as a borderline case: on the one hand, Kierkegaard took extensive notes to and made translations and excerpts from it.[21] On the other hand, the whole text is purely reproductive in nature.[22] Since it was probably written between October and November 1838,[23] and since, furthermore, Kierkegaard had promised his father in August 1838 (on the latter's deathbed) to pass his theological exams, the conclusion does not seem too far-fetched that Kierkegaard simply turned to the *Encyklopädie* as a first step in the direction of fulfilling his father's wish.

(5) Perhaps more surprising than the merely descriptive nature of Kierkegaard's reception is the normative aspect. Apart from the very few passages or entries of a more critical[24] or at least neutral kind,[25] a greater number of references to Rosenkranz and/or his works are unexpectedly positive or affirmative in nature. Kierkegaard often quotes his German contemporary at length or at least in full agreement and as a corroboration of his own views.[26] Moreover, some of these references are among the rare examples in Kierkegaard's entire *corpus*, where another author is explicitly and unironically praised.[27] Quite naturally these and other observations lead to the conclusion that Rosenkranz, despite the "grandiose"[28] Hegelian schema,

---

20 Of which the journal reference is highly unspecific, anyway: Kierkegaard may as well aim at Hegel here or at the (Danish) Hegelians in general. See also Stewart, *Kierkegaard's Relations to Hegel Reconsidered*, op. cit., pp. 368–77 (especially p. 371 and pp. 374f.).

21 *SKS* 18, 343–52, KK:4–KK:4.k [pp. 343–52] / *JP* 3, 2747.

22 See also *SKS* K18, 502f.

23 *SKS* 18, 352, KK:4.

24 See, for instance, *SKS* 4, 448n / *CA*, 148n.

25 See, for instance, *SKS* 4, 337 / *CA*, 30.

26 See, for instance, *Pap.* III B 41.9; *SKS* 17, 213, DD:1 and *SKS* 17, 234, DD:36.a; *SKS* 4, 448 / *CA*, 148.

27 For instance, *SKS* 4, 448 / *CA*, 148.

28 *SKS* 4, 448n / *CA*, 148n.

which sometimes—and to their disadvantage—dominates his presentations, is, in Kierkegaard's overall opinion, a thinker to be seriously reckoned with.

(6) Finally, and in typological terms, we may classify Kierkegaard's treatment of Rosenkranz as a borderline case between unproductive and productive reception.[29] A reception is unproductive, if and only if, although author A has evidently been taken note of by author B (be it ever so sporadically or briefly), this reception leaves no or only marginal (explicit and/or implicit) traces in B's writings.[30] A genuinely productive reception is distinguished by the more or less central or formative role that author A's work takes in author B's work *vis-à-vis* type, content and genesis, even when traces of the former are only recognizable in isolated passages of the latter. Thus, the relative infrequency of unambiguous references and allusions in Kierkegaard's reception of Rosenkranz suggests the unproductive variant. However, since there is more at stake with regard to the deeper affinities between Kierkegaard and his German contemporary, we may also be entitled to speak of a productive reception. That such a classification is in fact justified will become evident in the following.

III.

Given the relatively scanty references to Rosenkranz in Kierkegaard's works, it does not come as a surprise that very few scholars have touched upon possible connections between the two thinkers. And if they did, it was mostly in passing.[31] In my opinion,

---

29 This typology of reception is further explained in Heiko Schulz, "Die theologische Rezeption Kierkegaards in Deutschland und Dänemark. Notizen zu einer historischen Typologie," *Kierkegaard Studies. Yearbook*, 1999, pp. 220–44.

30 Such traces can be of the critical or (as is the case in Kierkegaard's reception of Rosenkranz) of a more or less affirmative sort.

31 Even the most elaborate accounts consist of no more than single passages or a few pages at best, and even these are frequently restricted to the most obvious references to Rosenkranz in Kierkegaard's works: namely, the latter's reception of *Psychologie oder die Wissenschaft vom subjectiven Geist* in *The Concept of Anxiety*. See, for instance, Michael Bösch, *Sören Kierkegaard: Schicksal—Angst—Freiheit*, Paderborn et al.: Ferdinand Schöningh 1994, p. 37; pp. 59ff.; p. 66; p. 69; p. 72; pp. 96f.; and p. 114; Anton Bösl, *Unfreiheit und Selbstverfehlung. Sören Kierkegaards existenzdialektische Bestimmung von Schuld und Sünde*, Freiburg et al.: Herder 1997, p. 49; p. 64; and pp. 119f.; Torsten Bohlin, *Kierkegaards dogmatische Anschauung in ihrem geschichtlichen Zusammenhange*, Gütersloh: Evangelischer Verlag 1927, p. 128; pp. 146f.; and p. 463; Walter Dietz, *Sören Kierkegaard. Existenz und Freiheit*, Frankfurt am Main: Anton Hain 1993, p. 126; p. 208; p. 255; p. 263; p. 269; p. 340; and p. 351; Stephen N. Dunning, *Kierkegaard's Dialectic of Inwardness. A Structural Analysis of the Theory of Stages*, Princeton: Princeton University Press 1985, p. 280; Wilfried Greve, *Kierkegaards maieutische Ethik. Von 'Entweder/Oder II' zu den 'Stadien,'* Frankfurt am Main: Suhrkamp 1990, p. 323 and p. 325; Alastair Hannay, *Kierkegaard. A Biography*, Cambridge: Cambridge University Press 2001, p. 218; p. 220; pp. 225f.; p. 300; and p. 467; Anton Hügli, *Die Erkenntnis der Subjektivität und die Objektivität des Erkennens bei Søren Kierkegaard*, Zürich: Editio Academica 1973, pp. 189; 192f.; 314

however, there are at least three characteristic features in Kierkegaard's reception of Rosenkranz which deserve a separate and more elaborate treatment: first, the influence on Kierkegaard of Rosenkranz's typology of religions (as introduced and explained in "Eine Parallele zur Religionsphilosophie"); secondly, the role of *Psychologie oder die Wissenschaft vom subjectiven Geist* in the authorship, particularly in *The Concept of Anxiety*; and finally, Kierkegaard's view of Schelling in its dependence on *Schelling. Vorlesungen, gehalten im Sommer 1842 an der Universität zu Königsberg*. Since the last point (apart from also being touched upon in the present volume) has already been dealt with elsewhere,[32] I need not go into detail here, but will instead, in the subsequent four sections of my account (III–VI)—concentrate on the first two aspects.

Kierkegaard's direct and explicit references to "Eine Parallele zur Religionsphilosophie" consist of (a) a brief quotation accompanied by a consenting comment[33] and (b) a fairly detailed paraphrase of the article's overall argument,[34] which also contains several quotations in German.[35] Both passages are located

---

and 316f.; Kresten Nordentoft, *Kierkegaard's Psychology*, Pittsburgh: Duquesne University Press 1981, pp. 21 and 389f.; Roger Poole, *Kierkegaard. The Indirect Communication*, Charlottesville and London: University Press of Virginia 1993, pp. 94–8 and p. 145. Further secondary sources include: Matthias Engelke, *Kierkegaard und das Alte Testament. Zum Einfluß der alttestamentlichen Bücher auf Kierkegaards Gesamtwerk*, Rheinbach: CMZ 1998, p. 63, pp. 73–7, p. 185 and p. 214 (on the impact of "Eine Parallele zur Religionsphilosophie" on Kierkegaard's writings); Carl H. Koch, *En flue på Hegels udødelige næse eller om Adolph Peter Adler og om Søren Kierkegaards forhold til ham*, Copenhagen: Reitzel 1990, p. 53 and p. 194 (on two implicit references to Rosenkranz in Kierkegaard); Gregor Malantschuk, *Kierkegaard's Thought*, 2nd ed., Princeton: Princeton University Press 1974, p. 35 and pp. 93ff. (as to the impact of "Eine Parallele zur Religionsphilosophie"); Tonny Aagaard Olesen, "Kierkegaards Schelling," op. cit., p. 29; p. 63; p. 67; p. 70; p. 72; and pp. 74–7 (as to the role of *Schelling. Vorlesungen, gehalten im Sommer 1842 an der Universität zu Königsberg* for Kierkegaard's reception of Schelling); Mark C. Taylor, *Journeys to Selfhood. Hegel and Kierkegaard*, Berkeley, Los Angeles, London: University of California Press 1980, p. 230 (Kierkegaard's theory of stages as dependent on Rosenkranz's reading of Hegel).

32 Tonny A. Olesen, "Kierkegaards Schelling," op. cit., especially the references given in the preceding footnote.

33 *SKS* 17, 213, DD:1 / *JP* 2, 2211: May 1837.

34 *SKS* 17, 219–22, DD:10 / *JP* 5, 5222: June 1837.

35 It is interesting to note that the latter (and much longer) passage consists of nothing but a mere paraphrase (plus some quotations). It does not contain any additions, comments or original ideas by Kierkegaard. By contrast, the earlier and much shorter entry invokes Rosenkranz's idea that Judaism, as a form of monotheism, can be reduced to the central claim "God is God" (see "Eine Parallele zur Religionsphilosophie," p. 1 and p. 12), as a corroboration for the genuinely Kierkegaardian idea that Judaism is a form of "*abstract* monotheism" (*SKS* 17, 213, DD:1/*JP* 2, 2211; my emphasis; as to the "abstract" character of Jewish monotheism, see also Rosenkranz, *Encyklopädie der theologischen Wissenschaften*, p. 143), which as such only admits of "tautological predications of God." (One may also think of Ex 3:14 here.) For Kierkegaard "this is also expressed indirectly by the fact that the Jews never dared utter" (ibid.) their God's name, and, furthermore, by an important stylistical feature of Old Testament texts, namely the so-called *parallelismus membrorum* (as to this, see *SKS* K17, 372).

within a context[36] in which Kierkegaard tries to come to terms with the relation of Christianity to non-Christian religions, in particular Paganism, Judaism and Islam.[37]

At least some of the ideas defended in Rosenkranz's essay apparently also left *implicit* traces in the later pseudonymous writings.[38] If I am not mistaken the most important one is to be found in a famous passage in Chapter Two of the *Fragments*.[39] Unfolding a fictitious love-story between a king and "a maiden of lowly station in life,"[40] Climacus examines the conditions of their mutual love to be or become a happy one. In his opinion, at least one important prerequisite is that the two lovers must understand or be fully transparent to each other; moreover, they must accept each other for what they are, and must also accept themselves, in relation to and in the mirror of the anticipated reciprocal judgment of the respective other. Thus, the love between the king and the maiden cannot be happy, unless the maiden knows and has the "bold confidence" [*Frimodighed*] to accept that (a) she is a maiden and her lover a king, and that (b) her lover knows and yet also accepts that he is a king and she, his beloved, nothing but "a lowly maiden." (Note that the same task is set for the king himself!) It is precisely this requirement which raises an anxious question in the king's mind: the question, namely, whether the girl can actually be made happy by their relationship; whether, in other words, she will be able to "acquire the bold confidence [*Frimodighed*] never to remember what the king only wished to forget—that he was the king and she had been a lowly maiden."[41]

Climacus invokes this fictitious setting in order to shed light both on the estranged relationship between God and a sinful humanity and the possible ways of overcoming it. According to the fundamental premise of his argument,[42] the love-story between

---

36 See, for instance, *SKS* 17, 218f., DD:7 / *JP* 3, 2734.

37 The only account of Rosenkranz's essay and its reflections in Kierkegaard that I know of is a passage in Matthias Engelke, *Kierkegaard und das Alte Testament*, op. cit., pp. 74–7.

38 Although I am not completely sure whether and to what extent the following examples are in fact characteristic of Rosenkranz, or whether he himself picked them up elsewhere, I mention some of those, which in my opinion are more or less clearly (if in part critically) reflected in Kierkegaard's later writings: the term "ethnic religion" ("Eine Parallele zur Religionsphilosophie," p. 1); the reflection of the tragic in the comic and vice versa (ibid., p. 8); the idea of love as the most fundamental attribute of God according to Christianity (ibid, p. 25); Christ as transcending the accidental elements of individuality (ibid., p. 29; see also *Encyklopädie der theologischen Wissenschaften*, p. 166 and *Kritische Erläuterungen des Hegel'schen Systems*, p. xxi); the worldview of Christianity as neither tragic (as in Greek religion) nor sad (as in Judaism), but rather as a "higher optimism," which as such presupposes "den absoluten Ernst" (ibid., p. 30).

39 *SKS* 4, 233–8 / *PF*, 26–32. That Rosenkranz's essay has left a few, if also implicit traces in other Kierkegaardian writings (such as *The Concept of Irony*, *The Sickness unto Death* and *Practice in Christianity*) is shown in Engelke, *Kierkegaard und das Alte Testament*, op. cit., pp. 76f.

40 *SKS* 4, 233 / *PF*, 26.

41 *SKS* 4, 234 / *PF*, 27.

42 Namely, Christianity rests on the belief that there is precisely one moment in time that has had (and so still has and will always have) eternally decisive significance: the moment of God's incarnation (*SKS* 4, 305 / *PF*, p. 109).

God and humanity is essentially unhappy from the outset, precisely because, due to Adam's fall, the conditions for mutual understanding and acceptance are lacking. As sinners, human beings neither can nor want to accept or understand themselves (as sinners) in relation to a (holy) god. And yet, the sinner is still "the object of the god's love. The god wants to be his teacher, and the god's concern is to bring about equality," for otherwise "the love becomes unhappy and the instruction meaningless, for they are unable to understand each other."[43] Thus, the situation is, at least to some extent, analogous to that of the king and the maiden; for here, too, what makes the understanding so difficult is precisely that by being reminded that he, the sinner, is nothing but a sinner over against a holy god, "he becomes nothing and yet is not annihilated; that he owes him [sc. god] everything and yet becomes boldly confident; that he understands the truth, but the truth makes him free, that he grasps the guilt of untruth, and then again bold confidence triumphs in the truth."[44]

Now, at first sight it may seem that Climacus envisages only two possible strategies,[45] which may be chosen by the god in order to reveal himself and his loving intentions to the sinner (and the sinner to himself) in the required way: on the one hand, he may bring about the missing unity "by an ascent";[46] on the other hand, the same may be accomplished "by a descent."[47] Closer scrutiny reveals, however, that paragraph A again has to be subdivided into *two* parts, each of which unfolds its own variant of the "ascent" strategy, so that, strictly speaking, we have to consider three possible modes of a divine revelation. Now, all I want to argue in the following is (a) that Climacus is alluding to what he takes to be the essence of Pagan (especially Greek), Jewish and Christian religion here, and (b) that the particular way in which he tackles these three (especially Judaism) is heavily indebted to Rosenkranz, especially the latter's essay from 1837.

Of course, the first part of my claim is in some sense far from being original: that Kierkegaard was of the (then as well as nowadays widely undisputed) opinion that Greek and Jewish thought function as formative powers and as major sources of Christianity is already evidenced in his second pseudonymous publication from 1844, *The Concept of Anxiety*.[48] And it is plain to see that Rosenkranz himself shared

---

43 *SKS* 4, 235 / *PF*, 28.

44 Ibid., pp. 30f.

45 See paragraph A and B: ibid., p. 29 and p. 30.

46 Ibid., p. 29.

47 Ibid., p. 31.

48 See especially *SKS* 4, 393 / *CA*, 90, where Haufniensis compares "the Greek, the Jewish, and the Christian views" of time and eternity. See also chapter III, § 2 and § 3 (*SKS* 4, 399–412 / *CA*, 96–110), where Paganism (= anxiety of fate) and Judaism (= anxiety of guilt) are juxtaposed; according to Haufniensis it "is precisely by the anxiety of guilt that Judaism is further advanced than Greek culture" (*SKS* 4, 406 / *CA*, 103)—further, namely, in the direction of Christianity, in which the whole development culminates (compare also Michael Bösch, *Sören Kierkegaard*, op. cit., pp. 113f.). Contrary to Hegel who places the Greek above the Jewish religion (see G.W.F. Hegel, *Vorlesungen über die Philosophie der Religion*, in *Werke*, ed. by Eva Moldenhauer and Karl Markus Michel, vols. 1–20, Frankfurt am Main: Suhrkamp 1986; vol. 17, pp. 50–184), Kierkegaard seems to follow Ferdinand C. Baur's ranking: see his *Die christliche Gnosis oder die christliche Religionsphilosophie in ihrer geschichtlichen*

this view.[49] However, *that* the three revelatory strategies, which Climacus takes to be exhaustive, do in fact correspond to the three religious standpoints described above, and *how* they are explained in the context of the *Fragments*, are much less self-evident; however, it becomes much more intelligible, if and as soon as we read the relevant passages in the light of Rosenkranz's essay from 1837.

My initial claim, according to which the third strategy (unity by descent) points to the Christian idea of the God-man, does not need any further explanation or corroboration, since it is evident from the context of the quoted passage.[50] Likewise Rosenkranz himself maintains that the judgment "God is man" in its proper sense is instantiated by Christianity alone and is as such based on the idea of the Incarnation.[51] To come to terms with the first variant of strategy one (unity by ascent) is relatively unproblematic, too: according to its basic idea (apotheosis of man), "god would...draw the learner up toward himself, exalt him,...let the learner forget the misunderstanding."[52] Since paganism as a whole and Greek religion in particular are lacking the decisive "distinguishing mark"[53] between the divine and the human,

---

Entwicklung, Tübingen: Osiander 1835, pp. 727–30 (*ASKB* 421). It is Baur also to whom Vigilius apparently refers by stating that it "is usually said that Judaism is the standpoint of the law" (*SKS* 4, 405 / *CA*, 103); cf. Baur, *Die christliche Gnosis*, op. cit., p. 733, where he calls Judaism "die Religion der Auctorität und des Gesetzes" (see also Rosenkranz, "Eine Parallele zur Religionsphilosophie," p. 12).

49 See, for instance, "Eine Parallele zur Religionsphilosophie," pp. 21–5 and pp. 30f.; further *Psychologie oder die Wissenschaft vom subjectiven Geist*, pp. 239f. Note also that Rosenkranz calls his article "Eine Parallele zur Religionsphilosophie," by which he probably means Hegel's lectures on the philosophy of religion (see "Eine Parallele zur Religionsphilosophie," p. 6 and pp. 8f.). However, whereas Hegel, in the second part of his lectures, distinguishes three types of positive or "determinate" religions (*Naturreligion, Religion der geistigen Individualität, absolute Religion*: see *Werke*, op. cit., vol. 16 and 17) and places the Greek (together with the Jewish and the Roman) religion under the second rubric, Rosenkranz favors another, if also triadic hierarchy, according to which Greek religion still belongs to the first type of religious judgment ("man is god"): see "Eine Parallele zur Religionsphilosophie," pp. 6ff. This deviation from his master's view might also be influenced by a pertinent Hegel critique that F.C. Baur had come up with two years prior to Rosenkranz's publication of "Eine Parallele zur Religionsphilosophie": see Baur's *Die christliche Gnosis*, op. cit., pp. 722–5.

50 *SKS* 4, 237f. / *PF*, 30ff.

51 See "Eine Parallele zur Religionsphilosophie," pp. 24–8. It should also be noted that Climacus calls the Incarnation "an absolute fact [*et absolut Faktum*]" (*SKS* 4, 297 / *PF*, 99), whereby he also seems to follow Rosenkranz who declares: Christianity's "*Factum ist das absolute Factum; caro Verbum factum est*" (*Psychologie oder die Wissenschaft vom subjectiven Geist*, p. 240; see also *Encyklopädie der theologischen Wissenschaften*, p. 40, where redemption is explained as the unity of an eternal and a temporal fact). However, it should just as little be overlooked that for Kierkegaard, contrary to Rosenkranz and the whole idealist tradition, the god-man does not simply represent the unity of god and *man*, but rather as the (paradoxical) unity of god and *a single individual*. As to this crucial difference, see Matthias Engelke, *Kierkegaard und das Alte Testament*, op. cit., p. 77.

52 *SKS* 4, 235 / *PF*, 29.

53 *SKS* 4, 250 / *PF*, 45.

namely sin,[54] a confusion between the two realms is the inevitable consequence: mankind as such—or at least mankind in its most striking individual manifestations (magicians, emperors, heros, and so on)—is erroneously mixed up with the divine through the "fantastical fabrication"[55] of elevating or exalting the former to the latter. Rosenkranz holds a similar view: "Ethnicism confuses the human and the divine in many ways and in innumerable degrees such that it ultimately arrives at a conception of God that is mere fancy."[56]

What about the second variant of the first strategy (unity by ascent)? In Climacus it is all but clear. He writes: "The unity could be brought about by the god's appearing to the learner, accepting his adoration, and thereby making him forget himself."[57] Not only in itself, but also as a description and assessment of (divine revelation within) Jewish thought, this formulation seems rather enigmatic at first sight. However, once we read it in the light of Rosenkranz's account of Judaism, it receives sharper contours and appears much less obscure. Rosenkranz contends that the judgment "god is god" functions as the basis for and the unifying element in all types of monotheism. Within Judaism in particular—judged by Rosenkranz as "the purest, most beautiful, most perfect development of monotheism"[58]—two basic aspects, both of which are connected with its concept of god, characterize its original outlook, as it is fully manifest in the Pentateuch: "Just as He [sc. God] as creator posits the world by his mere word…so also he commands absolutely without motivation. What he commands is sacred because He commands it. And human beings must obey the command because they are human beings and not God."[59] Being experienced both as the omnipotent creator and the holy, unconditionally authoritative lawgiver renders the Jewish god a totally transcendent Other, separated from the believer by an ontological and ethical abyss, which leaves the latter in a position of sheer awe and humble resignation over against the often inscrutable

---

54 See *SKS* 4, 400f. / *CA*, 97f.

55 *SKS* 4, 250 / *PF*, 45.

56 "Eine Parallele zur Religionsphilosophie," p. 11. See also ibid, p. 21: The pagan worldview as such "*ist in seinem Urtheil: der Mensch ist Gott; poetisch. Er dichtet dem ersteren alle Prädikate des letzteren an.*" Within the Greek "religion of art" (*Kunstreligion*), in particular, it is the tragic hero, "*der sich handelnd zum Göttlichen erhebt*" (ibid., p. 7). Elsewhere Rosenkranz calls the ethnic religion in general a religion of "*Anschauung*" (*Psychologie oder die Wissenschaft vom subjectiven Geist*, p. 239)—in contrast to both monotheism (as a religion of "*Vorstellung*," ibid.) and Christianity, which alone is based on the principles of thought and spirit (see ibid., pp. 239f.).

57 *SKS* 4, 236 / *PF*, 29.

58 "Eine Parallele zur Religionsphilosophie," p. 12. The reason for this preference is that Judaism, "*indem es Gott und Mensch auf das Entschiedenste auseinanderhält, zugleich von der Forderung, daß der Mensch nur dem Herrn leben solle, nicht einen Augenblick weicht*" (ibid., p. 12). It is interesting to note that in his earlier journal entry Kierkegaard, though paraphrasing Rosenkranz, simply omits Deism and Islam: "Rosenkranz…declares as a historical-religious judgment: *Gott ist Gott*, by which, of course, he means Judaism" (*SKS* 17, 213, DD:1 / *JP* 2, 2211). By contrast, see *SKS* 17, 220f., DD:10 / *JP* 5, 5222, p. 98, where all three types of monotheism are correctly mentioned.

59 Ibid., p. 12f.; emphasis added.

decrees of the former's will.[60] The fear of God is the beginning and the quintessence of wisdom—and such wisdom always keeps in mind as decisive that "God is God and Man is Man."[61] No doubt, this description meshes perfectly with what Climacus says when he, speaking in terms of the story of the king and the maiden, imagines that "the king could have appeared before the lowly maiden in all his splendor,"[62] thus leaving the latter in a state of awe and adoring admiration.

However, this being the case, how can we make sense of the additional claim that such a view of (the content of) divine revelation is part and parcel of an overall idea, according to which the unity between God and man can and must be brought about by an *ascent*? For, at first sight, it would seem that human beings, precisely by worshipping God as the omnipotent creator and holy lawgiver, are humiliated or even deliberately humiliate themselves to the utmost degree. Although this may—also for Rosenkranz himself[63]—be true in principle, we have to ask, first of all, whether Climacus is in fact (maybe even exclusively) speaking of a *human* ascent to God here and not (also) of the latter's own ascent. At least Rosenkranz's view of Judaism suggests that both ways of reading Climacus might be correct. In the former's opinion, contrary to the "Ethnicism, which takes the unity [sc. of God and man] lightly and superficially,"[64] the basic shortcoming of monotheism in comparison to Christianity lies in the fact that here the required unity is not realized at all. The fact that God is and remains the *totaliter aliter* separates him completely from the human realm, makes him vanish, as it were, into a sphere of sheer transcendence. God is thereby "honored" with an ascent, the price of which is his being put at a distance so great that it seems in fact unbridgeable. In this sense Judaism is, to use the Hegelian term, a "religion of the sublime" (*Religion der Erhabenheit*),[65] indeed.

However, this is not the whole story. For the discovery of this singular, omnipotent and absolutely sovereign god who, as such, demands absolute and totally unbiased obedience and worship on the part of the believer, strictly corresponds to and simultaneously goes along with another, no less far-reaching idea: the idea, namely, that the very same god has freely chosen the Israelite people to be the primary, if not the sole, addressee of his revelation to the world. In *Encyklopädie der theologischen Wissenschaften,* Rosenkranz puts the matter as follows:

---

60 See "Eine Parallele zur Religionsphilosophie," p. 15, where Rosenkranz calls Judaism "*eine Religion demüthiger Resignation*." (Perhaps this judgment is, at least terminologically, also the source for Kierkegaard's coining of the term "infinite resignation" in *Fear and Trembling*: see, for example, *SKS* 4, 133 / *FT*, 38).

61 "Eine Parallele zur Religionsphilosophie," p. 15. According to Rosenkranz, this "abstract monotheism" (see *Encyklopädie der theologischen Wissenschaften*, p. 143) basically remains the same throughout the whole Israelite history, although later, as being witnessed by the book of Job, the psalms and the prophets, in particular, its juxtaposition of god and man gradually begins to dissolve, until finally (namely in John the Baptist), the decisive insight begins to dawn: "*[W]eil Gott des* Menschen *Gott, so ist er selbst menschlich, und der Mensch, weil Gott* sein *Gott, göttlich*." ("Eine Parallele zur Religionsphilosophie," p. 15; my emphasis.)

62 *SKS* 4, 236 / *PF*, 29.

63 See, for example, *Encyklopädie der theologischen Wissenschaften*, p. 141 and p. 173.

64 "Eine Parallele zur Religionsphilosophie," p. 12.

65 See Hegel, *Werke*, op. cit., vol. 17, p. 50.

> The patriarchs were the first to whom God announced himself and manifested himself for their offspring. It is Abraham's, Isaac's, and Jacob's God in whom the people believe.... This coincidence of birth becomes a necessity here; the Jewish people are made noble people of born favorites of the Highest. Therefore, *Man in and for himself*, with all his sublimity, is, however, *not* the object in this religion; rather, a limitation of religion to this *particular* people takes place. All peoples are to praise the true God, but the real worship and glorification is limited to *One* people.[66]

Not only shall the Israelites worship and pay obedience to their god *alone*; rather, it is the *Israelites* alone who are granted the privilege of such worship and obedience. According to Rosenkranz, Judaism thus culminates in the highly ambivalent "Sensation as a slave to be absolutely nothing and then again as a servant to be everything."[67] And this unexpected human "ascent" is, if I am not mistaken, exactly what Climacus has in mind, when he, recounting the story of the king and the maiden, suggests that the former could have "appeared before the lowly maiden in all his splendor, could have let the sun of his glory rise over *her* hut, shine on the spot, where he appeared to *her*," and thus deceptively "let her forget herself in adoring admiration."[68]

IV.

The fact that Kierkegaard's private library contained several monographs on anthropology and psychology[69] may indicate how important the topic was for him—even more so, of course, when we take into account his own psychological works.

Furthermore, even a superficial survey of those journal entries in which the aforementioned authors are explicitly referred to reveals that, in comparison to the others, Rosenkranz clearly plays the most prominent role (apart from Hegel, of course).[70] However, the few explicit references do not do justice to the full extent of the former's impact on Kierkegaard. Most of these are to be found in *The Concept of Anxiety* and in a couple of accompanying journal entries. Here, at least two points need to be mentioned, if only in passing. On the one hand, Vigilius displays a *critical* attitude towards Rosenkranz, who in his opinion erroneously "admires

66 *Encyklopädie der theologischen Wissenschaften*, p. 139; see ibid., p. 173.

67 Ibid., p. 141.

68 *SKS* 4, 236 / *PF*, 29; my emphasis.

69 Apart from Hegel's *Encyklopädie* and Rosenkranz's *Psychologie oder die Wissenschaft vom subjectiven Geist*, Kierkegaard possessed: Carl Gustav Carus, *Psyche. Zur Entwicklungsgeschichte der Seele*, Pforzheim: Flammer und Hoffmann 1846 (*ASKB* 459); Johann Eduard Erdmann, *Leib und Seele. Ein Beitrag zur Begründung der philosophischen Anthropologie*, Halle: Schwetschke 1837 (*ASKB* 480); idem, *Grundriss der Psychologie*, Leipzig: Vogel 1840 (*ASKB* 481); idem, *Psychologische Briefe*, Leipzig: Geibel 1852 (*ASKB* 484); Heinrich Steffens, *Anthropologie*, vols. 1–2, Breslau: Max 1822 (*ASKB* 795–796); Theodor Waitz, *Lehrbuch der Psychologie als Naturwissenschaft*, Braunschweig: Vieweg 1849 (*ASKB* 852).

70 Compare the respective references (Carus, Erdmann, Rosenkranz, Steffens, Waitz) in Niels Jørgen Cappelørn's *Index* volumes to the *Papirer*.

Hegel,"[71] in particular for making implicit use of the leap within logic.[72] Later on Rosenkranz's overall proximity and obedience to his master is criticized again, even mocked in a more principled, methodological way. Vigilius notes that the former did not avoid "being ridiculous at times," since his book displays an almost "fanatical superstitious belief in an empty schema."[73] Due to the "grandiose"[74] Hegelian triad that Rosenkranz, according to Vigilius, all too slavishly clings to, his arguments tend to lose their thrust, whenever the concrete—and otherwise fully convincing—psychological analysis does not fit into the overarching dialectical framework, in which it is allegedly organically embedded.[75]

---

71 *SKS* 4, 337n / *CA*, 30n.

72 See *Psychologie oder die Wissenschaft vom subjectiven Geist*, p. 332: "*Man muß sich nur an die schöne Exposition Hegel's im ersten Teil der Logik erinnern, wo er zeigt, wie die Qualität durch die Veränderung ihrer Quantität in eine andere Qualität umschlagen kann. Die Steigerung erreicht endlich einen Grad, wo nicht mehr dasselbe in einer höheren Potenz, sondern zugleich etwas ganz Neues da ist.*" Kierkegaard alludes to this passage in *Pap.* V B 53.2. In the corresponding footnote of *The Concept of Anxiety* (*SKS* 4, 337; *CA*, 30) Vigilius refers to *Schelling. Vorlesungen, gehalten im Sommer 1842 an der Universität zu Königsberg* also—maybe to Schelling, pp. xxiii–xxx and pp. 179–82.

73 *SKS* 4, 448n / *CA*, 148n.

74 Ibid.

75 The passage that Vigilius invokes in order to support his claim is *Psychologie oder die Wissenschaft vom subjectiven Geist*, pp. 209ff. (see *SKS* 4, 448 / *CA*, 148). However, the notorious "schema" does not fully come across in the three subsection titles he quotes, since he omits a fourth one (see *Psychologie oder die Wissenschaft vom subjectiven Geist*, p. 211: "3. Die Aufhebung der Knechtschaft"), which, unless added to the two preceding ones (see ibid., p. 210: "1. Der Tod"; ibid., p. 211: "2. Der Gegensatz von Herrschaft und Knechtschaft"), leaves the Hegelian triad incomplete. All three of them are then placed by Rosenkranz under the more general heading "Das Selbst und das Selbst" (ibid., p. 209). This negligence notwithstanding, Vigilius is certainly right in highlighting Rosenkranz's "remorseless triads" (Roger Poole, *The Indirect Communication*, op. cit., p. 95): *Psychologie oder die Wissenschaft vom subjectiven Geist* is "divided into three massive parts. Each part is divided into three sections, and each section is laid out in three chapters. Most chapters are broken down into three subdivisions, and there are very often triadic subsections within these and even subsections of those again." (Ibid.) One important exception needs to be kept in mind, however: part three ("Pneumatologie") does not (*pace* Poole) consist of three, but only of two sections ("Der theoretische Geist" / "Der praktische Geist"). This can hardly be an accident, for in the second (Königsberg: Bornträger 1843) and third (Königsberg: Bornträger 1863)—otherwise substantially modified—editions of *Psychologie oder die Wissenschaft vom subjectiven Geist* this division remains unchanged. One possible explanation is that Rosenkranz wants to avoid a blurring of psychology and other (if dialectically related) philosophical disciplines (see *Psychologie oder die Wissenschaft vom subjectiven Geist*, pp. xf.). And since what is at stake at the end of part three, section two is precisely the quest for a transition from the emotional to the *moral* sphere of the subjective (*qua* practical) spirit, he may have been of the opinion that this could and should not be a proper theme of psychology as such. Thus at the very end of the book he writes: "*Die Psychologie hat nur mit dem Begriff der Individualität und Subjectivität zu thun. Mit dem Begriff der Persönlichkeit des Geistes beginnt eine andere [sc. ethische] Entwicklung.*" (*Psychologie oder die Wissenschaft vom subjectiven Geist*, p. 340; compare ibid., pp. x and xxviii; also Michael Bösch, *Sören Kierkegaard*, op. cit., p. 37.)

On the other hand, Vigilius explicitly praises *Psychologie oder die Wissenschaft vom subjectiven Geist* for being a truly "competent book";[76] and he also shows high regard for its author who, in his opinion, "distinguishes himself by his common sense and his humane interest in human life."[77] In particular, Rosenkranz is credited with having given an excellent account of disposition and also, though to a lesser degree and with some reservations, of habit, in relation to the former.[78] In *The Concept of Anxiety* the term disposition (*Gemyt*) is introduced for the purpose of giving a preliminary circumscription of inwardness.[79] Vigilius contends that although the term may be difficult to define, it—or at least one of its essential components—"is earnestness (*Alvor*)."[80] Now, a definition of earnestness turns out to be no less problematic—even though "in relation to existential concepts it always indicates a greater discretion to abstain from definitions,"[81] anyway. Thus, drawing on Rosenkranz, Vigilius takes refuge in the term "disposition"; for he believes that both concepts (earnestness and disposition) "correspond to each other," namely in such a way "that earnestness is a higher as well as the deepest expression for what disposition is."[82] Put another way, disposition is the *genus proximum* of earnestness, so that together with the respective *differentia specifica* we arrive at a quasi-definition that describes earnestness as "the *aquired* [*erhvervede*] originality of disposition, its originality *preserved* [*bevarede*] in the responsibility of freedom and its originality *affirmed* [*hævdede*] in the enjoyment of blessedness."[83] In order to make sense of this difficult remark, let us first return to Rosenkranz. Here, as Vigilius correctly states, disposition is defined as "the unity of feeling and self-consciousness,"[84] and this gives us a first hint as to the meaning of his former remark. Whereas animals, according to Rosenkranz, are restricted to the sphere of pure feeling (pain and pleasure, in particular), a human

---

A methodological parallel to this transition can be found in *The Concept of Anxiety*: Vigilius concludes his enquiry by contending that as "soon as psychology has finished with anxiety, it is to be delivered to dogmatics" (*CA*, 162; see also *SKS* 4, 322ff. / *CA*, 15ff. for an account of the relation between psychology and (first) ethics).

76 *SKS* 4, 447n / *CA*, 147n.

77 *SKS* 4, 447n / *CA*, 148n.

78 *SKS* 4, 447ff. / *CA*, 147ff.; furthermore, *Pap.* V B 67 and 69. Habit is the Hong's translation for "*Vane*" (see *SKS* 4, 448 / *CA*, 149); for "*Gemyt*" (see *SKS* 4, 448), which is a Danish assimilation of the German "*Gemüt*" (and is as such in fact hard to translate), they choose "disposition" (*CA*, 147). Mind, heart, soul, temper, and so on would count as possible alternatives. The Danish form must have been of quite recent use in Kierkegaard's time. Christian Molbech writes: "*Dette aldeles tydske Ord [sc. Gemyt] er især i nyere Tid indført og brugt for: Sind, Sindelav, Hjertelav, Sindsbeskaffenhed.*" (Christian Molbech, *Dansk Ordbog indeholdende det Danske Sprogs Stammeord*, Copenhagen: Gyldendal 1833, p. 354 (*ASKB* 1032).)

79 See *SKS* 4, 446–50 / *CA*, 146–50.

80 *SKS* 4, 446 / *CA*, 146.

81 *SKS* 4, 447 / *CA*, 147.

82 *SKS* 4, 448 / *CA*, 148.

83 *SKS* 4, 448 / *CA*, 149; my emphasis.

84 *SKS* 4, 448 / *CA*, 148. See *Psychologie oder die Wissenschaft vom subjectiven Geist*, p. 322: Disposition [*Gemüt*] is "*die Einheit des Gefühls und des Selbstbewußtseins*"; see also ibid., p. 319.

being has "Knowledge of feeling"[85] or "makes his feeling into an object by means of consciousness."[86] Accordingly, feeling functions as the medium of appropriation, as it were, of the content of (here, practical) self-consciousness. The proposition "I am in pain" can be uttered outside of a genuine first-person perspective: a child may babble these words without actually meaning them or without even understanding what they mean. By contrast, to say that the content of Peter's practical self-consciousness, expressed in the words "I am in pain," actually appears "as his own" (*als der seinige*)[87]—that is, in the genuine first-person-perspective—is tantamount to saying that what he is conscious of is actually (if not exclusively) felt by him, or that he is conscious of something that he himself actually feels. Thus, every instantiation of (spirit as) genuine practical self-consciousness connects and unifies at least two elements: both a cognitive or propositional element ("self-consciousness") and a non-propositional, emotional one ("feeling"). The former element refers to a given feeling as the "what" or the propositional *content*, the latter to the "how" or the non-propositional, self-appropriating *mode* of practical self-consciousness. Thus, we may speak of disposition only if (and yet also whenever) both elements are present:

> For, if the lucidity of cognition, the knowledge of sentiment, is lacking, then only the drive of the natural spirit, the turgor of immediacy, exists. If, however, sentiment is lacking, then only an abstract concept exists, which has not attained the last intimacy of the spiritual being (and) which has not merged with the self of the spirit.[88]

Rosenkranz's definition of disposition can, as Kierkegaard puts it in a draft, "be used as the foundation for earnestness, provided freedom is definitely included."[89] This is accomplished through the quasi-definition quoted above, according to which disposition becomes earnestness if and only if its originality (that is, the individual character and form of a dispositional unity between intellect and emotion) is both acquired, preserved and affirmed in a certain way. Which way? Vigilius' answer is threefold: first, the dispositional unity must be *repeatable*. In other words, it must have gained an inner stability which, as such, excludes the possibility of its being lost or dissolved again. This in turn is, according to Vigilius, tantamount to saying that it must exclude the possibility of becoming habitual. For habit[90] is precisely "the disappearance of self-awareness (*Selvfølelsens Forsvinden*)"[91] and, as such, signifies a loss of the original unity of disposition: wherever there is habit, there is loss of dispositional unity, and vice versa.[92] Correspondingly, if something can

85 *Psychologie oder die Wissenschaft vom subjectiven Geist*, p. 322.

86 Ibid., p. 321.

87 Ibid., p. 320.

88 Ibid., pp. 320f.

89 *Pap.* V B 67 / *CA*, Supplement, 209.

90 For "*Vane*," see *SKS* 4, 448 / *CA*, 149; also *SKS* 9, 43 / *WL*, 36.

91 *Pap.* V B 69 / *JP* 3, 3795.

92 That is the reason why Vigilius blames Rosenkranz for having dealt "with habit only in the 'Phenomenology,' not in the 'Pneumatology,'" although, correctly understood, "habit belongs in the latter [that is, in the doctrine of man as spirit] as well" (*SKS* 4, 448 / *CA*, 149). Accordingly, Vigilius himself discusses habit in a chapter that deals with "Freedom lost

become habitual, it cannot, for this very reason, be the proper object of earnestness. Or vice versa again, whatever it may be that makes a person earnest, it must be something that he or she can return to without ever becoming bored or frustrated, something that will never destroy the original dispositional unity by making that person susceptible to either an inappropriate sentimental or mocking mood.[93] Hence, the proper object of earnestness must be capable of being one and the same thing, for example, something to which the earnest person, as such, may easily "return in repetition."[94]

Secondly, nothing that fulfills the first requirement (whatever makes someone earnest must be repeatable) can *itself* be dispositional.[95] For "the inwardness of the feeling is a fire that may cool"; it "is uncertain in its mood, i.e., at one time it is more inward than at another."[96] Correspondingly, the original dispositional unity is inherently unstable, always in suspense and, as such, inevitably threatened by the possibility of being dissolved. As a consequence, that which makes someone truly earnest must be more than just a matter of disposition; rather, it must be something, the dispositional unity of which can be constantly acquired, preserved (that is reacquired) and affirmed. And this can only be the case if the object of earnestness admits of being taken seriously by means of a *free and deliberate inner act*.

Is there anything that actually fulfills both requirements? Vigilius answers in the affirmative, first by pointing to the eternal,[97] secondly to the self[98] and finally—both aspects taken together—to earnestness itself.[99] The true object of earnestness must itself be something *eternal*: for the eternal alone is unchangeable and as such admits of the possibility of unswervingly returning to it in *repetition*. Yet, what is eternally serious must also be part of the *self*: for only that which most intimately and non-contingently belongs to oneself may fully be realized by an inner *act* and by such an act *alone*. This holds true at least if (and only if) the self is conceived of not as a substance but rather as an infinitely repeatable inner act. If, however, both conditions obtain, then the conclusion that Vigilius considers himself entitled to draw seems less far-fetched: the conclusion, namely, that "this same thing to which earnestness is to return with the same earnestness can only be *earnestness itself*."[100]

Pneumatically" (*SKS* 4, 438 / *CA*, 137; my emphasis). The claim that Rosenkranz tackles the concept of habit in the second part of *Psychologie oder die Wissenschaft vom subjectiven Geist* (that is in the "Phenomenology") is wrong, however: it is actually discussed in the first part ("Anthropology": see *Psychologie oder die Wissenschaft vom subjectiven Geist*, pp. 157–62).

93 See *Pap.* V B 68; also *SKS* 4, 450 / *CA*, 150; the former indicating a disproportional predominance of feeling over intellect, the latter of intellect over feeling.

94 *SKS* 4, 448 / *CA*, 149.

95 Or habitual, for that matter: for habit is, as Rosenkranz puts it, "*als blos* formelle *Wiederholung der Tod des Geistes*" (*Psychologie oder die Wissenschaft vom subjectiven Geist*, p. 162; emphasis added).

96 *SKS* 4, 449 / *CA*, 149.

97 See *SKS* 4, 449 / *CA*, 149.

98 See *SKS* 4, 450 / *CA*, 150.

99 See *SKS* 4, 449 / *CA*, 149.

100 *SKS* 4, 449 / *CA*, 149; emphasis added.

As Vigilius points out, it is, for instance, not a matter of momentary enthusiastic mood or disposition which enables a preacher every Sunday to recite the prescribed common prayer or repeatedly to baptize children "in earnestness"; it is, rather, his willingness permanently and "in the responsibility of freedom"[101] to return to or to repeat (and thereby simultaneously to preserve and affirm) his original enthusiastic resolution to take these things seriously. It is, in short, his willingness to return to and reacquire his own earnestness, as part of his self, *vis-à-vis* the eternal.[102]

V.

In the preceding paragraph I have tried to show how and to what extent Vigilius, by *explicitly* drawing on *Psychologie oder die Wissenschaft vom subjectiven Geist*, borrows from (or even usurps) some of Rosenkranz's concepts and ideas for his own purposes, namely by integrating them into his own overall project. However, there is more to be said about the impact of Rosenkranz's psychological enquiry—at least with regard to some of its *implicit* traces in the Kierkegaardian corpus. As before, I will restrict my analysis to *The Concept of Anxiety*. To be sure, there are (as Kresten Nordentoft has rightly observed) a few early journal entries, which, although being mere preparatory studies to the essay on Mozart in *Either/Or*, Part One, are, on the one hand, perhaps "the most important rudimentary beginnings of the passage about Adam's anxiety in *The Concept of Anxiety*,"[103] and which, on the other hand, show striking similarities to some basic ideas in Rosenkranz's *Psychologie oder die Wissenschaft vom subjectiven Geist*.[104] Hence one might be tempted to conclude that Kierkegaard read and was influenced by the latter's book as early as 1837. However, this seems highly unlikely, given the fact that the respective entries were probably written in February 1837, so that even *if* Rosenkranz's book was already published at that time (which I doubt), it seems hardly possible that it was available in Denmark as early as that. Thus, when one considers the substantial similarities between the two authors, Nordentoft is probably right in presuming that Kierkegaard was simply "taking his point of origin in views which were well-known in his time."[105]

---

101 *SKS* 4, 448 / *CA*, 149.

102 Accordingly, Vigilius would probably criticize Schleiermacher's account of religion (in the latter's *Glaubenslehre*: see Friedrich D.E. Schleiermacher, *Der christliche Glaube nach den Grundsätzen der evangelischen Kirche im Zusammenhange dargestellt*, vols. 1–2, ed. by Martin Redeker, reprint of the 2nd ed., 1830, Berlin: Walter de Gruyter 1960; vol. 1, §§ 3–4, pp. 14–30 (*ASKB* 258)), arguing that it disregards one of its necessary preconditions or integral components, namely earnestness. In his opinion, religion is neither a matter of pure feeling nor of mere disposition, but rather of earnestness; it is, in other words, the freely acquired, preserved and affirmed originality of a (here, pious) disposition *vis-à-vis* the eternal.

103 Nordentoft, *Kierkegaard's Psychology*, op. cit., p. 21. Nordentoft refers to *SKS* 17, BB:24 and 25 / *JP* 4, 4397 and 4398 (1837) as germ-cells of *SKS* 4, 347–51 / *CA*, 41–6.

104 As to these parallels in detail, see Nordentoft, *Kierkegaard's Psychology*, op. cit., p. 21 and p. 389.

105 Nordentoft, *Kierkegaard's Psychology*, op. cit., p. 21.

This assumption is rendered even more probable if we consider what I take to be the first and rather obvious, if implicit, reflection of *Psychologie oder die Wissenschaft vom subjectiven Geist* in *The Concept of Anxiety*: Kierkegaard's and/or Vigilius' notion of psychology as "the doctrine of the subjective spirit."[106] Most commentators point to Hegel as the originator of this view. [107] They do so by following Rosenkranz's own lead who in justifying the title of his book (*Psychologie oder die Wissenschaft vom subjectiven Geist*) tells the reader that Hegel has "quite correctly and penetratingly designated the doctrine of subjective spirit as *everything* that the field of psychology is accustomed to include."[108] However, this judgment is question-begging, for it already presupposes and applies Rosenkranz's own terminology as authoritative, according to which both concepts (psychology/doctrine of subjective spirit) are coextensive. Without this presupposition, there would be no point in criticizing Hegel for having introduced a confusing and unnecessary terminological ambiguity, namely,[109] that of using the term "psychology" both in a wider sense, that is synonymous with "doctrine of subjective spirit *in general*," and in a more restricted sense, according to which it rather refers to the "doctrine of subjective spirit, *posited in and for itself*." However, Hegel is by no means guilty of such a "misunderstanding,"[110] for he does in fact *not* consider the terms "doctrine of subjective spirit" and "psychology" to be coextensive. By contrast, he has the latter designate the third and final part of the doctrine of subjective spirit *alone*.[111] In his opinion all psychology is a doctrine of subjective

[106] *SKS* 4, 331 / *CA*, 23. Although at first sight it may seem that Vigilius is simply reporting on somebody else's view here, so that one could be hesitant about ascribing the same view to him also, the context (together with a pertinent draft: see *Pap.* V B 49.17 / *CA*, Supplement, 183) renders it obvious that he actually subscribes to it himself. While focusing his methodological introduction on the problem of sin he only wants to inculcate that a psychology thus conceived (namely, as the doctrine of the subjective spirit) points beyond itself and is as such dialectically related both to dogmatics (as a form of "the doctrine of the absolute spirit": *SKS* 4, 331 / *CA*, 23) and to ethics (as "the doctrine of objective spirit": *Pap.* V B 49.17 / *CA*, Supplement, 183). It has also been rightly observed that, as a "psychologically orienting deliberation," *The Concept of Anxiety* is probably polemically directed against Heiberg who, being more Hegelian than his master, had banished psychology from "true" (that is, speculative) science (see Poole, *The Indirect Communication*, op. cit., pp. 96f.); moreover, that Kierkegaard, leaving behind Hegel's preference for a purely speculative doctrine of (here, subjective) spirit, introduces and applies a new, namely, empirical or "experimental" form of psychology (see Hannay, *Kierkegaard. A Biography*, op. cit., p. 225; also Bösl, *Unfreiheit und Selbstverfehlung*, op. cit., pp. 120f.); as to the limits of such an empirical discipline, see, for instance, *SKS* 4, 330; *CA*, 22f.

[107] See, for instance, Josef Leonhard Blaß, *Die Krise der Freiheit im Denken Sören Kierkegaards*, Ratingen: A. Henn 1968, p. 240; Dietz, *Existenz und Freiheit*, op. cit., p. 263; Hügli, *Die Erkenntnis der Subjektivität und die Objektivität des Erkennens*, op. cit., p. 314; Malantschuk, *Kierkegaard's Thought*, op. cit., p. 35.

[108] *Psychologie oder die Wissenschaft vom subjectiven Geist*, p. 8; my emphasis.

[109] See ibid., p. xxviii and p. 8.

[110] Ibid.

[111] Its first part (focusing on the concept of the soul) being the anthropology, its second part (concentrating on consciousness) being the phenomenology: see G.W.F. Hegel, *Werke*, op. cit., vol. 10, p. 38 (= *Enzyklopädie*, Part Three, § 387); as to the third part ("psychology,"

spirit, but not vice versa. This being the case, it seems obvious that Kierkegaard's own terminology is dependent on Rosenkranz rather than on Hegel—whether he himself was actually aware of it or not.[112]

The second implicit reflection of *Psychologie oder die Wissenschaft vom subjectiven Geist* in *The Concept of Anxiety* that I want to call attention to is methodological in nature. In the introduction to his book Vigilius takes great pains to unmask what he takes to be a fatal blurring of the boundaries between the various scientific disciplines.[113] Such a blurring, which, in his opinion, primarily Hegel and his successors have brought on, bears on the relation between, in particular, logic and metaphysics, logic and dogmatics, logic and ethics and ethics and dogmatics. The conceptual and methodological analysis is not an end in itself, though. Addressing the problem of (hereditary) sin, Vigilius tries to persuade his reader that this term has no proper place in either of these disciplines; rather, "it is the subject of the sermon, in which the single individual speaks as the single individual to the single individual."[114] If, however, sin is to be tackled "within the limits of scientific reasoning" at all, then, in his opinion, one ought to favor a kind of complementary model, in which psychology, (first and second)[115] ethics, metaphysics and dogmatics contribute to

---

with its focus on the spirit, as being posited in and for itself) see also ibid., pp. 229ff. (= *Enzyklopädie*, part three, § 440); see also Michael Bösch, *Sören Kierkegaard*, op. cit., p. 61 (note 132). Hegel also has good reasons not to adopt the term "pneumatology" for this latter part (as Rosenkranz does in order to avoid Hegel's purported ambiguity: see *Psychologie oder die Wissenschaft vom subjectiven Geist*, p. xxix and p. 8): see Hegel, *Werke*, op. cit., vol. 10, pp. 11f. (= *Enzyklopädie*, Part Three, § 378). For a survey of Hegel's doctrine of subjective spirit (with special emphasis on his anthropology) see Manfred Baum, "Georg Wilhelm Friedrich Hegel. Geist und Seele in der Anthropologie," in *Philosophische Anthropologie im 19. Jahrhundert*, ed. by Friedhelm Decher/Jochem Hennigfeld, Würzburg: Königshausen und Neumann 1991, pp. 51–66; see also Hermann Drüe, *Psychologie aus dem Begriff. Hegels Persönlichkeitstheorie*, Berlin and New York: Walter de Gruyter 1976. As to Rosenkranz's psychology in comparison to Hegel's, see, for instance: Karl Löwith, "Die Ausführung von Hegels Lehre vom subjectiven Geist durch Karl Rosenkranz," in *Hegels philosophische Psychologie*, ed. by Dieter Henrich, Bonn: Bouvier 1979, pp. 227–34.

112 See also Greve's apt remark as to the consequences of this particular use of language: "*Hegel benutzt den Begriff 'Anthropologie' nur für den ersten Teil seiner Philosophie des subjectiven Geistes, die zu 'Phänomenologie des Geistes' und 'Psychologie' fortschreitet.... Da Vigilius diesen letzten Begriff zum Gesamtbegriff ausweitet—im Anschluß an K. Rosenkranz's 'Psychologie oder die Wissenschaft vom subjectiven Geist'—hat er selber für den Terminus 'Anthropologie' keine Verwendung. Er spielt bei Kierkegaard überhaupt keine Rolle*" (Greve, *Kierkegaards maieutische Ethik*, op. cit., p. 323). It should also be noted that Rosenkranz's terminology is far from idiosyncratic; on the contrary, it seems to be firmly rooted in a *communis opinio* within mid-ninteenth-century philosophy. Thus, for instance, Carl Ludwig Michelet defines psychology as "*Philosophie des Geistes*..., und zwar näher des menschlichen, d.h. des einzelnen oder *subjectiven* Geistes" (Michelet, *Anthropologie und Psychologie oder die Philosophie des subjectiven Geistes*, Berlin: Sander 1840, p. 7).

113 *SKS* 4, 317–31 / *CA*, 9–24.

114 *SKS* 4, 323 / *CA*, 16.

115 As to the difference between first and second ethics, see *SKS* 4, 323–6 and 328f. / *CA*, 16–19 and 20f.

a common overarching project, the unifying perspective of which always keeps in mind that these different (and in fact irreducible, interdependent and irreconcilable) contributions can never hope to arrive at a complete and scientifically fully adequate picture of the phenomenon.

Now, these methodological considerations echo similar views put forward and defended in the introduction to Rosenkranz's *Psychologie*. For Rosenkranz, too, is concerned about the widespread "Confusion of the different spheres"[116] within contemporary, particularly post-Hegelian philosophy. And although he does not deal with the problem of sin (and, accordingly, does not discuss the methodological status of dogmatics), he takes equally great pains to determine the method and content of psychology in relation to the other (philosophical) disciplines—especially aesthetics, ethics, philosophy of history and logic.[117] In this context a brief comparative look at the two authors' accounts of the relation between (first) ethics and psychology proves particularly illuminating. Vigilius considers the former to be a strictly *prescriptive* science. As such, "(it) proposes to bring ideality into actuality"—more exactly, it "points to ideality as a task and assumes that every man possesses the requisite conditions"[118] to fulfill this task. If I am not mistaken, Rosenkranz fully agrees with this view: "Ethics presupposes that spirit can subject its corporality to its will; ethics demands this obedience in the name of freedom."[119] By contrast, psychology, according to Rosenkranz, can only be conceived and properly practiced as a strictly *descriptive* science. Its double task is, first, to show that and in which sense "*in itself*...nature…as the *organ* of spirit, constitutes an essential element of it";[120] and, secondly, to describe the gradual process from (subjective) spirit in itself to spirit (in and) for itself.[121] Now, even though Vigilius would certainly not subscribe to

---

116 *Psychologie oder die Wissenschaft vom subjectiven Geist*, p. x.

117 See ibid., pp. xf.; also *Encyklopädie der theologischen Wissenschaften*, pp. xxivf. Even Vigilius' insistence that the ability to address a scientific problem adequately requires a certain "mood [*stemning*] that properly corresponds to the correct concept" (*SKS* 4, 322 / *CA*, 14)—for instance, earnestness in the case of hamartiology—has its prototype in Rosenkranz. He contends that proper philosophical writing requires a certain stylistical sensitivity and competence; however, "*für diese Seite einer philosophischen Production bedarf es ebensowohl der Stimmung, als für die Realisierung eines Kunstwerks*" (*Psychologie oder die Wissenschaft vom subjectiven Geist*, p. xxii). See also ibid., pp. 11f., where mood is defined as a "*Zustand des* ganzen *Menschen, der allen besonderen Empfindungen und Gedanken eine spezifische Färbung gibt*"; therefore, mood is "*mehr und weniger als Empfindung; mehr, wegen der Totalität, womit sie den Menschen in Beschlag nimmt; weniger, weil sie abstracter und unbestimmter ist*" (ibid., p. 12; see also ibid., pp. 88f).

118 *SKS* 4, 323 / *CA*, 16.

119 "*Die Ethik setzt voraus, daß der Geist seine Leiblichkeit seinem Willen unterwerfen kann; die Ethik fordert diesen Gehorsam im Namen der Freiheit*" (*Psychologie oder die Wissenschaft vom subjectiven Geist*, p. 105; my emphasis).

120 Ibid.

121 Put another way, the central task of psychology is to describe and analyze what it means to be and become subjective spirit, precisely by describing and analyzing in which way an individual "*da ist, lebt, den Gebrauch aller seiner Sinne gewinnt, seiner Anlagen inne wird, die sich ihm darbietende Welt im Bewußtsein erfaßt,... denkt und begehrt*" (*Psychologie oder die Wissenschaft vom subjectiven Geist*, pp. xviif.).

the speculative implications of a psychology, thus conceived (in particular, the idea of an inevitable transition from soul to consciousness to spirit[122]), it seems quite obvious that he would consider himself in full agreement with Rosenkranz's, in that the "subject of which psychology treats must be something in repose that remains in a restless repose."[123] In other words, it must be something that is and remains in a state of transition or a transitional state and as such admits of and calls for psychological observation and description. By contrast, ethics, due to its purely prescriptive nature, "is never observing but always accusing, judging, and acting"[124] and thus does not have states, but rather events or acts (as a subclass of events) as its proper object.

The claim of such a mutual, if tacit, methodological agreement can be further corroborated by a look at the strikingly similar way in which the two authors tackle the paradigmatic issue of evil. Rosenkranz reminds his reader, "psychology has nothing to do with the concept of ethical division,"[125] for "evil in itself is purely an act of spirit"[126]; it is rooted, in other words, in a voluntary act of wickedness, not in an involuntary state of sickness.[127] Thus, even though Rosenkranz admits that, psychologically speaking, evil may subsequently *lead to* a "spirit falling ill,"[128] and that, for this very reason, it might have seemed appropriate to incorporate it into *Psychologie oder die Wissenschaft vom subjectiven Geist*, he declares that in the end he deemed it necessary to abstain from the idea—"for the sake of clear treatment of science which respects the rights of each sphere."[129] However, these considerations are, at least methodologically, very close to how Vigilius puts the matter with regard to the possibility of a psychological treatment of sin. For he, too, claims that sin is

---

122 See, for instance, *Psychologie oder die Wissenschaft vom subjectiven Geist*, p. 180: "*Der Geist wird durch die Natur bestimmt. Er ist aber von vornherein an sich Subject und sucht daher die Natürlichkeit durch sich zu bestimmen. Da nun dieselbe gegen ihn nicht als Subject sich setzen kann, so muß ihm die Bemächtigung seiner Leiblichkeit gelingen. Der Sieg über sie ist ihm vor dem Kampf garantirt.*" See also ibid., p. xxvi, and, furthermore, Bösch, *Sören Kierkegaard*, op. cit., p. 97. Likewise Kierkegaard and/or Vigilius would probably reject Rosenkranz's Hegelian claim as rash and one-sided that "*[d]ie Objectivität [sc. the 'objective spirit' qua morality, law and the ethical life] ist die Wahrheit der Subjectivität*" (ibid., p. xxvii).

123 *SKS* 4, 329 / *CA*, 21.

124 *SKS* 4, 330 / *CA*, 22.

125 *Psychologie oder die Wissenschaft vom subjectiven Geist*, p. xxxi.

126 Ibid., p. xxx.

127 In fact, Rosenkranz defines evil (*das Böse*) as "*die durch die Freiheit gegen ihr Wesen gesetzte Unfreiheit*" (*Psychologie oder die Wissenschaft vom subjectiven Geist*, p. xxxii; see also *Encyklopädie der theologischen Wissenschaften*, p. 67 and p. 86); as to a comparison, see Climacus' account of the sinner as a person who "uses the power of freedom in the service of unfreedom" (*SKS* 4, 225f. / *PF*, 17).

128 Ibid., p. xxxi.

129 Ibid., p. xxx. That Rosenkranz was very well aware of the paradoxical character of sin (as being both hereditary and actual, fate and guilt, state and act, quasi-natural and spiritual) is evidenced, for instance, by a number of pertinent passages in *Encyklopädie der theologischen Wissenschaften*. Here (see particularly ibid., pp. 68f.) Rosenkranz maintains that sin, although being a matter of inheritance, is nevertheless brought about by every individual again, and this in exactly the same way as in Adam.

"not a state" or is not *as* a state, but, on the contrary, is only "*de actu* or *in actu*… again and again."[130] Thus, it can be no proper object of psychology—much less of metaphysics or aesthetics or logic.[131] However, due to his insight into the necessity of a complementary treatment of the phenomenon, Vigilius picks up where Rosenkranz leaves off: although never letting the reader forget that the subject of sin first and foremost needs to be couched in ethical and dogmatic terms, he nevertheless goes into a "psychologically orienting deliberation," which is supposed to describe how psychological factors may influence and shape both the genesis and the consequences of sinful acting (including the consequences of a suppressed sin *consciousness*).

I conclude with a few observations as to the more substantial, if implicit, "material" reflections of *Psychologie oder die Wissenschaft vom subjectiven Geist* in *The Concept of Anxiety*. Before I do so, let me first recall the basic triadic structure of Rosenkranz's book.[132] It appears as follows:

Part One: Anthropology	**Part Two: Phenomenology**	**Part Three: Pneumatology**
The spirit in immediate unity with its naturalness (For instance, mood and character (as influenced by certain planetary and racial factors), temperament, sexuality, sleep, sensation.)	Consciousness as such	The Theoretical Spirit (Namely, perception, idea (memory, imagination, recollection), thought.)
The struggle of the spirit with its corporeality (For instance, dream, vision, clairvoyance, melancholy.)	Self-Consciousness	The Practical Spirit (For instance, pain and pleasure, desire, passion.)
The symbolic appearance of the spirit in its corporeality (Namely, mimic, physiognomical and craniological expression.)	Rational Self-Consciousness	

The few explicit references to part three (concerning Rosenkranz's concept of disposition) notwithstanding, we cannot help but notice that Vigilius is almost exclusively drawn to part one of the former's work: the anthropology, in which "the somatic…enters in its entire force."[133] Consequently, Kierkegaard and/or Vigilius do not engage in a discussion of those various parts, sections and paragraphs of the book, in which its author addresses basic problems of "cognitive psychology," as

130 *SKS* 4, 323 / *CA*, 15.

131 See *SKS* 4, 320ff. / *CA*, 12ff.

132 See *Psychologie oder die Wissenschaft vom subjectiven Geist*, pp. xxxvii–xliv.

133 Ibid., p. xxix. As to Rosenkranz's anthropology, in relation to both Hegel and Kierkegaard, see Bösch, *Sören Kierkegaard*, op. cit., pp. 59–62.

it were—in other words, the forms and developmental stages of human cognition. Thus, for instance, the (Hegelian) transition from sense certainty to perception and, finally, to understanding—a transition which dominates the first section of the *Phenomenology* (corresponding to part two) and is shown here both to posit and to presuppose a split between consciousness as such and its object[134]—plays no significant role in either Vigilius or Kierkegaard himself.[135] Thus, although it might be tempting to draw parallels either between the latter's doctrine of the (aesthetic, ethical and religious) stages of existence or between, for instance, the immediate, reflective and post-reflective level of the self in Anti-Climacus, on the one hand, and, on the other hand, Rosenkranz's transition from a level of subjective spirit "in itself" (anthropology), via "for itself" (phenomenology) to, finally, "in and for itself" (pneumatology), such a maneuver appears to me to be rather misleading. It is misleading, first, because, as mentioned already, Rosenkranz explicitly excludes the ethical dimension of existence from the domain of psychology, *qua* doctrine of subjective spirit.[136] Secondly, and pretty much for the same reason, there can be no parallel for reflective or conscious despair, that is, for the idea of a volitionally potentialized misrelation of the self to itself *vis-à-vis* the eternal,[137] in Rosenkranz. To use the latter's terminology, the possibility of such despair would presuppose or at least go along with a conscious relation to the eternal, *qua* "objective spirit" in its various forms and degrees—and this dimension, too, is fully (and also, in Kierkegaardian terms, correctly) absent from his book.[138]

---

134 *Psychologie oder die Wissenschaft vom subjectiven Geist*, pp. 181ff. and p. 185.

135 Likewise the whole first section of part three, spelling out the forms and the dialectical development of the major theoretical faculties of spirit (perception, idea, thought: see *Psychologie oder die Wissenschaft vom subjectiven Geist*, pp. 242–311) has apparently left no traces in *The Concept of Anxiety* or in the Kierkegaardian *corpus* as a whole. One exception that comes to mind, though, is the distinction between recollection (*erindring*) and memory [*hukommelse*], as being introduced and explained in the *Stages on Life's Way*: see *SKS* 6, 17–26 / *SLW*, 9–19. It corresponds to Rosenkranz's distinction between *Erinnerung* and *Gedächtnis* (see *Psychologie oder die Wissenschaft vom subjectiven Geist*, pp. 252–7 and pp. 296–305, respectively).

136 This notwithstanding, Bösl has persuasively argued that Vigilius builds on the triadic Rosenkranzian pattern by distinguishing three "anthropological spheres": the somatical (corresponding to the latter's anthropology), the psychical (corresponding to the phenomenology) and the pneumatical (corresponding to the pneumatology): see Bösl, *Unfreiheit und Selbstverfehlung*, op. cit., pp. 119f.

137 See, for example, *SKS* 11, 145, 157, 175ff. / *SUD*, 29, 42 and 60ff.

138 This notwithstanding, it can hardly be overlooked that Rosenkranz's "dynamical" (and in fact Fichtean and Hegelian) notion of consciousness, according to which "[d]as Bewußtsein keine *seiende* Qualität, wie etwa das Temperament u. dgl [ist], sondern die *Thätigkeit* des Geistes, wodurch er sich als Subject *setzt*" (*Psychologie oder die Wissenschaft vom subjectiven Geist*, p. 181; see also ibid., p. 144 and p. 225), is clearly echoed in Kierkegaard's pseudonymous authorship, especially in Judge William, Vigilius Haufniensis and Anti-Climacus. In addition, Rosenkranz also operates with a notion of (the feeling (!) [*Empfindung*] of) despair, which, in his opinion, expresses the "*Widerspruch, daß das, was nicht sein sollte, ist, und daß das, was sein sollte, nicht ist*" (*Psychologie oder die Wissenschaft vom subjectiven Geist*, p. 154). A

This general proviso notwithstanding, the unbiased reader may nevertheless discover a number of significant "material" similarities or parallels between *Psychologie oder die Wissenschaft vom subjectiven Geist* and *The Concept of Anxiety*—parallels, to be sure, which do not prove, but just as little exclude the possibility or even probability of a direct dependence of Kierkegaard on Rosenkranz. For instance, the idea that to be human is to be spirit "all the way down" and thus to be qualitatively different from other animals from the very beginning;[139] the corresponding idea of a sexual and, more generally, a spiritual development of human existence in various stages;[140] the notion of individuality as a dialectical unity of itself and the species;[141] the insistence on both inevitable and irreducible psychosomatical implications of mental diseases;[142] and the claim that, in ethical terms, feminity culminates in "procreation."[143]

By far the most important of these parallels, however, bears on the transition from, in Rosenkranzian terms, the spirit "in itself" to the spirit "for itself" or from possibility to actuality of consciousness. In order to make sense of this transition, let me briefly return to the basic tasks and themes of anthropology. According to Rosenkranz, anthropology investigates "spirit as soul, i.e., in its immediacy, in its original interrelation with nature."[144] Referring to its initial task of investigating the immediate *unity* of spirit and nature (*qua* soul), it describes, for instance, various *outer*, in particular planetary or racial, factors that determine human subjectivity (for example, by triggering certain moods),[145] and likewise a number of *inner* factors that function accordingly (for instance, temperaments, dispositions and character traits).[146] It also treats of the "natural *modifications*" of the spirit, *qua* soul, inasmuch as they pertain to the different stages of life, the fundamental sexual difference and the difference between sleeping and waking. Common to these and other related

---

further reflection of Rosenkranz in *Sickness* is pointed out by Engelke, *Kierkegaard und das Alte Testament*, op. cit., p. 76.

139 *Psychologie oder die Wissenschaft vom subjectiven Geist*, p. xxvi, p.6 and p. 223.

140 Ibid., pp. 6f.; p. 53; p. 55; and pp. 227f.

141 Ibid., p. 54; also *Encyklopädie der theologischen Wissenschaften*, p. 82. The passage deserves to be quoted in full: "*Das Individuum ist in seiner Existenz durch die Thätigkeit der Gattung vermittelt. Es ist an sich, als identisch mit der Gattung, zur Allgemeinheit derselben bestimmt; sie ist ihm immanent. Aber zugleich ist es als ein Eins für sich. Also ist es der Widerspruch seiner Einzelheit gegen die Allgemeinheit.*" (*Psychologie oder die Wissenschaft vom subjectiven Geist*, p. 54; see also ibid., p. 33.) Needless to say Rosenkranz, in contrast to Vigilius, does not discuss the consequences of this view as they pertain to dogmatics and/or ethics. In other words, he is not and cannot be interested (here) in the problem of (hereditary) sin.

142 Ibid., pp. 144ff.

143 *SKS* 4, 369 / *CA*, 65; compare *Psychologie oder die Wissenschaft vom subjectiven Geist*, p. 66.

144 *Psychologie oder die Wissenschaft vom subjectiven Geist*, p. 180; see also ibid., pp. 5 and passim.

145 See ibid., pp. 11f.

146 Vigilius speaks of innocence here, thereby highlighting only the ethico-religious implications of such a state: "In innocence, man is not qualified as spirit, but is psychically qualified in immediate unity with his natural condition" (*SKS* 4, 347 / *CA*, 41).

phenomena is their corporeality or their natural, irreducibly somatical basis. For even sensation (*Empfindung*), as the highest and ultimate form of the individual psycho-physical unity, "is a qualitative determination penetrating spirit and body."[147]

Now, in all dialectical consistency, this initial psycho-physical unity calls for being dissolved or negated—though also preserved on a higher level—in order to give way for the actualization of spirit, *qua* consciousness. Such a transition, which is spelled out in full detail in part two of the *Psychologie oder die Wissenschaft vom subjectiven Geist*, the phenomenology, goes along with and presupposes a conscious separation or distancing of the individual both from itself, the world and other minds. Hence it entails and at the same time cultivates basic forms of reflective subjectivity, objectivity and intersubjectivity. However, the result of this transition is preceded and made possible only by what Rosenkranz calls "the *struggle* of spirit with its corporeality."[148] It is precisely this aspect which reveals another significant parallel to Vigilius—here with regard to the concept of *dreaming*, which in Rosenkranz functions as the first and obviously most important,[149] if not principal and exclusive,[150] mediator of the final victory of spirit, *qua* consciousness over its (dependence on its) own natural basis. In considering it the first step of such a mediation, Rosenkranz makes use of the notion of dreaming in a *literal*, non-metaphorical sense: dreaming is, by definition, the unity of sleeping and waking.[151] Or more specifically: "If...the state of wakefulness is the positing of difference of subjectivity and objectivity and sleep the elimination of this difference, then the state of dreaming is the immediate mixing of the two conditions."[152] And since in dreaming neither the subject nor its object, although already in principle being related to each other, can become fully transparent as such, we may as well speak of a "flowing of subjectivity into an indeterminate objectivity, which does not stand *vis-à-vis* the subjects as a true object."[153] However, strictly speaking, such a qualification pertains to *all* forms of spirit in its gradual transition from soul to consciousness. Accordingly, Rosenkranz utilizes the notion of dreaming *metaphorically*, also. Thus conceived, it is supposed to designate an overall feature of spiritual development as such; it functions as a symbol for a number of principal ("dreamlike") characteristics of the transition just mentioned. "Spirit dreams as soul,"[154] so that what is true for dreaming is also and in

147 *Psychologie oder die Wissenschaft vom subjectiven Geist*, p. 10.

148 Ibid., p. 105.

149 The pertinent section in *Psychologie oder die Wissenschaft vom subjectiven Geist* comprises three chapters of about 50 pages altogether (see *Psychologie oder die Wissenschaft vom subjectiven Geist*, pp. 105–57), by far the lengthiest of which is the one on dreaming (see Ibid., pp. 108–42).

150 For, according to Rosenkranz, even habit (as the final form of the spiritual struggle with nature) is "*als Product der Gewöhnung...wieder ein traumhafter Zustand*" (*Psychologie oder die Wissenschaft vom subjectiven Geist*, p. 5; for an explanation of this apparently odd idea, see ibid., p. 107).

151 Ibid., p. 106.

152 Ibid., p. 109.

153 Ibid.

154 Ibid., p. 5; my emphasis.

general true for the "spirit as dreamer"[155]: it immediately suspends "the opposition of subjectivity and objectivity."[156]

Now, although it goes without saying that Vigilius draws on these and related ideas (*if* he does so at all) by freely adopting them for his own purposes—purposes which integrate them into a highly original account of (sin and) *anxiety*—we should not underestimate the fact that some of his views put forward in the context of this project clearly echo some of the ideas just mentioned. Thus, it makes sense to presume that (other possible sources notwithstanding) he may well have picked them up from Rosenkranz. For one thing he, too, contends that within the state of an immediate unity between spirit and nature "[t]he spirit in man is dreaming."[157] Moreover, his account of the relation between sleeping, dreaming and waking spirit mirrors the one defended by Rosenkranz: "Awake, the difference between myself and my other is posited, sleeping, it is suspended, dreaming, it is an intimated nothing."[158] The latter formulation points to a third parallel. Just as in Rosenkranz the dreaming spirit can neither reach an adequate grasp of its object nor of itself as the subject and medium of envisaging that object (although it is in principle the actuality of spirit itself, which is already, if tacitly, at work here), so too, in Vigilius: the dreaming spirit does not realize that it is in fact *itself* (its own actualized freedom, or spirit's "own actuality")[159] that it is anxiously "dreaming" of; nor does it realize that it is only *dreaming* of it or that this dreaming is in fact already a first, albeit imperfect *actualization* of what it is dreaming of.[160]

But the parallel goes even further. According to Vigilius, the dreaming spirit, as a, *sit venia verbo*, "state of transition," is an ontologically paradoxical phenomenon. However, as previously described, it is and is also experienced as a highly ambivalent phenomenon and thus a proper object for psychology. *Anxiety* is the psycho-physical expression that corresponds to the ontological transition from possibility to actuality of spirit, and anxiety is indeed an ambivalent or even apparently contradictory state of mind, owing to the fact that it is "*a sympathetic antipathy* and *an antipathetic sympathy*."[161] Now, it would certainly be pointless to look for anything even remotely reminiscent in Rosenkranz of the central role of anxiety in Vigilius.[162] Hence there can be no question whatsoever of any direct dependence, much less of an imitation

155 Ibid., p. 158.

156 Ibid.

157 *SKS* 4, 347 / *CA*, 41.

158 *SKS* 4, 347 / *CA*, 41f.

159 *SKS* 4, 347 / *CA*, 41.

160 *SKS* 4, 347 / *CA*, 41f. The fact that within dreaming—and thus also within actualized consciousness, as being mediated by the former—there is a priority of *self*-consciousness over consciousness of other objects, including other minds, is also conceded by Rosenkranz (*Psychologie oder die Wissenschaft vom subjectiven Geist*, p. 121). In other words, there is only one hero in dreaming, and that is the dreamer himself!

161 Ibid., p. 42.

162 On the one hand, there is a short paragraph on (apathy) antipathy and sympathy (*Psychologie oder die Wissenschaft vom subjectiven Geist*, pp. 51f.), but Rosenkranz does not refer to anxiety here. On the other hand, we do in fact find a small number of passages where he mentions or even briefly discusses the concepts of fear and anxiety, but they do not—or more

or even plagiarism here. This notwithstanding, there are some significant parallels to be found in the *Psychologie oder die Wissenschaft vom subjectiven Geist*—parallels, which might have led Rosenkranz to consider his own theory at least compatible with, if not supported by, the one vindicated by Vigilius, had he known the latter's book. Let us take a brief look at this parallel.

Rosenkranz's theory of sensation [*Empfindung*] distinguishes between outer and inner and, within the latter, between abstract/general and concrete/individual sensations.[163] Moreover, if "the universal content of spirit is perceived [*empfunden*] in opposites, in *concrete individualization*, then sensation [*Empfindung*] can either be affirmative, negative or mixed."[164] For instance, courage and joy are affirmative or "sthenic,"[165] whereas fear and sadness count as "asthenic"[166] or negative sensations. However, there is a third class (called "mixed sensations"), the explanation of which gives rise to certain logical difficulties since they presuppose "the possibility of the coexistence of opposite sensations in one temporal moment."[167] The manner in which Rosenkranz tries to cope with this logical problem need not interest us here. The fact is that he considers those states of mind—for example, "timid courage,... sweet anxiety [!],...despondent defiance."[168]—as a psychological reality; and he insists, furthermore, that we cannot account for their possibility by merely taking refuge in the idea of their *temporal* succession.[169] By contrast, if such sensations are actualized, "such a tension of sensation is posited, which is contradiction itself."[170] A suggestion with which Vigilius would, I suppose, agree.[171]

A final observation: in Chapter II, § 2 of *The Concept of Anxiety* Vigilius unfolds the history of sin in terms of its subjective aspect, namely, with regard to the psychological differences between Adam and each subsequent human individual.[172] The crucial, albeit in effect merely quantitative, difference lies in the increasing degree of subjective reflectiveness of anxiety, such that eventually its "nothing" becomes "a complex of presentiments (*Ahnelser*), which, reflecting themselves in themselves, come nearer and nearer to the individual, even though again, when viewed essentially in anxiety, they signify a nothing."[173] It turns out, then, that these "presentiments"

---

exactly, at least not explicitly (see below)—bear on the ambivalence of antipathy and sympathy (*Psychologie oder die Wissenschaft vom subjectiven Geist*, pp. 96ff.; p. 211; and p. 332).

163 *Psychologie oder die Wissenschaft vom subjectiven Geist*, pp. 94ff.

164 Ibid., p. 95.

165 Ibid., p. 96.

166 Ibid.

167 Ibid., p. 98.

168 Ibid.

169 Ibid.

170 Ibid.

171 See, for instance, *SKS* 4, 348 / *CA*, 42, where he refers the reader to the ordinary language used as evidence for the ambivalent or even paradoxical character of anxiety: "One speaks of a pleasing anxiety, a pleasing anxiousness" (ibid.; see also *SKS* 4, 365f. / *CA*, 61). As to the proximity between Rosenkranz and Vigilius at this point, see Bösch, *Sören Kierkegaard*, op. cit., pp. 72f.

172 *SKS* 4, 365–83 / *CA*, 60–80.

173 *SKS* 4, 366 / *CA*, 61f.

refer to sensuousness and/or sinfulness as their proper, though prior to the qualitative leap of sin consciousness, still vague and indefinite "objects."[174] This distinction between two subsequent stages or forms of anxiety—one less and one more reflected (presentiment)—corresponds to what Rosenkranz distinguishes as dreaming in general and "dream-wakefulness" [*Traumwachen*][175]—the latter being a borderline case between dreaming and waking, because it "presupposes wakefulness and passes over into the condition of a dream without sleep."[176] As usual, Rosenkranz argues for three subtypes of such a state: presentiment, vision and deuteroskopy.[177] All three of these bear witness to the peculiar fact that "in dreams a *simultaneous* fact or a fact that enters into existence only *later* can be anticipated."[178] Rosenkranz's account of the first form (presentiment), in particular, reveals interesting parallels to Vigilius' view of reflective anxiety. Presentiment itself unfolds in three stages, reaching from a mere "presentiment" [*Vorgefühl*][179] to presentiment in a stricter sense and, finally, to a definite prediction [*Voraussage*]. The first form is tantamount to "an *undetermined* restlessness";[180] for "in the presentiment the content is not yet determined; it presents itself merely as an excitement without object."[181] This notwithstanding, such a "prophetic" feeling has already distanced itself from the complete indefiniteness of dreaming, the object of which (in Haufniensis' terms) dissolves into a mere nothing, while simultaneously remaining inextricably bound up with a subject not being aware of itself, yet. Whenever the indefinite feeling receives a more specific, though still in some respect vague, content, "*there arises a* determinate indeterminacy,"[182] and this "nebulous sensation is the usual presentiment."[183] For instance, someone has a presentiment of a friend visiting soon, but which one remains unknown to him. The final stage of a subjectively as well as objectively "determinate determinacy"[184] is reached, as soon as the content of the expected event becomes fully specified: "The presentiment can…turn into a prediction, which, for example, expects this specific friend on this specific day."[185] Now, even though, especially in the age of Romanticism, such an account of presentiment can hardly be judged as singular, much less as a complete novelty, its basic ideas and concepts (anticipation, indeterminate

174 *SKS* 4, 377 / *CA*, 73f.

175 *Psychologie oder die Wissenschaft vom subjectiven Geist*, p. 122.

176 Ibid.

177 Ibid., pp. 122–31.

178 Ibid., p. 119. Although as a psychologist Rosenkranz resists the temptation to invoke "die Reflexion auf die *Vorsehung Gottes*" (ibid., p. 123), in order—via divination or revelation—to account for such phenomena in a theological way, he nevertheless does not in principle deny their possibility or veridicality. As for his own explanation, see ibid., pp. 119–22 and p. 124.

179 Ibid., p. 123.

180 Ibid.

181 Ibid.

182 Ibid.

183 Ibid.

184 Ibid., pp. 123f.

185 Ibid., p. 124.

restlessness, excitement without object, determinate indeterminacy) may at least have a significantly familiar ring to the reader of *The Concept of Anxiety*.

VI.

Although there are several points of comparison that I could only touch upon marginally in the preceding paragraphs, and although there are quite a few others left which I can also just mention in passing,[186] I hope that I have succeeded in delivering a fairly comprehensive and reliable picture of Kierkegaard's reception of Rosenkranz, and that my account has at least gathered enough evidence to convince the reader that this reception is (and presumably remains for the time being) a topic worth pursuing in some detail. Let me conclude by briefly summing up the results of the preceding analysis with a few theses—partly in addition to, partly as a corroboration of the ones already formulated at the beginning of my paper on the basis of a first, superficial glance at the pertinent references: (1) Kierkegaard's reception of Rosenkranz is mainly documented in the pseudonymous authorship. (2) The pseudonyms are primarily interested in Rosenkranz as a philosopher and/or theologian, not as a literary critic or as a political, historical and/or pedagogical thinker. (3) Typologically speaking, their treatment of Rosenkranz may be classified as a borderline case between unproductive and productive reception. (4) Some critical remarks notwithstanding, the pseudonyms' assessment of the German contemporary is mostly positive. (5) References to *Psychologie oder die Wissenschaft vom subjectiven Geist*, *Schelling. Vorlesungen, gehalten im Sommer 1842 an der Universität zu Königsberg*, "Eine Parallele zur Religionsphilosophie" and, to some extent, *Encyklopädie der theologischen Wissenschaften* bear witness to the fact that they are sources, which obviously had a deeper, if frequently non-explicit, impact on the pseudonyms. (6) Implicit traces of "Eine Parallele zur Religionsphilosophie" are to be found in the *Fragments*, in particular; they document that Kierkegaard's and/or Climacus' view of (the relation between) Paganism, Judaism and Christianity

[186] See, for instance: *Psychologie oder die Wissenschaft vom subjectiven Geist*, p. 20 (speculative philosophy is not and cannot be interested in the individual as such); p. 50 (a genius has no advantage in the realm of the ethical); p. 54 (appearances to the contrary notwithstanding, "[hat] *im Zeugungsact die Thätigkeit der Gattung ihre Spitze erreicht*"); p. 76 and p. 84 (hearing as the deepest human sense); pp. 148–52 (madness as a "collateral" phenomenon); p. 170 (thinking, willing and feeling as universal and non-contingent human capacities); p. 227 (spirit and freedom as coextensive; see also *Encyklopädie der theologischen Wissenschaften*, p. 309); p. 284 (God as the originator of language); p. 323 and p. 333 (passion as infinite interest in any object). See, furthermore, *Encyklopädie der theologischen Wissenschaften*, p. 6 (all purported proofs of God's existence are circular); p. 19 (for God everything is possible); p. 21 (actuality as a unity of the accidental and the substantial); p. 26 (God's will as a unity of absolute freedom *qua* love and absolute necessity *qua* justice; see also p. 166); p. 32 (man as spirit is not born, but rather reborn); p. 48 (god must become his teacher, if man is to recognize him); p. 55 and p. 66 (freedom and the good as coextensive); pp. 80f. (despair as a defiant opposition against oneself); p. 242 and p. 344 (the misled contemporary tendency to aestheticize and philosophize preaching); p. 243 (Christ as having established the possibility of an immediate relationship to God).

is heavily indebted to Rosenkranz. (7) With regard to both its explicit and its implicit reception within the pseudonymous authorship, *Psychologie oder die Wissenschaft vom subjectiven Geist* obviously had the greatest impact on Kierkegaard. (8) With other relevant sources aside, *The Concept of Anxiety* shows the most distinctive traces of this impact. (9) Vigilius explicitly concedes his indebtedness to his German contemporary, in particular by referring to and freely drawing on Rosenkranz's theory of disposition and habit. (10) The implicit reflections of the *Psychologie oder die Wissenschaft vom subjectiven Geist* in *The Concept of Anxiety* prove to be no less important than the explicit ones: they are both conceptual (concept of psychology), methodological (theory of sciences) and material (dreaming, mixed sensations and presentiment).

Bibliography

I. Rosenkranz's Works in The Auction Catalogue *of Kierkegaard's Library*

Encyklopädie der theologischen Wissenschaften, Halle: C.A. Schwetschke und Sohn 1831 (*ASKB* 35).

"Eine Parallele zur Religionsphilosophie," *Zeitschrift für spekulative Theologie*, vols. 1–3, ed. by Bruno Bauer, Berlin: Dümmler 1836–38, vol. 2, no. 1, 1837, pp. 1–31 (*ASKB* 354–357).

"Die Verklärung der Natur. Eine skeptische Untersuchung," *Zeitschrift für spekulative Theologie*, op. cit., vol. 2, no. 2, 1837, pp. 257–96.

[Review of] "*Die Religions-Systeme der heidnischen Völker des Orients*, dargestellt von P.F. Stuhr, Berlin 1836. XII und 448 S. 8.," *Zeitschrift für spekulative Theologie*, op. cit., vol. 3, no. 2, 1838, pp. 457–84.

Erinnerungen an Karl Daub, Berlin: Duncker und Humblot 1837 (*ASKB* 743).

Psychologie oder die Wissenschaft vom subjectiven Geist, Königsberg: Bornträger 1837 (*ASKB* 744).

Kritische Erläuterungen des Hegel'schen Systems, Königsberg: Bornträger 1840 (*ASKB* 745).

"Erindringer om Karl Daub," *Tidsskrift for udenlandsk theologisk Litteratur*, vol. 1–20, ed. by Henrik Nikolai Clausen and Matthias Hagen Hohlenberg, Copenhagen: C.A. Reitzel 1833–52, vol. 5, 1837, pp. 534–76 (*ASKB* U 29).

"Hegel's Levnet," *Tidsskrift for udenlandsk theologisk Litteratur*, op. cit., vol. 12, 1844, pp. 511–636 (*ASKB* U 29).

[ed.] *Schelling: Vorlesungen, gehalten im Sommer 1842 an der Universität zu Königsberg*, ed. by Karl Rosenkranz, Danzig: Gerhard 1843 (*ASKB* 766).

[ed.] *Georg Wilhelm Friedrich Hegel's philosophische Propädeutik*, ed. by Karl Rosenkranz, Berlin: Duncker und Humblot 1840 (vol. 18, in *Georg Wilhelm Friedrich Hegel's Werke. Vollständige Ausgabe*, ed. by Philipp Marheineke et al., Berlin: Duncker und Humblot 1832–45) (*ASKB* 560).

II. Works in The Auction Catalogue *of Kierkegaard's Library that Discuss Rosenkranz*

Baader, Franz von, *Ueber die Incompetenz unsrer dermaligen Philosophie, zur Erklärung der Erscheinungen aus dem Nachtgebiete der Natur*, Stuttgart: Brodhag 1837, p. 19 (*ASKB* 411).

Chalybäus, Heinrich Moritz, "Natur- und Geistesphilosophie," *Zeitschrift für Philosophie und spekulative Theologie*, op. cit., vol. 3, 1839, pp. 160–95.

Erdmann, Johann Eduard, *Vorlesungen über Glauben und Wissen als Einleitung in die Dogmatik und Religionsphilosophie*, Berlin: Duncker und Humblot 1837, p. 271 (*ASKB* 479).

Fichte, Immanuel Hermann, "Zu Hegels Charakteristik, mit Rücksicht auf 'G.W.Fr. Hegels Leben, beschrieben von Karl Rosenkranz 1844,'" *Zeitschrift für Philosophie und spekulative Theologie*, op. cit., vol. 8, 1844, pp. 295–311.

—— *System der Ethik*, vols. 1–2.1, Leipzig: Dyk 1850–51 (*ASKB* 510–511), vol. 2.2, Leipzig: Dyk 1853 (*ASKB* 504), vol. 2.1, p. 287n.

Günther, Anton, *Die Juste-Milieus in der deutschen Philosophie gegenwärtiger Zeit*, Vienna: Beck 1838, pp. 4–6; p. 123n. (*ASKB* 522).

Günther, Anton and Johann Heinrich Pabst, *Janusköpfe. Zur Philosophie und Theologie*, Vienna: Wallishausser 1834, pp. 80–8 (*ASKB* 524).

Helfferich, Adolph, *Die christliche Mystik in ihrer Entwickelung und in ihren Denkmalen*, vols. 1–2, Gotha: Friedrich Parthes 1842, vol. 1, p. 32 (*ASKB* 571–572).

Michelet, Carl Ludwig, *Geschichte der letzten Systeme der Philosophie in Deutschland von Kant bis Hegel*, vols. 1–2, Berlin: Duncker und Humblot 1837–38, vol. 2, p. 613; p. 633; p. 648; pp. 657f.; pp. 659f.; pp. 662ff.; pp. 679f. (*ASKB* 678–679).

—— *Vorlesungen über die Persönlichkeit Gottes und Unsterblichkeit der Seele oder die ewige Persönlichkeit des Geistes*, Berlin: Verlag von Ferdinand Dümmler 1841, pp. 184–91 (*ASKB* 680).

Mynster, Jakob Peter, *Blandede Skrivter*, vols. 1–3, Copenhagen: Den Gyldendalske Boghandlings Forlag 1852–53 [vols. 4–6, Copenhagen: Den Gyldendalske Boghandlings Forlag 1855–57], vol. 1, p. 209n; vol. 2, p. 100 (*ASKB* 358–363).

Schelling, Friedrich Wilhelm Joseph, *Vorlesungen von Karl Rosenkranz*, Danzig: Gerhard 1843 (*ASKB* 766).

Steenstrup, Mathias G.G., *Historisk-kritisk Oversigt over Forsøgene paa at give en Historiens Filosofi*, Copenhagen: C.A. Reitzel 1854, p. 14; p. 54n; p. 69; p. 112; p. 118; p. 122n (*ASKB* 792).

Strauss, David Friedrich, *Fremstilling af den christelige Troeslære i dens historiske Udvikling og i dens Kamp med den moderne Videnskab*, vols. 1–2, trans. by Hans Brøchner, Copenhagen: Forlagt af H.C. Klein 1842–43 (*ASKB* 803–804).

Zeuthen, Ludvig, *Humanitet betragtet fra et christeligt Standpunkt, med stadigt Hensyn til den nærværende Tid*, Copenhagen: Gyldendalske Boghandling 1846, p. 32; p. 62n (*ASKB* 915).

III. Secondary Literature on Kierkegaard's Relation to Rosenkranz

Bösch, Michael, "Der Hegelsche Begriff der Seele in Karl Rosenkranz' *Psychologie*," in his *Søren Kierkegaard: Schicksal—Angst—Freiheit*, Paderborn et al.: Ferdinand Schöningh 1994, pp. 59–62.

Engelke, Matthias, *Kierkegaard und das Alte Testament. Zum Einfluß der alttestamentlichen Bücher auf Kierkegaards Gesamtwerk*, Rheinbach: CMZ 1998, 74–7.

Schulz, Heiko, "Die spekulative Verflüchtigung des Christentums. Philipp Marheinekes System der christlichen Dogmatik und seine Rezeption bei Søren Kierkegaard," *Kierkegaard Studies. Yearbook*, 2003, pp. 20–48.

Schleiermacher:
Revisiting Kierkegaard's Relationship to Him

Richard E. Crouter

> [Socratic ignorance] is a religious ignorance which seeks its edification and manifests its piety in a total ignorance, just as Schleiermacher, for example, in a much more concrete development locates the edifying in a feeling of absolute dependence. This, too, conceals within itself a polemic and becomes a terror [*Forfærdelse*] for everyone who finds repose in some finite relation to the deity.
>
> Kierkegaard, *The Concept of Irony*, 1841

At age 64 and at the height of his fame Friedrich Schleiermacher (1768–1834) made a Scandinavian tour that brought him to Copenhagen, 22–29 September 1833, where the Plato translator and Christian theologian was highly feted, accorded academic honors, held private talks with cultural luminaries as well as students, and preached in the Vor Frue Kirke.[1] The visit, less than five months before his death, was certainly extraordinary. The *Copenhagen Post* noted, "His whole effectiveness is so significant and influential, that he would have to be an object of interest for anyone, who did not wish to hold himself aloof from the most important movements of the age."[2] The young Kierkegaard, then a student at the university, appears to have held himself aloof on this occasion. He thus missed the

---

I am grateful to Gordon Marino and Cynthia Lund for use of the Kierkegaard Library at St. Olaf College and to Jon Stewart for inviting me to revisit these issues.

1 On Schleiermacher's *Confidential Letters*, see also Richard Crouter, "Kierkegaard's Not so Hidden Debt to Schleiermacher," *Zeitschrift für Neuere Theologiegeschichte / Journal for the History of Modern Theology*, vol. 1, no. 2, 1994, pp. 205–25, reprinted as Chapter 4 in *Friedrich Schleiermacher: Between Enlightenment and Romanticism*, Cambridge: Cambridge University Press 2005; and Richard Crouter, "More than Kindred Spirits: Schleiermacher and Kierkegaard on Repentance," in *Proceedings of the Schleiermacher-Kierkegaard Congress, Copenhagen, October 9–13, 2003*, ed. by Niels Jørgen Cappelørn, Richard Crouter, Theodor Jørgensen, and Claus-Dieter Osthövener, Berlin: Walter de Gruyter, 2006. For a vivid account of the visit that includes source documents, see Jon Stewart, "Schleiermacher's Visit to Copenhagen in 1833," *Zeitschrift für Neuere Theologiegeschichte / Journal for the History of Modern Theology*, vol. 11, no. 2, 2004, pp. 279–302. An account of the *Copenhagen Post* for 28 September is found in *Aus Schleiermachers Leben. In Briefen*, vols. 1–4, ed. by Ludwig Jonas and Wilhelm Dilthey, Berlin: de Gruyter 1974, vol. 2, pp. 502–3.

2 *In Briefen*, op. cit., vol. 2, p. 503.

poet Adam Oehlenschläger's (1779–1850) lyrical song that deftly celebrated the visitor's many gifts. By giving Plato and Socrates to the Germans, Oehlenschläger opined, Schleiermacher had connected the Baltic Sea with the Archipelagos. His words recognized Schleiermacher for having turned Plato, if not also Socrates, into German contemporaries of Golden Age Denmark, a major feat of cultural transmission that will gain our attention in what follows.

Despite the sure sense we have that the 20-year-old Kierkegaard had to have been aware of the Schleiermacher festivities, direct evidence to that effect does not exist. Kierkegaard's youthful theological, literary, and philosophical studies, recorded in meticulous journals and notebooks, were only just getting underway. An argument about how Kierkegaard came to view Schleiermacher and the role that Schleiermacher's work played in his development must begin with a survey of his private journals, notebooks, as well as relevant published works, especially, for reasons adduced below, *The Concept of Irony* and *The Concept of Anxiety*. Although Kierkegaard owned some collections of Schleiermacher's sermons, and it is possible that they exercised an influence on him, the key Schleiermacher texts that pertain to this relationship are *On Religion: Speeches to its Cultured Despisers*, read not in the 1799 edition but in the third (1821) and fifth (1843) editions, the *Confidential Letters on Schlegel's Lucinde* (1800), read in the 1835 edition reissued by the young poet Karl Gutzkow, and the second edition of his dogmatics and *magnum opus*, *The Christian Faith* (1830–31). Among philosophical works, Kierkegaard owned Schleiermacher's translation of the works of Plato (1817–28) as well as the Ludwig Jonas (posthumously published) edition of the *Dialectics* (1839). But the setting for examining how knowledge of these texts influenced Kierkegaard can best be established if we first take a glance at the reception of Schleiermacher's teaching among Kierkegaard's Danish contemporaries.

I. Schleiermacher among the Danes

It is doubtful that any account of Schleiermacher's reception in early nineteenth-century Denmark can be decisive for our grasp of the ways that Kierkegaard's work draws upon the German writer. Yet some awareness of this reception offers clues regarding the theological culture that Kierkegaard faced in Copenhagen as he sought to come to his own terms with Schleiermacher. In fact, individual philosophers, writers, and theologians, persons closely involved with Kierkegaard, had been exposed to, and sometimes deeply touched by, Schleiermacher's work as well as his person. That list includes the philosopher Frederik Christian Sibbern (1785–1872) and the theologian Henrik Nikolai Clausen (1793–1877) (who were involved in the 1833 visit) but also the natural scientist and philosopher Hans Christian Ørsted (1777–1851), who came to know Schleiermacher in Germany in 1802. Each of them had a special relationship to Schleiermacher, as did Hans Lassen Martensen (1808–84), through a friendship with Henriette Herz (1764–1847), and the future bishop

Jakob Peter Mynster (1775–1854), who studied his works from afar.[3] Examining Schleiermacher's reception by this circle of Danes at a symposium in 1984, Helge Hultberg makes clear that, despite the fame of the German theologian and the impressiveness of his personality, Denmark was on the whole reserved towards him. It is not surprising if his earliest works, *On Religion*, the *Monologues*, and the *Confidential Letters* made the Danes suspicious of his philosophical position as well as his theology. At the time, this was also his fate in Germany.

The suspicion of pantheism in the young Schleiermacher grated against more empirical views of the natural order, which, even if it embodies spirit, is not itself divine. In addition, Schleiermacher's most rhapsodic work, the *Monologues* (1800), easily left an impression of self-indulgence, while his version of Christianity seemed suspect. That suspicion was shared by Mynster. When Georg Brandes (1842–1927) looked back on Denmark in the 1870s, he lamented that the critical spirit of Lessing had never taken root and added: "Mynster was our Schleiermacher, but one knows what a distance there is between the liberality [*Frisind*] of Schleiermacher and the ecclesiastical faith of Mynster."[4] When the future bishop Mynster borrowed a copy of the *Monologues* from Ørsted in 1806, he returned it, saying: "You were exactly right when you found Schleiermacher to be laboring in intellectual arrogance."[5] As a young pastor in Spjellerup, Mynster found Schleiermacher's sermons interesting, yet they did not please him very much.[6] In the same letter to Ørsted in which he complains about the *Monologues*, Mynster adds that "there is still much that is interesting in it, which had undeniably come forth from a noble, deep, and free nature."[7] The estimates of Schleiermacher's work held by the eventual primate of the Danish Church never overcame a deep ambivalence.[8]

The Danish Schleiermacher reception also included significant teachers of Kierkegaard. From studies with Schleiermacher in 1818–19 H.N. Clausen was influenced by his personality as well as his theology.[9] In reaction to Schleiermacher's *Hermeneutik und Kritik* (1838) Clausen published his own hermeneutic of the New Testament.[10] Even if Clausen felt that Schleiermacher's hermeneutic fell more in the field of philosophy than theology, he drew inspiration from him in taking a position against N.F.S. Grundtvig's (1783–1872) unscientific approach to Scripture

---

3 Niels Munk Plum, *Schleiermacher i Danmark*, Copenhagen: Bianco Lunos Bogtrykkeri 1934.

4 Helge Hultberg, "Schleiermacher und die dänische Romantik," in *Schleiermacher im besonderen Hinblick auf seine Wirkungsgeschichte in Dänemark*, ed. by Hultberg et al., Munich: Wilhelm Fink Verlag and Copenhagen: Text and Kontext 1986, p. 127, citing Brandes' *Samlede Skrifter*, vols. 1–18, Copenhagen: Gyldendal 1899–1910, vol. 4, p. 7.

5 Hultberg, "Schleiermacher und die dänische Romantik," op. cit., p. 126.

6 Ibid., p. 127.

7 Ibid., p. 128, citing *Breve fra og til Hans Christian Ørsted*, vols. 1–2, ed. by Mathilde Ørsted, Copenhagen: Th. Lind 1870, vol. 1, pp. 183f.

8 Hultberg, "Schleiermacher und die dänische Romantik," op. cit., pp. 128–130.

9 Bernhard Eric Jensen, "Hermeneutik und Historik. Schleiermacher, Dilthey und das Problem des Historismus," in *Schleiermacher im besonderen Hinblick*, op. cit., pp. 10–13.

10 Clausen, *Det Nye Testaments Hermeneutik*, Copenhagen: Jens Hostrup Schultz 1840 (a work of over 500 pages).

as well as against Martensen for failing to secure the independence of theology from philosophy.[11] A perceived vacillation between monism and dualism in the thought of Clausen contributed to the view, certainly held by Grundtvig, that Schleiermacher was nothing more than a covert sort of rationalist.[12] Alongside Clausen as a teacher of Kierkegaard, Sibbern had been deeply impressed by the theologian during his 1811 studies in Berlin and remained in touch with his work. (We will shortly say more on Sibbern and Martensen as mediating Schleiermacher to Kierkegaard.)

Hultberg characterizes the intellectual climate in the first decades of the nineteenth century as a "synthesis of the Enlightenment, Christianity, and moderate Platonism" in which "the monistic tendencies" of the young Schleiermacher could have no effect.[13] Hultberg's judgment that "the Danes found Schleiermacher simply too bold, too much convinced of the possibilities of the human spirit" may well capture the ambivalence of his reception.[14] Apart from the poet Adam Oehlenschläger, no figures in Denmark appear to register unqualified enthusiasm for Schleiermacher. In Oehlenschläger's case, admiration rested more on Schleiermacher's noble bearing and liberality of mind than on the Christian orthodoxy of his theological teachings.[15] The only Dane who truly grasped the ground-breaking nature of Schleiermacher's work was his lifelong friend, Henrik Steffens (1773–1845), once a cultured despiser of religion who, under Schleiermacher's tutelage, moved to Christianity from natural science and taught alongside the theologian briefly in Halle (1804–06) before returning to Denmark. Yet even Steffens ended up endorsing a version of Christianity that consisted of his own synthesis of elements from Luther and German idealism.[16]

> I must not conceal the fact that the view of how Christian doctrine was conceived, how it had to develop and be shaped historically, which is the proper view for me, was not his. But he was a *Christian.* What penetrated him inwardly he called feeling. Yet this feeling was deeper, more powerful, than the clarity of the thought, which he sought to interpret.[17]

For Helge Hultberg the Steffens citation typifies the Danish view of Schleiermacher as heterodox, though somehow still a Christian.

---

11 Jensen, "Hermeneutik und Historik. Schleiermacher, Dilthey und das Problem des Historismus," op. cit., p. 12.

12 Hultberg, "Schleiermacher und die dänische Romantik," op. cit., p. 130.

13 Ibid., p. 125.

14 Ibid., p. 126; on Schleiermacher and Grundtvig, see Theodor Jørgensen, "Schleiermachers und Grundtvigs Verständnis vom Heil in Bezug auf die Versöhnungslehre unter besonderer Berücksichtigung ihrer Bestimmung des Bösen," in *Schleiermacher im besonderen Hinblick*, op. cit., pp. 82–101.

15 Ibid., p. 132, notes that after Schleiermacher's death Oehlenschläger wrote a tragedy called *Socrates*, in which one can recognize features of the recently deceased.

16 Ibid., pp. 133–7.

17 Henrick Steffens' graveside address for Schleiermacher, February 1834, from *Drei Reden am Tag der Bestattung des Prof. u. Predigers Herrn Dr Schleiermacher am 15ten Febr. 1834*, Berlin: Reimer 1834, pp. 33f. cited in Hultberg, "Schleiermacher und die dänische Romantik," op. cit., p. 138.

The Danish reception of Schleiermacher was generally respectful, aware of the weight of his various positions and works in Germany, yet held back from the theological revolution that established the German as the premier theologian of Protestant liberalism. Writing at the end of the century, long before his countrymen had acknowledged the philosophical significance of Kierkegaard, Harald Høffding (1843–1931), expressed profound doubts about the adequacy of Schleiermacher's theological as well as his philosophical teaching. Høffding's Schleiermacher was much too this-worldly, much too engaged with discussions of human conscious self-awareness to stake out the objective truth of the claims he wished to espouse.[18] The pervasive Danish unease with regard to Schleiermacher, echoed at the end of the century, must have made him appear all the more intriguing and challenging a figure for the critical imagination of the young Kierkegaard.

II. Four Hermeneutical Asides

At the outset of the discussion that follows I wish to note four sorts of methodological challenges, each of which presents difficulties to interpreters.

(1) The theological background in which Kierkegaard is the protector of orthodox Protestant Christian teaching against the slippery slope of Schleiermacher's alleged rationalism still dominates writing about their relationship. The initial pairing of the two figures arose from passionate debates regarding the nature of a proper Reformation theology versus a theology that had sold out to the Enlightenment. In the received version of this theology the twentieth-century Swiss theologian, Karl Barth (1886–1968), whose *Römerbrief* and other early works were inspired by Kierkegaard, was the dedicated nemesis of Schleiermacher and of liberal theology.[19] In what follows I write from a conviction that seeks to move away from

---

18 Harald Høffding, *A History of Modern Philosophy: From the Close of the Renaissance to Our Own Day*, vols. 1–2, trans. by B.E. Meyer, New York: The Humanities Press 1905 [1900], vol. 2, pp. 208–13; for a similar view, see Anton Thomsen in *Salmonsens store illustrerede Konversationsleksikon En nordisk Encyklopædi*, vols. 1–19, Copenhagen: Brødrene Salmonsens Forlag 1893–1911, vol. 15, p. 776.

19 The weight of Barth's polemical view of Schleiermacher partly explains the long-standing preoccupation with the category of sin as a basis of comparison between the two figures. See the classic study by Hermann Fischer, *Subjektivität und Sünde: Kierkegaards Begriff der Sünde mit ständiger Rücksicht auf Schleiermachers Lehre von der Sünde*, Itzehoe: Die Spur 1963; Henning Schröer, "Wie verstand Kierkegaard Schleiermacher?" in *Internationaler Schleiermacher Kongreß Berlin 1984*, vols. 1–2, ed. by Kurt-Victor Selge and Hermann Fischer, Berlin: de Gruyter, 1985, vol. I.2, pp. 1147–55, asks whether Barth is correct in seeing them as diametrically opposed, charts the way forward by study of Kierkegaard's journal entries, and sees three phases in the relationship that range from (1) early critical and questioning journal entries by Kierkegaard, (2) a positive view of Schleiermacher's anti-Hegelian grounding of theology on the distinction between knowledge and faith, and (3) a sharp criticism during the time of the attack on the Church; the essay also offers a sketch of further issues and calls for nuanced judgments. Wilhelm Anz, "Schleiermacher und Kierkegaard. Übereinstimmung und Differenz," *Zeitschrift für Theologie und Kirche*, vol. 82, no. 4, 1985,

the theological assumptions that govern much of the secondary literature that seeks to relate Kierkegaard to Schleiermacher. Of course, those debates remain significant. But they will be better informed when a more historical lens is brought to bear on these materials.

(2) The diverse nature of Kierkegaard's references or allusions to Schleiermacher, both in the *Nachlaß* as well as in published pseudonymous or non-pseudonymous works, constitutes a challenge. Formidable methodological problems present themselves, beginning with the question of how to take Kierkegaard's journal entries which, unless multiply attested, backed up by published works, or held in a consistent pattern, pose a major challenge. Often one does not know whether such entries are espousing a studied position, just comparing impressions, marking out a potential intellectual quandary, or putting forth a lifelong *Tendenz* of thought.[20] Schleiermacher became a significant figure for Kierkegaard, highly influential, but also pointedly criticized. The Danish writer had little reason to single out Schleiermacher for extended commentary, even if he did, as I shall argue, find in his work many positions that were fruitful for his own writing. Faced with this second difficulty I have attempted to study the journal and notebook entries one-by-one in order to retrace (and rethink) the problem of how Schleiermacher surfaces in Kierkegaard's evolving body of work. In proceeding in this direction one becomes aware that Schleiermacher's studied positions on issues (Socrates, the nature of dogmatics, sin, ethics) feed the one or other aspect of the authorship, even without being fully assimilated or emulated by Kierkegaard. Only this approach can begin to break up the logjam, as it were, between the high praise as well as the sharp criticism that Kierkegaard expresses in relation to Schleiermacher.

(3) In addition, it is necessary to remind ourselves that Schleiermacher's teaching is hugely varied. Like the work of Kierkegaard, it also consists of pseudonymous works, student notebooks, and transcripts of lectures (hermeneutics

---

pp. 409–29, evaluates (1) the appearance of a fundamental difference between Schleiermacher and Kierkegaard, (2) a common orientation in relation to the philosophical tradition, and (3) the consequences that follow for a Christian dogmatics. Anz deliberately excludes from his purview Schleiermacher as Plato interpreter and the influence of the *Confidential Letters* on Kierkegaard (p. 415); the paper repays careful study in laying out similarities and differences. Although focused exclusively on a comparison of their views of sin, Christine Axt-Piscalar argues that Schleiermacher's view of sin is closer to Kierkegaard in *The Sickness unto Death* than in *The Concept of Anxiety*; see "Das Selbst in der Selbstverstrickung: Eine vergleichende Betrachtung zu Schleiermachers und Kierkegaards Sündenlehre," in *Kierkegaard Studies. Yearbook*, 2004, pp. 452–72.

[20] On the pitfalls as well as yield of studying the journals, see Alastair Hannay, "Kierkegaard's Journals and Notebooks as Interpretative Tools for the Published Works," and Richard Purkarthofer, "'Suppose I would die tomorrow': Possible Uses of Kierkegaard's Journals and Notebooks for Research," *Kierkegaard Studies. Yearbook*, 2004, pp. 189–201 and pp. 202–13 respectively.

and dialectics) that never achieved final form in his lifetime.[21] Moreover, the many-sided nature of Schleiermacher's work encompasses interests that fall in the fields of theology, philosophy, as well as the history of those disciplines, plus his work as philologist and translator of Plato into German.[22] Readers of Kierkegaard must pay careful attention to *which* Schleiermacher texts and teachings are drawn into the discussion. Neither Schleiermacher nor Kierkegaard can be approached as a finished thinker with a settled body of writing that counts as the writer's essential thought or position. Settled interpretations of either writer scarcely exist and fresh perspectives on their work continue to be developed.

(4) Finally, though this comment relates not just to the present essay, I wish to be on record as holding the view that some of the most profound intellectual debts are held tacitly and hence not subject to scrutiny. In that position I have been influenced by the work of Harold Bloom, *Anxiety of Influence* (1973), which argues cogently that "strong poets" are, by their very nature, individuals who rise above their influences in ways that covertly supplant them. Put this way, I wish to be on record as espousing the view that no individual writer, philosopher, or theologian is ever the mere sum of influences. This last point serves to warn us that any writing about influences should be greeted with a raised eyebrow. If we are successful in tracking any influences, then this success throws a deeper light on teachings or forms of inquiry that are larger than any one given writer, which both proponents, and perhaps we ourselves, may also come to value.

III. Earliest Encounters with Schleiermacher's Teaching

Only when we are aware of the cluster of issues running through the mind of Kierkegaard at distinct times of his life are we able to see a living Kierkegaard at his writing desk and assess how he views Schleiermacher's teaching, or aspects of that teaching. All in all, there are some 94 references or allusions to Schleiermacher in the authorship as a whole.[23] These break down into 36 references or allusions to Schleiermacher in *The Concept of Irony*, 23 in the other published works, and some 35 in the papers, journals, and notebooks. In what follows I seek to give a running

---

21 The contribution of early German Romanticism to philosophy as well as literature is increasingly recognized. See Manfred Frank, *The Philosophical Foundations of Early German Romanticism*, trans. by Elizabeth Millán-Zaibert, Albany: State University of New York 2004; Terry Pinkard, *German Philosophy 1760–1860: The Legacy of Idealism*, Cambridge: Cambridge University Press 2002, writes of the Romantic appropriation of Kant; Philippe Lacoue-Labarthe and Jean-Luc Nancy, *The Literary Absolute: The Theory of Literature in German Romanticism*, trans. by Philip Barnard and Cheryl Lester, Albany: State University of New York 1988.

22 Becoming aware of the full range of Schleiermacher's work is the best antidote against treating him solely within the parameters of twentieth-century theological debates.

23 The actual number will vary slightly, depending upon how clusters of references are counted. Only a monograph could do full justice to the many traces of Schleiermacher within the authorship.

account, as it were, of the most significant of these references, while weighing the evidence in light of the questions: What is known to Kierkegaard of Schleiermacher's work? What use does he make of these materials in his own writing? Does he have a considered judgment of the worth of Schleiermacher as theologian or philosopher, or in some other fashion, as a spur to his own work? Only the first of these questions has thus far been raised. A citation index alone can tell us little about the relative use and influence of Schleiermacher on the body of Kierkegaard's work and provide answers to the next two questions. But when we look at the references in the context of Kierkegaard's developing body of work, the contours of his interest in, and relationship to, Schleiermacher become clear.

Although no evidence exists to suggest that Kierkegaard was involved in the September 1833 Schleiermacher festivities in Copenhagen, the visit of the theologian and his death in February 1834 form the backdrop for Kierkegaard's initial encounter with his teaching. The status of Schleiermacher's work among his teachers must have been in play when, in July 1834, Kierkegaard signed on for a tutorial on Schleiermacher's *The Christian Faith* with his theological and philosophical teacher at the university, Martensen. Notes on his reading of *The Christian Faith* and queries about its implications are among Kierkegaard's 1834 journal entries. One entry muses over the apparent failure of theologians to push the "unrestricted grace" of the New Testament even further in recognition of Jewish particularism (8 July).[24] Passages or theses copied from the *The Christian Faith* have the appearance of memory jogs or reader notes regarding what understandings of human nature are compatible with the need (and reality) of redemption.[25] Apparent seeds of future concerns are seen in an undated entry from 1834 where Kierkegaard wonders how Schleiermacher's teaching on "the feeling of absolute dependence" as well as the characterization of Christianity as "teleological" relates to Schleiermacher's apparent view of "predestination," which appears to threaten human nature's free interaction with divine agency. With regard to prayer he wonders whether, "if the feeling of absolute dependence is the highest...then prayer is regarded merely as a fiction."[26] An even longer journal entry the next year, 17 October 1835, on philosophy as it relates to theology and a need for redemption [*Trang til Forløsning*] draws heavily from his teacher F.C. Sibbern's philosophy and contains formulations that call *The Christian Faith* to mind. The contrast drawn between "basic feeling" [*først føles*] and knowing or doing sets forth Schleiermacher's distinctive teaching in *The Christian Faith* § 8, while Sibbern's insistence upon the relative independence of theology from philosophy also mirrors Schleiermacher.[27] The encounter with Schleiermacher took a different turn that same October 1835 when Kierkegaard read the young German

24 *Pap.* I A 4 / *JP* 1, 410.

25 *Pap.* I C 23 / *JP* 4, 3844.

26 *Pap.* I C 20 / *JP* 4, 3843.

27 See *SKS* 17, 31, AA:13. I wish to thank Jon Stewart for his paper discussing this journal entry that he presented at the October 2003 Schleiermacher–Kierkegaard Congress in Copenhagen.

poet Karl Gutzkow's edition of Schleiermacher's *Confidential Letters on Schlegel's Lucinde*.[28]

The Gutzkow edition deserves highlighting, not only because of its effect on Kierkegaard, but for its place in the Schleiermacher reception generally. Karl Gutzkow (1811–78), soon prominent in the "Young Germany" movement, had attended Schleiermacher's Trinity Church as a youth and heard his lectures at the university. He reissued the book after hearing that the executors of Schleiermacher's literary estate did not plan to include it among his collected works. A 38-page preface opens with the words of a pupil, still grieving for the master: "I present here an offering as a token for love to lay upon the winter snow of the grave that will soon have enclosed the memory of Schleiermacher for a year."[29] The literary–theological plaidoyer that follows gives an impassioned recollection of Schleiermacher's illustrious career, including the theologian's acknowledgment of earthly love as a component of religion.

Though he makes no explicit reference to the Gutzkow preface, the work did get the attention of Kierkegaard. In his journal from October 1835 (a scant year and a half after Schleiermacher's death) Kierkegaard refers to the theologian's youthful "Lucinde Letters:"

> These letters are written about a book, *Lucinde*, published at one time by F. Schlegel. It is not known for sure whether or not this book is by Schl.[eiermacher], but Gutzkow puts the burden upon everyone to prove that it is not by him.[30]
>
> Surely on the basis of internal evidence alone it is incontestable; the characteristically Schl. dialectical-polemical language is unmistakable throughout, just as in, for example, "*Versuch über die Schamhaftigkeit*" ["*Essay on the Sense of Shame*"]. It is probably a model review and also an example of how such a thing can be most productive, in that he constructs a host of personalities out of the book itself and through them illuminates the work and also illuminates their individuality, so that instead of being faced by the reviewer with various points of view, we get instead many personalities who represent these various points of view. But they are complete beings, so that it is possible to get a glance into the individuality of the single individual and through numerous yet merely relatively true judgments to draw up our own final judgment. Thus it is a true masterpiece.[31]

---

28 Friedrich Schleiermacher, *Schleiermachers Vertraute Briefe über die Lucinde mit einer Vorrede von Karl Gutzkow*, Hamburg: Hoffman und Campe 1835, pp. v–xxxviii. Gutzkow's preface is reprinted in Gisela Dischner, *Friedrich Schlegels 'Lucinde' und Materialien zu einer Theorie des Müßiggangs*, Hildesheim: Gerstenberg Verlag 1980, pp.161–7.

29 Gutzkow's *Vorrede* in *Vertraute Briefe*, p. v. Gutzkow's obituary remembrance of Schleiermacher as preacher and teacher appeared in the *Allgemeine Zeitung*, 23 February 1834, reprinted in *Karl Gutzkows ausgewählte Werke*, vols. 1–12, ed. by Heinrich Hubert Houben, Leipzig: Max Hesse 1908, vol. 8, pp. 97–104.

30 Kierkegaard's remark reflects earlier speculation about the anonymously published 1800 edition; Schleiermacher's name is on the 1835 title page and Gutzkow's preface never places authorship in doubt.

31 Cited from *SKS* 19, 99, Not3:2 / *CI*, Supplement, p. 425. In commenting on this passage Emanuel Hirsch writes that Kierkegaard's "own pseudonymous authorship later does the same in a deeper sense. One may venture the thesis that the literary form of the first part of *Either/Or* is largely an imitation of [Schlegel's] *Lucinde*, in its second part an imitation of

Indeed, it *was* an interesting way to write.[32] That the work served as one such model for creating pseudonymous masks is little in doubt.[33] Kierkegaard's joy in giving full admiration to certain literary works of others was expressed early in the New Year.[34] The "Lucinde Letters" constitute a form of indirect communication about oneself, one's relationship to Friedrich Schlegel and to the projects of Romanticism. Indirection provided Schleiermacher with the fictional tools to defend as well as criticize his friend Schlegel's *Lucinde*, a book that stunned its German contemporaries with its rapturous celebration of erotic love between Schlegel and his (married) friend, Dorothea Veit. In the end, we can judge that Schleiermacher is less rhapsodic than Schlegel and puts realistic limits to Schlegel's ecstatic utterances about a new religion of love, as a fusion of "spiritual voluptuousness and sensual beatitude."[35] The form of these fictive letters underscores what I am saying. The idea that you can engage in telling criticism by *concealing* your own persona was an unusual and startling notion of Romantic literary theory. As a term "Romantic" still has connotations that derive from the German *Roman* or novel, where authors invent characters. As the *Athenaeum* (Critical Fragments # 26) puts it: "Novels are the Socratic dialogues of our time."[36] Like Kierkegaard's pseudonymous works, Schleiermacher's *Confidential Letters* were novelistic.

As Plato translator, Schleiermacher is, after all, the emulator of dialogical thinking. This is seen not just in the rhetorical art form of *On Religion: Speeches to its Cultured Despisers* (1799, 1806, 1821) but also in the *Letters on the Occasion of the Political-Theological Task and the Open Letter of Jewish Householders* (1799) on David Friedländer and Jewish emancipation in Prussia,[37] *On the Liturgical Right of Evangelical Princes: A Theological Reflection* by Pacificus Sincerus (1824), *Conversation about Scripture of Two Self-Preeminent Evangelical Christians. Luther with Respect to the New Prussian Order of Worship: A Last Word or a First*

Schleiermacher's *Lucinde* letters," *Kierkegaard-Studien*, vols. 1–2, Gütersloh: Bertelsmann 1933, vol. 2, p. 33, note 6 [479, note 6]. (Reprinted, Vaduz, Liechtenstein: Toposverlag 1978. First published in *Studien des apologetischen Seminars in Wernigerode*, nos. 29, 31, 32, 36, 1930–33. The reprint retains the pagination of the first publication, giving the page numbers of the 1933 edition in square brackets. This convention is followed here.)

32 Elsewhere I have tried to tease out of the *Confidential Letters* what it is that Kierkegaard so very much admires in this way of writing. See above, note 1.

33 A marginal note added to the entry regarding Schleiermacher's *Confidential Letters* (February 1836) cites a work by Poul Martin Møller, who was himself a master at "the literary dramatization of philosophical problems," Joakim Garff, *Søren Kierkegaard: A Biography*, trans. by Bruce H. Kirmmse, Princeton: Princeton University Press 2005, p. 94. See *SKS* 19, 99, Not3:2.a / *JP* 4, 3847.

34 *Pap.* I A 118 / *JP* 5, 5117 notes that in addition to the Schleiermacher letters, Kierkegaard had been reading E.T.A. Hoffmann, Herder, and Poul Martin Møller.

35 *Friedrich Schlegel's 'Lucinde' and the Fragments*, ed. and trans. by Peter Firchow, Minneapolis: University of Minnesota Press 1971, p. 44.

36 Ibid., p. 145.

37 See David Friedländer, Friedrich Schleiermacher, and Wilhelm Abraham Teller, *A Debate on Jewish Emancipation and Christian Theology in Old Berlin*, ed. and trans. by Richard Crouter and Julie Klasssen, Indianapolis: Hackett Publishing 2004.

(1827)[38] on liturgical controversies within the Prussian Church Union. Each of these works, plus the better known translated work *The Celebration of Christmas: A Conversation* (1806), makes use of anonymity, pseudonymity, and fictional voices to gain a hearing for distinctive points of view that deeply reflect Schleiermacher's engagement with his contemporaries.[39]

Further journal entries from 1836 deal with Schleiermacher's sense of human nature, the Romantic imagination, his position on "relative predestination," and his view of religion. The single sentence, "Schleiermacher is Stoicism reborn in Christianity"[40] remains cryptic, but nonetheless shows (at a minimum) that Kierkegaard had discovered the deep confidence and inwardness of the theologian's anthropological teaching. One must wonder whether Kierkegaard's own sense of Stoicism as a form of robust aestheticism may have been fed from this source, including an appreciation of the allure of the Stoic alternative to Christianity. Two entries (12 June and 4 August) picture Romanticism, with its sense of wonder and miracles, in decline in the face of a classicism and sense of necessity that Kierkegaard associates with Hegel and Schleiermacher.[41] The lone entry disassociates Schleiermacher from early Romanticism, despite awareness of the *Confidential Letters*. But if Kierkegaard was perplexed about Schleiermacher's relationship to early German Romanticism, he shares company with most subsequent interpreters. Kierkegaard did not own the first edition of *On Religion*; nor, for all his interest in Friedrich Schlegel in *The Concept of Irony*, does he appear to cite articles from the Schlegel brothers' literary journal *Athenaeum*, to which Schleiermacher also contributed. In a similar vein of thought, what Schleiermacher calls "religion" is associated with what Hegelian dogmaticians, like Marheineke, call "faith;" in both cases it is seen as a first immediacy, a vital fluid, thus again showing that Kierkegaard seems to place Schleiermacher within the larger camp of German idealists, whose world view espouses a kind of subliminal monism.[42]

But it was not just Martensen who served as a link to *The Christian Faith*. A spur to his investigations was provided by the son of Johann Gottlieb Fichte (1762–1814), Immanuel Hermann Fichte (1796–1879) whose journal, *Zeitschrift für Philosophie und spekulative Theologie*, was owned by Kierkegaard.[43] The younger Fichte made a career interpreting his father's work, while relating it to the philosophy of the later Schelling and Hegel. An entry from January 1837 shows that Kierkegaard, in reading notes on I.H. Fichte, refers to the younger Fichte, along with Schleiermacher and Schelling, within categories of German idealism, in which the individual threatens

38 *Kritische Gesamtausgabe*, Abteilung 1, vol. 9, *Kirchenpolitische Schriften*, ed. by Günter Meckenstock with Hans-Friedrich Traulsen, Berlin: Walter de Gruyter 2000, pp. 211–69; pp. 381–472; the works are not available in English.

39 Published in English as *Christmas Eve: Dialogue on the Incarnation*, ed. and trans. by Terrence N. Tice, San Francisco: EM Texts 1990.

40 *Pap*. I 305 / *JP* 4, 3848.

41 *Pap*. I A 170 / *JP* 2, 1563 and *Pap*. I A 216 / *JP* 3, 3809.

42 *Pap*. I A 273 / *JP* 2, 1096.

43 *Zeitschrift für Philosophie und spekulative Theologie*, vols. 1–16, ed. by Immanuel Hermann Fichte and Christian Hermann Weiße, Bonn et al.: Eduard Weber et al. 1837–46 (*ASKB* 877–911).

to be lost in a system of infinite multiplicity, becoming, and completeness.[44] In the same year Kierkegaard also records his belief that Schleiermacher's definition of religion is pantheistic, thus producing a religion that fuses the infinite and the finite.[45] The charge of pantheism in *On Religion* hovered in the air in the work's German reception, even if a case can be made, and was by Schleiermacher, that *On Religion* (1799) stops short of espousing such a view. In the earlier Schleiermacher journal entries Kierkegaard pays close attention to Schleiermacher's lively sense of human consciousness as primary (which he admires, but fears may veer towards pantheism) while noting the need for a proper sense of the truth of theology that will not become ossified in dogmatic systems.

Just prior to the end of 1837 on 7 December Kierkegaard wrote a journal entry that, in its nuanced eloquence, further captures the tensions in his understanding of Schleiermacher.

> Schleiermacher's is basically the first level of genuine orthodox dogmatics (and therefore he will come again to have great importance), however heterodox his position is in many respects, and his position will naturally be significantly modified in that the dogmatic content will be given a completely different, objective qualification and determinateness. Yet in many points his position is right—for example, he has incorporated the concept of wonder in its inwardness within the system rather than, as before, keeping it outside as a prolegomenon; his whole position is that of wonder, and his entire self-awareness is a completely new Christian self-awareness.[46]

The quotation requires us to puzzle over the initial depiction of a "genuine orthodox dogmatics" which is evaluated positively, before being juxtaposed with Schleiermacher's "heterodoxy." The paragraph is less than fully transparent. But I take the first level of dogmatics to refer to the fact that Schleiermacher makes the case for theology as independent from philosophy. At the outset dogmatics presupposes the faith of the community. That enterprise may well risk undercutting the ability of the theologian to defend Christian teaching in its objectivity. But the endorsement of wonder [*Under*] within Schleiermacher's system and building a system directly upon a "new Christian self-awareness" outweigh, as it were, the

---

44 *SKS* 17, 41f., AA:22 / *JP* 2, 1096.

45 *SKS* 17, 219, DD:9 / *JP* 4, 3849. Kierkegaard gives no specific cross-reference to Schleiermacher's works. At the time Kierkegaard was very likely reading J.E. Erdmann, "Pantheismus die Grundlage der Religion," *Zeitschrift für spekulative Theologie*, vols. 1–3, ed. by Bruno Bauer, Berlin: Dümmler 1836–38 (*ASKB* 354–357), vol. 1, no. 2, p. 143, where the Hegelian leaning journal criticizes pantheism in Schleiermacher. Erdmann takes the doctrine of absolute dependence on God to constitute a subjective pole of pantheism, as if one were merging with an indescribable one and all in this feeling. See *SKS* K17, pp. 384–6 as well as *SKS* 19, p. 169, for the notebook entry on Kierkegaard's reading of Erdmann's *Glauben und Wissen*.

46 *SKS* 17, 249, DD:86 / *JP* 4, 3850. In the Hong edition of *JP*, a note on the first sentence of the 1837 entry links it with the subsequent 1851 entry in which Kierkegaard maintains that Schleiermacher's sense of being precludes a proper sense of human agency and becoming. I see no reason to associate the subsequent idea with this passage.

risks of heterodoxy.[47] In addition, the entry reveals that Kierkegaard has given up his earlier association of Schleiermacher with Hegel under the classic, a stance that has no room for miracles.[48] To have systematically captured "the concept of wonder in its inwardness" is no small achievement if you are Kierkegaard. Eight months later, in August 1838, an entry speaks of Schleiermacher's restoration of a "common consciousness of the faith" prior to Holy Scripture becoming an article of faith within dogmatic systems.[49] Just as the sense of wonder in Schleiermacher enabled him to stand against wooden systems of dogmatics, the same consciousness of faith could not be sustained merely by Scripture being given doctrinal status.

Journal entries from December 1838 and from February and May 1839 show Kierkegaard engaging in reading and debates that draw from *The Christian Faith* and contemporary questions of dogmatic theology. Even if incomplete in the information they convey, the entries make clear that his preoccupation with Schleiermacher's teaching extends well beyond the 1834 summer tutorial with Martensen. The first of these entries notes with tacit approval Schleiermacher's view that the doctrine of the Trinity arose from Platonizing within the Alexandrian school.[50] An entry from 25 February 1839 has Schleiermacher in mind when Kierkegaard writes about "the increasing loss of the teleological moment, which belongs with a life-view."[51] For Schleiermacher the abstract "teleological type" of Christian religion is connected with a distinctive life-view "by the fact that in it everything is related to the redemption accomplished by Jesus of Nazareth."[52] An entry on the theme of John 4:16, the idea that "God is love" (12 May 1839), does not directly cite Schleiermacher. But *The Christian Faith* highlights this teaching in a striking manner in §167, under the heading "God is love," where readers are told that this is the only expression concerning God that fully responds to God's nature.[53] An entry from 20 May that probably alludes to contemporary dogmaticians, K.G. Bretschneider

---

47 The term used here (*Under*) differs from the meditation on wonder, in the sense of surprise or astonishment [*Forundringen*], that is celebrated in "On the Occasion of a Confession," in *Three Discourses on Imagined Occasions* (*SKS* 5, 399–405 / *TD*, 18–25). Like the German *Wunder*, the Danish *Under* admits of being translated as "wonder" or "miracle." See Schleiermacher, *On Religion: Speeches to its Cultured Despisers*, ed. and trans. by Richard Crouter, Cambridge: Cambridge University Press 1996, p. 49: "Miracle is merely the religious name for event, every one of which, even the most natural and usual, is a miracle as soon as it adapts itself to the fact that the religious view of it can be the dominant one."

48 See *Pap*. I A 216 / *JP* 3, 3809.

49 *SKS* 17, 258, DD:125 / *JP* 4, 3851.

50 *SKS* 18, 354, KK:5. The passage indicates that Kierkegaard had read Schleiermacher's treatise, "Ueber den Gegensatz zwischen der Sabellianischen und der Athanasianischen Vorstellung von der Trinität," *Theologische Zeitschrift*, ed. by F. Schleiermacher, W.M.L. de Wette and Fr. Lücke, 3 Hefte, Berlin: Reimer 1822, pp. 295–408.

51 See *SKS* 18, 15, EE:29: "*Vor Tid taber mere og mere det teleologisk Moment, der hører med til en Livs-Anskuelse*."

52 See *SKS* K18, 30, which refers to *The Christian Faith*, § 11, p. 52.

53 *SKS* 18, 27, EE:62, and *The Christian Faith*, § 167, p. 730, "Hence it is in this exclusive form that our paragraph has to be established and justified, namely, that love alone and no other attribute can be equated thus with God."

(1776–1848) and K.A. Hase (1800–90) approves of Schleiermacher's preference for the Augsburg Confession over the Formula of Concord.[54] In another direct allusion to Schleiermacher's dogmatics, (22 May 1839) Kierkegaard writes with apparent approval that "every dogma is nothing other than a concrete expression of general human consciousness."[55]

IV. Two Schleiermachers, One Danish Authorship

As we follow the Schleiermacher references into the 1840s it behooves us to be aware of journal entries as they co-exist with his chief publications. As we shall see, for the "main period" of Kierkegaard's writing in the 1840s, two Schleiermachers—the Plato scholar, interpreter, and translator, as well as the theologian whose dogmatics wrestles with the doctrines of sin, grace, and redemption—compete for attention. In the history of Schleiermacher reception the two dimensions of his work are typically held apart; theologians rarely probe his Plato work, philosophers rarely attend to his dogmatic theology. Kierkegaard's authorship is exceptional in bringing together the two sides of Schleiermacher's legacy, where the common ingredient is a penchant for self-examination.

Among all of Kierkegaard's published works, his 1841 master's dissertation, *The Concept of Irony with Continual Reference to Socrates*, contains the most overt and frequent references to Schleiermacher. In calling attention to its centrality in this inquiry, we revert to the poet Oehlenschläger's view that Schleiermacher turned Plato (and thereby Socrates) into Denmark's German contemporaries. Depending upon how they are enumerated, there are some 32 direct references or allusions to Schleiermacher's Plato edition as well as several references to his 1815 lecture to the Berlin Academy of Sciences, "On the Worth of Socrates as Philosopher."[56] Not incidentally (in view of earlier journal entries) *The Concept of Irony* also includes two overt and approving references to teachings in *The Christian Faith*, each of which is brought to bear on the analysis of Socrates in the Platonic corpus.

The first and abiding sense of *The Concept of Irony* with respect to Schleiermacher is that it deeply shares his quest to take Socrates seriously philosophically, while placing his achievement within the history of ancient Greek philosophy. Within its own problematic *The Concept of Irony* asks the same question posed by

---

54 *SKS* 18, 31, EE:75.

55 *SKS* 18, 32, EE:80, refers to the basic orientation of *The Christian Faith*, § 15, p. 76, "Christian doctrines are accounts of the Christian religious affections set forth in speech."

56 A detailed examination of each of these references in *The Concept of Irony* exceeds the bounds of this article. Schleiermacher references in the work are comprised of informational annotations, historical and philological asides, as well as substantive philosophical comments on his work as Plato scholar and interpreter. Schleiermacher's "On the Worth of Socrates as Philosopher," in *Xenophon's Memorabilia of Socrates*, ed. by Charles Anthon, New York: Harper & Brothers 1848, pp. 443–57, was written to counter contemporary German classical philologists who asserted either that Socrates belongs to the end of a previous age of philosophy (Krug) or that he stands as precursor to Plato, though not as a significant thinker in his own right (Ast).

Schleiermacher's "On the Worth of Socrates as Philosopher." That 1815 lecture seeks to resolve the contradiction between the universal acclaim for Socrates as a monumental influence in the history of philosophy and depictions of Socrates by Xenophon (or by contemporary philologists, Friedrich Ast and W.T. Krug) that fail to credit him with a teaching that could have launched a new philosophical era in the first place. Thesis III of Kierkegaard's dissertation similarly tries to reconcile the rival pictures of Socrates put forth by Xenophon and Plato.[57] Schleiermacher sees Socrates' philosophical worth in his dogged insistence upon placing the idea of knowledge (science) in the forefront and in depicting the quest for knowledge through the positive method of learning how to divide and combine concepts properly (*Phaedrus* 266b-c), the art which we call dialectic.[58] Schleiermacher's understanding of Socratic dialectic may end with a doctrine of knowledge that, on Kierkegaard's reading, is more positive and less paradoxical than his own. In the dissertation Kierkegaard uses the problem of extracting a consistent teaching from Socrates to develop his theory of irony which, unlike speculative or abstract unity, can hold unity together "invisibly and imperceptively."[59] Their sheer love of Socrates united the German with the Dane. On the matter of Socrates' philosophical significance they are in basic accord, even if on Kierkegaard's reading the emphasis is put on what Gregory Vlastos calls "the strangeness of Socrates."[60] As translator, not just philologist, Schleiermacher's authority provides Kierkegaard with just the body of work that was needed in order to pursue his own thought.

Secondly, *The Concept of Irony* gives abundant testimony to Schleiermacher's hermeneutical principles that bestow order on the Platonic corpus by viewing it in a developing scheme. The book attests to the weight of Schleiermacher's effort to render the Platonic corpus intelligible by proposing a scheme of ordering the dialogues by placing what Schleiermacher takes as the more mythic and metaphorical works, that is, the more Socratic works, first.[61] In reviewing the respective positions of Ast and Schleiermacher on the order of the dialogues, Kierkegaard sides with

57 "If a comparison is made between Xenophon and Plato, one will find that the first takes too much from Socrates, the second raised him too high; neither of them finds the truth." See *SKS* 1, 259 and 263 footnote / *CI*, 214 and 219 footnote.

58 The art of pursuing philosophical questions through conversation, vividly accomplished in the *Confidential Letters*, was further enhanced by Schleiermacher's work as Plato translator. Not just the words, but the form and style of interrogation cannot but have left a profound mark on the Dane.

59 *SKS* 1, 113–6 / *CI*, 53–5.

60 Gregory Vlastos, *Socrates: Ironist and Moral Philosopher*, Cambridge: Cambridge University Press 1991. Vlastos' asides regarding Kierkegaard's reading of Socrates suggest how very much the paradoxicality of Socratic thought in the hands of Kierkegaard is nurtured by Romantic sources, pp. 43–4.

61 On Schleiermacher as Plato interpreter, see Julia A. Lamm, "Schleiermacher as Plato Scholar," *Journal of Religion*, vol. 80, no. 2, 2000, pp. 206–39, and "Reading Plato's Dialectics: Schleiermacher's Insistence on Dialectics as Dialogical," *Zeitschrift für Neuere Theologiegeschichte / Journal for the History of Modern Theology*, vol. 10, no. 1, 2003, pp. 1–25.

Schleiermacher.[62] He generally agrees with Schleiermacher's arrangement of the dialogues, despite problems critics had seen in the fact that the first book of the *Republic* (written later) emulates the Socrates of earlier dialogues.[63] Kierkegaard holds (against Ast) that the *Apology* is not a mere invention of Plato, even if he stops short of Schleiermacher's view that it is a recollection of Socrates' actual defense.[64] Kierkegaard also defends the more philological approach of Schleiermacher to Plato as philosophically significant against the reproaches of Hegel.[65]

Thirdly, two references to Schleiermacher's theological *magnum opus* in a work that constitutes an inquiry into irony and Socrates speak to the ways that a close reading of *The Christian Faith* informed his thinking. The ease with which Kierkegaard moves from intense discussion of Socrates and Plato to Schleiermacher's dogmatics is surprising, unless Kierkegaard had, so to speak, internalized the teachings of *The Christian Faith* that caught his fancy. The first such reference draws from Kierkegaard's wrestling with the Socratic view that virtue is one and everywhere the same.[66] He refers to Schleiermacher's "penetrating judgment" [*skarpsindige Bedømmelse*] regarding the significance of number in the case of God, namely, that to attribute unity to a being can only be done with reference to some still higher category and hence is, strictly speaking, illicit in the case of God.[67] Presumably, Kierkegaard also agrees with Schleiermacher's point that, even if illicit, the popular needs of religious devotion do nonetheless speak of deity as one, just as we continue to think of virtue as one. Even apart from its content, the passage honors Schleiermacher's mental acumen. In addition, further on in *The Concept of Irony*, Kierkegaard again turns to the dogmatics. While representing Socrates' theoretical ignorance as a religious ignorance, he writes:

> This theoretical ignorance for which the eternal essence of the deity remained a mystery must naturally have had its counterpart in a corresponding religious ignorance respecting divine providence and guidance for mankind. This is a religious ignorance which seeks its edification and manifests its piety in a total ignorance, just as Schleiermacher, for example, in a much more concrete development locates the edifying in a feeling of absolute dependence. This, too, conceals within itself a polemic and becomes a terror [*Forfærdelse*] for everyone who finds repose in some finite relation to the deity.[68]

---

62 *SKS* 1, 113 and 113–6 / *CI*, 53 and 53–5.

63 *SKS* 1, 164 and 172 / *CI*, 111 and 120. On the early criticism of Schleiermacher's dating of the dialogues, see Lamm, "Schleiermacher as Plato Scholar," *Journal of Religion*, op. cit., and Peter M. Steiner, "Zur Kontroverse um Schleiermachers Platon," in Friedrich Daniel Ernst Schleiermacher, *Über die Philosophie Platons*, ed. by Peter M. Steiner, Hamburg: Felix Meiner 1996, pp. xxiii–xliv.

64 *SKS* 1, 138 / *CI*, 79f.

65 *SKS* 1, 266 / *CI*, 222.

66 *SKS* 1, 119 / *CI*, 59.

67 See *The Christian Faith*, p. 229 and the explanatory note in *CI*, 493, which quotes *The Christian Faith*, "strictly taken it can never be an attribute of a thing that it only exists in a definite number."

68 *SKS* 1, 223 / *CIC*, 201.

The passage (used above as epigraph) parallels Socratic ignorance with the central idea of Schleiermacher's dogmatics, the "feeling of absolute dependence." Such a teaching, Kierkegaard writes, conceals within itself a polemic that "becomes a terror for everyone who finds repose in some finite relation to the divine."[69] Here Kierkegaard acknowledges that the central point of Schleiermacher's theology ensures the radical transcendence and strict unknowability of deity, positions with which Kierkegaard, as philosopher, has considerable sympathy. After noting with approval the Christian appropriation of Socratism, Kierkegaard expands on the point by calling Xenophon to mind, "where Socrates relates how the gods have reserved to themselves the most important secrets...."[70] Like Socrates, Schleiermacher had glimpsed the hidden abyss that threatens efforts to find security in our finitude.

A broad view of *The Concept of Irony* will see the work as juxtaposing the Platonic side of Schleiermacher's legacy with the theologian's own involvement in early German Romanticism. At times *The Concept of Irony* seems like a virtual replication of debates within Schleiermacher's youthful circle. The work's prolonged interrogation of Friedrich Schlegel's teaching on irony is steeped in the literary theory of the German movement. Today we are more aware than ever of the philosophical significance of early German Romanticism, with its teaching regarding the inexpressibility of being, as well as the sheer radicality of the movement as it brought criticism to bear on the received teachings of Kant and the development of German idealism.[71] Read through the eyes of Kierkegaard one attains fresh appreciation for the role of Schleiermacher's Plato in connection with his early Romanticism.

If a preoccupation with Schleiermacher's Plato scholarship, including the Academy Address on Socrates, pervades *The Concept of Irony*, this is less apparent in Kierkegaard's subsequent works. Some journal entries in the next few years continue to attest to Schleiermacher's Plato as silent companion. An undated entry from 1841 cites dialogues in the Schleiermacher edition that illustrate the insistence of Socratic dialectic on "the basic law of the dialectical movement," that is, that of the excluded middle, or view that "only two things can be opposite of each other."[72] Kierkegaard agrees with Schleiermacher on the spurious status of the *Alcibiades primus*.[73] An entry in 1843 on the *Cratyllus* cross-references the exact point in Plato's work where Socrates sets forth an insight that runs deep in Kierkegaard's imagination: "What Socrates says in the *Cratyllus* is beautiful— namely, that to be deceived by oneself is the worst of all, for when the deceiver does not go away even for a moment but is constantly present, how could it fail to be terrifying?"[74]

---

69 As represented in 1841 in *The Concept of Irony*, Schleiermacher's central theological claim would appear to forestall the sort of cultural Protestantism that Kierkegaard appears to charge him with in 1850; see below, under "*Late Encounters in the Journals*."

70 *SKS* 1, 223 / *CIC*, 201.

71 See Manfred Frank, *The Philosophical Foundations of Early German Romanticism*, op. cit., pp. 65–85.

72 *Pap.* III B 27 / *JP* 4, 4245, citing passages in Schleiermacher's Plato from *Phaedrus*, *Protagoras*, the *Republic*, and the *Sophist*.

73 *Pap.* IV A 203 / *JP* 4, 4250.

74 *SKS* 18, 183, *JJ*:131 / *JP* 4, 4260 altered; where Kierkegaard cites: *Cratyllus* § 428 in Schleiermacher's translation, *Platons Werke*, Part II, vol. 2, p. 104.

Initially it seems as if Schleiermacher's impact declines after the master's dissertation. But the ways Schleiermacher's presence continues once the literary works proper get underway can still be seen and inferred from the evidence at hand. Our task, as interpreters, is neither to claim too much nor too little. Only two relatively explicit Schleiermacher allusions occur within the two volumes of *Either/Or*. A passage in *Either/Or*, Part One alludes to Socrates on Heraclitus, while a passage in the work of the Judge in *Either/Or*, Part Two on the Judge's teaching about history and ethics as unfolding organically recalls views of Schleiermacher.[75] Meanwhile, however, I have noted the conjectural, but not implausible, judgment of Emanuel Hirsch that *Either/Or*, Part One emulates Schlegel's *Lucinde* in its bohemian self-obsessiveness, while *Either/Or*, Part Two emulates the epistolary model and subtle ethical caution of Schleiermacher's *Confidential Letters*.[76] Initially, too, Schleiermacher appears to be well hidden in *Fragments* behind its pervasive reflection on Socrates. At least one reference in *Philosophical Fragments* to the "pugnacious proposition" (*Meno* 80) and a reference to *Clitophon* as spurious reflect an ongoing immersion in the Plato translation.[77] Schleiermacher is similarly concealed in *Concluding Unscientific Postscript* where the text speaks about theological introductions and apologetics versus lived appropriations of faith, refers to Schleiermacher's reading of the *Apology* 36a where Socrates is condemned by three (not 30) votes, comments on the Sophists' view that "everything is true" (which parallels a reference in *De Omnibus* that associates the view with Schleiermacher's view of "feeling") and expresses doubts about "Christians among the cultured in Christendom" in a possible allusion to the "cultured despisers" of *On Religion*.[78] All of this, of course, seems like minimal influence of Schleiermacher on two of Kierkegaard's most significant philosophical books. Yet one may also be permitted to think that none of the reflections on Socrates in *Philosophical Fragments* or the extension of that interrogation in *Concluding Unscientific Postscript* would have occurred if Kierkegaard had not encountered Schleiermacher's Plato/Socrates and appropriated deep strands of those interpretations about lived existence and the life of the mind for his own purposes.

In turn, when we look closely at the philosophical themes and theological orientations of *Philosophical Fragments* and *The Concept of Anxiety*, as paired books from 1844, the complementary inquiries of Johannes Climacus and Vigilius Haufniensis appear to have brought together the two sides of Schleiermacher. Published on 13 June, *Philosophical Fragments* juxtaposes Socratic self-discovery of truth with a hypothetical Christian self-consciousness that presupposes (though does not yet analyze) the category of sin. *The Concept of Anxiety*, published 17 June is dedicated to a psychological examination of inherited sin and accords Schleiermacher his most notable accolade within the Kierkegaardian *corpus*. Near the start of that

---

75 *SKS* 2, 24 / *EO1*, 26. *SKS* 3, 160 / *EO2*, 163.

76 See above, note 32. On the *Vertraute Briefe* and Kierkegaard, see Crouter, note 1.

77 *SKS* 4, 218 / *PF*, 9 and *SKS* 4, 221 / *PF*, 12.

78 *SKS* 7, 24 / *CUP1*, 15. *SKS* 7, 137 / *CUP1*, 147. See also the explanatory note in *CUP2*, 219. *SKS* 7, 272 / *CUP1*, 298–9. See also *Pap.* IV B 1, p. 146 / *JC*, 167. See the accompanying explanatory note, *JC*, 330. *SKS* 7, 533 / *CUP1*, 587.

work, after a section that assaults the Hegelian smugness of contemporaries who associate faith with simple immediacy, Haufniensis turns to the requirements of a proper dogmatics, "which begins with the actual in order to raise it up into ideality. It does not deny the presence of sin; on the contrary, it presupposes it and explains it by presupposing hereditary sin."[79] Being able to presuppose and write about sin is, we are told, comparable to Greek speculation concerning nature, "a moving something that no science can grasp."[80] He continues in the next paragraph:

> That such is the case with dogmatics will readily be granted if once again time is taken to understand Schleiermacher's immortal service to this science. He was left behind long ago when men chose Hegel. Yet Schleiermacher was a thinker in the beautiful Greek sense, a thinker who spoke only of what he knew. Hegel, on the contrary, despite all his outstanding ability and stupendous learning, reminds us again and again by his performance that he was in the German sense a professor of philosophy on a large scale, because he *à tout prix* must explain all things.[81]

The tribute simply could not be higher in the eyes of its author. The two Schleiermachers—the Greek thinker and admirer of Socrates and the Christian analyst of human sin—are again brought together in a single passage. In speaking only about what he knows, Schleiermacher brings the spirit of Socrates (see *Fragments*) to bear on the actual sinfulness of individual persons (see *The Christian Faith*). The contrast with Hegel is deliberate and breaks with earlier journal entries that placed Schleiermacher and Hegel in the same idealist philosophical camp. Indeed, the passage that immediately follows makes it clear that dogmatics of the sort recommended by Kierkegaard does not leave ethics behind, even though it is no longer an "immanental science."

> So the new science begins with dogmatics in the same sense that immanental science begins with metaphysics. Here ethics again finds its place as the science that has as a task for actuality the dogmatic consciousness of actuality. This ethics [now construed within dogmatics] does not ignore sin, and it does not have its ideality in making ideal demands; rather, it has its ideality in the penetrating consciousness of actuality, of the actuality of sin, but note carefully, not with metaphysical light-mindedness or with psychological concupiscence.[82]

In fact, Schleiermacher's dogmatics does not leave ethics behind, but rests upon the coming together of human sinfulness and ethics in the activity of repentance. Indeed, in the thematizing of repentance one can see even richer and wider parallels between Kierkegaard and Schleiermacher.

---

79 *SKS* 4, 326f. / *CA*, 19; for *The Concept of Anxiety*, the Schleiermacher references in Torsten Bohlin, *Kierkegaards dogmatische Anschauung in ihrem geschichtlichen Zusammenhange*, trans. by Ilse Meyer-Lüne, Gütersloh: C. Bertelsmann 1927, continue to repay careful study.

80 *SKS* 4, 327 / *CA*, 20.

81 *SKS* 4, 327f. / *CA*, 20.

82 *SKS* 4, 328 / *CA*, 20.

I have noted that explorations of the two thinkers' views of sin are in the forefront of comparisons.[83] Such comparisons will doubtless continue to be made. But the references and teachings within *The Concept of Anxiety*, like other texts we are analyzing, should be understood in the context of that book as well as the developing body of Kierkegaard's work.[84] The frequent observation that Schleiermacher views sin as a condition [*Zustand*],[85] while Kierkegaard sees sin and grace qualitatively, obscures the complementarity of their teachings on sin and grace. For Schleiermacher, as for Kierkegaard, sin cannot be given "an objective elucidation" but requires us to attend to "personal self-consciousness."[86] In fact, Schleiermacher's teaching on sin, remorse, and the self-examination of repentance basically accords with the views of Kierkegaard's pseudonymous masks.[87] Elsewhere I have argued that the depictions of the crucial category of repentance in the two authors are wholly compatible. The parallels strikingly convey what we might take to be the "cash value" of Kierkegaard's deep reading of *The Christian Faith*. In "More than Kindred Spirits: Kierkegaard and Schleiermacher on Repentance,"[88] I show that Kierkegaardian masks as varied as "A", the Judge, Johannes de silentio, William Afham, Quidam, Frater Taciturnus, all speak on behalf of views of repentance that resonate with

---

83 See above, note 19. On the doctrine of sin, the received view in secondary theological literature inspired by Barth maintains that Kierkegaard posited a more serious and traditional understanding of sin, while Schleiermacher's teaching lacks the Pauline-Augustinian dimension of Christian teaching.

84 *SKS* 4, 328 / *CA*, 20. *SKS* 4, 333 / *CA*, 27. *SKS* 4, 334 / *CA*, 28. *SKS* 4, 339 / *CA*, 32. *SKS* 4, 386 / *CA*, 83. *SKS* 4, 387 / *CA*, 84. A passage on the Lord's Supper as a potential spiritual trial may well echo *The Christian Faith*, § 142.2, p. 656 on the Supper and worthy or unworthy participation; see *SKS* 4, 443 / *CA*, 143.

85 *The Christian Faith*, § 62.1, pp. 259–60, in speaking about a "more or less" of sin and grace seems to quantify, but in fact contends that Christian self-awareness hovers and oscillates between the two poles, hence is never a static state of being. On this see Axt-Piscalar, "Das Selbst in der Selbstverstrickung," op. cit., p. 453, note 4.

86 Ibid., § 66.1, p. 271.

87 See note 1 for reference to my study of repentance in Schleiermacher and Kierkegaard. In the literature on the *The Christian Faith* more has been written on the understanding of sin (§§ 65–85) as well as on the person and work of Christ (§§ 86–105) than on the explication of grace in the work of redemption as it plays out in the individual soul (§§ 106–112).Yet it is precisely the account of the interplay of sin and grace in the regenerate individual soul that bears comparison with Kierkegaard.

88 The comparison is undertaken under six perspectives or theses that Schleiermacher's dogmatics shares with Kierkegaard's pseudonymous masks: (1) repentance directly relates to the good, that is, to ethics, though it does so as a thoroughly religious category; (2) repentance is directed toward sin that is ideal and pervasive, and clings to our condition, not toward actual sins; (3) repentance is necessarily the act of a private individual and a pivotal, that is, dialectical, category; (4) although it is highest, repentance is a passive act within human psychology, only partly within our power and control; (5) if it does not lead to a true change of heart, repentance becomes stuck in remorse where it is negative, painful, and demonic; (6) no timetable can be established for repentance, or for other moments in the process of redemption, despite the fact that the work of redemption is ordained by God.

views put forth in *The Christian Faith*.[89] Granted, the teachings are expressed the way that a novelist, not a dogmatic theologian, would do. Like Schleiermacher, the master of concealment consistently views repentance as the highest self-activity prior to faith. If an argument made elsewhere can be assumed here, it shows that (1) Schleiermacher's theology continues to play a significant role in the authorship, and (2) the main works of the 1840s have indeed internalized the teaching of the German predecessor's much admired dogmatics. Of course, nuances distinguish the two writers; a dogmatics is not a philosophical novel. But Schleiermacher, like Kierkegaard, refuses to be prescriptive about possible patterns and paths of coming into the Christian life. He tells us that, "Undeniably there are types of conversion which seem to be mainly a happy rescue from despair. But there are others in which no such agonizing crisis occurs."[90] Kierkegaard must have been pleased to read that a happy rescue from despair is possible but also taken pleasure in the way that his predecessor acknowledges the reality of shipwrecked and despairing lives. I am not arguing for a full convergence of their teachings. Kierkegaard is ever the pessimist about the possibilities of the human condition in ways that may well have shocked his predecessor. Yet on the pivotal significance of repentance in the Christian life, their views agree more than they differ.

Kierkegaard's turn to the niceties of Christian theology never moves too far away from the figure of Socrates. The Greek's penchant for self-examination became personalized and Christianized at another level in the authorship. At a time of greatest questioning concerning the purpose and fate of his literary productions, which coincides with the crisis over pseudonymity brought on by the *Corsair* affair, an undated entry from 1846 shows how deeply Kierkegaard takes the admonitions of Socrates to heart and applies them as a justification for the duplicity in his own life and art: "I decided to do the imprudent thing and disdain the appearance of being somebody, which Socrates develops so beautifully in the *Republic*."[91] After an undated marginal note informs us that the reference was marked in his copy of Schleiermacher's translation,[92] the passage continues:

> But that all this is in the service of the idea, is my highest interest, my artistic exertion in order to sustain my productivity, something I could scarcely dare confide to Spang that

---

89 The paper from which I cite draws from the following references to repentance in Kierkegaard's works: "A" (*SKS* 2, 147–8 / *EO1*, 148–9); the Judge (*SKS* 3, 207–9, 215, 230 / *EO2*, 216–8, 224, 241); William Afham (*SKS* 6, 162 / *SLW*, 174), Quidam (*SKS* 6, 412–3, 418 / *SLW*, 446–7, 452; Frater Taciturnus (*SKS* 6, 437–46 / *SLW*, 474–85, which lead directly to the book's conclusion); Johannes de silentio (*SKS* 4, 186, 188n, 191 / *FT*, 96, 98n. 102).

90 *The Christian Faith*, p. 488; *Glaubenslehre*, vol. 2, p. 162. To maintain with Fischer, *Subjektivität und Sünde*, p. 116, that "*Angst und Verzweiflung als Interpretationsbegriffe der Sünde in Schleiermachers Aufriß sind undenkbar*," does not wholly preclude the lived reality of despair within the dogmatics.

91 *SKS* 20, 24, NB:13a / *JP* 5, 5892 (n.d., 1846). In the passage from *Republic* II, 360c–361d, the speech of Glaucon observes that since even the unjust seek to appear just, how one appears in the public eye is not the crucial test of character.

92 See *SKS* K20 for *SKS* 20, 24, Kierkegaard's copy of the *Republic* has not been able to be acquired.

> my only justification is that I acted against the understanding, that without it I would have been a prolific wordgusher as authors these days are, to whom it never occur to realize one jot of what they write....[93]

The reference again illustrates the once-removed but not insignificant nature of Schleiermacher's presence. Kierkegaard's intense appropriation of Socratism benefited from having on hand such artful German formulations of the Greek text that carried over so readily into Danish.

The same lurking presence of Schleiermacher behind Plato informs not just the more avowedly philosophical works, but also the non-pseudonymous *Upbuilding Discourses in Various Spirits* published on 13 March 1847. Although the allusions are hidden behind slightly veiled references to "a simple man" or locutions like "from olden times it is said,"[94] a series of passages bring the moral and philosophical rigor of Socrates directly to bear upon the complacency and sophistry that Kierkegaard perceives in contemporary life.[95] Indeed, a relentless philosophical defense of the good stands at the heart of these theological and ethical meditations. In addition to drawing from Schleiermacher's German Plato, the *Upbuilding Discourses*, when it claims that agreement is needed at some level before disputes can arise, may well be borrowing hermeneutical insight from Schleiermacher's *Dialectics* in the Ludwig Jonas edition that was owned by Kierkegaard.[96]

V. Late Encounters in the Journals

Following the writing of *The Point of View for My Work as an Author* and *The Sickness unto Death* in 1848–49, Kierkegaard's references to Schleiermacher become increasingly sporadic, appear only in the journals, and suddenly take on a mood of critical defiance. Several of the entries charge his German predecessor with an error in his dogmatics and with having falsified Christianity. The earlier appreciation of Schleiermacher's Plato scholarship is now forgotten or perhaps just irrelevant. For reasons we must now explore, Kierkegaard distances himself from Schleiermacher, as if he holds him responsible for the plight of the Danish church.[97] His deep sympathies with Schleiermacher somehow shift amid the rising sense of self-martydom that coincides with the attack upon the bourgeois state-dominated Christianity of Bishop Mynster. A possible harbinger of the impending shift occurs in 1849 when Kierkegaard finds a warrant for asceticism in the third edition of *On*

---

93 *SKS* 20, 24, NB:13 / *JP* 5, 5892. Kierkegaard refers to Peter Johannes Spang (1796–1846), his chaplain and later pastor of the Holy Ghost church.

94 See *SKS* 8, 149–50 / *UD*, 37. *SKS* 8, 161 / *UD*, 50.

95 *SKS* 8, 176 / *UD*, 68. *SKS* 8, 200 / *UD*, 95–6. *SKS* 8, 232 / *UD*, 133. *SKS* 8, 178 / *UD*, 180. *SKS* 8, 228 / *UD*, 191.

96 *SKS* 8, 226 / *UD*, 126. *SKS* K8, 256, cites *Dialektik. Aus Schleiermachers handschriftlichem Nachlasse*, ed. by L. Jonas, Berlin: Reimer 1839, §§ 45–46, pp. 17f.

97 Although this was not always the case, it is now widely recognized that the last phase of Kierkegaard's work takes a distinctive turn. Cf. the 1951–52 debate between Knud Hansen and Anna Paulsen on "Der andere Kierkegaard," in *Sören Kierkegaard*, ed. by Heinz-Horst Schrey, Darmstadt: Wissenschaftliche Buchgesellschaft 1971, pp. 120–54.

Religion and believes it most excellent when Schleiermacher says: "Every person of depth has his asceticism."[98] We may doubt, however, whether they understood the same thing by the term *Askese*. Two undated entries,[99] the first from 1850, signal a rejection of Schleiermacher's theology that reverses the affirmation of the dogmatics in the 1840s. In the journals we read:

> The error in Schleiermacher's dogmatics is that for him religiousness is always really a condition, *it is*; he represents everything in the sphere of being, Spinozian being. How it becomes in the sense of coming to exist and in the sense of being maintained does not really concern him. This is why he can take up so little of the dogmatical. Every Christian qualification is characterized by the ethical oriented to striving. From this comes fear and trembling, and the *you shall*; from this also the possibility of offense etc. This is of minor concern to Schleiermacher. He treats religiousness in the sphere of being.[100]

Kierkegaard continues:

> From this also comes his thesis that feeling is always true. Considered more closely, its truth is actually the truth that it *is*. The whole battle begins with becoming. The question considered in the sphere of "becoming" is: But is that which is—true? In the sphere of being the truth is that it is.[101]

Here Schleiermacher is supposed to have viewed not just the sense of sin, but religiousness itself as a condition. With regard to sin, the issue has been addressed above; a further effort to cast religion as a static condition seems at best to be a tendentious reading of Schleiermacher. Beginning with *On Religion*, the German theologian teaches that, even though a capacity for religion belongs to our nature as humans, "religion never appears in a pure state."[102] What Kierkegaard has in mind under the label "dogmatical" that is too little taken up by Schleiermacher is unspecified. One hears no echo of the 1844 utterance regarding Schleiermacher's "immortal service" to dogmatics. The potential terror associated with the feeling of absolute dependence is now forgotten as are the profound commonalities between the pseudonyms and Schleiermacher on the understanding of repentance in the process of coming into the Christian life. In the middle of the previous journal entry Kierkegaard added a marginal note sometime before his death:

> This [religiousness as a condition, as a form of being] also explains Schleiermacher's stipulation of the feeling of absolute dependence as the principle of all religion, for this is again a condition of religiousness in the sphere of being. As soon as the question becomes

---

98 *SKS* 22, 395, NB14:88.a / *JP* 1, 173. The term *Askese* occurs only once in the work, where it was added to a revised version of the first edition: "Each religious person fashions his own asceticism according to his need." *On Religion: Speeches to its Cultured Despisers*, trans. by John Oman, Louisville: Westminster/John Knox 1957, p. 62.

99 *SKS* 23, 58, NB15:83.b / *JP* 4 3853 is a marginal note and comment on *SKS* 23, 58, NB15:83 / *JP* 4, 3852.

100 *SKS* 23, 58, NB15:83 / *JP* 4 3852.

101 Ibid.

102 *On Religion*, trans. by Richard Crouter, op. cit., p. 21.

> ethical, consequently a question of the becoming of this condition, how it comes into existence, what I have to do in order that it can come into existence, also how it is to be maintained or how I am to be maintained in it, which also is becoming, then the mark of religiousness is changed. I think it is precisely in this way that Schleiermacher may be said to have falsified Christianity, because he had conceived it esthetically-metaphysically merely as a condition, whereas Christianity is essentially to be conceived ethically, as striving. S. conceives of religiousness as completely analogous to erotic love. But this is a misunderstanding. Erotic love essentially has nothing to do with a striving. But Christianity is in the sphere of becoming. As soon as this is understood, every single Christian qualification is characterized differently than in S. And not only this, but only then do the most decisive qualifications of Christianity appear, and they are lacking in S., or in S. they lack the decisive quality.[103]

One can scarcely take the polemical entry at face value. If there is no ethical dimension to the Christian life for Schleiermacher, then Vigilius Haufniensis' contrast in *The Concept of Anxiety* between Schleiermacher's dogmatics and those of Hegelian theologians, a theme central to Kierkegaard's argument, must be ignored. The reader of these late entries has difficulty squaring them with Kierkegaard's apparent endorsement of Schleiermacher's emphasis on new Christian self-awareness or the account of "wonder in its inwardness" within his system. To think that Schleiermacher's view of religion, whether in *On Religion* (1799) or *The Christian Faith* (1830–31), lacks a sense of striving, awakening, or becoming, seems extraordinary. Schleiermacher's debt to Romanticism ensures the very qualities of personal growth and discovery that the journal entry seems to deny. The charge in 1850 that Schleiermacher "represents everything in the sphere of being, Spinozian being" reverts to the 1837 suspicion about the theologian's alleged pantheism.[104] The polemic against Schleiermacher continued during 1851. In another journal entry, Kierkegaard comments on Schleiermacher's phrase, "the Christian consciousness," and notes that Neander associates it with the Reformation. He adds: "That may be all right, but there is something very dubious about it" and relates the notion to the Christian diffusion and collective consciousness "that is supposed to be Christianity—no thanks."[105] If the Christianity of the New Testament no longer exists, neither apparently should the Christianity of Friedrich Schleiermacher.

Given this evidence, how shall the contradictory and tension-filled views be resolved? To my mind the situation requires a threefold response. (1) It might be possible to discount all the earlier favorable references to Schleiermacher and privilege the late journal citations. To do so, however, would take the intemperate attack on Schleiermacher as Kierkegaard's definitive view, while ignoring the weight of the positive elements outlined here. (2) To avoid simply declaring that

---

103 *SKS* 23, 58, NB15:83.b/ *JP* 4, 3853, 14f.

104 *SKS* 23, 58, NB15:83 / *JP* 4, 3852, 14; see *SKS* 17, 219, DD:9 / *JP* 4, 3849. A surface reading of such an entry of the late authorship conceals the fact of Spinoza's own influence on the edifying discourses. See Purkarthofer, "'Suppose I would die tomorrow': Possible Uses of Kierkegaard's Journals," op. cit., pp. 207–13.

105 *Pap.* X–4 A 232 / *JP* 3, 2822.

Kierkegaard is muddled or contradictory requires the approach taken here, which attends to his contexts and development. (3) We can think that after the *Corsair* affair when Kierkegaard desperately turns against what he takes to be the smug theology of the Danish Church, he reverts to his earliest 1837–38 suspicions about Schleiermacher and reads him in light of his deepening polemic against cultural and state-dominated Protestantism of the Danish Church. We have seen that Bishop Mynster—his arch-nemesis until his death in January 1854—had lifelong reservations about Schleiermacher's teaching. Mynster's noble bearing, cultivated faith, and theological intransigence, so Kierkegaard may well have imagined, must have been aided and abetted by post-Reformation forms of Christianity that also make too much peace with the world. On this reading, the last encounters with Schleiermacher reflect local meaning and purpose and are not to be taken as negating Kierkegaard's earlier indebtedness to the work of his German predecessor.

VI. A Concluding Word

The evidence presented here shows that Kierkegaard has a significant relationship to Schleiermacher, which is differentiated within the authorship's life settings and immediate ends. The relationship begins with significant study and questions, moves to a serious appropriation of ideas, and ends with criticism that concurs with Kierkegaard's increasingly hostile attitude to the existing Danish Church. Little exists post-1847 to rival the impact of Schleiermacher the Plato scholar or the dogmatic theologian in contributing to the main literary works. Yet even in 1854 Kierkegaard can still glean useful insight from Schleiermacher for the attack on a complacent Church. Though he no longer remembers the exact source (a passage from *On Religion*), he writes in a journal entry entitled "The Church. The Forgery": "Presumably it is as Schleiermacher says somewhere that it certainly is not man's idea in the discovery of lightning rods to sit securely behind them and laugh at God." Like the false security of a lightning rod, the Church is not a "folding screen behind which the Christian evades the real strenuousness of being a Christian."[106] The writer of *On Religion* with whom he now quarrels remains a useful ally in his struggle. By sketching the historical matrix of Kierkegaard's relationship to Schleiermacher, I believe that the various levels and sorts of relationship to the German theologian can be approached fruitfully.

While writing his multi-volume *History of Modern Protestant Theology* over 50 years ago, Emanuel Hirsch, translator of Kierkegaard and lifelong student of both thinkers, summed up the relationship:

---

[106] See *Pap.* XI–2 A 229 / *JP* 1, 603 and *On Religion*, trans. by Oman p. 64: "When you stand under your lightning conductors, have you, perhaps, a laugh ready wherewith to mock the thunder?" The image was used earlier in *SKS* 6, 441 / *SLW*, 479: "Schleiermacher so enthusiastically declares that knowledge does not perturb religiousness, and that the religious person does not sit safeguarded by a lightning rod and scoff at God."

> It cannot be denied that Kierkegaard's thesis that truth is subjectivity takes up and carries further in the sharpest conceivable form the basic thought of Schleiermacher about the relationship of religion to knowledge and piety to expressions of dogma. To that extent, Kierkegaard is in his generation the only authentic pupil of Schleiermacher.[107]

To my mind, the formulation of Hirsch still has merit, even if we are tempted to qualify it to read "in his generation of Danes." If it is true that Schleiermacher, generally speaking, was too bold for the Danes, it was just this quality of mind that drew Kierkegaard to his work. Schleiermacher influences the work of Kierkegaard decisively in at least three ways: by providing a model for indirect communication, by transmitting the Plato *corpus* and the figure of Socrates as philosopher, and by developing a system of dogmatic theology in which Christian faith begins and ends with the self-awareness of Christian existence. All three areas lie near the heart of Kierkegaard's fundamental concerns.

Today it can scarcely be denied that Schleiermacher's legacy had a significant, though highly nuanced, impact on issues of momentous concern to Kierkegaard. Despite their different social locations, vehicles of communication, and the details of their mature arguments, a set of formal as well as substantive concerns unites far more than it divides the two thinkers. The result should not surprise us. Like Kierkegaard, Schleiermacher was viewed by contemporaries as holding uncommon insight into the vagaries of individual human lives. Among German theologians of his day, he was the apostle of *Inderlighed.* Discussing his "Essay on the Sense of Shame" with Henriette Herz, 16 April 1799 (later incorporated into the *Confidential Letters*) he writes: "Actually I believe I know a good deal about the human, especially about his inner being, which is where I have a clear intuition; but in that which one calls the world, in practical knowledge, in routine and its little tricks, there I am an awful bungler."[108] The sentence might well have been an entry in the *Papirer*. The argument I have made recognizes the powerful intellectual movements in which Schleiermacher functions for Kierkegaard as mentor and pathfinder, not necessarily as constant beacon of light.

---

[107] *Geschichte der neuern evangelischen Theologie*, vols. 1–5, Gütersloh: C. Bertelsmann 1949, vol. 5, pp. 453–4. For an account of the process of Kierkegaard carrying Schleiermacher further with regard to the dialectic of existence, see Hermann Deuser, "Existenz-Mitteilung–nicht unmittelbares Selbstbewusstsein. Kierkegaards Kritik transzendentaler Religionsbegründung," in *Subjectivity and Truth. Proceedings of the Schleiermacher-Kierkegaard Congress in Copenhagen, October 9–13, 2003*, op. cit., pp. 197–215.

[108] *Briefe* 1, p. 219, cited in *Kritische Gesamtausgabe*, Abteilung 1, vol. 3, *Schriften aus der Berliner Zeit 1800–1802*, ed. by Günter Meckenstock with the assistance of Hans-Friedrich Traulsen, Berlin: Walter de Gruyter 1988, p. LI.

Bibliography

I. Schleiermacher's Works in The Auction Catalogue *of Kierkegaard's Library*

Predigten von Friedrich Schleiermacher, vols. 1–4, new ed., Berlin: G. Reimer 1834–35 (vols. 1–4, in *Friedrich Schleiermacher's sämmtliche Werke, Zweite Abtheilung. Predigten*, Abtheilungen 1–3, Berlin: G. Reimer 1834–64) (*ASKB* 238–241).

Prædikener om det christelige Huusliv, trans. by Christian Winther, Copenhagen: P.G. Philipsen 1839 (*ASKB* 242).

Der christliche Glaube nach den Grundsätzen der evangelischen Kirche, vols. 1–2, 3rd ed., Berlin: G. Reimer 1835 (*ASKB* 258).

Ueber die Religion. Reden an die Gebildeten unter ihren Verächtern, 5th ed., Berlin: G. Reimer 1843 (*ASKB* 271) [cf. *ASKB* A I 40].

Dialektik. Aus Schleiermachers handschriftlichem Nachlasse, ed. by L. Jonas (vol. 2, Section 2 in *Friedrich Schleiermacher's literarischer Nachlaß. Zur Philosophie* (vol. 4, Part 2, in *Friedrich Schleiermacher's sämmtliche Werke. Dritte Abtheilung. Zur Philosophie*, Abtheilungen 1–3, Berlin: G. Reimer 1834–64)), Berlin: G. Reimer 1839 (*ASKB* 769).

Ueber die Religion, 3rd ed., Berlin: G. Reimer 1821 (*ASKB* A I 40) [cf. *ASKB* 271].

"Prædikener med Hensyn til den Augsburgske Confessions Jubelfest," *Tidsskrift for udenlandsk theologisk Litteratur*, vols. 1–20, ed. by Henrik Nikolai Clausen and Matthias Hagen Hohlenberg, Copenhagen: C.A. Reitzel 1833–52, vol. 1, no. 1, 1833, pp. 160–92 (*ASKB* U 29).

"Prædikener med Hensyn til den Augsburgske Confessions Jubelfest," *Tidsskrift for udenlandsk theologisk Litteratur*, op. cit., vol. 1, no. 2, 1833, pp. 109–54.

"Bemærkninger om den fælleds Samvirken af geistlige Mænd i kirkelige Anliggender," *Tidsskrift for udenlandsk theologisk Litteratur*, op. cit., vol. 2, 1834, pp. 386–94.

"Den praktiske Theologie efter den evangeliske Kirkes Grundsætninger" [Part One], *Tidsskrift for udenlandsk theologisk Litteratur*, op. cit., vol. 18, 1850, pp. 603–714.

"Den praktiske Theologie efter den evangeliske Kirkes Grundsætninger" [Part Two], *Tidsskrift for udenlandsk theologisk Litteratur*, op. cit., vol. 19, 1851, pp. 195–343.

[ed.] *Magazin von Fest-, Gelegenheits- und andern Predigten und kleineren Amtsreden.* Neue Folge, vols. 1–6, ed. by Johann Friedrich Röhr, Friedrich Schleiermacher and Jonathan Schuderoff. Magdeburg: Wilhelm Heinrichshofen 1823–29 (*ASKB* A I 77–82).

[trans.] *Platons Werke*, vols. 1–6, trans. by Friedrich Schleiermacher, Berlin: In der Realschulbuchhandlung 1817–28 (*ASKB* 1158–1163).

II. Works in The Auction Catalogue *of Kierkegaard's Library that Discuss Schleiermacher*

Baur, Ferdinand Christian, *Die christliche Gnosis: oder, die christliche Religions-philosophie in ihrer geschichtlichen Entwiklung*, Tübingen: C.F. Osiander 1835, pp. 626–68 (*ASKB* 421).

—— *Das Christliche des Platonismus oder Sokrates und Christus. Eine religionsphilosophische Untersuchung*, Tübingen: Ludwig Friedrich Fues 1837, p. 20n; p. 85n; p. 88n; pp. 93f.; p. 109; p. 123; p. 125; p. 148n (*ASKB* 422).

—— "Die Schleiermacher'sche Glaubenslehre, ihre Freunde und Gegner," in his *Die christliche Lehre von der Versöhnung in ihrer geschichtlichen Entwicklung von der ältesten Zeit bis auf die neueste*, Tübingen: Osiander 1838, pp. 614–48 (*ASKB* 423).

Biedermann, A. Emanuel, *Die freie Theologie oder Philosophie und Christenthum in Streit und Frieden*, Tübingen: Ludwig Friedrich Fues 1844, p. 131; pp. 142–3; p. 149; p. 175n; pp. 179–80; p. 192n (*ASKB* U 20).

[Billroth, Johann Gustav Friedrich], *Vorlesungen über Religionsphilosophie gehalten von Dr. Joh. Gust. Friedr. Billroth*, ed. by Johann Eduard Erdmann, Leipzig: Friedrich Christian Wilhelm Vogel 1837, p. 37 (*ASKB* 428).

Bruch, Johann Friedrich, *Die Lehre von den göttlichen Eigenschaften*, Hamburg: Friedrich Perthes 1842, pp. 3–6; p. 8; p. 11; pp. 15–6; p. 19; p. 46n; p. 67n; p. 75; p. 83n; pp. 85–6; p. 93; p. 97; pp. 101–3; p. 106; p. 154n; p. 156n; p. 157; p. 160n; p. 161n; p. 163n; p. 175n; p. 177n; p. 189n; pp. 190f.; p. 197n; p. 199n; p. 204n; p. 205; p. 241; p. 255n; p. 257n; p. 280; p. 283; pp. 287–8; pp. 290–2; p. 297 (*ASKB* 439).

Chalybäus, Heinrich Moritz, *System der speculativen Ethik, oder Philosophie der Familie des Staates und der religiösen Sitte*, vols. 1–2, Leipzig: F.A. Brockhaus 1850 (*ASKB* 463–464).

Clausen, Henrik Nikolai, *Det Nye Testaments Hermeneutik*, Copenhagen: Jens Hostrup Schultz 1840, p. 363 (*ASKB* 468).

Diesterweg, F.A.W., "Om Schleiermachers Læremethode," *Tidsskrift for udenlandsk theologisk Litteratur*, op. cit., vol. 2, 1834, pp. 718–27 (*ASKB* U 29).

Erdmann, Johann Eduard, *Vorlesungen über Glauben und Wissen als Einleitung in die Dogmatik und Religionsphilosophie*, Berlin: Duncker und Humblot 1837, p. 124; pp. 250–4 (*ASKB* 479).

Fichte, Immanuel Hermann, "Der bisherige Zustand der praktischen Philosophie in seinen Umrissen. Ein kritischer Versuch....I. Kant, J.G. Fichte, Hegel, Schleiermacher," in *Zeitschrift für Philosophie und spekulative Theologie*, vols. 1–16, ed. by Immanuel Hermann Fichte and Christian Hermann Weiße, Bonn et al.: Eduard Weber et al. 1837–46, vol. 11, 1843, pp. 161–202 (*ASKB* 877–911).

—— "J.G. Fichte und Schleiermacher, eine vergleichende Skizze," *Zeitschrift für Philosophie und spekulative Theologie*, op. cit., vol. 15, 1846, pp. 112–46.

—— *Die speculative Theologie oder allgemeine Religionslehre*, Heidelberg: Akademische Buchhandlung von J.C.B. Mohr 1846 (vol. 3, in *Grundzüge zum Systeme der Philosophie*), pp. 413ff.; p. 428 (*ASKB* 509) (vols. 1–2 (*ASKB* 502–503)).

—— "Friedrich Schleiermacher (1768–1834)," in his *System der Ethik*, vols. 1–2.1, Leipzig: Dyk 1850–51, vol. 1, *Die philosophischen Lehren von Recht, Staat und Sitte in Deutschland, Frankreich und England von der Mitte des Achtzehnten Jahrhunderts bis zur Gegenwart*, 1850, pp. 277–353; vol. 2.1, *Die allgemeinen ethischen Begriffe und die Tugend- und Pflichtenlehre*, 1851, p. 116; p. 207; pp. 270–1; pp. 291–3; vol. 2.2, p. 10n; p. 385; p. 412 (*ASKB* 510–511) [vol. 2.2, Leipzig: Dyk 1853, (*ASKB* 504)].

Fischer, Carl Philipp, *Die Idee der Gottheit. Ein Versuch, den Theismus speculativ zu begründen und zu entwickeln*, Stuttgart: S.G. Liesching 1839, p. 11n; p. 14; pp. 70–71 (*ASKB* 512).

Grundtvig, N.F.S., [Review of] "F. Delbrück, *Erörterungen einiger Hauptstücke in Schleiermachers Glaubenslehre*. 1827," *Theologisk Maanedsskrift*, ed. by Nikolaj Frederik Severin Grundtvig and Andreas Gottlob Rudelbach, Copenhagen: Wahlske Boghandling, vol. 12, 1828, pp. 231–9 (*ASKB* 346–351).

Guerike, Heinrich Ernst Ferdinand, *Handbuch der Kirchengeschichte*, vols. 1–2, 3rd revised and enlarged ed., Halle: in der Gebauerschen Buchhandlung 1838, vol. 2, p. 1161 (*ASKB* 158–159).

Hagen, Johan Frederik, *Ægteskabet. Betragtet fra et ethisk-historiskt Standpunct*, Copenhagen: Wahlske Boghandels Forlag 1845, p. 159 (*ASKB* 534).

Hahn, August (ed.), *Lehrbuch des christlichen Glaubens*, Leipzig: Friedrich Christian Wilhelm Vogel 1828, p. 9; p. 46; p. 425 (*ASKB* 535).

Hase, Karl, *Kirkehistorie. Lærebog nærmest for akademiske Forelæsninger*, trans. by C. Winther and T. Schorn, Copenhagen: C.A. Reitzel 1837, p. 602; p. 604; p. 614 (*ASKB* 160–166).

—— *Hutterus redivivus oder Dogmatik der evangelisch-lutherischen Kirche. Ein dogmatisches Repertorium für Studirende*, 4th revised ed., Leipzig: Breitkopf und Härtel 1839, p. 3; pp. 11–7 passim; p. 79; p. 91; p. 101; p. 103; p. 118; pp. 131–9 passim; p. 149; pp. 185f.; p. 217; p. 239; p. 249; p. 256; p. 275; p. 287 (*ASKB* 581).

[Hegel, Georg Wilhelm Friedrich], *Georg Wilhelm Friedrich Hegel's vermischte Schriften*, vols. 1–2, ed. by Friedrich Förster and Ludwig Boumann, Berlin: Duncker und Humblot 1834–35 (vols. 16–7 in *Georg Wilhelm Friedrich Hegel's Werke. Vollständige Ausgabe*, ed. by Philipp Marheineke et al., Berlin: Duncker und Humblot 1832–45), vol. 2, pp. 295ff. (*ASKB* 555–556).

Heine, Heinrich, *Die romantische Schule*, Hamburg: Hoffmann und Campe 1836, pp. 116f. (*ASKB* U 63).

Helfferich, Adolph, *Die christliche Mystik in ihrer Entwickelung und in ihren Denkmalen*, vols. 1–2, Gotha: Friedrich Parthes 1842, vol. 1, pp. 41–2; p. 51; p. 54 (*ASKB* 571–572).

Hundeshagen, Carl Bernhard, "Den tydske Protestantisme, dens Fortid og dens nuværende Livsspørgsmaal," *Tidsskrift for udenlandsk theologisk Litteratur*, op. cit., vol. 16, 1848, pp. 125–240.

Lücke, F., "Minder om Dr. Fr. Schleiermacher," *Tidsskrift for udenlandsk theologisk Litteratur*, op. cit., vol. 2, 1834, pp. 652–717.

Martensen, Hans Lassen, "Theologia sensus," in his *De autonomia conscientiae sui humanae in theologiam dogmaticam nostri temporis introducta*, Hauniae: I.D. Quist 1837, pp. 86–129 (*ASKB* 648).

—— "Følelsestheologien," in his *Den menneskelige Selvbevidstheds Autonomie i vor Tids dogmatiske Theologie*, trans. by L.V. Petersen, Copenhagen: C.A. Reitzel 1841, pp. 71–105 (*ASKB* 651).

—— *Den christelige Dogmatik*, Copenhagen: C.A. Reitzel 1849, p. 7; p. 11; p. 65; p. 110n; p. 127; p. 161; p. 189; p. 192; p. 208; p. 221; p. 227; p. 229; pp. 296f.; pp. 322–3; p. 399: p. 408; pp. 436–7; p. 573 (*ASKB* 653).

Menzel, Wolfgang, *Die deutsche Literatur*, vols. 1–4, 2nd revised ed., Stuttgart: Hallberg'sche Verlagshandlung 1836, vol. 1, pp. 140ff.; pp. 235ff. (*ASKB* U 79).

Michelet, Carl Ludwig, "Schleiermacher," in his *Geschichte der letzten Systeme der Philosophie in Deutschland von Kant bis Hegel*, vols. 1–2, Berlin: Duncker und Humblot 1837–38, vol. 2, pp. 46–114 (*ASKB* 678–679).

—— *Vorlesungen über die Persönlichkeit Gottes und Unsterblichkeit der Seele oder die ewige Persönlichkeit des Geistes*, Berlin: Ferdinand Dümmler 1841, pp. 158f.; pp. 210–11; p. 214 (*ASKB* 680).

Møller, Jens, "Om Religionens Væsen, hvori det bestaaer og hvor det maa søges. (Især efter Dr. Schleiermacher og Dr. Twesten)," *Nyt theologisk Bibliothek*, ed. by Jens Møller, Copenhagen: Andreas Seidelin, vol. 17, 1830, pp. 233–82 (*ASKB* 336–345).

Müller, Julius, *Die christliche Lehre von der Sünde*, vols. 1–2, 3rd revised and enlarged ed., Breslau: Josef Max und Komp. 1849, vol. 1, pp. 55–65; pp. 477–94; vol. 2, pp. 1–5; pp. 152–5; pp. 245–51; pp. 432–5 (*ASKB* 689–690).

Mynster, Jakob Peter, *Blandede Skrivter*, vols. 1–3, Copenhagen: Den Gyldendalske Boghandlings Forlag 1852–53 [vols. 4–6, Copenhagen: Den Gyldendalske Boghandlings Forlag 1855–57], vol. 1, p. 47; p. 50n; p. 65n; pp. 67–9; p. 77n; p. 88n; p. 151n; p. 163n; pp. 190f.; p. 245n; p. 269; p. 463; p. 470; vol. 2, pp. 105–6; p. 139; p. 241; vol. 3, p. 42n (*ASKB* 358–363).

Nielsen, Rasmus, *Forelæsningsparagrapher til Kirkehistoriens Philosophie. Et Schema for Tilhørere*, Copenhagen: P.G. Philipsens Forlag 1843, p. 92 (*ASKB* 698).

Ørsted, Anders Sandøe, *Af mit Livs og min Tids Historie*, vols. 1–2, Copenhagen: Gyldendalske Boghandling 1851–52 [vols. 3–4, Copenhagen: Gyldendalske Boghandling 1855–57], vol. 1, pp. 151–2 (*ASKB* 1959–1960).

Petersen, August, *Die Idee der christlichen Kirche. Zur wissenschaftlichen Beantwortung der Lebensfrage unserer Zeit. Ein theologischer Versuch*, vols. 1–3, Leipzig: bei Friedr. Christ. Wilh. Vogel 1839–46, vol. 1, pp. 205–9 (*ASKB* 717–719).

Romang, Johann Peter, *Ueber Willensfreiheit und Determinismus, mit sorgfältiger Rücksicht auf die sittlichen Dinge, die rechtliche Imputation und Strafe, und auf das Religiöse. Eine philosophische Abhandlung*, Bern: C.A. Jenni, Sohn 1835, p. 55; p. 238n; p. 246n; p. 268n (*ASKB* 740).

Rosenkranz, Karl, *Erinnerungen an Karl Daub*, Berlin: Duncker und Humblot 1837, pp. 14f.; p. 19; p. 21; p. 38; p. 40; pp. 42f.; p. 52 (*ASKB* 743).

—— *Psychologie oder die Wissenschaft vom subjectiven Geist*, Königsberg: Bornträger 1837, pp. 63–4; p. 266; p. 272 (*ASKB* 744).

—— [ed.] *Schelling. Vorlesungen, gehalten im Sommer 1842 an der Universität zu Königsberg*, Danzig: Fr. Sam. Gerhard 1843, p. xix; p. 199; p. 207 (*ASKB* 766).

Rudelbach, Andreas, *De ethices principiis hucusque vulgo traditis, disquisito historico-philosophica, quæ systematum ethicorum secundum primas causas amplioris criseos introductionem continet*, Copenhagen: Hartv. Frid. Popp 1822, p. 15n; p. 20n; p. 26; p. 38n; p. 46; p. 52; p. 71n; p. 72; p. 77n; p. 130; p. 138; p. 146; pp. 163–4; p. 213; p. 215 (*ASKB* 750).

Sack, Karl Heinrich, *Christliche Apologetik, Versuch eines Handbuchs*, Hamburg: bei Friedrich Perthes 1829 (*ASKB* 755).

Schlegel, Friedrich, *Philosophische Vorlesungen aus den Jahren 1804 bis 1806*, ed. by C.J.H. Windischmann, vols. 1–2, Bonn: Weber 1836, vol. 2, p. 271; p. 449 (*ASKB* 768-68a).

Schopenhauer, Arthur, *Die Welt als Wille und Vorstellung*, vols. 1–2, 2nd revised and enlarged ed., Leipzig: F.A. Brockhaus 1844 [1819], vol. 1, p. 59; vol. 2, p. 85 (*ASKB* 773–773a).

—— *Parerga und Paralipomena: kleine philosophische Schriften*, vols. 1–2, Berlin: A.W. Hayn 1851, vol. 2, p. 8 (*ASKB* 774–775).

Schweitzer, Alexander, "Schleiermachers Virksomhed som Prædikant," *Tidsskrift for udenlandsk theologisk Litteratur*, op. cit., vol. 3, 1835, pp. 225–71.

Sibbern, Frederik Christian, *Logik som Tænkelære fra en intelligent Iagttagelses Standpunct og i analytisk-genetisk Fremstilling*, 2nd enlarged and revised ed., Copenhagen: Paa Forfatterens Forlag trykt hos Fabritius de Tengnagel 1835, pp. 173f. (*ASKB* 777).

Steffens, Henrich, *Christliche Religionsphilosophie*, vols. 1–2, Breslau: im Verlage bei Josef Max und Komp. 1839 (vol. 1, *Teleologie*; vol. 2, *Ethik*), vol. 1, p. 11; p. 243; vol. 2, pp. 13f. (*ASKB* 797–798).

—— *Was ich erlebte. Aus der Erinnerung niedergeschrieben*, vols. 1–10, Breslau: Josef Max und Comp. 1840–44, vol. 1, p. 198; vol. 4, p. 91; p. 155; p. 254; p. 277; p. 310; vol. 5, p. 81; pp. 141–149; p. 152; p. 161; p. 164; p. 172; pp. 191–200; pp. 205–8; p. 212; pp. 216–24; p. 227; vol. 6, p. 3; p. 138; p. 140; p. 142; p. 146; pp. 150–2; p. 172; p. 175; p. 283; p. 313; vol. 7, p. 3, p. 13; p. 264; vol. 9, p. 35; vol. 10, p. 51; pp. 59–61; pp. 107–8 (*ASKB* 1834–1843).

Strauß, David Friedrich, *Fremstilling af den christelige Troeslære i dens historiske Udvikling og i dens Kamp med den moderne Videnskab*, vols. 1–2, trans. by Hans Brøchner, Copenhagen: Forlagt af H.C. Klein 1842–43 (*ASKB* 803–804).

Trendelenburg, Adolf, *Logische Untersuchungen*, vols. 1–2, Berlin: G. Bethge 1840, vol. 2, p. 86; p. 148n; pp. 165f. (*ASKB* 843).

—— *Die logische Frage in Hegel's System. Zwei Streitschriften*, Leipzig: F.A. Brockhaus 1843, pp. 36–7; p. 50 (*ASKB* 846).

Twesten, August Detlef Christian, *Vorlesungen über die Dogmatik der Evangelisch-Lutherischen Kirche: nach dem Compendium des Herrn Dr. W.M.L. de Wette*, vols. 1–2, 4th ed., Hamburg: Friedrich Perthes 1837–38, vol. 1 [vol. 1, 1838; vol. 2, 1837] (*ASKB* 849–849a).

Usteri, Leonhard, *Udvikling af det Paulinske Lærebegreb i dets Forhold til det Ny Testamentes bibelske Dogmatik. Et exegetisk-dogmatisk Forsøg*, trans. by W.J.J. Boethe, Copenhagen: Philipsen 1839 (*ASKB* 850).

Weiße, Christian Hermann, "Die philosophische Literatur der Gegenwart. Erster Artikel. Schleiermacher. Hegel. Steffens," *Zeitschrift für Philosophie und spekulative Theologie*, op. cit., vol. 6, 1840, pp. 267–309.

—— "Ueber das Verhältniß der Glaubenslehre zur Philosophie. Mit Beziehung auf Schleiermacher und andere Zeiterscheinungen," *Zeitschrift für Philosophie und spekulative Theologie*, op. cit., vol. 16, 1846, pp. 1–38.

Wette, Wilhelm Martin Leberecht de, *Ueber Religion und Theologie. Erläuterungen zu seinem Lehrbuche der Dogmatik*, Berlin: Realschulbuchhandlung 1815, p. 65 (*ASKB* A I 34).

—— *Christliche Sittenlehre*, vols. 1–3, Berlin: G. Reimer 1819–23, vol. 1, p. 247n (*ASKB* U 110).

Wolff, Oskar Ludwig Bernhard, *Handbuch deutscher Beredsamkeit enthaltend eine Uebersicht der Geschichte und Theorie der Redekunst, zugleich mit einer vollständigen Sammlung deutscher Reden jedes Zeitalters und jeder Gattung*, vols. 1–2, Leipzig: Carl B. Lorck 1845–46, vol. 1, pp. 272–84; pp. 448–59; vol. 2, pp. 499–508 (*ASKB* 250–251).

Zeuthen, Ludvig, *Om den christelige Tro i dens Betydning for Verdenshistorien. Et Forsøg*, Copenhagen: Gyldendalske Boghandels Forlag 1838, p. 20n (*ASKB* 259).

—— *Humanitet betragtet fra et christeligt Standpunkt, med stadigt Hensyn til den nærværende Tid*, Copenhagen: Gyldendalske Boghandling 1846, p. 5 (*ASKB* 915).

III. Secondary Literature on Kierkegaard's Relation to Schleiermacher

Anz, Wilhelm, "Schleiermacher und Kierkegaard. Übereinstimmung und Differenz," *Zeitschrift für Theologie und Kirche*, vol. 82, no. 4, 1985, pp. 409–29.

Axt-Piscalar, Christine, *Ohnmächtige Freiheit. Studien zum Verhältnis von Subjektivität und Sünde bei A. Tholuck, Julius Müller, Sören Kierkegaard und F. Schleiermacher*, Tübingen: J.C.B. Mohr (P. Siebeck) 1996.

—— "Das Selbst in der Selbstverstrickung. Eine vergleichende Betrachtung zu Schleiermachers und Kierkegaards Sündenlehre," *Kierkegaard Studies. Yearbook*, 2004, pp. 452–72.

Bohlin, Torsten, *Kierkegaards dogmatische Anschauung in ihrem geschichtlichen Zusammenhange*, trans. by Ilse Meyer-Lüne, Gütersloh: C. Bertelsmann 1927.

Cappelørn, Niels Jørgen, Richard Crouter, Theodor Jørgensen and Claus Osthövener (eds), *Schleiermacher und Kierkegaard. Subjektivität und Wahrheit. Subjectivity and Truth. Proceedings of the Schleiermacher-Kierkegaard Congress in Copenhagen 2003*, Berlin: Walter de Gruyter 2006 (*Kierkegaard Studies Monograph Series*, vol. 11).

Crouter, Richard, "Kierkegaard's Not so Hidden Debt to Schleiermacher," *Zeitschrift für Neuere Theologiegeschichte / Journal for the History of Modern Theology*, vol. 1, no. 2, 1994, pp. 205–25. (Reprinted as Chapter 4 in *Friedrich Schleiermacher: Between Enlightenment and Romanticism*, Cambridge: Cambridge University Press 2005.)

—— "More than Kindred Spirits: Schleiermacher and Kierkegaard on Repentance," in *Subjectivity and Truth. Proceedings of the Schleiermacher-Kierkegaard Congress in Copenhagen 2003*, ed. by Niels Jørgen Cappelørn et al., op. cit., pp. 673–86.

Dalferth, Ingolf, "'Die Sache ist viel entsetzlicher': Religiösität bei Kierkegaard und Schleiermacher," in *Subjectivity and Truth. Proceedings of the Schleiermacher-Kierkegaard Congress in Copenhagen 2003*, ed. by Niels Jørgen Cappelørn et al., op. cit., pp. 217–64.

DeHart, Paul, "Absolute Dependence or Infinite Desire? Comparing Soteriological Themes in Schleiermacher and Kierkegaard," in *Subjectivity and Truth. Proceedings of the Schleiermacher-Kierkegaard Congress in Copenhagen 2003*, ed. by Niels Jørgen Cappelørn et al., op. cit., pp. 561–76.

Despland, Michael Samuel, *The Idea of Divine Education: A Study in the Ethical and the Religious as Organizing Themes for the Interpretation of the Life of the Self in Kant, Schleiermacher and Kierkegaard.* Ph.D. Thesis, Harvard University, Cambridge, Massachusetts 1966.

Dierkes, Hans, "Friedrich Schlegels *Lucinde*, Schleiermacher und Kierkegaard," *Deutsche Vierteljahrsschrift für Literaturwissenschaft und Geistesgeschichte*, vol. 57, 1983, pp. 431–49.

Dietz, Walter, "Die Stellung von Vigilius Haufniensis' *Begrebet Angest* im Kontext der Sündenlehre des 19. und 20. Jahrhunderts," *Kierkegaard Studies. Yearbook*, 2001, pp. 96–128.

Ferreira, M. Jamie, "The Single Individual and Kinship: Reflection on Kierkegaard and Schleiermacher," in *Subjectivity and Truth. Proceedings of the Schleiermacher-Kierkegaard Congress in Copenhagen 2003*, ed. by Niels Jørgen Cappelørn et al., op. cit., pp. 125–43.

Fischer, Hermann, *Subjektivität und Sünde. Kierkegaards Begriff der Sünde mit ständiger Rücksicht auf Schleiermachers Lehre von der Sünde*, Itzehoe: Verlag Die Spur 1963.

Frawley, Matthew J., "Human Nature and Fall in Schleiermacher and Kierkegaard," in *Subjectivity and Truth. Proceedings of the Schleiermacher-Kierkegaard Congress in Copenhagen 2003*, ed. by Niels Jørgen Cappelørn et al., op. cit., pp. 145–58.

Gerdes, Hayo, *Das Christusbild Søren Kierkegaards. Vergleich mit der Christologie Hegels und Schleiermacher*s, Düsseldorf und Köln: Eugen Diederichs 1960.

—— *Der geschichtliche biblische Jesus oder der Christus der Philosophen. Erwägungen zur Christologie Kierkegaards, Hegels und Schleiermachers*, Berlin: Verlag Die Spur 1974.

Hirsch, Emanuel, *Kierkegaard-Studien*, vols. 1–2, Gütersloh: Bertelsmann 1933, vol. 2, pp. 21–4 [pp. 467–70] (reprinted, Vaduz, Liechtenstein: Toposverlag 1978. First published in *Studien des apologetischen Seminars in Wernigerode*, nos. 29, 31, 32, 36, 1930–33. The reprint retains the pagination of the first publication, giving the page numbers of the 1933 edition in square brackets).

—— *Geschichte der neueren evangelischen Theologie*, vols. 1–5, Gütersloh: C. Bertelsmann, 1949.

Hulteberg, Helge, Karsten Friis Johansen, Theodor Jørgensen and Friedrich Schmöe (eds), *Schleiermacher im besonderen Hinblick auf seine Wirkungsgeschichte in Dänemark*, Munich: Wilhelm Fink Verlag and Copenhagen: Text & Kontext 1986.

Janus, Richard, "Über den Werth des Sokrates als Philosophen: Einige Anmerkungen und Kierkegaard," in *Subjectivity and Truth. Proceedings of the Schleiermacher-Kierkegaard Congress in Copenhagen 2003*, ed. by Niels Jørgen Cappelørn et al., op. cit., pp. 733–40.

Kangas, David, "The Metaphysics of Interiority: The Two Paths of Schleiermacher and Kierkegaard," in *Subjectivity and Truth. Proceedings of the Schleiermacher-Kierkegaard Congress in Copenhagen 2003*, ed. by Niels Jørgen Cappelørn et al., op. cit., pp. 655–72.

Moretto, Giovanni, "Der Augenblick bei Sören Kierkegaard und Friedrich Schleiermacher," in *Subjectivity and Truth. Proceedings of the Schleiermacher-Kierkegaard Congress in Copenhagen 2003*, ed. by Niels Jørgen Cappelørn et al., op. cit., pp. 299–312.

Munster, H.A. van, "Marheineke, Martensen, Schleiermacher," *Søren Aabye Kierkegaard*, Den Haag: Lannoo 1963, pp. 109–17.

Niedermeyer, Gerhard, "Kierkegaard als Überwinder der Romantik," in his *Sören Kierkegaard und die Romantik*, Leipzig: Verlag von Quelle & Meyer 1909 (*Abhandlungen zur Philosophie und ihrer Geschichte*, vol. 11), pp. 45–61.

O'Connor, D.T., "Schleiermacher and Kierkegaard: The Odd Couple of Modern Theology," in *Religion in Life*, no. 41, 1972, pp. 8–17.

Plum, Niels Munk, *Schleiermacher i Danmark*, Copenhagen: Biano Lunos Bogtrykkeri A/S, 1934.

Ruttenbeck, Walter, *Kierkegaard, der christliche Denker und sein Werk*, Berlin and Frankfurt an der Oder: Trowitzsch 1929.

Schröer, Henning, "Wie verstand Kierkegaard Schleiermacher?" in *Internationaler Schleiermacher Kongress Berlin 1984*, Berlin and New York: Walter de Gruyter 1985 (*Schleiermacher-Archiv*, vol. 1, no. 2), pp. 1147–55.

Spera, Salvatore, "Kierkegaard e Schleiermacher," *Archivio di Filosofia*, vol. 52, nos. 1–3, 1984, pp. 435–63.

—— "Le Carte schleiermacheriane di Kierkegaard," *Aquinas*, vol. 28, 1984, pp. 287–316.

Sponheim, Paul Ronald, *The Christological Formulations of Schleiermacher and Kierkegaard in Relation to Fundamental Options Discernible in Divergent Strands in Their Discussion of God and Man*, Ph.D. Thesis, University of Chicago 1961.

Stewart, Jon, "Schleiermacher's Visit to Copenhagen in 1833," in *Zeitschrift für neuere Theologiegeschichte / Journal for the History of Modern Theology*, vol. 11, no. 2, 2004, pp. 279–302.

Stucki, Pierre-André, "Schleiermacher ou la théologie régnante," in his *Le christianisme et l'histoire d'après Kierkegaard*, Basel: Verlag für Recht und Gesellschaft 1963, pp. 41–45.

Suances Marcos, Manuel, *Sören Kierkegaard*, vols. 1–2, Madrid: Universidad Nacional de Educación a Distanca 1997, vol. 2 (*Trayectoria de su pensamiento filosófico*), pp. 39–45.

Thulstrup, Niels, "Kierkegaards Kenntnis der philosophischen und theologischen Tradition," *Theologische Zeitschrift*, vol. 35, 1979, pp. 351–62.

Tielsch, Elfriede, "Die Stellung von Kierkegaards wertschöpferischem Glauben, der seine 'zweite' Ethik ausmacht, zu der 'autonomen,' imperativistischen Soll- und Gesetzesethik seiner Zeit, zu Freud, Schleiermacher und Fichte," in her *Kierkegaards Glaube. Der Aufbruch des frühen 19. Jahrhunderts in das Zeitalter moderner, realistischer Religionsauffassung*, Göttingen: Vandenhoeck & Ruprecht 1964, pp. 43–50.

Tornøe, Caspar Wenzel, "The Changeless God of Schleiermacher and Kierkegaard," in *Subjectivity and Truth. Proceedings of the Schleiermacher-Kierkegaard Congress in Copenhagen 2003*, ed. by Niels Jørgen Cappelørn et al., op. cit., pp. 265–78.

Vahrmeyer, Marcia Morgan, "The Role of Music in Schleiermacher's and Kierkegaard's Writings," in *Subjectivity and Truth. Proceedings of the Schleiermacher-Kierkegaard Congress in Copenhagen 2003*, ed. by Niels Jørgen Cappelørn, et al., op. cit., pp. 93–105.

Voskanian, Ashot, "Der Begriff der Individualität bei F. Schleiermacher und S. Kierkegaard im Lichte der geistigen Situation der Nachmoderne," in *Subjectivity and Truth. Proceedings of the Schleiermacher-Kierkegaard Congress in Copenhagen 2003*, ed. by Niels Jørgen Cappelørn et al., op. cit., pp. 503–19.

D.F. Strauss:
Kierkegaard and Radical Demythologization

George Pattison

For any theological student of Kierkegaard's generation David Friedrich Strauss was an unavoidable phenomenon. The book by which he was to be chiefly—often solely—remembered, *The Life of Jesus Critically Examined*, was published in its first and second editions in 1835 and 1836 respectively, right in the middle of Kierkegaard's time as a theology student. This work, developing a thorough-going and consistent application of contemporary biblical scholarship with the help of some inspiration from Hegelianism, both established Strauss as a figure of European stature and, at the same time, effectively destroyed his career as a theologian. The whole affair epitomized what has since come to be a recurrent crisis within the life of the Christian Church, as scholarly theological thinking finds itself being drawn to challenge what are widely regarded as central elements of Christian faith and ethics. Kierkegaard himself saw a parallel with the affair of the Hegelian Danish priest Adolph Peter Adler (1812–69). Although the circumstances were rather different, in that Adler came to public attention when a nocturnal appearance of Jesus led him to renounce Hegelianism, both cases do illustrate the extreme tensions of the cohabitation of modern scholarly enquiry and traditional ecclesiastical faith.[1]

Long before Strauss there had been attacks on the historicity of the Church's founding texts, even on the gospels, but these attacks had mostly been explicitly intended as attacks upon the substance of Christian faith. What distinguished Strauss' work was, firstly, that it came from the pen of one who was himself a Church theologian and seemed to wish to continue to be so (that is, who understood himself as interpreting, not attacking Christianity) and, secondly, that it argued its case for a mythical interpretation of the gospel with previously unmatched detail and consistency. It is an irony of history that the period after Strauss was to see the great flowering of lives of Jesus, since Strauss' achievement had already shown that there was little if anything in the gospel narratives that could safely be used to reconstruct a psychological portrait of Jesus. What he did was, at a stroke, to unsettle what had previously been regarded as the sure historical base of Christian doctrine.

---

1 *Pap*. VIII–2 B 27.

As his biographer, Horton Harris wrote, "Voltaire and his friends had merely denied the traditional doctrines; Strauss had destroyed the foundations on which those doctrines stood."[2] In the wave of critical reappraisals of Christianity coming from the radical "young Hegelian" left, the sheer scholarly authority of his work as well as its controversial thesis ensured that Strauss became one of the figureheads of the new movement, even if politically and in other respects he soon became outstripped by yet more radical voices. *The Life of Jesus* was one of those works that were discussed across society with passion and acrimony, not only by scholarly specialists and not only by those who actually read them. So, for example, we learn that the Jewess Naomi, the main female figure in Hans Christian Andersen's *Only a Fiddler*,[3] was a partisan of radical thinking, succumbing to "the Straussian evaporation that dissolves everything historical into myths," a quotation cited by Kierkegaard in his dissection of Andersen's work.[4]

Testimony to the importance of Strauss' role at this pivotal moment in the development of modern religious thought can be culled from many quarters, and includes those such as Karl Barth who were to be the doughtiest opponents of this kind of anthropologization of religion (as Barth saw it). Barth wrote, "It is simply a matter of fact that, besides Feuerbach, Strauss was the most characteristic exponent of the situation of theology in the period after Schleiermacher's death; that it quite simply was down to him that theology was confronted with that question, the question of history, in all its fundamental rigor."[5] Or Harris again: "Strauss was not merely the most notorious theologian of the century; he was also unquestionably the most consequent. Other theologians might go only half-way; he could not. For him it was all or nothing and no half-and-half solutions for the theological problems of the time could satisfy him."[6] Or, as Kierkegaard's own contemporary, Hans Lassen Martensen (1808–84), put it, "His significance is that he confronted us with a great and decisive either/or."[7]

It is, then, almost surprising that Kierkegaard says virtually nothing about Strauss in the published work, although we may well guess that he is comprised in such general formulations as "the whole newer development" of *From the Papers of One Still Living*[8] or "the modern mythical allegorizing trend" of the *Concluding Unscientific Postscript*,[9] and, broadly speaking, is assumed to be part of the development of left-Hegelianism that Kierkegaard repeatedly castigates. For it is clear that Kierkegaard was not ignorant of Strauss. He made extensive excerpts and summaries from Julius

---

2 Horton Harris, *David Friedrich Strauss and his Theology*, Cambridge: Cambridge University Press 1973, p. 42.

3 Hans Christian Andersen, *Kun en Spillemand*, Copenhagen: C.A. Reitzel 1837 [in English as *Only a Fiddler*, trans. by Mary Howitt, London: H.G. Clarke and Co. 1845].

4 *SKS* 1, 49n / *EPW*, 94n.

5 Karl Barth, *Die Protestantische Theologie im 19ten Jahrhundert*, Zollikon and Zürich: Evangelischer Verlag 1947, p. 514.

6 Harris, *David Friedrich Strauss and his Theology*, op. cit., p. ix.

7 Hans Lassen Martensen, *Af mit Levnet*, vols. 1–3, Copenhagen: Gyldendalske Boghandels Forlag 1882–83, vol. 1, p. 134.

8 *SKS* 1, 17 / *EPW*, 61.

9 The Hongs explicitly connect this phrase with Strauss. See *CUP2*, 230, note 305.

Schaller's *The Historical Christ and the Philosophical Criticism of the Basic Idea of the Work: The Life of Jesus by Dr. D.F. Strauss*,[10] and there are also important references to Strauss in the lectures by Marheineke, which he attended in Berlin.[11] Kierkegaard also owned a set of unofficially circulated lecture notes on Hans Lassen Martensen's lectures on the history of philosophy that contained references to Strauss.[12] The auction catalogue of his library does not indicate that he actually owned *The Life of Jesus* itself, but he did own the two-volume *Christian Dogmatics* which were also translated into Danish by his relative and friend Hans Brøchner (but, although Brøchner recalls their having frequently discussed Feuerbach, he says nothing about Strauss).[13] We can minimally say that Strauss' thought was known by and of interest to Kierkegaard. The limitations of explicit references, however, suggest that it would be unwise to mount too strong a case for the encounter with Straussian thought being in any way decisive in Kierkegaard's intellectual development. Even though there is therefore every reason to be cautious, I propose that the lecture and reading notes do allow us to say that if Strauss was far from being the only or even the major representative of left-Hegelianism in Kierkegaard's developing intellectual universe, he typified what Kierkegaard found disturbing in that movement. In this regard we can show how some of the issues that come to the fore in Schaller's book in particular provide one of the earliest statements of themes that will become central in Kierkegaard's mature theological—and especially Christological—thinking.

In what follows, then, I shall, firstly, summarize the main points of Strauss' career, focusing chiefly on the period of the 1830s and early 1840s. Then I shall turn to Kierkegaard and examine more closely the evidence for his acquaintance with and opinion of Strauss before commenting on the nature of the differences and similarities between them. In terms of this last operation, I shall largely focus on the question of Christology which, I believe, is clearly the most important point at issue in the encounter between the two thinkers. However, I shall also use material from Strauss' *Christian Dogmatics* to show how consistently the Straussian and Kierkegaardian approaches relate to each other, with particular reference to the question of immortality. Finally, I shall attempt to comment on what this historical footnote implies for our own contemporary reading of Kierkegaard and, more broadly, of the religious debates of the 1830s and 1840s.

---

10 Julius Schaller, *Der historische Christus und die Philosophie. Kritik der Grundidee des Werks: das Leben Jesu von Dr. D.F. Strauss*, Leipzig: Verlag von Otto Wigand 1838 (*ASKB* 759).

11 For these notes, see *SKS* 19, 249–77, Not9:1 and 389–401, Not10:8–9.

12 *Pap*. II C 25, in *Pap*. XII, pp. 280–331.

13 Strauss, *Die christliche Glaubenslehre in ihrer geschichtlichen Entwicklung und im Kampfe mit der modernen Wissenschaft dargestellt*, vols. 1–2, Tübingen and Stuttgart: Osiander 1840–41 [in Danish as *Fremstilling af den christelige Troeslære i dens historiske Udvikling og i dens Kamp med den moderne Videnskab*, vols. 1–2, trans. by Hans Brøchner, Copenhagen: H.C. Klein 1842–1843 (*ASKB* 803–804)].

I. David Friedrich Strauss (1808–74)

Born in the town of Ludwigsburg near Stuttgart in 1808, Strauss, like many other talented young Swabian men of the period, became a theological student at the famous Tübingen Stift (or Seminary), where he read widely in Romantic and idealist philosophy and literature, as well as pursuing his theological studies. Somewhat curiously he wrote a prize essay in 1828 for the Catholic faculty (then, as now, Tübingen had both Catholic and Protestant faculties) on the resurrection of the flesh of which he famously wrote, that "as soon as I made the last full-stop, it was clear to me that there was nothing in the whole idea of resurrection."[14] Shortly afterwards, Strauss began to read Schleiermacher and Hegel—at that time virtually unread in his own alma mater. In 1831 Strauss took a parish post whilst continuing to wrestle with the religious significance of key Hegelian ideas, especially the tension between representational and conceptual thinking (*Vorstellung* and *Begriff*), and the implications of this for popular religion with its penchant for plastic, narrative representation. At the same time he worked on his doctoral dissertation *The Doctrine of the Restoration of all Things in its Religious-Historical Significance*,[15] a topic that allowed him to think further the choices to be made between a Schleiermacherian and an Hegelian approach. In the autumn of 1831 he managed to secure a period of study in Berlin, where he learned from Schleiermacher that Hegel had just died, to which news Strauss famously and ineptly replied, "But it was for his sake that I came here!"

It seems to have been about this time that Strauss began seriously to plan *The Life of Jesus*. An important feature of the original conception was that it would be a work in two parts, constructed under the inspiration of a rather loose version of Hegelian dialectic. In part one Strauss would enact the negation of the traditional historical basis of Christianity, in part two he would reinstate this in a speculative manner. This division survives in the published work, although the concluding dissertation on "The Dogmatic Import of the Life of Jesus" is quantitatively little more than a footnote to the main bulk of the "negative" historical work. It was therefore not implausible for Ferdinand Christian Baur (1792–1860), whose own work was very much on the liberal wing of scholarship and who had been Strauss' teacher, to contrast his "positive" method with Strauss' "negative" criticism.

What, then, was Strauss' method in his "negative" treatment of the historical materials of the life of Jesus. It was summarized in his own phrase "the mythical view," but what did this mean?

Strauss' "Introduction" to *The Life of Jesus* contains an admirable survey of the development of historical criticism of the biblical sources. Strauss' illustrations reach back to the ancient world, but there is, naturally, a special emphasis on the most recent, German discussion. The stage for this is shown to have been set by the emergence of deist and naturalist reinterpretations of Scripture in the seventeenth and eighteenth centuries. Typical of these is the view Strauss ascribes to Bolingbroke, that the Bible

---

14 Harris, *David Friedrich Strauss and his Theology*, op. cit., p. 19.

15 Strauss, *Die Lehre von der Wiederbringung aller Dinge in ihrer religionsgeschichtlichen Entwicklung*, doctoral dissertation, University of Tübingen 1831.

is "a collection of unauthentic and fabulous books."[16] Both the miraculous element of Scripture and the supposed moral shortcomings of biblical teaching were ridiculed. The climax of this movement came with Hermann Samuel Reimarus (1694–1768), extracts from whose researches on the gospels were published posthumously by Gotthold Ephraim Lessing (1729–81) as the renowned *Wolfenbüttel Fragments*. Typical of Reimarus' approach was the depiction of Moses as an impostor and "the despotic ruler of a free people" and of the resurrection of Jesus as a "fraudulent pretence" on the part of the disciples.[17] Elements of this naturalistic method were taken over into what Strauss calls the rationalist interpretation of Scripture. The rationalists generally shared the view that the Bible, *qua* historical text, should be treated in the same way as all other ancient texts, and that one should bring to it a general acceptance of the universal validity of the laws of nature. However, they did not ascribe attributions of miracles to deliberate deception. Rather, one had imaginatively to consider such reports as reflecting the effect that certain marvellous events had on the observers, so that "[t]he shining of [Moses'] countenance was the natural effect of being over-heated: but it was supposed to be a divine manifestation, not only by the people, but by Moses himself, he being ignorant of the true cause."[18] At first these methods were largely limited to the Old Testament, but in figures such as Johann Gottfried Eichhorn (1752–1827) and Heinrich Eberhard Gottlob Paulus (1761–1851), they begin also to be applied to the New.

Typical for the rationalistic commentators is the broad acceptance of a model of divine providence akin to Lessing's idea of an "education of the human race," in which, over the course of centuries and millennia, initially crude misconceptions and superstitions about the natural and moral universe are refined into the elements of a religion of reason. In such a process sacrifice is replaced by moral conversion and improvement, and miracles by explanations. No less important for the distinctive rationalist position, however, was the acceptance of the idea that the biblical text was, more or less, an accurate portrayal of the events they describe, if not as they happened then in terms of the effect they had on those who witnessed them. As in a previous example, the assumption was that Moses' face really was shining when he came down from the mountain, and the question was only to decide what the true explanation for this unusual phenomenon was. But was this kind of assumption safe and, if not, how might one begin to separate out what really belonged to the historical event reported in the text from what the text itself added?

This is where the idea of myth begins to come into its own. Starting with critics such as Julius August Ludwig Wegscheider (1771–1849) the idea that there was an element of myth in the biblical narrative began to gain ground and preliminary taxonomies of myths began to be drawn up. Strauss mentions historical, philosophical and poetic myths, of which the first were "narratives of real events colored by the light of antiquity, which confounded the divine and the human, the natural and the supernatural"; the second "such as clothe in the garb of historical narrative a simple thought, a precept, or an idea of the time"; and the third a blending of these, but

16 Ibid., p. 45.
17 Ibid., p. 46.
18 Ibid., p. 48.

so embellished by the imagination as to almost totally obscure the idea or event underlying it.[19]

Strauss proceeds to set out his own case for the presence of myth in the New Testament with his customary clarity and vigor. As he represents the case, it is not a matter of ascribing intentional fictions to the evangelists, as the older naturalists had done, but simply of recognizing that the early Christians' belief that Jesus was the Messiah led them to see all his words and actions through the filter of Messianic myths. The application of this method is clearly exemplified in the first piece of the narrative to which Strauss turns his attention, namely, the birth of John the Baptist. Pulling to pieces the attempts by various commentators to find a rational explanation for the miraculous elements in the narrative, Strauss finally brushes them aside to conclude that:

> we stand here upon purely mythical-poetical ground; the only historical reality which we can hold fast as positive matter of fact being this: —the impression made by John the Baptist, by virtue of his ministry and his relation to Jesus, was so powerful as to lead to the subsequent glorification of his birth in connection with the birth of the Messiah in the Christian legend.[20]

It is perhaps hard for us now to recapture the shock-value of such a conclusion—coming from one assumed to be a Christian theologian—but shocking it was, and especially when Strauss went on to deal in the same way with the birth, ministry, death and resurrection of Jesus himself. With regard to the resurrection, Strauss typically concludes that whatever their more precise content, the appearances to the disciples were essentially of the same kind as the appearance to Paul, that is, as impossible to regard "as an external, objective appearance of the real Christ."[21]

As Strauss himself noted in the opening sentence of the "Concluding Dissertation":

> The results of the enquiry which we have now brought to a close, have apparently annihilated the greatest and most valuable part of that which the Christian has been wont to believe concerning his Savior Jesus, have uprooted all the animating motives which he has gathered from his faith, and withered all his consolations.[22]

However, he now proposes to restore with his right hand what he has taken away with his left (he several times claimed that his basic interests were dogmatic rather than historical), and, by means of the speculative method to offer a Christology that can be meaningful in the modern world. Again he proceeds by running through—rather more cursorily this time—the previous history of orthodox, rationalist and other Christologies. He pauses to take particular issue with Schleiermacher, and the latter's idea that Jesus is to be seen as the one in whom there existed the maximum

---

19 Strauss, *The Life of Jesus Critically Examined*, trans. by George Eliot, ed. by Peter C. Hodgson, Ramsey, New Jersey: Sigler Press 1994 [1972], p. 53.

20 Ibid., p. 107.

21 Ibid., p. 741.

22 Ibid., p. 757.

level of God-consciousness and that it is in the influence of this God-consciousness that his redemptive power continues to be experienced. But, says Strauss,

> ...it would be contrary to the laws of all development to regard the initial member of a series as the greatest—to suppose that in Christ, the founder of that community, the object of which is the strengthening of the consciousness of God, the strengthening of this consciousness was absolute, a perfection which is rather the infinitely distant goal of the progressive development of the community founded by him.[23]

As he goes on to add that no individual in particular can ever "present the perfect ideal,"[24] we begin to see where he is going. The "truth" of Christology is the idea of the unity of the divine and human. But representing this unity in the form of an individual life is only an inadequate representation of what is true only when predicated of the human race as a whole. "In an individual, a God-man, the properties and functions which the church ascribed to Christ contradict themselves; in the idea of the race, they perfectly agree."[25] That the divine attributes are attributed only to one man is simply a "necessary result of the historical circumstances" under which Christology developed.[26] It is humanity, not the individual man Jesus, that:

> ...is the union of two natures—God become man, the infinite manifesting itself in the finite, and the finite spirit remembering its infinitude....It is Humanity that dies, rises, and ascends to heaven, for from the negation of its phenomenal life there ever proceeds a higher spiritual life; from the suppression of its mortality as a personal, national, and terrestrial spirit, arises its union with the infinite spirit of the heavens.[27]

But what exactly does this somewhat flowery language mean? Strauss is candid enough to tell us, as he goes on to ask:

> And shall we interest ourselves more in the cure of some sick people in Galilee, than in the miracles of intellectual and moral life belonging to the history of the world—in the increasing, the almost incredible dominion of man over nature—in the irresistible force of ideas, to which no unintelligible matter, whatever its magnitude, can oppose any enduring resistance....Our age demands to be led in Christology to the idea in the fact, to the race in the individual...[28]

—of which we may say that if Kierkegaard did not read it, it nevertheless *answers* perfectly to what he many times unmasks as "what the age demands," namely, the subordination of the individual to "the race"!

But back, briefly, to Strauss. The controversy over *The Life of Jesus* led, unsurprisingly, to his being relieved of his post as tutor in the Tübingen Stift. Not only were subsequent Church posts closed to him, so too were academic positions. Elected to a professorship in Zürich, the election was overturned in a popular

23 Ibid., p. 771.
24 Ibid., p. 772.
25 Ibid., p. 780.
26 Ibid.
27 Ibid.
28 Ibid., p. 781.

referendum. After a third edition of *The Life of Jesus* in 1838 in which Strauss partially back-pedalled on the radical position of the earlier editions, his *Dogmatics* of 1841—or to give the book its full title, *Christian Dogmatics Presented in its Historical Development and in Conflict with Modern Science*—offered a two-volume reinterpretation of the main headings of Christian teaching which, as Harris wrote, was "an exposition of the Christian faith without a personal God, without a divine and supernatural Jesus, without any miraculous events and without any life after death"[29]—or, as Peter C. Hodgson put it more drily, "The philosophical perspective of the book is that of a monistic pantheism."[30]

Strauss' life continued to be controversial, and in a variety of ways. After a disastrous marriage to an opera singer, Agnese Schebert, he was elevated to the Wittenberg Assembly in 1848, where he experienced what many erstwhile young firebrands have discovered—that they did not have the stomach for the yet more radical ideas and actions of the new generation waiting in the wings. His attack on a left-wing journal, *The Neckar Steamboat*, could almost be mistaken for an extract from Kierkegaard's attack on the "rabble-barbarism" of *The Corsair*, when Strauss spoke of

> ...its insolent scorn, its abandoned character which bares its envious teeth, with its deep hatred against every educated man who has raised himself above the masses, not to speak of the cynical loathsome tone of its pages. It is well known throughout the country that the best men who rise up against such mischief are branded as aristocrats, pulled into the dung heap and doused with filthy water.[31]

Yet Strauss' self image as one "who has raised himself above the masses" was rudely punctured by Nietzsche, when, in the last year of Strauss' life, he lambasted the latter's last major theoretical work, *The Old and the New Faith*,[32] as exemplifying the cultural philistinism of a spiritless age. Here, it is Nietzsche who reminds us of Kierkegaard, for what Nietzsche sees in Strauss is profoundly akin to what Kierkegaard portrayed in *A Literary Review* and other works of *Zeitkritik*, namely a bourgeois world that, having left both Christianity and the sterner discipline of an age of warfare behind, still wants to regard itself as cultured, as aspiring to ideals, and productive of genius—a claim that both Kierkegaard and Nietzsche deride.

II. Kierkegaard's Knowledge of Strauss

I shall come back to Schaller's critical study of Strauss, which provides the most substantial presentation of the latter's thought in Kierkegaard's journals, but first I turn to the "Lectures on the History of Dogma" by Philipp Marheineke (1780–1846),

---

29 Harris, *David Friedrich Strauss and his Theology*, op. cit., p. 139.

30 In his Introduction to Strauss, *The Life of Jesus Critically Examined*, 1994, op. cit., p. xlv.

31 Harris, *David Friedrich Strauss and his Theology*, op. cit., p. 169.

32 Strauss, *Der alte und der neue Glaube*, Leipzig: Hirzel 1872 [in English as *The Old and the New Faith*, trans. by Mathilde Blind, introduced and annotated by G.A. Wells, Amherst et al.: Prometheus Books 1997 [New York: H. Holt 1873]].

lectures which Kierkegaard began attending shortly after his arrival in Berlin in 1841. Marheineke is generally known in the history of ideas as the most prominent of the so-called right Hegelians, who attempted to argue for the compatibility of Hegelianism with mainstream Christian belief. By the time of these lectures, however, many were presuming that "Hegelianism" was more likely to provide an inspiration to the radical left than to the Church, and Marheineke therefore had not only to apply the insights of Hegel but also to defend them against what he regarded as misinterpretations.

The context in which Marheineke turns his attention to Strauss is the discussion of Christology and, especially, the Christological idea of Christ as the God-man. In Kierkegaard's clipped notes, we hear Marheineke give a clear warning: Strauss has gone too far, or, more precisely, Strauss has overlooked something essential in Christology. And what is that? It is precisely the individuality of Christ. Strauss, he says, does not doubt the unity of the divine and human, but he will not allow this unity to occur "in one individual" but only in a succession of examples that reciprocally complement one another. But this is to fail to grasp the genuine historicity of Christ. If the speculative starting-point is that of the abstract, "in-itself" unity of the divine and the human—the idea that is to be realized in historical time—then Strauss' view merely takes us back to the beginning. Marheineke concedes that Strauss is correct in rejecting any kind of portrayal of the Incarnation that would make it *ex abrupto* without any real connection with the rest of history, some supernatural *Deus ex machina*. Nevertheless, the idea of humanity itself, which requires the affirmation of the individual, is occluded in Strauss' thought.

> With the thought of humanity one does indeed stand in infinity, because one has the abstract manifold; if one then turns to the concrete, the unsatisfactory [aspect of this] shows itself, and only the individual (*Einzelne*) is the true infinite. Divine and human nature are united in Christ as never before and never afterwards; for neither can the Christian community take Christ's place, since in that case one would confuse the incarnation with the indwelling of Christ's Spirit in the individual. The congregation is confused with its center. The truth of the doctrine of the incarnation is that Christ came as this singular person, this individual.[33]

If one does not allow this and says, with Strauss, that "humanity" is the collective Son of God, "then real historicality is done away with." "Christ is humanity, but in individuality."[34]

Marheineke returns to his criticism of Strauss when he comes to the topic of "the goal of reconciliation." Here, Strauss' flight from historicality has further consequences for the believer. Instead of a concrete, individual mediator between God and humanity, Strauss has only an idea, something which, Marheineke says, cannot serve to bring about a sense of reconciliation in the individual. But, Marheineke argues, reconciliation depends on Christ's actual obedience, in the flesh. "Obedience in the individual person must have its basis in the obedience Christ showed to his

33 *SKS* 19, 271, Not9:1.

34 Ibid.

Father."[35] But Christ's obedience is only the objective condition of our obedience, and it must be realized by each individual believer before reconciliation can be deemed complete. Even his death did not complete this, since real reconciliation must be appropriated by each individual. Thus too, we must not understand his death as a substitutionary sacrifice, but as the fulfillment of his obedience, and "obedience is more precious to God than sacrifice."[36] We are reconciled with God when the reconciling characteristics of Christ's own life enter into us. But, for Strauss, all of this can only be rhetoric.

Kierkegaard was well prepared to understand Marheineke's criticisms of Strauss, if only from his own reading of Julius Schaller's *The Historical Christ and Philosophy* of 1838. As the editors of *SKS* remark in their explanatory notes, Schaller distinguished himself from many of Strauss' critics by the objectivity of his approach to the issue and by the fact that he did not simply dismiss the idea of using Hegelian thought to help understand Christianity, but rather sought to show how this did not necessarily require understanding the New Testament text as mythical in the way that Strauss does. It is, of course, not Schaller himself we are concerned with here, but Kierkegaard, and Kierkegaard's response to Strauss, and I shall follow only his notes, rather than attempting to give a more general summary of Schaller's argument.

Kierkegaard's marginal dating at the top of these notes suggests that he read Schaller in the summer of 1838, from 23 July to 21 August to be precise. The timing is of interest. In the Winter Semester of 1837–38, Hans Lassen Martensen, at this point a charismatic young lecturer in theology, who had just returned from a tour of Germany where he discovered Hegelianism and met several of the leading figures associated with it, including Strauss (whom he spoke of as radiating "humanity"),[37] gave a series of lectures on "Introduction to Speculative Dogmatics," which continued through the Summer Semester of 1838. Kierkegaard attended these lectures, which some contemporaries and later commentators have regarded as one of the high-water marks of Hegelianism in Denmark. Whether Martensen ever was 100 per cent Hegelian is another matter, but in 1838 he was certainly willing to use—indeed he largely introduced—the language of speculative thought into the service of theology. Although Martensen was subsequently to distance himself from Hegelianism—not least because of the "excesses" associated with left Hegelians such as Strauss, it is clear that, for this year at least, the question as to the implications of the new philosophy for Christian faith was very much a question of the hour. It is in this context that Kierkegaard sits down with Schaller's book. What does he find in it that merits excerpting or noting?

He begins by writing out a series of quotations, translated by him into Danish from the German original (with just a few words remaining untranslated), that set out the Straussian critique of traditional faith. The nub of this, familiar from the polemic of German idealists from Kant onwards against "positive" religion, is that faith must cease to be an "act of submission to an alien hostile dominion, but much

35 *SKS* 19, 292, Not10:8.

36 Ibid.

37 Hans Lassen Martensen, *Af mit Levnet*, op. cit., vol. 1, p. 131.

more the content-filled act of becoming free from, of negating, of overcoming every preceding alienation, the subject coming to consciousness of its own inwardness."[38] In this perspective it is an error to exclude knowledge from faith or to say with Tertullian *Credo quia absurdum.* To insist on "the facts" is to insist on what can only be an object of consciousness but not a part of self-consciousness,

> Purely historical knowledge is empty and devoid of content, spirit is here altogether outside itself, without being turned back on the content-rich certainty and knowledge of itself, and there can therefore be no greater *Entgeistung* [de-spiritualization] in the realm of theoretical knowledge than this simple knowing or cognizing a mass of unrelated atoms.[39]

Against this concern with facts is to be set the centrality of Christ's person, which is, indeed, at the heart of his own teaching. However, and this is now Schaller's objection, even focusing on the person is a kind of "fact" that has concrete, historical consequences. As he puts it, one could not believe Christ to be the God-Man and remain a Jew.

The insistence of the mythical conception on the sacred narrative being merely "the sensuous garb of the religious ideas" in such a way that the supposed historical facts are irrelevant leads it to commence with demonstrating that these supposed facts are actually false or unprovable historically. Strauss' presupposition that the Idea cannot "pour its entire fullness into one exemplar" and that "the predicates that the Church ascribes to Christ's person cannot be united in one individual" leads him "on dogmatic and philosophical grounds alone" to refuse to see the divine element in Christ in the same way as the Bible.[40] Strauss' understanding of the place of "facts" in the overall system of knowledge leads him to the view that even if miracles were to be proved, they would have nothing to offer to faith, which must be concerned with the Idea, the person to which the miracles were to point. But, says Schaller, even if Strauss were to have shown that the text was unhistorical, this still does not prove it to be mythical. That requires something more, namely, to show how the supposed facts could function as expressions of the religious self-consciousness, that is, a self-consciousness that knew itself to be permeated by the divine Idea. The problem is that if, as the mythical view argues, the New Testament simply used the prevailing Jewish Messianic framework, this does not explain the distinctiveness of the Christian conception. If Judaism already, in its own way, expressed the idea of divine–human reconciliation in, for example, its cult, the mythical view must explain why this needed to be surpassed, which it does not. Not only is history downgraded, argues Schaller, but myth itself, that is, the forms of the actual religious consciousness, are not taken really seriously.

But there is a more fundamental question, namely, whether Strauss is correct in his view that "sensuous, factual immediacy is actually inessential to the idea of reconciliation"—a form that can be skimmed off from the essential content—"or

38 *SKS* 18, 318, KK:2.

39 *SKS* 18, 319, KK:2.

40 *SKS* 18, 320, KK:2.

whether that immediate reality might not rather be conceived as a moment of the content itself."

What, then, is the fundamental view of the human being that is presupposed in Strauss' thought? As Schaller summarizes it, it goes like this. The state of nature is one in which Spirit and reality are divided, in which the human subject experiences nature as something alien or external to it, yet, also, something by which it itself is limited and dominated. As a raw, empirical individual the human subject is bound to this state of natural alienation from itself. As Spirit, however, it knows itself as responsible for itself and, in so doing, both integrates its natural state as a subordinate element as well as recognizing its community with all other rational beings. In the realm of Spirit, then, the relation of the individual to society or to the species is essentially different from that of individual and species in any merely natural kind. Spirit, the free human subject, knows itself as a member of a community of free subjects, although "immediately" this "is only present in the mode of possibility and not in accordance with its actuality," that is, as a state to be achieved through historical action.[41]

The different stages of this realization are reflected in the history of religions and, of special interest in this context, the transition from Judaism to Christianity. Judaism, on this view, ascribes all divinity exclusively to God, over against whom "the human being is lost in his finitude" or, in the language of speculation,

> Consciousness and self-consciousness fall apart. The absolute is the object of my consciousness and I recognize it as all that is true and actual, but in what is thus an object of my consciousness I no longer know myself, and nor does the self-consciousness of my finitude find fulfillment in this object, but I rather know myself as utterly annihilated in this object that is the absolute essence.[42]

This division is overcome for the Jew by the idea of the special relationship of belonging to the chosen people, but this idea is inherently incapable of expressing the true universality of spiritual existence, that is, humanity.

But how is reconciliation to be understood in its divine aspect? Are we to imagine that the change is merely a change in human consciousness, "so that one simply removes the idea one once had of God's wrath"? Kierkegaard's notes leave the question unanswered at this point, but the issue of God's wrath is one to which, as we shall see, he returns.

When we move to a section entitled "Critique of the Straussian Christology," Kierkegaard notes that "Its chief failing is its lack of definition."

> [T]he denial of the historical Christ's personal divine-humanity has the additional consequence of denying the personal divine-humanity altogether...as soon as we start consistently using the relationship of species and individual in relation to Spirit, Spirit as such and all spiritual interest, especially personality, are annihilated from the ground up.[43]

---

41 *SKS* 18, 322f., KK:2.

42 *SKS* 18, 324, KK:2.

43 *SKS* 18, 326, KK:2.

But, on the other hand, if we were really to take seriously the idea of Spirit as self-conscious individual identity, then "the concept of divine-humanity deriving from that is so far from dispensing with the God-man's historical appearance that it rather also includes the proof for the necessity of the historical appearance."[44] If, with Strauss, we speak only of the species as divine–humanity, "there must nevertheless always be a point at which the individual participates in divine-humanity."[45] Or, looking at it from another side, the Straussian emphasis on the species, the universal, in fact institutionalizes the impossibility of the individual becoming free from sin, even though Strauss denies the idea of sin, since it is only the species that is united with the divine in such a way that the individual will never entirely overcome its state of separateness. All in all, "the shaky deployment of the category 'species' is precisely the chief moment and the chief failing in Strauss."[46]

This criticism relates also to the next heading in Kierkegaard's notes, "The Idea of Reconciliation." Here Schaller opposes two quite distinct views. On the one side is the view that "The new relation to God must in the first instance essentially take its point of departure from the side of God, for without this it becomes an empty movement within subjectivity's own limits....For in our knowledge truth is the absolute '*prius*' which we do not invent but discover...."[47] Over against this is the view that Schaller takes to be that of speculative Christology, namely, "that in knowing God, humanity is actually knowing itself."[48] The paradoxical outcome of this latter is that it actually has the same effect as Judaism. Where Judaism forced the finite individual back onto himself, so too does subjective idealism "break off every actual relationship and thus, despite all its efforts and longings, remain stuck in its firm and insuperable finitude."[49] Only the recognition of genuine substantial difference on each side of the relation between spiritual beings opens the way for genuine self-knowledge.

Although we might have thought that there was much in this that Kierkegaard would welcome and, indeed, much that clearly anticipates many of his own later attacks on "the system" and "speculation," especially the issue of the subordination of the individual to the species, he breaks off his notes at this point and remarks, in the typically condescending young Kierkegaard fashion that

> ...the reason why many of the writings produced by recent philosophy leave behind so little by way of outcome that is really satisfying, after the admiration that their displays of talent must elicit from all sides has subsided, is that their attention is turned towards questions that have never been voiced in the Christian consciousness.[50]

This seems to be aimed not only at Strauss but also, and more particularly, at Schaller. The problem seems to be that Schaller has developed only "the possibility of God's

44 *SKS* 18, 326f., KK:2.
45 *SKS* 18, 327, KK:2.
46 Ibid.
47 *SKS* 18, 328f., KK:2.
48 *SKS* 18, 329, KK:2.
49 *SKS* 18, 330, KK:2.
50 Ibid.

relation to human beings." Schaller's point that God must be regarded as personal is merely a presupposition that faith itself always makes. What matters to faith is rather the more concrete configuration of this relationship, that is, whether "the wrathful God" is actually reconciled.

However, Kierkegaard returns to his note-taking, jotting down Schaller's reiterated argument that "only that religion can be called the absolute revelation in which God is revealed as a person and enters human consciousness as he is in and for himself." Only this religion, Schaller argues, really annihilates the opposition between God and the world. But, once more, Kierkegaard interrupts himself with the remark that "this indeed shows that the opposition was purely logical and that the opposition that comes under the rubric of religious-moral views (sin, etc.) has not been touched on."[51]

The next section of Schaller's book that he comes to is that of "The Personality of Christ." Many of the substantial points, such as the need for a concrete, individual and personal revelation of the God-man, are by now familiar. Kierkegaard, more appreciative of Schaller's endeavors, now notes, "Against the mythical volatilization of the historical Christ the point has rightly been established that every spiritual step forward proceeds from the energy of individuality."[52] In words that could almost be taken from *Philosophical Fragments* Kierkegaard notes, "That one person is to combine two within himself, namely his own and an alien nature, seems the hardest contradiction that can be offered to thought, but this is precisely the concept and essence of the person, that it does not have its existence in itself but in an Other...."[53] The movement of faith is correspondingly one in which both "the difference from Christ and the union with him are made to appear more and more deeply."

The next section deals with the question of miracles, where there seems once again (though not entirely clearly) to be an analogy between speculation and Judaism in the sense that both make it hard to accept not merely this or that individual miracle, but the whole miracle of Christ's appearing. The final section, which Kierkegaard breaks off after a few lines, deals with Christian life and philosophy, asserting that, as it developed historically, Christian faith did not "have the form of philosophical thinking, since it took its departure from what it felt and not from thinking about thinking."[54] Even in the Middle Ages, theology was not philosophical but "believing and meditative thinking"—philosophy was not subordinated to faith, but there was simply no urge towards philosophizing as an essential element in the spiritual life. Although the notes do not go on to develop the point, this, of course, undercuts one of the repeated claims made by Strauss, namely, that the true essence of Christian thought always had been essentially philosophical.

We can then see that Kierkegaard could have found many themes that were to reappear centrally and repeatedly in his later work. Even if he seems to limit Schaller's contributions to the level of prolegomena to true Christian thinking, he himself will take up themes such as that of the principle of concrete individual

51 *SKS* 18, 331, KK:2.

52 *SKS* 18, 335, KK:2.

53 Ibid.

54 *SKS* 18, 337, KK:2.

personality, both with regard to the believer and to Christ, the God-man. Moreover, lining up against Straussian speculation, we can see the emergence of such concepts as the absurd, sin, "the hardest contradiction that can be offered to thought," the priority of God in reconciliation, and the rejection of "thinking about thinking" as a medium of Christian reflection. Kierkegaard's own opposition to speculation, then, has clear affinities with the moderate Christian idealism of theologians such as Schaller and Marheineke. We could add that analogous points are also to be found in Martensen's lectures on "Speculative Dogmatics," which indicate that even at this stage Martensen was by no means a radical Hegelian in the manner of a Strauss. At the same time it is clear that Kierkegaard too, like the speculative theologians, including Strauss, sought to formulate the questions of Christology in such a way that detailed questions of historical fact are assiduously avoided. Clearly his emphasis on the individual humanity of the God-man (and his acceptance that this would be offensive to reason) was antithetical to Strauss' definition of the God-man in terms of the race or universal humanity and, basically, reaffirms Schaller's view that a spiritual relationship can only exist where there are two distinct spiritual individualities. Yet Kierkegaard shares with the speculative theologians a conviction that the real interest of Spirit lies elsewhere than in the proof or disproof of historical facts. These elements combine into the well-known assertion from *Philosophical Fragments* that "The historical fact that the God has been in human form is the main thing, and the rest of the historical detail is not even as important as if, instead of the God, we were talking about a human being."[55] Or, as he put it in *Stages on Life's Way*, "Spirit asks these two things: (1) Is that which is said possible? (2) Can I do it? But it shows lack of Spirit to ask these two things: (1) Is it real? (2) Has my neighbor, Christopherson, done it ...?"[56] Although later texts, such as *Judge for Yourself!*, will go further in sketching elements of the life of Jesus that indicate the fittingness of his having been the God-man and that provide matter for imitation, here too there is an avoidance of detail and the focus is kept firmly on those moments in the life that have a strong archetypal or symbolic dimension. One example would be the story of Jesus' acceptance of the tears and anointing by the woman who was a sinner, which enacts such parables as that of the Pharisee and the tax-collector.

A similar pattern of difference and similarity appears if we turn to an area of doctrine that was of especial importance to Kierkegaard, not least in the context of his critique of Hegelianism, namely, immortality.

III. The Question of Immortality

We have already seen that, in 1828, Strauss had written a prize essay on the resurrection, only to realize as he finished writing that he did not believe a single word of it. In this connection it is striking that when Martensen met Strauss in the course of his tour of Germany, he reported Strauss as saying that Hegel's singular service was to have "annihilated the dream of a beyond, an other-world," to the

55 *SKS* 4, 300 / *PF*, 103f.

56 *SKS* 6, 407 / *SLW*, 440 (translation modified).

extent (and Martensen emphasizes that this was Strauss' expression) "there wasn't a table or chair left." With particular regard to the doctrine of immortality, Martensen reports Strauss as saying "I had scarcely finished reading Hegel's *Phenomenology of Spirit*, before that belief fell away from me like a dead leaf."[57]

In accordance with the method he follows throughout the *Dogmatics*, Strauss begins this final topic by giving an overview of the Church's historical teaching, before examining modern revisionist approaches and concluding with his own speculative resolution (or, as his critics would see it, dissolution) of the matter in question. So, here, he spends the 70 pages of his first main section summarizing biblical and ecclesiastical eschatology before turning to the second main section, "The Doctrine of Immortality of Modern Reflection." Any reader who has followed Strauss thus far will be unsurprised by the opening words of this section, in which Strauss states that, "The modern 'I' lets the whole rich dowry of ecclesiastical eschatology be put on the fire of criticism without any particular emotion, content to hold back only its own bare survival after death."[58] This residual faith is, he points out, the most important of the three elements of religious ideals accepted by Kant: God, freedom and immortality. Now, however, Strauss will proceed to reductively reinterpret even this last remaining vestige of supernaturalism and to expose it as mere "egoism." The "I" is, he concedes, justified in seeing itself as on an equal footing with the chief representational forms of religion, other-worldly divine beings, angels, a Christ who will return at the end of time. But has it grasped its own infinity in the correct manner or is it guilty of postulating an "eternity" that is, in fact, essentially "finite" in character? That this is actually the case is seen by Strauss in the predominance of modern enlightened thought of the motif, "We shall see each other again," which, having occupied a strictly subordinate place in ecclesiastical eschatology, has now become the chief point of modern eschatology. However, Strauss is convinced that such a falling-back into finite modes of thinking can only be an interim solution, and he hails the work of Friedrich Richter and Ludwig Feuerbach as signalling the true meaning of the speculative principle for faith in immortality, namely, "the breaking open of the final sanctuary" and the destruction of "the newest deity, the immortal I."[59]

To secure this point Strauss goes back over recent attempts to ground the doctrine in moral, teleological, metaphysical and even speculative arguments. In these last, Strauss sees a final, vestigial effort to interpret death as the liberation of the isolated self for a life of genuine universality. Yet such attempts obscure what Strauss sees as the inexorable conclusion of Hegel's *Phenomenology of Spirit*, that the idea of Absolute Spirit does not offer hope of survival to individuals but, instead, absolutely requires there to be an infinite succession of individuals in and through which Spirit gradually or progressively realizes its infinite potential.[60] One such speculative argument (which, in connection with process theology, has since come to be known as the idea of objective immortality) is that human subjects are preserved as such,

---

57 Hans Lassen Martensen, *Af mit Levnet*, op. cit., vol. 1, p. 131.

58 David Friedrich Strauss, *Die christliche Glaubenslehre*, op. cit., vol. 2, p. 697.

59 Ibid., p. 703.

60 Ibid., p. 728.

that is, in their subjectivity, in the mind of God. Strauss is not overly impressed by this. As he sees it, individuation is entirely a modification of the universal human qualities of consciousness, will, freedom by the conditions of organic existence, and the individual is thus inherently limited by the law-bound materiality that is the basis of this modification. What lives as individual *must* pass away. Citing Feuerbach, Strauss comments "You yourself, *qua* determinate person, are only the object of consciousness, not consciousness itself, and you will depart from consciousness just as you once entered it, and in your place a new, fresh personality will enter into the world of consciousness."[61] Nor does he yield anything to another "speculative" view which argues that those who have in this life learned to identify their true selves with the interests of Spirit will pass over into eternal life, leaving the merely "animal" remainder of humanity to perish. Strauss regards it as patently implausible that any degree of moral activity could bring about a transformation in the metaphysical definition of any being, nor could any single species have two such contrary attributes as mortality and immortality and remain a single species. Even where Christ's own word is invoked as a ground for hope in immortality, Strauss directs his reader back to Schleiermacher, who, he claims, allowed no other immortality to Christ himself than the latter's continuing influence in the life of the Church.[62]

And what is the positive dialectical countermovement to such a consistent rebuttal of all attempts to argue for individual immortality? It is "that immortality is not primarily to be conceived as something future, but as a present quality of Spirit, as its inner universality, the strength by which it raises itself above everything finite to the idea."[63] That the names of great men live on "eternally" is merely the reflex of the fact that in this life they were concerned with what had the here-and-now character of eternity. Once more teasingly citing Schleiermacher, Strauss concludes:

> In the midst of the finite to be one with the infinite, and to be eternal in every moment is all that modern science has to say about immortality. With this our business is, for now, ended. For the beyond is indeed the One in all things, but in the form of the future [life] it is the last enemy against which speculative criticism has to struggle and, if possible, overcome.[64]

If we now turn back to Kierkegaard, it is perhaps the points of difference that most immediately leap out. Was it not precisely the incapacity of speculative thought to engage with the question of personal immortality that provided Kierkegaard with the guiding thread for his critique of the system in *Concluding Unscientific Postscript*. Here, in the section "Becoming Subjective," Kierkegaard opposes to the pretensions of "objective" or "world-historical" knowledge a series of issues and questions that become completely altered when shown in the prism of subjectivity. These include what it is to die and what it means to be immortal. With regard to this latter, he insists that it is simply not a matter for objective knowledge. It is a matter, as he puts it, in which "instruction must be dialectically qualified in relation to the learner's

61 Ibid., p. 731.
62 Ibid., p. 736.
63 Ibid., p. 737.
64 Ibid., p. 739.

qualifications."[65] Noting that "some have found immortality in Hegel; others have not," he argues that even if the system does have a place for eternity, it is not eternity of the kind that really interests one who is eager to learn about immortality.[66] The problem is not the difficulty of the question. Indeed, the problem really only comes to the fore as and when the question is made simple, a point which he acknowledges came to be recognized by Poul Martin Møller (1794–1838) in a treatise on immortality (a treatise that has often been regarded as anticipating Kierkegaard's own attack on the system, not only in terms of content but also in terms of Møller's resorting to humorous episodes interspersed with philosophical argumentation).[67] And what is the simple version of the question? It is this: "Do *I* become immortal or am *I* immortal?"[68]

> In all simplicity, then, the existing subject asks not about immortality in general, because a phantom such as that does not exist at all, but about his immortality. He asks about his immortality, about what it means to become immortal, whether he can do anything to become immortal or whether he becomes that automatically, or if he is immortal and remains so.[69]

Once the question is regarded in this way, it becomes clear that the question concerning immortality is and has to be inextricably bound up with subjectivity. It is "the subjective individual's most passionate interest"[70] on which the whole construction of his ethical life hangs and, as the preceding pages of "Becoming Subjective" have told us, it is precisely the ethical that should be the absolute for the individual, as it is the ethical that keeps any purely "systematic" or "world-historical" approach in its place. To ask about immortality without asking it subjectively, without asking what it would mean for me, now, in the way I live my life, is to manifest absentmindedness. And that, complains Kierkegaard, is what a philosophical—read "objective," "systematic," "world-historical"—approach invariably does. Indeed, part of the task of learning rightly—subjectively—to live with the question of immortality is to learn how to keep a metaphysical approach at bay or how not to philosophize about it. Nor, it should quickly be added, is this concern with the question of immortality a quirk of the writings ascribed to the pseudonym Johannes Climacus. The theme of "the expectation of an eternal happiness" is equally—if unsurprisingly—central to the whole program of upbuilding discourses with which Kierkegaard accompanied the pseudonymous works.

In these terms, then, Strauss' approach would seem to exemplify everything against which Kierkegaard is directing his attack. For Strauss it is precisely an article of faith that the individual consciousness must perish, that the aim of treating the

---

65 *SKS* 7, 158 / *CUP1*, 171.

66 *SKS* 7, 158f. / *CUP1*, 171.

67 Poul Martin Møller, "Tanker over Muligheden af Beviser for Menneskets Udødelighed," in *Maanedsskrift for Litteratur*, no. 17, 1837, pp. 1–72; pp. 422–53. (Reprinted in Møller's *Efterladte Skrifter*, vols. 1–3, Copenhagen: C.A. Reitzel 1839–43, vol. 2, pp. 158–272.)

68 *SKS* 7, 160 / *CUP1*, 173.

69 *SKS* 7, 161 / *CUP1*, 174 (adapted).

70 Ibid.

topic at all is, so to speak, to cure the individual of the longing for immortality—whereas for Kierkegaard the aim is to help the individual to raise that very same question in such a way as to make it the pivot of his whole existence. And as was also the case with regard to Christology, the issue seems precisely to center on the nature of the concrete individual person and speculative thought's presumed indifference or hostility towards such concrete personality.

Yet, once more, it would be wrong to draw a simple line between a "positive" Kierkegaardian "personalist" faith and Straussian negation. For just as Kierkegaard's defence of the historical *fact* of the incarnation went hand in glove with a denial of the importance of the historical details of the life of Jesus, so too his insistence on the centrality of the question concerning immortality is joined with a complete disinterest in reflecting on what the post-mortem condition of human beings might be or be like. Having noted that the theme of immortality can be found in Kierkegaard's upbuilding writings just as much as in his pseudonymous works, it is in fact in one of his *Christian Discourses* of 1848 that he makes the clearest distinction between a proper religious concern with eternal life and inappropriate speculations about the actual configuration of such a life. The discourse in question is entitled "The Resurrection is at Hand, for the Just—and for the Unjust."[71] Here Kierkegaard asserts the view that, for Christianity, the idea of resurrection (and, hence, of immortality[72]) is inseparable from the idea of judgment. This means that any attempt to discuss "survival" is totally irrelevant, since the only thing that should concern us is how we will fare in the judgment, whether we are here and now living our lives in such a way as to merit inclusion with the just—or not.

> Immortality and judgement are one and the same. One can only speak rightly about immortality, when one speaks about judgement, and, naturally, when one speaks about judgement, one speaks about immortality....Immortality is judgement. There is not a single word more to say about immortality. He who says one word more, or takes the matter in another direction, had better watch out for the judgement.[73]

Kierkegaard, in other words, seems to set himself against any kind of discourse about "survival" outside the context of the ethical demand placed upon the individual in the "now," the "moment of decision." And putting it like this seems, again, to narrow the gap between Kierkegaard and Strauss, for Kierkegaard, no less than Strauss, seems to want to talk about something quite different from the kind of consolatory talk about "meeting again" in the beyond that Churchgoers might have expected to hear from the representatives of established Christendom.

In one of the few full-length articles previously devoted to the relationship between Kierkegaard and Strauss, F.L. Jackson seizes upon the analogies between Kierkegaard and Strauss to argue that, in the end, they are both manifestations of "the new faith"

---

71 *SKS* 10, 211 / *CD*, 202. This is translated by the Hongs as "There will be the Resurrection of the Dead, of the Righteous—and of the Unrighteous."

72 I am aware that the Christian idea of the resurrection of the body and the idea of the immortality of the soul are both different and, arguably, incompatible. However, in the present context I do not regard the differences as decisive.

73 *SKS* 10, 214 / *CD*, 205f.

that emerged in the nineteenth century. This new faith was not the simple abandonment but rather the transformation of Christianity, and expressed itself in two main forms. The first—which clearly enough has Strauss as one of its representative men—pins its colors to the mast of humanity, conceived "as the objective totality of human activity, the material-historical process in which all individuals seek collectively to overcome the limitedness of their natural particularity through participation in a common technological, economic and cultural-scientific enterprise."[74] The other form—with Kierkegaard as prototype—transposes "the concept of the spiritual to refer to particular human subjectivity; to the immediate inward relation to self and this-worldly inwardness of the existing, self-conscious individual...."[75] As Jackson goes on to claim, "For Kierkegaard no less than for humanist theologians, reality is self-consciousness and God is spoken of only by the way,"[76] and "Jesus Christ is for Kierkegaard no less than for Strauss a mere archetype: in this case the archetype of 'the individual in particular' who is 'higher than the universal'...."[77] Thus, if Strauss reduced Christianity to the collective history of "humanity," Kierkegaard reduced it to individual psychology and, Jackson claims, seen from the perspective of classical Christian thought, this amounts to pretty much the same thing. In Kierkegaard no less than in Strauss "the older Christian terminology of God, faith, redemption and the rest are brought into play only as a kind of allegory."[78]

Such an assertion clearly raises far-reaching questions about the overall interpretation of Kierkegaard. Properly to assess it would require a careful and extensive weighing of Kierkegaard's whole engagement with past and present Christian thought. Such an assessment lies beyond the scope of this comparative study, where the question must be limited to the justifiability of twinning Kierkegaard and Strauss as representing the new anthropological transformation of Christianity. Here, however, we have to say that, purely as anthropology, the thought of Kierkegaard and Strauss is scarcely reconcilable. As we have seen with regard both to Christology and the question of immortality, they have profoundly different views as to the constitution of the person. Kierkegaard's "individualism" is not merely an individualizing of the humanist idea found in Strauss, but rather a struggle to articulate a far more concrete idea of embodied personality, in which the decisive religious relationship is not between the individual and the collective but, as Schaller had already suggested, between concrete existing individuals. Yet—and we recall Kierkegaard's impatient interruption of his own notes on Schaller's book—the attempt philosophically to articulate the idea of personality, even when directed against the "absentmindedness" of a Strauss, is incapable of giving a place for what the Christian consciousness finds truly decisive, namely the dialectic of sin and holiness. Kierkegaard's "I" is an "I" that, in facing the question of immortality, must ethically engage itself to prepare for judgment and that, in face of its repeated

---

74 F.L. Jackson, "The New Faith: Strauss, Kierkegaard and the Theological Revolution," in *Dionysius* (Halifax), vol. 12, 1988, p. 111.

75 Ibid.

76 Ibid., p. 125.

77 Ibid., p. 130.

78 Ibid., p. 134.

failure to do enough to merit counting itself amongst the "just," finds atonement in a determinate relation to another concrete existing "I," the "I" of the individual divine–human person, Jesus Christ. It is not only the concept of the person that divides Kierkegaard and Strauss, but the very questions about human existence that are worth asking. But, for all Kierkegaard's own impatience with it, even the philosophical clarification of the idea of personhood in terms of concrete individuality (rather than of a merely individualized case of universal freedom) holds open, as Strauss does not, the possibility both of genuinely ethical interpersonal human relations and of our highest good being compatible with a relation of absolute dependence on one who precedes all human relations. In the situation of modern philosophical pluralism, it would seem harsh on the part of Christian theology to expect more from a thinker (rather than, say, from an apostle) than to hold such a possibility open.

Jürgen Habermas has said that we are all still contemporaries of the generation after Hegel, and if many of the details of the debates covered by this article are in the process of becoming of purely antiquarian interest, the central questions around which those debates took shape remain urgent in the philosophy and theology of today. For we too know the tension between, on the one hand, the quest to become free from heteronomous religion and to affirm the total freedom and openness of human self-invention, and, on the other hand, the sense of the claim upon us of each concrete Other and, in that claim, of a possible—perhaps the only possible—return of God to philosophy.

Bibliography

I. Strauss' Works in The Auction Catalogue *of Kierkegaard's Library*

Fremstilling af den christelige Troeslære i dens historiske Udvikling og i dens Kamp med den moderne Videnskab, vols. 1–2, trans. by Hans Brøchner, Copenhagen: H.C. Klein 1842–43 (*ASKB* 803–804).

"*Jesu Liv, kritisk bearbeidet* af D.F. Strauß, Dr. Phil., 2 Dele. Tübingen 1835–1836," *Tidsskrift for udenlandsk theologisk Litteratur*, vols. 1–20, ed. by Henrik Nikolai Clausen and Matthias Hagen Hohlenberg, Copenhagen: C.A. Reitzel 1833–52, vol. 4, 1836, pp. 80–221 (*ASKB* U 29).

"Monolog om det Forgjængelige og det Blivende i Christendommen," *Tidsskrift for udenlandsk theologisk Litteratur*, op. cit., vol. 7, 1839, pp. 330–49.

"Den christelige Troeslære i sin historiske Udvikling og i Kamp med den moderne Videnskab," *Tidsskrift for udenlandsk theologisk Litteratur*, op. cit., vol. 9, 1841, pp. 181–268.

II. Works in The Auction Catalogue *of Kierkegaard's Library that Discuss Strauss*

Adler, Adolph Peter, *Populaire Foredrag over Hegels objective Logik*, Copenhagen: C.A. Reitzel 1842, p. 20 (*ASKB* 383).

Baader, Franz, *Vorlesungen über speculative Dogmatik*, vol. 1, Stuttgart und Tübingen: Cotta'sche Buchhandlung 1828 [vols. 2–5, Münster: Theissing 1830–38], vol. 4, 1836, p. 125; p. 127 (*ASKB* 396).

—— *Über das Leben Jesu von Strauß*, Munich: Franz 1836 (*ASKB* 407).

—— *Ueber den Paulinischen Begriff des Versehenseyns des Menschen im Namen Jesu vor der Welt Schöpfung*, vol. 3, Würzburg: In Commission der Stahel'schen Buchhandlung 1837, p. 30n (*ASKB* 413) (vols. 1–2 (*ASKB* 409–410)).

—— *Revision der Philosopheme der Hegel'schen Schule bezüglich auf das Christenthum. Nebst zehn Thesen aus einer religiösen Philosophie*, Stuttgart: S.G. Liesching 1839, p. 36; p. 43n; p. 44n (*ASKB* 416).

—— *Ueber die Nothwendigkeit einer Revision der Wissenschaft natürlicher, menschlicher und göttlicher Dinge, in Bezug auf die in ihr sich noch mehr oder minder geltend machenden Cartesichen und Spinozistischen Philosopheme*, Erlangen: bei J.J. Palm und Ernst Enke 1841, p. 3; p. 6 (*ASKB* 418).

Bauer, Bruno, "Die Glaubwürdigkeit der evangelischen Geschichte zugleich eine Kritik des *Lebens Jesu* von Strauß. Dargestellt von Dr. A. Tholuck. Hamburg, bei F. Perthes 1837. XVI, 463. S.," *Zeitschrift für spekulative Theologie*, vols. 1–3, ed. by Bruno Bauer, Berlin: Dümmler 1836–38, vol. 2, no. 2, 1837, pp. 405–25 (*ASKB* 354–357).

Baur, Ferdinand Christian, *Das Christliche des Platonismus oder Sokrates und Christus. Eine religionsphilosophische Untersuchung*, Tübingen: Ludwig Friedrich Fues 1837, p. 107n; p. 108n (*ASKB* 422).

Beck, Frederik, *Begrebet Mythus eller den religiøse Aands Form*, Copenhagen: P.G. Philipsens Forlag 1842 (*ASKB* 424).

[Kein Berliner], "Luther als Schiedsrichter zwischen Strauß und Feuerbach," in *Anekdota zur neuesten deutschen Philosophie und Publicistik*, vols. 1–2, ed. by Arnold Ruge, Zürich and Winterthur: Verlag des literarischen Comptoirs 1843, vol. 2, pp. 206–8 (*ASKB* 753).

Biedermann, A. Emanuel, *Die freie Theologie oder Philosophie und Christenthum in Streit und Frieden*, Tübingen: Ludwig Friedrich Fues 1844, p. 2; p. 192n; p. 264 (*ASKB* U 20).

Brøchner, Hans, *Nogle Bemærkninger om Daaben, foranledigede ved Professor Martensens Skrift: Den christelige Daab*, Copenhagen: P.G. Philipsens Forlag 1843, pp. 7f.; pp. 10f.; pp. 20–22; pp. 26f.; p. 31; p. 33; p. 56 (*ASKB* U 27).

Bruch, Johann Friedrich, *Die Lehre von den göttlichen Eigenschaften*, Hamburg: Friedrich Perthes 1842, p. 4; p. 8; pp. 17–18; p. 20n; p. 27n; p. 29n; p. 83n; p. 120n; p. 123; p. 124n; p. 125n; p. 126; p. 130n; p. 139n; p. 150n; p. 152n; p. 160n; p. 179; p. 184n; p. 188n; p. 244n; p. 248n; p. 278n; p. 281 (*ASKB* 439).

Chalybäus, Heinrich Moritz, "Philosophie der Geschichte und Geschichte der Philosophie in Bezug auf: Hegels *Vorlesungen über die Philosophie der Geschichte*...L. Feuerbach *Geschichte der neurern Philosophie*," *Zeitschrift für Philosophie und spekulative Theologie*, vols. 1–16, ed. by Immanuel Hermann Fichte and Christian Hermann Weiße, Bonn et al.: Eduard Weber et al. 1837–46, vol. 1, 1837, pp. 301–38 (*ASKB* 877–911).

Clausen, Henrik Nicolai, *Det Nye Testaments Hermeneutik*, Copenhagen: Jens Høstrup Schultz 1840, pp. 374–5 (*ASKB* 468).

Erdmann, Johann Eduard, *Vorlesungen über Glauben und Wissen als Einleitung in die Dogmatik und Religionsphilosophie*, Berlin: Duncker und Humblot 1837, p. 38 (*ASKB* 479).

Fichte, Immanuel Hermann, "Einige Bemerkungen über den Unterschied der immanenten und der Offenbarungstrinität nach Lücke und Nitzsch, auch mit Beziehung auf Hegel und Strauß," *Zeitschrift für Philosophie und spekulative Theologie*, op. cit., vol. 7, 1841, pp. 224–54.

—— "Nogle Bemærkninger om Forskjellen imellem den immanente Trinitet og Aabenbaringstriniteten, efter Lücke og Nitzsch, samt med Hensyn til Hegel og Strauß," *Tidsskrift for udenlandsk theologisk Litteratur*, op. cit., vol. 10, 1842, pp. 546–76.

—— *Die speculative Theologie oder allgemeine Religionslehre*, Heidelberg: Akademische Buchhandlung von J.C.B. Mohr 1846 [vol. 3, in *Grundzüge zum Systeme der Philosophie*], pp. 242ff.; p. 373; p. 415; p. 498 (*ASKB* 509) (vols. 1–2 (*ASKB* 502–503)).

Fischer, Kuno F., "Kritik af den Strauß'iske Dogmatik," *Tidsskrift for udenlandsk theologisk Litteratur*, op. cit., vol. 12, 1844, pp. 197–251.

Helfferich, Adolph, *Die christliche Mystik in ihrer Entwickelung und in ihren Denkmalen*, vols. 1–2, Gotha: Friedrich Parthes 1842, vol. 1, p. 89 (*ASKB* 571–572).

Hundeshagen, Carl Bernhard, "Den tydske Protestantisme, dens Fortid og dens nuværende Livsspørgsmaal," *Tidsskrift for udenlandsk theologisk Litteratur*, op. cit., vol. 16, 1848, pp. 125–240.

Martensen, Hans Lassen, *Den christelige Dogmatik*, Copenhagen: C.A. Reitzel 1849, p. 29; p. 95n (*ASKB* 653).

Menzel, Wolfgang, *Die deutsche Literatur*, vols. 1–4, 2nd revised ed., Stuttgart: Hallberg'sche Verlagshandlung 1836, vol. 1, pp. 207ff. (*ASKB* U 79).

Michelet, Carl Ludwig, *Vorlesungen über die Persönlichkeit Gottes und Unsterblichkeit der Seele oder die ewige Persönlichkeit des Geistes*, Berlin: Verlag von Ferdinand Dümmler 1841, p. 185; p. 189; p. 239n (*ASKB* 680).

Mynster, Jakob Peter, *Blandede Skrivter*, vols. 1–3, Copenhagen: Den Gyldendalske Boghandlings Forlag 1852–53 [vols. 4–6, Copenhagen: Den Gyldendalske Boghandlings Forlag 1855–57], vol. 2, pp. 100–3 passim (*ASKB* 358–363).

Neander, August, "Erkläring med Hensyn til en Beretning i *Allgemeine Zeitung*," *Tidsskrift for udenlandsk theologisk Litteratur*, op. cit., vol. 4, 1836, pp. 221–30.

Nielsen, Rasmus, *De speculativa historiæ sacræ tractandæ methodo*, Copenhagen: Fabritius de Tengnagel 1840; pp. 121–35; pp. 142–4 (*ASKB* 697).

—— *Evangelietroen og Theologien. Tolv Forelæsninger holdte ved Universitetet i Kjøbenhavn i Vinteren 1849–50*, Copenhagen: C.A. Reitzel 1850, pp. 81–5 (*ASKB* 702).

Schaller, Julius, *Der historische Christus und die Philosophie. Kritik der Grundidee des Werks: das Leben Jesu von Dr. D.F. Strauss*, Leipzig: Verlag von Otto Wigand 1838 (*ASKB* 759).

Schmidt, Karl, *Das Verstandesthum und das Individuum*, Leipzig: Otto Wigand 1846 (*ASKB* 868).

Schopenhauer, Arthur, *Die Welt als Wille und Vorstellung*, vols. 1–2, 2nd revised and enlarged ed., Leipzig: F.A. Brockhaus 1844 [1819], vol. 2, p. 613; p. 627 (*ASKB* 773–773a).

—— *Parerga und Paralipomena: kleine philosophische Schriften*, vols. 1–2, Berlin: A.W. Hayn 1851, vol. 2, p. 319 (*ASKB* 774–775).

Steffens, Henrich, *Christliche Religionsphilosophie*, vols. 1–2, Breslau: im Verlage bei Josef Max und Komp. 1839 [vol. 1, *Teleologie*; vol. 2, *Ethik*], vol. 1, p. 284 (*ASKB* 797–798).

—— *Was ich erlebte. Aus der Erinnerung niedergeschrieben*, vols. 1–10, Breslau: Josef Max und Comp. 1840–44, vol. 5, p. 316; vol. 9, p. 144 (*ASKB* 1834–1843).

Stilling, Peter Michael, "Den 'moderne Videnskab' i Relation til sig selv, eller dens indre Historie gjennem Michelet, Strauss og Feuerbach," in his *Den moderne Atheisme eller den saakaldte Neohegelianismes Conseqvenser af den hegelske Philosophie*, Copenhagen: C.A. Reitzel 1844, pp. 48–74 (*ASKB* 801).

Tholuck, August, "Den evangeliske Histories Troværdighed, tillige en Kritik over Strauß's *'Jesu Liv.'* af Dr. A. Tholuck, Prof. i Theologien i Halle," *Tidsskrift for udenlandsk theologisk Litteratur*, op. cit., vol. 5, 1837, pp. 107–79.

Trendelenburg, Adolf, *Die logische Frage in Hegel's System. Zwei Streitschriften*, Leipzig: F.A. Brockhaus 1843, pp. 8–9 (*ASKB* 846).

Ullmann, Carl, "Dr. Strauß's *Jesu Liv*," *Tidsskrift for udenlandsk theologisk Litteratur*, op. cit., vol. 4, 1836, pp. 447–90.

Vorländer, Friedrich, "Ueber die philosophisch-theologische Theorie des Dr. Strauß, Verfasser des Leben Jesu," *Zeitschrift für Philosophie und spekulative Theologie*, op. cit., vol. 3, 1839, pp. 69–100.

Weiße, Christian Hermann, "Recensionen: *Die Glaubwürdigkeit der evangelischen Geschichte, zugleich eine Kritik des Leben Jesu von Strauß, für theologische und nicht theologische Leser* dargestellt von Dr. A. Tholuck. Hamburg, Perthes, 1837. XVI. 464 S. gr. 8," *Zeitschrift für Philosophie und spekulative Theologie*, op. cit., vol. 1, 1837, pp. 255–300.

—— "Om det philosophiske Grundlag for Strauß's *Jesu Liv*," *Tidsskrift for udenlandsk theologisk Litteratur*, op. cit., vol. 5, 1837, pp. 88–106.

—— "Den evangeliske Histories Troværdighed, tillige en Kritik over Strauß's *Jesu Liv*," *Tidsskrift for udenlandsk theologisk Litteratur*, op. cit., vol. 5, 1837, pp. 107–79.

—— "Die philosophische Literatur der Gegenwart. Die jüngere Hegelsche Schule. Die Hallischen Jahrbücher. Feuerbach. Strauß. Frauenstädt," *Zeitschrift für Philosophie und spekulative Theologie*, op. cit., vol. 7, 1841, pp. 103–50.

—— "Strauß und Bruno Bauer. Eine kritische Parallele," *Zeitschrift für Philosophie und spekulative Theologie*, op. cit., vol. 10, 1843, pp. 40–82.

Wirth, Johann Ulrich, *Die speculative Idee Gottes und die damit zusammenhängenden Probleme der Philosophie. Eine kritisch-dogmatische Untersuchung*, Stuttgart and Tübingen: J.G. Cotta'scher Verlag 1845, pp. 393f. (*ASKB* 876).

Wolff, Oskar Ludwig Bernhard, *Handbuch deutscher Beredsamkeit enthaltend eine Uebersicht der Geschichte und Theorie der Redekunst, zugleich mit einer vollständigen Sammlung deutscher Reden jedes Zeitalters und jeder Gattung*, vols. 1–2, Leipzig: Carl B. Lorck 1845–46, vol. 1, pp. 421–30 (*ASKB* 250–251).

Zeuthen, Ludvig, *Humanitet betragtet fra et christeligt Standpunkt, med stadigt Hensyn til den nærværende Tid*, Copenhagen: Gyldendalske Boghandling 1846, p. 66 (*ASKB* 915).

III. Secondary Literature on Kierkegaard's Relation to Strauss

Hjell, Richard, "Søren Kierkegaard och David Friedrich Strauss," in *Edda*, vol. 27, no. 40, 1940, pp. 43–51.

Jackson, F.L., "The New Faith: Strauss, Kierkegaard and the Theological Revolution," *Dionysius* (Halifax), vol. 12, 1988, pp. 111–42.

Index of Persons

Subject Index